THE OPENING-UP OF CHINA'S FINANCIAL MARKET

POLICY AND EMPIRICAL ANALYSIS

THE OPENING-UP OF CHINA'S FINANCIAL MARKET

POLICY AND EMPIRICAL ANALYSIS

Xuechun Zhang
Ruihui Xu
People's Bank of China, China

World Scientific
NEW JERSEY • LONDON • SINGAPORE • BEIJING • SHANGHAI • HONG KONG • TAIPEI • CHENNAI

Published by

World Scientific Publishing Co. Pte. Ltd.
5 Toh Tuck Link, Singapore 596224
USA office: 27 Warren Street, Suite 401-402, Hackensack, NJ 07601
UK office: 57 Shelton Street, Covent Garden, London WC2H 9HE

Library of Congress Cataloging-in-Publication Data
Names: Zhang, Xuechun, Ph. D., author. | Xu, Ruihui, author.
Title: The opening-up of China's financial market : policy and empirical analysis /
Xuechun Zhang, Ruihui Xu, People's Bank of China, China.
Description: New Jersey : World Scientific, [2025] | Includes bibliographical references.
Identifiers: LCCN 2024053282 | ISBN 9789819803217 (hardcover) |
ISBN 9789819807093 (paperback) | ISBN 9789819803224 (ebook) |
ISBN 9789819803231 (ebook other)
Subjects: LCSH: Finance--China--History. | Capital market--China--History. |
Investments, Foreign--China--History. | China--Economic policy.
Classification: LCC HG187.C6 Z365 2025 | DDC 332.0951--dc23/eng/20250108
LC record available at https://lccn.loc.gov/2024053282

British Library Cataloguing-in-Publication Data
A catalogue record for this book is available from the British Library.

For any available supplementary material, please visit
https://www.worldscientific.com/worldscibooks/10.1142/14093#t=suppl

Desk Editors: Soundararajan Raghuraman/Kura Sunaina

Typeset by Stallion Press
Email: enquiries@stallionpress.com

About the Authors

Xuechun Zhang, Ph.D. in Economics, is deputy director general of the Research Bureau, People's Bank of China (PBC). She currently leads research and policy studies in monetary policy, macroeconomics, international trade and finance, and green finance.

She joined the PBC in 2007, and had held positions in the Research Institute, Frankfurt Representative Office and Monetary Department II of PBC. In addition to research works, she was in charge of policy design and implementation related to the RMB international use such as international monetary cooperation, financial market integration, cross-border capital flow, exchange rate policy analysis, and the like.

Dr. Zhang has published extensively in China, and won the first Sun Yefang Financial Award in 2015, the highest academic award for research in finance and economics in China.

Prior to joining the PBC, she held various positions in the Asian Development Bank, the International Monetary Fund, the Federal Deposit Insurance Corporation, and the Federal Reserve Board. She received her Ph.D. in economics in 1997.

Ruihui Xu, Ph.D. in Finance, is currently an Associate Researcher in the Research Institute of the People's Bank of China. Her research interests covers financial markets, banking, monetary policy, and macroeconomics.

Dr. Xu has published more than 20 papers in both Chinese and English. She won the first prize of Best Paper Award at the 2016 Annual Conference of Global Chinese Real Estate Congress and the first prize for Financial Research Projects of the People's Bank of China in 2019. She received her Ph.D. in Finance in 2017.

Contents

List of Abbreviations

ABS	Asset-Backed Securities
ADB	Asian Development Bank
ADR	American Depository Receipt
AFRE	Aggregate Financing to the Real Economy
AHFCAA	Accelerating Holding Foreign Companies Accountable Act
AMEX	American Stock Exchange
AIM	Alternative Investment Market
AMEX	American Stock Exchange
BIS	Bank for International Settlements
BRI	Belt and Road Initiative
BSE	Beijing Stock Exchange
CBPC	China Bond Pricing Center
CBIRC	China Banking and Insurance Regulatory Commission
CCDC	China Central Depository and Clearing
CCMC	Communist Chinese Military Company
CDR	China Depositary Receipt
CFETS	China's Foreign Exchange Trade System
CFTC	Commodity Futures Trading Commission
CGB	Chinese Government Bond
CHIPS	Clearing House Interbank Payment System
CIBM	China Interbank Bond Market
CICC	China International Capital Corporation
CIPS	Cross-border Interbank Payment System
CIRC	China Insurance Regulatory Commission

CIRP	Covered Interest Rate Parity
CMIC	Chinese Military Industrial Complex Company
CNAPS	China National Advanced Payment System
CNY	Chinese Yuan (Renminbi)
COFER	Currency Composition of Official Foreign Exchange Reserves
CSDC	China Securities Depository and Clearing Corporation Limited
CSRC	China Securities Regulatory Commission
DR	Depositary Receipt
ETF	Exchange Traded Fund
FASB	Financial Accounting Standards Board
FCA	Financial Conduct Authority
FDI	Foreign Direct Investment
FINRA	Financial Industry Regulatory Authority
FSDC	Financial Stability and Development Commission
FTZ	Free Trade Zone
GAAP	Generally Accepted Accounting Principles
GDR	Global Depositary Receipt
GEB	Growth Enterprise Board
GEM	Growth Enterprise Market
HFCAA	Holding Foreign Companies Accountable Act
HKEX	Hong Kong Stock Exchanges and Clearing Limited
HKSCC	Hong Kong Securities Clearing Company Limited
IMF	International Monetary Fund
IOSCO	International Organization of Securities Commissions
IPO	Initial Public Offering
IRP	Interest Rate Parity
JPX	Japan Exchange Group
LSE	London Stock Exchange
MoF	Ministry of Finance
MSRB	Municipal Securities Rulemaking Board
NAFMII	National Association of Financial Market Institutional Investors
NASD	National Association of Securities Dealers
NASDAQ	National Association of Securities Dealers Automated Quotations
NCD	Negotiable Certificate of Deposit
NDAA	National Defense Authorization Act

NDF	Non-Deliverable Forward
NDRC	National Development and Reform Commission
NEEQ	National Equities Exchange and Quotations
NFA	National Futures Association
NYSE	New York Stock Exchange
OFAC	Office of Foreign Assets Control
OTC	Over-the-Counter
OTCBB	Over-the-Counter Bulletin Board
PBC	People's Bank of China
PRC	People's Republic of China
PCAOB	Public Company Accounting Oversight Board
QFII	Qualified Foreign Institutional Investor
QDLP	Qualified Domestic Limited Partner
QDIE	Qualified Domestic Investment Enterprise
QDII	Qualified Domestic Institutional Investor
RMB	Renminbi; Chinese Yuan
RQDII	Renminbi Qualified Domestic Institutional Investor
RQFII	Renminbi Qualified Foreign Institutional Investor
RTGS	Real-Time Gross Settlement
SAC	Securities Association of China
SAFE	State Administration of Foreign Exchange
SAIC	State Administration for Industry and Commerce
SAMR	State Administration for Market Regulation
SAT	State Administration of Taxation
SDR	Special Drawing Right
SEC	Securities and Exchange Commission
SFC	Securities and Futures Commission
SGE	Shanghai Gold Exchange
SGX	Singapore Exchange
SIFMA	Securities Industry and Financial Markets Association
SIIO	State Internet Information Office
SIX	Swiss Stock Exchange
SMEB	Small-and-Medium Enterprise Board
SOE	State-Owned Enterprise
SPE	Special Purpose Entity
SSE	Shanghai Stock Exchange
STAR	Science and Technology Innovation Board
SWIFT	Society for Worldwide Interbank Financial Telecommunications

SZSE	Shenzhen Stock Exchange
TBM	Third Board Market
UIRP	Uncovered Interest Rate Parity
USD	US Dollar
VIE	Variable Interest Entity
WFE	World Federation of Exchanges
WTO	World Trade Organization
WVR	Weighted Voting Rights

Part I

Introduction

Chapter 1

Opening-up for Financial Market Reform and Development

Opening-up is a precondition for successful financial market reform and development in China. The reform and opening-up are mutually reinforcing, as reform necessitates opening-up, and opening-up requires reform. Opening-up encompasses two levels: first, introducing foreign-funded institutions to the domestic market or allowing domestic institutions to expand internationally, and second, developing the domestic financial market in accordance with the rules of the market, respecting and adapting to international market rules and conventions. The second level represents a higher level of opening-up. China's financial market was established and developed after the implementation of the reform and opening-up policy in 1978. The market exemplifies how opening-up can promote reform and development. Following international rules leads to rapid financial market growth, but not following such rules could lead to problems or even necessitate a fresh start. As the scope and depth of opening-up continue to expand, our understanding of its importance deepens, and opening-up itself becomes an indispensable aspect of reform. Over the more than 40 years of reform and opening-up, it has become evident that opening-up can drive domestic reform, which leads to significant progress in economic and social development in a short period of time. By continuing to make good use of this valuable experience and elevating the level of opening-up of the economy, China can gain a competitive edge in global competition.

China is currently the second-largest economy in the world, as well as a middle-income country, although its per capita GDP still lags behind those of other developing countries. The economy is undergoing a profound structural transition from extensive to intensive, from investment-driven and external demand-driven to innovation-driven, focusing more on structure, quality, and efficiency. This transition is a necessary step toward a more advanced phase. In this critical stage of upgrading the growth model, it is essential to actively promote supply-side structural reforms, eliminate various price distortions, and further utilize market forces in resource allocation. Throughout this process, it is crucial to enhance the financial market system, fully leverage the financial market to serve the real economy, and optimize resource allocation. Meanwhile, only an open financial market can possess true broadness and depth, and only the price signals generated by an open financial market can have true representativeness and influence, attracting more capital and investors to support the development of the real economy. As China becomes increasingly integrated into the world economy, the current development stage necessitates a steadily opening financial market that is progressively integrated into international financial orders. The internationalization of the RMB also requires further financial market opening up to provide multiple investment opportunities for the offshore RMB. For the RMB to become an international reserve currency, it must first be widely accepted as a trade and investment currency worldwide. In this context, it is crucial to adhere to the principles of promoting reform and development through opening-up, emphasizing top-level design and comprehensive arrangements, strengthening macroprudential management, and establishing a modernized financial market system that is compatible with China's status as a major open economy. This system should be comprehensive, well structured, efficient, secure, robust, inclusive, competitive, and supportive of the sustainable development of the real economy.

1. Milestones in China's Financial Market Development

Since 1978, China's financial market has been gradually established, developed, and expanded. At present, China has essentially formed a relatively comprehensive multitiered financial market system covering currency, bonds, stocks, insurance, gold, foreign exchange, and derivative markets. China's financial market is a good example of promoting reform and development through opening-up and abiding by international financial rules. However, there were some detours in the early phase, when problems arose due to not adhering to the laws of the financial market, even necessitating a fresh start. To better analyze the current status and future prospects of China's financial market, it is essential to understand the history of financial market development and learn from both experience and lessons.

In the course of development over the past few centuries, the financial systems of the United Kingdom and the US have also encountered various issues. For instance, after the Great Depression, the US introduced the *Glass-Steagall Act*. Following the crisis of the American Savings and Loans Association, the US implemented the *Financial Institutions Reform, Recovery, and Enforcement Act* in 1989, a comprehensive financial reform package. As integrated financial operations expanded, the US introduced the *Financial Services Modernization Act* at the beginning of the 21st century. After the Enron scandal, the *Sarbanes–Oxley Act* was enacted to strengthen corporate governance and auditing systems, along with improvements to accounting statements. In the wake of the subprime mortgage crisis, the *Dodd–Frank Act* was introduced. This development pattern in the US illustrates that financial market legislation often emerges as a responsive action to problems that arise within the financial market. Regulatory authorities examine these issues, analyze their causes, and subsequently enact legislative and institutional adjustments to address them.

China's financial market development took place within a relatively short time in the context of rapid economic development. First, during the initial stages of the implementation of the reform and opening-up policy, there was a need for significant development across various sectors. However, the government faced severe financial constraints, as even the issuance of treasury bills was challenging and required mandatory allocation. In the early 1990s, the establishment of the Shanghai Stock Exchange (SSE) and the Shenzhen Stock Exchange (SZSE) played a crucial role in driving state-owned enterprise reform. As a result, China's financial market was developed predominantly under government initiatives rather than a gradual process of marketization. Second, China's financial market development took a different path than its economic reform.

Economic reform typically started from the private sector, driven by market forces, and then progressed through summary and expansion. However, the primary function of China's financial market in early times was to serve the real economy, leading to several detours and even a restart in a few sections. Finally, China's financial market emerged amid an underdeveloped credit system. In China's early days of reform and opening-up, credit primarily relied on collective trust rather than individual creditworthiness. Essentially, the more significant an entity's "official stamp" was (meaning the higher the level of the entity within the administration), the higher its perceived creditworthiness. Nevertheless, the development of financial markets requires a foundation built on individual credit, as a system solely reliant on collective trust would cause significant problems in the financial system. However, it is worth noting that during the transition from a planned economy to a market economy and before the establishment of a comprehensive individual credit system, collective trust did indeed play a crucial role. With continuous developments in accounting, credit reporting, and credit ratings in recent years, China's individual credit system has gradually improved, providing favorable conditions for the development of the financial market. In fact, many of the issues currently observed in the financial market are related to the incompleteness of the individual credit system and the lack of sound intermediary systems, such as accounting, auditing, and credit ratings.

Reflecting on the development of financial markets, it follows the principles of financial market development and adheres to international rules resulting in faster progress in domestic financial market growth. Conversely, deviating from these principles can lead to problems and sometimes even require a restart (Xu *et al.*, 2017). Prior to the 1996 Asian Financial Crisis, a significant irregularity occurred in China's government bond futures market. The largest bond firm at the time, Wanguo Securities, faced bankruptcy due to risky futures investments. The "3·27" government bond futures incident highlighted the inadequate consideration of market conditions and lack of gradual progression when introducing financial market products. These introductions were driven by regulatory authorities' subjective thoughts, leading to lack of foresight and consistency that eventually triggered the incident. The key reasons for the incident were as follows: First, China's interest rates were far from being market-driven; second, there was a lack of transparency in the Ministry of Finance's rate hedging policy; and third, there was an inadequate understanding of government bond futures risks from the exchanges. Overall, the incident underscored the unstable foundation of the government bond futures market at the time.

These risks spurred the Chinese government to commit to developing a more unified, healthy, and transparent market. Regarding bond markets, the State Council approved the establishment of China's new interbank bond market in 1997, accompanied by a series of policy measures. This laid the groundwork for the rapid development of the bond market in the subsequent two decades. The interbank bond market primarily caters to institutional investors, while the SSE and SZSE are dominated by individual investors. The interbank market facilitates over-the-counter price inquiries, whereas the exchanges enable centralized matching transactions. With institutions as the major participants, the interbank market is well suited for large-scale fund transactions, facilitating the rollout of many innovations. Regarding the stock market, comprehensive reforms have led to the establishment of a robust multitiered market system. The introduction of the National Equities Exchange and Quotations and the Science and Technology Innovation Board (SSE STAR Market), along with the establishment of the Beijing Stock Exchange, marked significant breakthroughs in the reform of the stock market registration-based system. This has deepened market-oriented issuance and significantly enhanced the efficiency and predictability of review and registration. Critical aspects such as trading and delisting procedures have been further improved, resulting in enhanced investment and financing functions within the stock market. Various cross-border trading mechanisms have been introduced, including Shanghai–Hong Kong Stock Connect, Shenzhen–Hong Kong Stock Connect, and Shanghai–London Stock Connect. Additionally, the rules for qualified foreign institutional investors (QFII), renminbi-qualified foreign institutional investors (RQFII), qualified domestic institutional investors (QDII), and renminbi-qualified domestic institutional investors (RQDII) have been continuously refined. The reform of overseas listing regulations has progressed steadily, cross-border investment and financing facilitation have significantly improved, and A-shares have increasingly gained prominence in international benchmark indices. Consequently, the international attractiveness and influence of China's capital market have greatly increased.

At the end of 1997, the first National Conference on Financial Work explicitly proposed the development of the capital market and the expansion of direct financing. Relevant authorities accelerated the promotion of capital market development, strengthened the establishment of fundamental institutional frameworks, and improved market functionality. The development of China's stock market and bond market have achieved significant growth. By the end of 2023, the outstanding balance of bonds in custody amounted to RMB 157.9 trillion. China's bond market size ranks second globally and first in Asia, as does the balance of China's corporate credit bonds. Among these, the interbank bond market has a complete product sequence and a rich variety of trading instruments, making it the core of China's bond and other financial markets. According to Wind Economic Database, as of the end of 2023, the total number of listed companies in the SSE and SZSE was 5,346, with a total market value of RMB 77.76 trillion. Among them, there were 2,263 companies listed in SSE, 2,844 in SZE, and 239 in Beijing Stock Exchange. According to statistics from the World Federation of Exchanges (WFE), in 2022, the Chinese stock market's total market capitalization ranked second in the world, below only that of the US.

Over the past two decades, China's financing products have become more diversified, and the financing structure has significantly improved. The reliance on indirect financing has steadily shifted. In terms of total amount, from 2002 to 2023, the aggregate financing to the real economy (AFRE)[1] increased from RMB 2 trillion to RMB 35.6 trillion, with an average annual growth rate of 17.7%, which was 3.07 percentage points higher than the average annual growth of RMB loans over the same period. In 2023, the ratio of AFRE to GDP was 28.2%, 10.05 percentage points higher than that in 2002. In terms of structure, from 2002 to 2023, the proportion of loans (excluding entrusted and trust loans) in the AFRE decreased from 95.5% to 61.8%, and the proportion of direct financing by enterprises[2] experienced an inverted W-shaped trend, increased from

---

[1]AFRE (stock) refers to the outstanding of financing provided by the financial system to the real economy at the end of a period. The data are released by the PBC.

[2]That is, the total proportion of corporate bond financing and nonfinancial domestic stock financing in the AFRE. In recent years, the PBC made efforts to improve the statistical method of AFRE. Since July 2018, the PBC incorporated "Asset-backed Securities of Depository Financial Institutions" and "Loans Written off" into AFRE, which is reflected as a sub-item of "Other Financing". Since September 2018, the PBC incorporated "Local Government Special Bonds" into AFRE. Since September 2019, the PBC incorporated "Asset-backed Securities of Non-Financial Enterprises" into "Net Financing of Corporate Bonds". Since December 2019, the PBC introduced "Treasury Bonds" and "Local Government General Bonds" into AFRE and merged with "Local Government Special

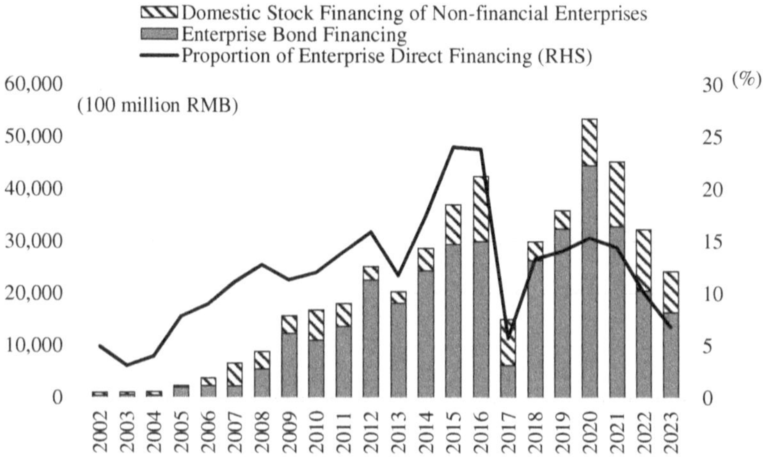

Figure 1. The proportion of direct financing for enterprises to AFRE.

Note: The black line indicates the proportion of direct financing for enterprise (RHS). Direct financing for enterprises = enterprise bond financing + domestic stock financing of non-financial enterprises.
Source: Wind Economic Database.

4.9% to 24.0% in 2015 and decreased to 6.8% in 2023 (see Figure 1). The changes are related to the adjustments of the statistical method of AFRE. By the end of 2023, the proportion of government bonds reached 27%.

The Chinese bond market can be broadly divided into exchange-traded markets and over-the-counter markets, with the latter primarily serving institutional investors. Currently, the market for institutional investors follows a global trading model. The over-the-counter market (interbank market) is dominated by institutional investors, accounting for approximately 87% of the bond market nationwide. The SSE and the SZSE, which were originally centralized trading markets for individual investors, did not previously conform to the dynamics of bond trading and had slow development. Only after transitioning to over-the-counter inquiry-based trading for institutional investors did they experience rapid growth.

Bonds" into "Government Bonds", which is recorded at face value at depositories. The historical data were traced back to January 2017. As of January 2023, three kinds of non-depository financial institutions, i.e., the Consumer Finance Companies, the Wealth Management Companies, and the Financial Asset Investment Companies, were included in the coverage of financial statistics of PBC.

The total size of the Chinese bond market has grown rapidly over the past decade, with the proportion of the bond market size to GDP continually increasing and its growth surpassing that of GDP. In 2001, the ratio of the bond market size to GDP was less than 20%, and it stands at approximately 125% in 2023. From a global perspective, the ranking of China's bond market size has significantly risen. According to statistics from the Bank for International Settlements (BIS), China ranked 25th in the world in terms of total bond market size in 1997. According to the Securities Industry and Financial Markets Association (SIFMA) data, as of the end of 2022, the largest national bond market in the world was the US, with a total balance of approximately 51.9 trillion USD, accounting for 40.0% of the global total. The second-largest bond market was China, with a balance of approximately 21.7 trillion USD, accounting for 16.7% of the global total. Currently, the third-largest bond market globally is Japan, with a bond market balance of approximately 12.1 trillion USD. Japan's bond market structure, shaped by prolonged economic stagnation, differs notably from China. According to Asian Development Bank (ADB) statistics, government bonds account for over 90% of the bond balance in Japan.

Generally speaking, China's bond market has been established and developed in the process of resolving various contradictions and has been driven by market demands, not by certain administrative authorities or thinkers. In the process of addressing these contradictions, China has not relied on administrative intervention but rather fostered an open bond market through more profound reforms. The practice of the past two decades has shown that the most challenging times often present the best opportunities for reforms. It is during difficulties that consensus on reforms can be more easily achieved. The ultimate way of solving various issues lies in deepening reforms rather than regressing. This is the key takeaway from China's experience with its bond market.

First, for a new bond market to advance, it must be market-oriented rather than relying on increased administrative approvals or various restrictions. Reducing administrative approvals does not equate to relaxing regulations. In fact, China has tightened the corporate bond issuance regulations over time rather than reducing them. If a company does not maintain good credit, it is difficult for the company to issue new bonds in the market today. If an issuer provides false or fake information, investors will immediately sell off the bonds, making it challenging for the issuer to raise funds again. Another important lesson in bond market development is the value of reducing implicit government guarantees. The overarching direction of reform is to reduce administrative approvals while strengthening market-oriented regulations. These market-oriented regulations encompass information disclosure, accounting, audits, and arrangements for custody and clearing.

Second, over the past decade, institutional investors have made a significant breakthrough in China's bond market. While individuals may not directly access the institutional market, they can still invest in bonds. Individuals can engage in bond investments through funds, bank wealth management products, or other institutional investors. These institutional investors can manage risks more effectively in the market and achieve relatively higher returns than individuals could. Access to the financial market requires specialized knowledge, and institutional investors can professionally assess the risks of various financial and bond products, which is challenging for individual investors. Of course, individual investors can also purchase government bonds over the counter, but these products are unlikely to yield high returns. The growth of institutional investors has allowed the public's extensive savings to flow into the interbank bond market, fostering its diversification. This accelerates the development of the bond market while simultaneously addressing the issue of limited bond knowledge among individual investors and preventing fraudulent sales. The characteristics of the bond market are somewhat different from those of certain stock exchanges. China has essentially followed the development patterns of major global bond markets in building its own bond market, making significant progress over the past decade. In the future, the development of the bond market should continue in this direction to make further progress.

Despite the substantial number of bond products in the market, this number still falls far short of meeting the demands. To fulfill and adapt to market needs, various types of corporate credit bonds should be gradually introduced. The introduction of related products is not done for the sake of innovation itself but rather to cater to the requirements of the real economy and continuously improve the financial services for the real economy. This marks a significant difference between the development of China's bond market and that of some Western countries. The experience of the past decade tells us that in the bond market, the government should step back and allow intermediary institutions and self-regulatory organizations to play larger roles. For instance, in 2007, China established the National Association of Financial Market Institutional Investors (NAFMII) as a self-regulatory agency. As of January 5, 2024, NAFMII has 9,632 member institutions. Certain crucial financial products are not proposed by the People's Bank of China (PBC) or a specific regulatory authority; rather, they originate from members of NAFMII. After proposing financial products, members of NAFMII, along with lawyers and accountants, engage in discussions to balance various interests and contradictions, restrain risks, and finally, formulate product rules and design concepts. These are then submitted for filing with market regulatory authorities. Regulatory authorities primarily inspect the process by which the financial product was developed and whether it complies with existing regulations and risk control provisions. They evaluate whether the product represents the will of individuals or a few specific institutions or if it reflects the consensus of all market participants. Market entities have increasingly played pivotal roles in innovation. This process has not involved traditional approval mechanisms, as the market entities are directly involved stakeholders. Some are issuers seeking more convenient financing, while others are investors demanding better safeguards. Ultimately, a balance of various interests has been reached. The design concept and process of these products are much more mature than what individual government officials might come up with. This is also a key factor for the success of China's bond market. Moving forward, this approach should be upheld to drive the innovation of bond products.

2. China's Financial Market Structures and International Comparisons

2.1 *Direct and indirect financing*

Over the past decade, the proportion of direct financing in China has risen rapidly but is still low compared with that in other countries. As shown in Figure 2, the proportion of direct financing by enterprises in AFRE experienced an inverted W-shaped trend, which increased from 9% in 2006 to 24.0% in 2015 and decreased to 6.8% in 2023, with the proportion of bond financing varying from 5.4% to 4.6%. The ratio of direct financing to indirect financing in China is not only lower than that in mature markets in countries such as the US and Singapore but also lower than that in countries such as South Korea, Malaysia, and Japan (see Figure 3).

2.2 *Broad bond market (corporate bonds + ABS)*

China's broad bond market has expanded rapidly, but the proportion of structured financing remains relatively low. From 2006 to 2023, the scale

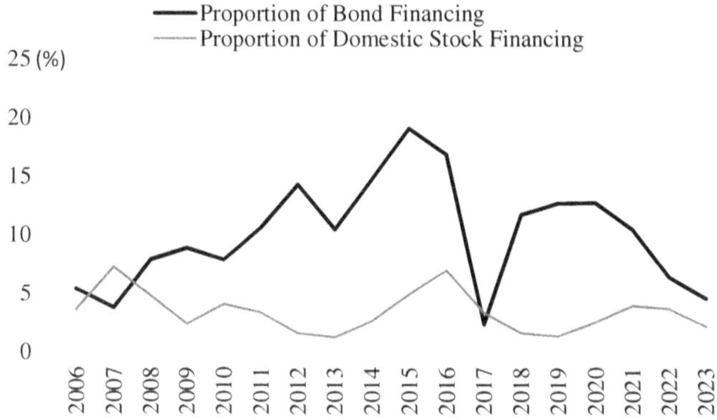

Figure 2. The proportion of China's direct financing to AFRE.

Source: Wind Economic Database.

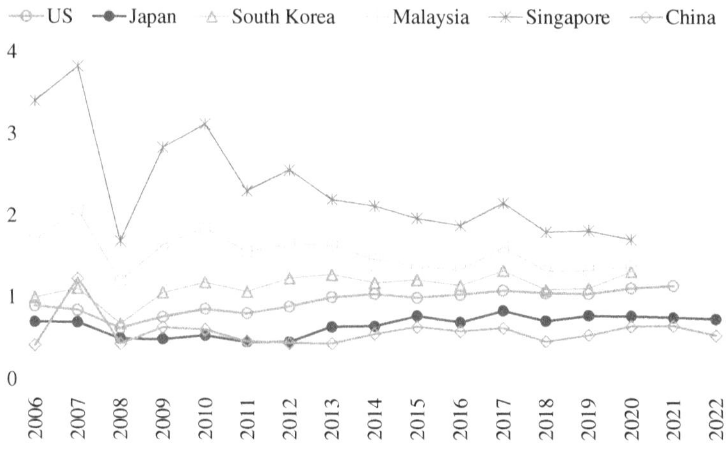

Figure 3. The ratio of direct and indirect financing in different countries.

Note: Indicators = (total market value of listed companies + outstanding balance of corporate bonds)/ outstanding balance of credit to the private sector.

Source: SIFMA, ADB, Wind Economic Database, the World Bank.

of China's broad bond market increased from RMB 0.75 trillion to RMB 43.96 trillion, growing more than fifty-fold (see Figure 4). Within the market, enterprise bonds increased by 58 times, and asset-backed securities (ABS) increased by 46 times. Although ABS has grown quickly since 2013, its low initial base means it still comprises a small portion of the bond market. In 2021, ABS accounted for 10.5% of the broad bond, which

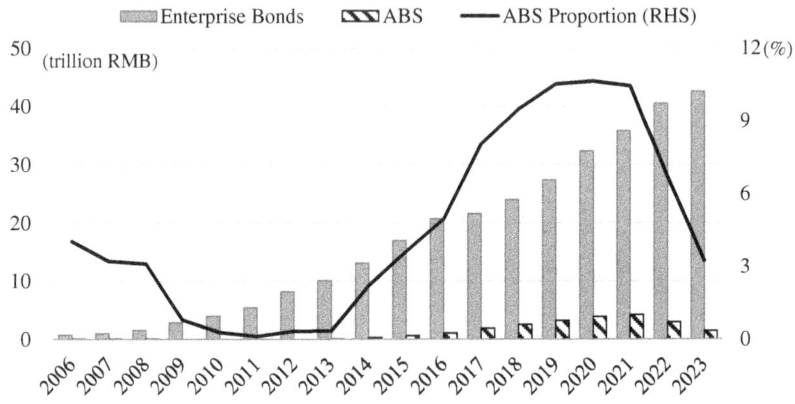

Figure 4. The scale of China's broad bond market.

Note: Enterprise bonds = financial bonds – policy-based bank debts + corporate bonds + corporate debenture bonds + debt financing instruments.
Source: Wind Economic Database.

was significantly lower than figures in Japan (nearly 25%) and the US (58%, Figure 5).

2.3 *Broad bond market and shadow banking*

While China's direct financing market has developed rapidly and the broad bond market has expanded, shadow banking surged for a period of time, bringing with it increased potential risks. Figure 6 shows that from 2009 to 2022, China's shadow banking market (narrow measure of NBFI) increased from USD 0.21 trillion to USD 10.3 trillion, surpassing a 3:2 ratio to the broad bond market scale since 2012.

In terms of shadow banking market structure, according to the FSB classification,[3] fund products (EF1) account for more than three-quarters

[3]FSB proposes a dichotomy definition of shadow banking. In a broad sense, it is the financing intermediation activities of all informal banks and is a full-aperture measurement index of all non-bank financial intermediation activities. Shadow banking in the narrow sense refers to non-bank financial institutions that participate in credit intermediation activities and may bring financial stability risks similar to commercial banks. According to economic function (EF), shadow banking is classified into five categories: fund (EF1), loan companies (EF2), brokerage financing (EF3), guarantee company (EF4), and securitization platform (EF5). Since 2015, the Financial Stability Board has officially defined shadow banking as "non-bank financial intermediation" (NBFI) and

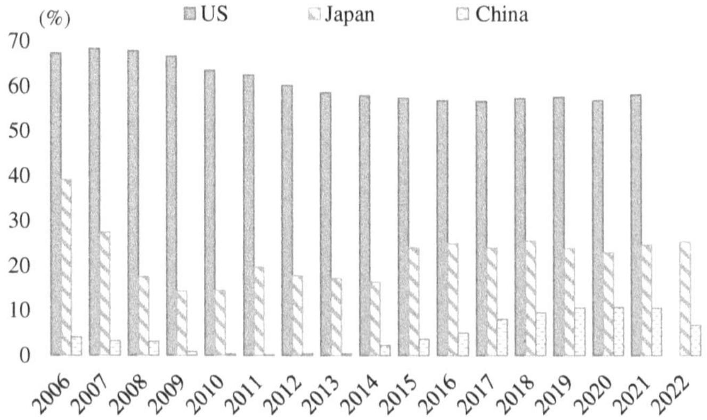

Figure 5. International comparison of the proportion of ABS in the broad bond market.

Source: Japan Securities Dealers Association, SIFMA, ADB, Wind Economic Database.

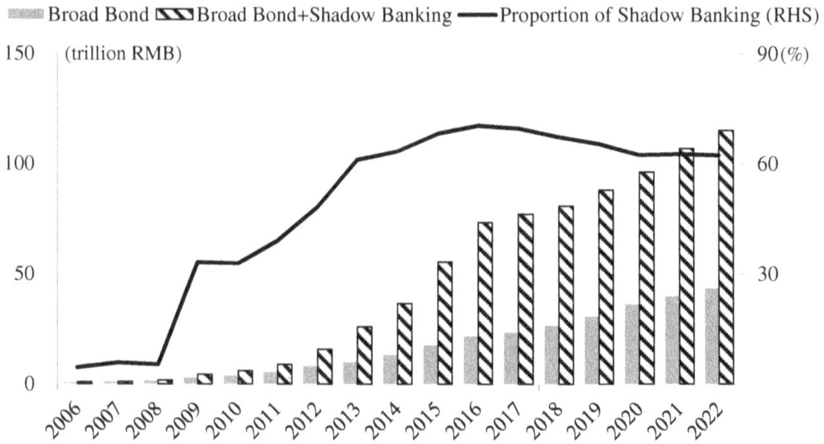

Figure 6. Comparison of shadow banking and broad bond scale in China.

Note: Narrow measure of NBFI is valued in USD trillions in FSB report, and converted to RMB with year-end foreign exchange rate.
Source: FSB, Wind Economic Database.

of the market. In 2022, according to FSB classification, EF1 (bond funds, mixed funds, credit hedge funds, and real estate funds) accounted for

proposed three metrics to measure the size of shadow banking. Starting with its 2018 annual report, FSB has fully changed the name of "shadow banking" to "nonbank financial intermediation".

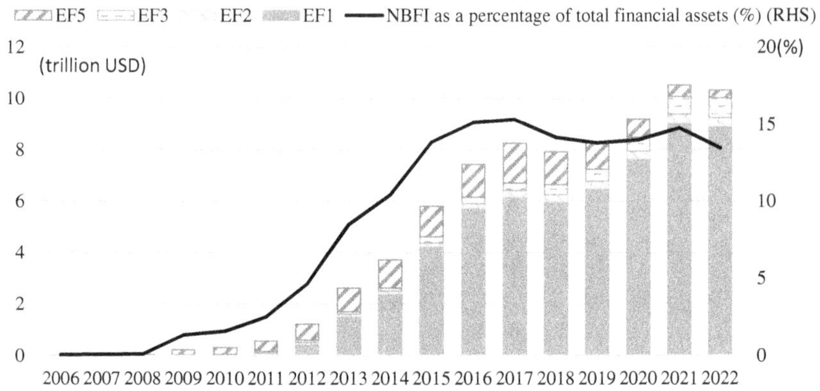

Figure 7. Scale and structure of shadow banking in China.

Source: FSB.

86.4%, EF2 (financial companies, leasing companies, factoring companies, and consumer credit companies) accounted for 3.2%, EF3 (securities brokers and underwriters) accounted for 7.5%, and EF5 (asset securitization platforms) accounted for 2.9% (see Figure 7).

In recent years, with efforts to mitigate aggregate risks, the total scale of shadow banking in China has stabilized. The scale of high-risk shadow banking has decreased by approximately RMB 25 trillion[4] from its historical peak. In April 2018, the *Guiding Opinions on Regulating Asset Management Business of Financial Institutions* (also known as the "*New Asset Management Regulations*") was promulgated. This regulation, which included a transitional period,[5] changed the practice of rigid redemption, unified regulatory standards, and prevented arbitrage. It helped eliminate both clear and implicit guarantees provided by banks to investors when issuing wealth management products, effectively curbing the rapid expansion of shadow banking. As a result, the relative importance of NBFI in China has decreased. China's shadow banking has shown a relative contraction compared with the global market. At the end

[4]CSRC (2022).

[5]The transition period was scheduled to conclude at the end of 2020. To ease the pressure of the transformation of financial institutions' asset management business during the COVID-19 pandemic, the CBIRC announced in July 2020 that the transitional period of the *New Asset Management Regulations* would be extended to the end of 2021.

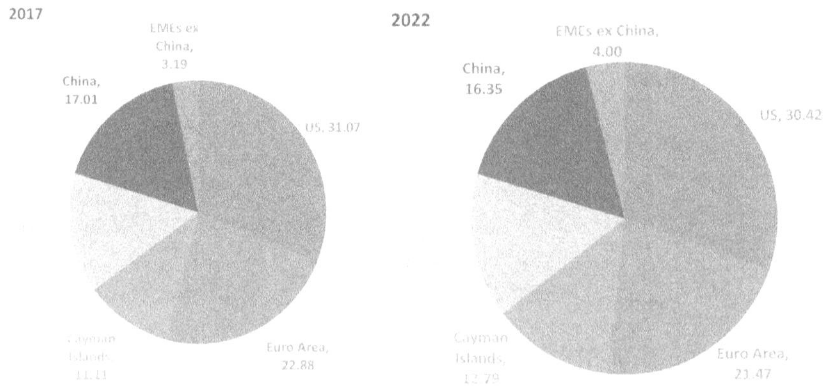

Figure 8. The share of China's shadow banking in the global market.
Source: FSB.

of 2017, China's shadow banking accounted for 17.01% of the global market; by 2022, this ratio had decreased to 16.35% (Figure 8).

2.4 *International comparison of bond market indicators*

2.4.1 *Outstanding bonds*

China's bond market has developed rapidly over the past decade, with both the absolute scale of the bond market and the bond market/GDP ratio experiencing rapid growth. However, China's government bond/GDP ratio is still lower than that of countries such as the US and Japan, and the corporate credit bond/GDP ratio also lags behind that of the US market (see Figures 9–11).

2.4.2 *Bond issuance*

China's bond issuance has seen a significant increase in recent years, with an optimized structure, particularly in the government and corporate bond sectors. According to the ADB data, in the government bond market, due to the rapid growth of local government bond issuances, the issuance scale increased from nearly 0.7 trillion USD in 2014 to 3.26 trillion USD in 2022 (see Figure 12). The issuance of corporate credit bonds has also

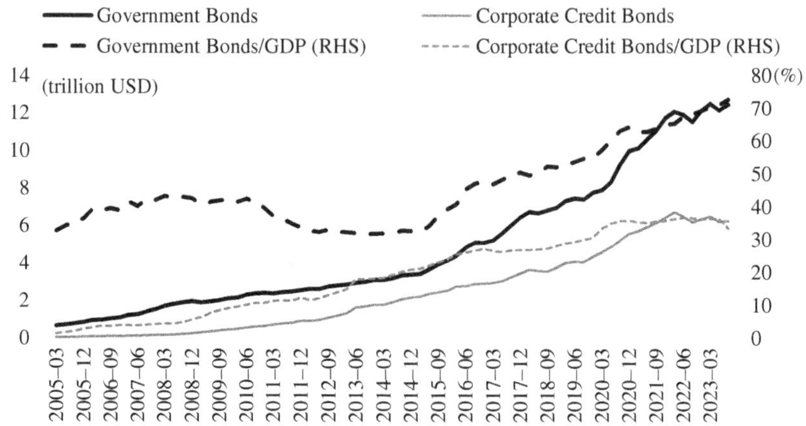

Figure 9. The outstanding scale of China's bond market.

Note: According to the statistics from the ADB, government bonds include central government bonds, local government bonds, central bank notes, and policy financial bonds. Corporate credit bonds include corporate debenture bonds, corporate bonds, non-financial companies' debt financing instruments, and bonds issued by financial institutions. In China, the bonds issued by financial institutions are not included in corporate credit bonds.

Source: ADB.

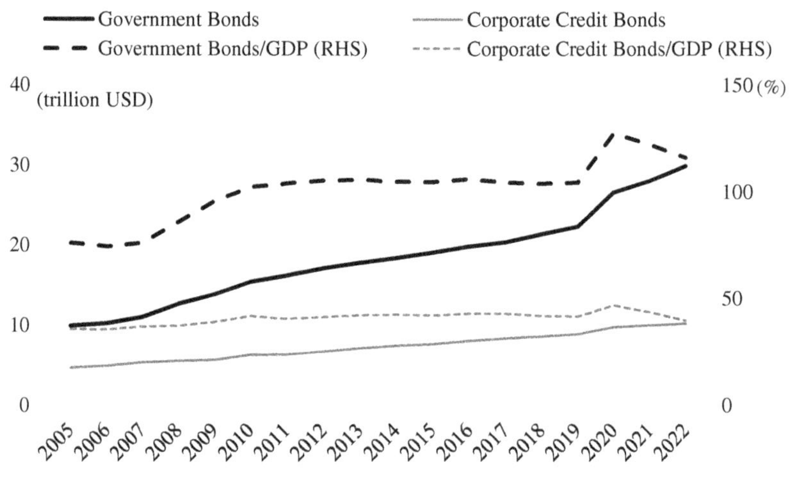

Figure 10. The outstanding scale of the US bond market.

Source: SIFMA.

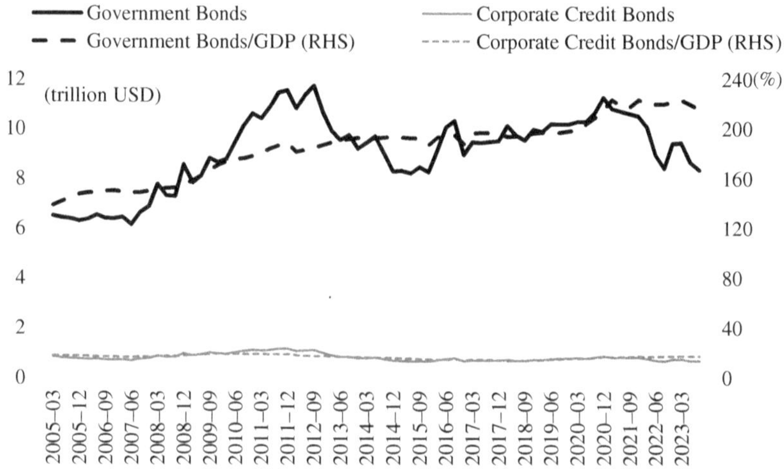

Figure 11. The outstanding scale of Japan's bond market.

Source: ADB.

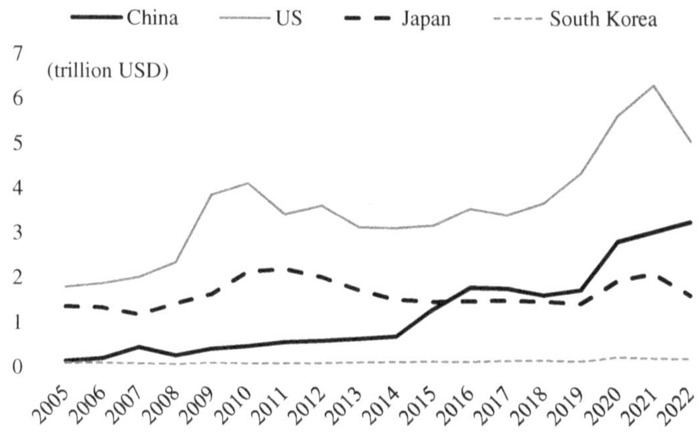

Figure 12. International comparison of the scale of government bond issuance.

Source: ADB, SIFMA.

grown rapidly, from 0.93 trillion USD in 2014 to 2.56 trillion USD in 2022 (see Figure 13).

2.4.3 *Turnover and liquidity*

China's bond market trading scale rapidly increased from RMB 40 trillion in 2005 to over RMB 1,000 trillion in 2016, reaching RMB 2628 trillion

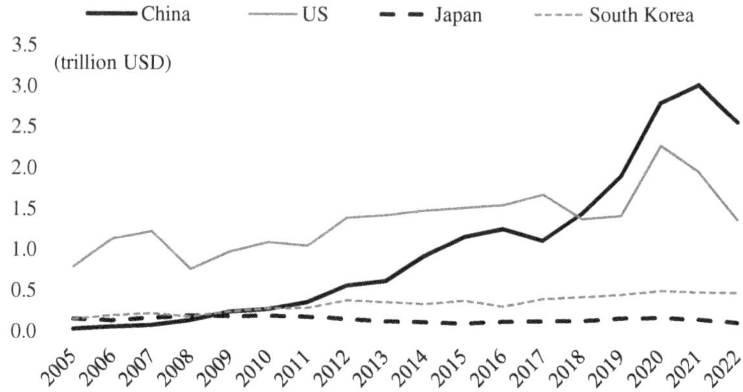

Figure 13. International comparison of the scale of corporate credit bond issuance.
Source: ADB, SIFMA.

in 2023. Given that this period also coincided with the rapid growth of China's outstanding bonds, we have chosen the relative value of turnover (namely, annual turnover/average outstanding bonds) as an indicator in this section. We find that despite the significant increase in bond turnover, the turnover rate suggests that although the liquidity level of government bonds has improved, that of corporate credit bonds has not.

In terms of cross-market comparison (as shown in Figures 14–16), China's government bond market enjoys better liquidity than those of Japan and South Korea, but there is still considerable space for improvement compared with the bond market in the US. The liquidity of corporate credit bonds in China is not on par with that of the US or South Korea.

2.5 *Multitiered bond market*

China's bond market operates as a multitiered system, dominated by interbank and exchange markets with the over-the-counter market playing a supplementary role. These markets collaborate to fully meet the needs of various participants in the financial market. The China Interbank Bond Market (CIBM), established in 1997, is the largest and most liquid segment of the Chinese bond market, accounting for approximately 86% of the outstanding volume. The CIBM stands as the main trading venue for Chinese government bonds (CGBs), policy bank bonds, and negotiable certificates of deposit (NCDs), which are popular among overseas

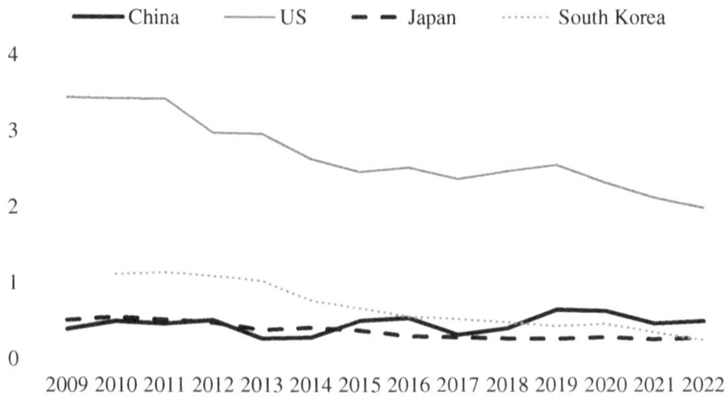

Figure 14. Government bond trading volume (relative value).

Note: Trading volume (relative value) = trading volume of the year/(the average of the balance at the end of the previous year and the balance at the end of the year). US government bonds include treasury bonds and municipal bonds, with the former possessing higher liquidity.
Source: ADB, SIFMA.

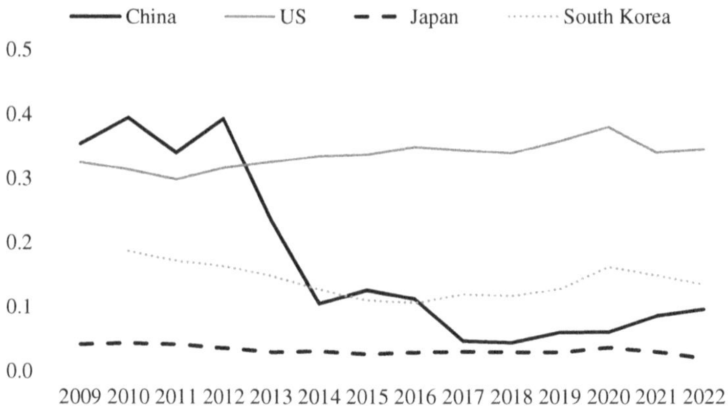

Figure 15. Corporate credit bond trading volume (relative value).
Source: ADB, SIFMA.

investors. The interbank bond market serves as an over-the-counter trading platform for institutional investors and is regulated by the PBC. In contrast, the exchange market mainly operates as a centralized matching trading market for retail investors and is regulated by the China Securities

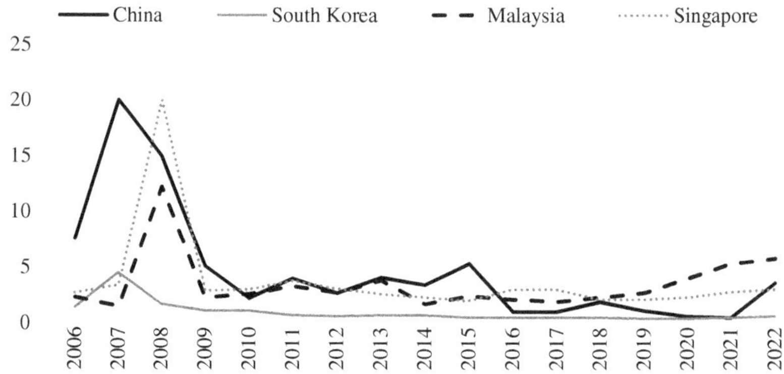

Figure 16. Government bond bid ask spreads.

Source: ADB.

Regulatory Commission (CSRC). The bond issuance of the interbank bond market accounts for 86% of China's total bond market size, making it the primary market for bonds. In 2022, the interbank market accounted for 87.6% of the total bond trading volume, while the exchange market accounted for 12.3%, serving as an important complement to the interbank market.

The offering credit bond products continue to innovate with increasing diversity. China's bond market includes various types of bonds, such as government bonds, policy financial bonds, local government bonds, central bank bills, corporate debenture bonds, corporate bonds, short-term commercial papers, medium-term notes, and asset-backed securities. Innovative bond products, including SME collective bonds, commercial bank subordinated bonds, Panda bonds, convertible bonds, exchangeable bonds, perpetual bonds, project revenue bonds, green bonds, and special drawing rights (SDR)-denominated bonds, have emerged, catering to the diverse needs of investors. The wide variety of bonds caters to the needs of different types of investors. In terms of trading venues, the interbank market offers a complete range of bond varieties, with abundant types of interest rate bonds and credit bonds. The exchange market primarily deals with corporate debenture bonds and corporate bonds, as well as some government bonds and local government bonds. Government bonds, local government bonds, and corporate debenture bonds eligible for exchange listing can be cross-listed and traded between the interbank market and the exchange market.

The following are the main credit bonds.

Corporate debenture bond: China's corporate debenture bond market began in the 1980s and has undergone several regulatory changes. In 1987, the State Council issued the *Interim Administrative Measures of Corporate Debenture Bonds*, requiring approval from the PBC for issuance. Building on this, in August 1993, the State Council released the *Administrative Measures for Corporate Debenture Bonds*, which standardized the issuance approval process, issuance quotas, industries targeted, and interest rates for corporate debenture bonds. It was stipulated that the State Planning Commission, in conjunction with the PBC, the Ministry of Finance, and the CSRC, would propose the annual scale and various indicators for national corporate debenture bond issuance for approval by the State Council. During this period, administrative oversight was prominent in corporate debenture bonds. Due to their high yields, transfer difficulty, and low liquidity, corporate debenture bonds had relatively low turnover. The SSE and SZSE allowed corporate debenture bonds with a face value of over RMB 100 million to be listed for trading on the exchanges in 1996 and 1997, respectively, which improved bond liquidity. From 2000, issuance quotas of corporate debenture bonds were subject to special approvals from the State Council. In January 2008, the National Development and Reform Commission (NDRC) issued a *Circular on Promoting the Development of the Corporate Debenture Bond Market and Simplifying Issuance Approval Procedures*, streamlining the process for approving issuance after the quota's determination to one single step. This change facilitated the expansion of corporate debenture bond issuance. In 2015, while the NDRC continued to handle the acceptance, review, and supervision of corporate debenture bond issuance, it entrusted third-party market professionals to assess aspects such as compliance and financial indicators during the review process. In March 2020, the NDRC released a circular clarifying that corporate debenture bond issuance would be shifted from an approval-based system to a registration-based system.

Corporate bonds: Corporate bonds were established on the foundation of corporate debenture bonds. In recent years, the market orientation of corporate bond issuance has gradually increased. In August 2007, the CSRC promulgated and implemented the *Trial Measures for the Issuance of Corporate Bonds*, allowing listed companies to apply to the CSRC for the issuance of corporate bonds. Hindered by factors such as the complexity of the bond approval process, only 1,472 corporate bonds were issued from 2007 to 2014. In January 2015, the CSRC issued a revised version of the *Administrative Measures for the Issuance and Trading of Corporate Bonds*, reforming the relevant system by significantly simplifying the approval process, expanding the scope of issuing entities, enriching issuance methods, and increasing trading venues, resulting in a surge in the issuance of corporate bonds (see Figure 17). Subsequently, the issuance volume of corporate bonds gradually exceeded that of similar corporate financing instruments, such as medium-term notes and short-term financing bonds. The market now includes a range of innovative bonds such as bonds for innovative and entrepreneurial companies, poverty alleviation bonds, housing rental bonds, green bonds, renewable bonds, exchangeable bonds, Panda bonds, and Belt and Road bonds. In February 2021, in accordance with the requirements of the revised *Securities Law* in 2019, the CSRC revised the *Administrative Measures for the Issuance and Trading of Corporate Bonds*, implementing a registration-based system for the public issuance of corporate bonds.

Debt financing instruments: Debt financing instruments generally correspond to corporate debenture bonds regulated by the NDRC and corporate bonds regulated by the CSRC. NAFMII, under the PBC's regulations, introduced short-term financing notes, ultra-short-term financing notes, medium-term notes, SME collective notes, privately placed targeted debt

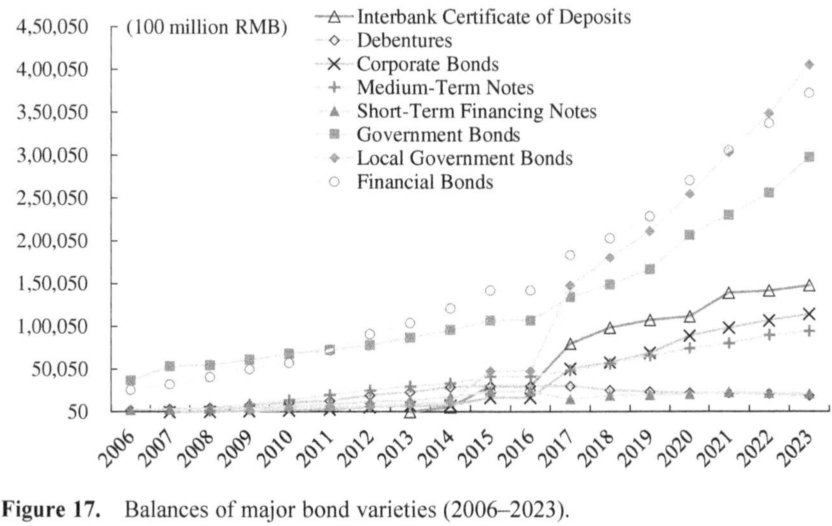

Figure 17. Balances of major bond varieties (2006–2023).

Source: Wind Economic Database.

financing instruments, asset-backed securities, and more. These are collectively referred to as debt financing instruments. China's corporate short-term financing notes originated in 1987 as tools for raising short-term funds for enterprises. Building on this pilot program, in 1989, the PBC successively issued a *Circular on Issues Related to Corporate Short-Term Financing Notes* and *Supplementary Circular on Issues Related to Corporate Short-Term Financing Notes*, allowing enterprises to issue short-term financing notes after approval from the central bank. Rules were introduced on bond interest rates, issuance quotas, and other aspects. However, the funds raised could only be used for short-term financing needs, not for long-term funding purposes or fixed asset investment. In 2005, the PBC issued the *Administrative Measures for Short-term Financing Notes*, allowing qualified nonfinancial enterprises[6] to issue short-term financing notes on the interbank bond market, subject to a filing-based issuance system. In 2007, NAFMII was established, and it took the initiative in managing the issuance of non-financial corporate debt financing instruments, such as medium-term notes and short-term financing notes. A registration-based system was introduced, which activated the market. Short-term financing notes have since made significant contributions to expanding direct financing channels for enterprises.

Interbank certificates of deposit: In December 2013, the PBC introduced interbank certificates of deposit in the interbank bond market. Its investment and trading entities include members of the interbank money market, fund management companies, and fund products. Due to their transferability and liquidity, interbank certificates of deposit offer commercial banks higher liquidity than interbank deposits. The issuance of the former has rapidly increased, contributing to the improvement of the short-term interest rate system. The volume of interbank certificates of deposit has largely increased since 2017.

All regulatory authorities have vigorously developed the bond markets (or similar markets) in China, especially the corporate credit bond

---

[6] Short-term financing securities of financial enterprises are mainly used by securities companies. In October 2004, the PBC and the CSRC issued the *Administrative Measures for the Short-term Financing Securities of Securities Companies*, clarifying that short-term financing securities of securities companies shall be jointly administered by the PBC and the CSRC, and other short-term financing securities shall be administered by the PBC. In 2006, due to changes in the market environment and other reasons, the securities company did not issue short-term financing bonds again, and it did not resume until 2012 (Xie Duo, 2014).

market, including the corporate bonds regulated by the CSRC and the bond investment plans regulated by the China Insurance Regulatory Commission (CIRC). These authorities have established different agencies for issuance, trading, and registration custody. In addition to the types of bonds or bond-like financing mentioned in Figure 18, there are also direct financing tools supervised by the China Banking Regulatory Commission (CBRC).

In addition to corporate credit bonds, the asset securitization market is also managed by different regulators and self-regulatory organizations, including asset-backed special plans, credit asset-backed securities, asset-backed notes, asset-backed plans, and credit asset circulation (see Figure 19). In addition to there being five types of asset-backed securities (ABS) mentioned above, such securities can also be listed and traded on the National Equities Exchange and Quotations (NEEQ), the National Interbank Private Equity Products Quotations and Services, and securities firms' over-the-counter markets.

On July 19, 2020, the PBC and the CSRC jointly issued Notice No. 7 of 2020, agreeing to facilitate cooperation between infrastructure

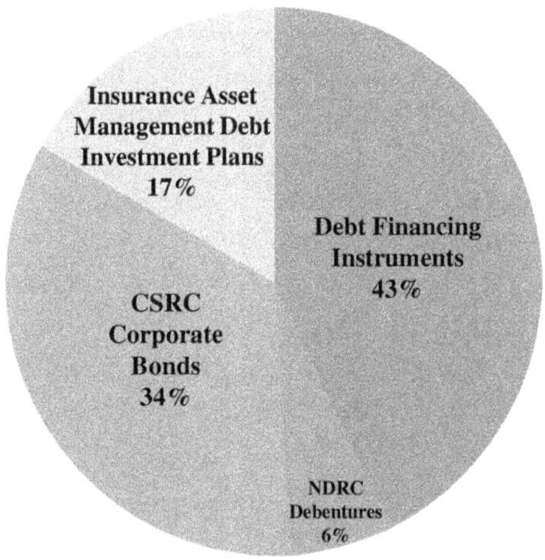

Figure 18. China's corporate credit bond market structure at the end of 2023.

Notes: Due to data availability, the insurance asset management debt investment plans in this figure are aggregate registration amounts by the end of April 2023. They are not equal to the real stock amounts and include a small portion of equity projects. Thus, the data are overvalued.

Source: IAMAC website, Wind Economic Database.

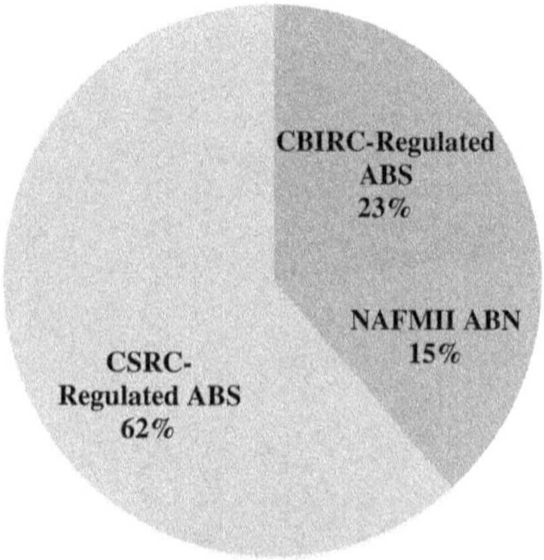

Figure 19. Market structure of asset securitization at the end of 2023.

Notes: The data on the size of the asset-backed plan of the CBIRC are as of the end of August 2021.
Source: Banking Credit Asset Registration and Circulation Center Co. Ltd. Website, Wind Economic Database.

institutions in the interbank market and the exchange market. Subsequently, the SSE, the SZSE, China Foreign Exchange Trade System & National Interbank Funding Center (CFETS), Shanghai Clearing House, and China Securities Depository and Clearing Co. Ltd. (CSDC), jointly formulated and published the *Interim Measures for Mutual Market Access Between the Interbank Bond Market and the Exchange Bond Market*. These measures aim to enhance the efficiency of bond market operations. However, China Central Depository & Clearing Co. Ltd. (CCDC) does not participate in mutual market access.

2.6 *Investor structure of the securities market*

2.6.1 *Investor structure of government bonds*

The investor structure of Chinese government bonds went through positive changes from 2006 to 2023. One such change was a significant increase in the proportion of fund investors (unincorporated products), rising from 1% to 6.9%. The proportion of holdings by overseas institutions also increased from zero to 8.3% (see Figures 20 and 21). However, issues remain. For instance, a relatively high proportion of government

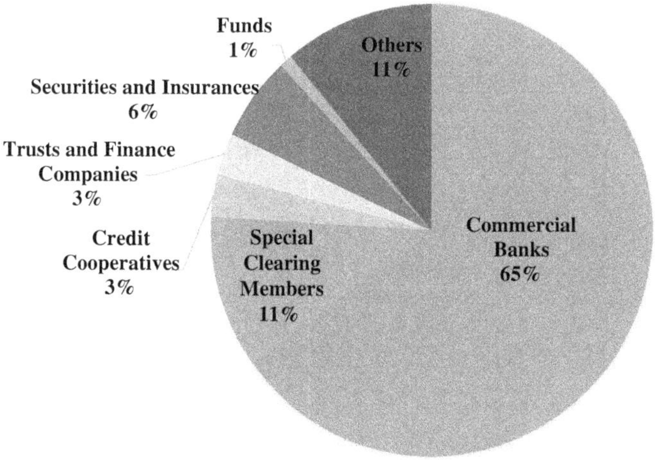

Figure 20. Structure of the holders of Chinese government bonds at the end of 2006.
Source: CCDC.

bonds are held by banks, which contributes to a lack of diversified risk preferences, negatively affecting the liquidity of government bonds. Among banks, the proportion of government bonds held by bank wealth management products has been rising rapidly. If this portion is separated from unincorporated products, the actual proportion of government bonds held by bank proprietary funds would significantly decrease.

In comparison, banks in the US hold 6.7% of US Treasury bonds, while the proportion held by banks in Japan is 11%, and in South Korea, it is 21.6% by the end of September 2023 (see Figures 22–24). In mature international markets, central banks, insurance companies, pension funds, mutual funds, and foreign institutions are all significant investors in government bonds. In China, banks have a relatively high proportion of holdings of government bonds. In the future, China can improve its investor structure by, in particular, attracting long-term institutional investors, such as pension funds, insurance companies, and foreign institutions.

2.6.2 *Investor structure of stocks*

The investor structure of the stock market (see Table 1) reveals that individual investors have 46 million stock accounts opened on the SSE, representing 99.7% of the total accounts, and their ownership constitutes 22.2% of the total amount of stocks in 2022. Accounts with holdings

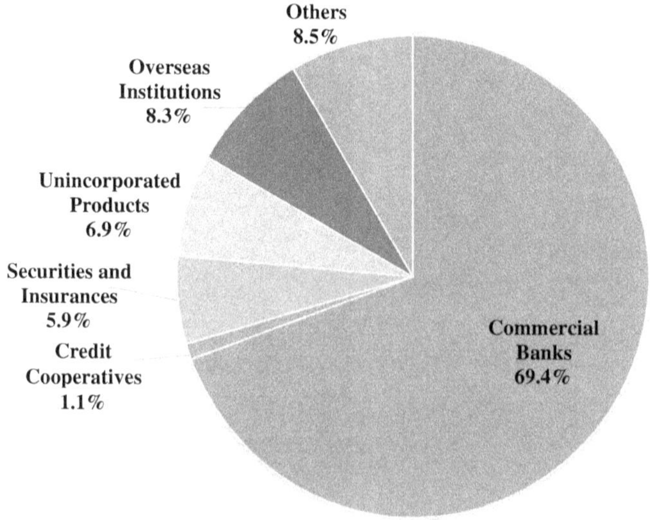

Figure 21. Structure of the holders of Chinese government bonds registered in custody with the CCDC at the end of 2023.

Notes: According to the *Regulations on the Account Management of Unincorporated Products of the China Central Depository & Clearing Co. Ltd.*, issued in 2014, unincorporated products include securities investment funds, national social security funds, trust plans, enterprise annuity funds, insurance products, asset management plans of securities companies, specific asset management portfolios of fund companies, and financial products of commercial banks.
Source: CCDC.

below 100,000 RMB account for about 50% of the total. These data illustrate that China's stock market is primarily composed of retail investors with relatively limited investment experience. As shown in Table 2, individual investors have short holding periods and high turnover rates, indicating their speculative nature.

According to Jones *et al.* (2020)[7] based on trading and holding data from approximately 53.4 million accounts on the SSE from January 2016 to June 2019, all individual investors experienced losses, with larger individual investors experiencing relatively smaller average losses. On average, individual investors with account values below 100,000 RMB experienced a loss of 20.53%, while those with account values above RMB 10 million only incurred a 1% loss. Institutional investors and corporate accounts gained profits of 11% and 6%, respectively (Table 2).

[7] Jones *et al.* (2020).

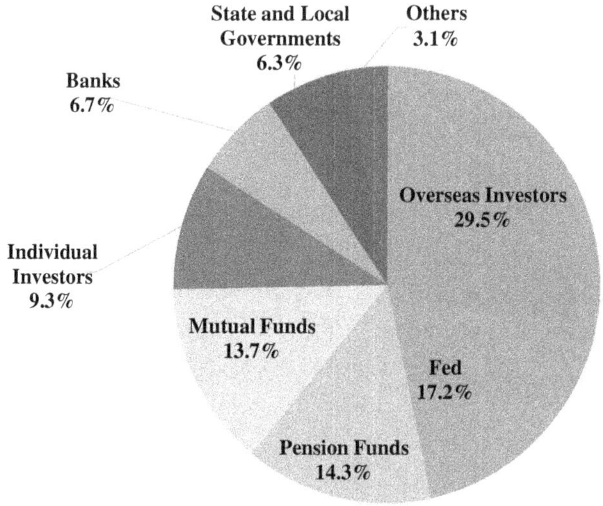

Figure 22. Structure of US treasury bond holders at the end of September 2023.
Source: SIFMA.

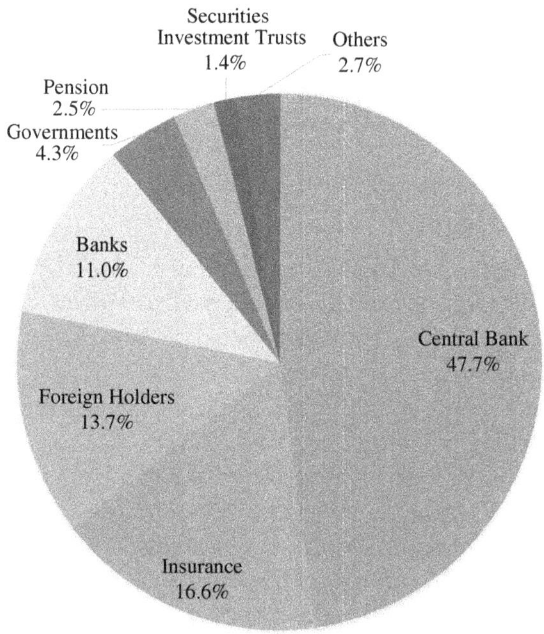

Figure 23. Structure of Japanese government bond holders at the end of September 2023.
Source: ADB.

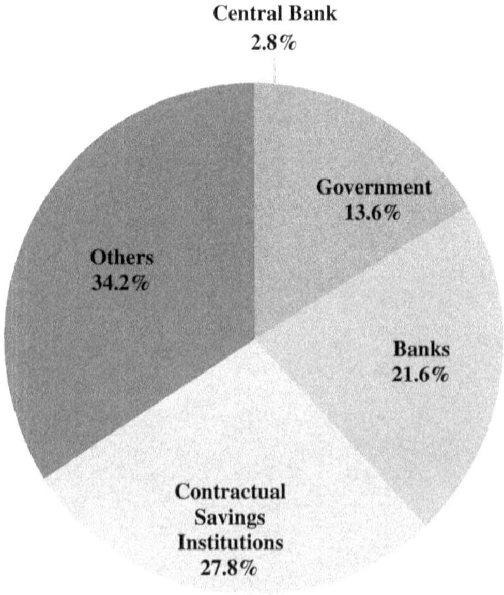

Figure 24. Structure of South Korean government bond holders at the end of September 2023.

Source: ADB.

Table 1. Shares held by types of investors on the SSE at the end of 2022.

Investor Types	Hold Value (RMB 100 million)	Ratio (%)	Number of Hold Accounts (10 thousand)	Ratio (%)
Natural persons	107381	23.19	4625.87	99.73
Among them: less than 100,000 RMB	3252	0.7	2305.25	49.7
100,000–500,000 RMB	11119	2.4	1404.28	30.28
500,000–1 million RMB	9168	1.98	430.7	9.29
1 million–3 million RMB	15426	3.33	339.13	7.31
3 million–10 million RMB	13901	3	111.65	2.41
Above 10 million RMB	54515	11.77	34.85	0.75
General legal persons	255189	55.12	5.81	0.13
Professional institutions	100411	21.69	6.68	0.14
Among them: SSE Stock Connect	12415	2.68	0	0
Mutual funds	28665	6.19	0.66	0.01

Source: 2023 Shanghai Stock Exchange Statistical Yearbook.

Table 2. Average holdings and transactions by investor type (January 2016–June 2019).

	Individual Investors (Grouped by account market value)						
Holdings and Transactions	**Below 100,000 RMB**	**100,000–500,000 RMB**	**500,000–3 million RMB**	**3 million–10 million RMB**	**Above 10 million RMB**	**Institutional Investors**	**Corporate Investors**
Number of Accounts	31,409,950	15,282,005	5,826,800	734,705	235,420	39,547	46,882
Trading Amount (billion RMB)	9	35	54	27	37	35	3
Share (%)	5	17	27	13	19	17	2
Holdings Market Value (billion RMB)	336	951	1,566	840	1,794	4,201	15,547
Share (%)	1	4	6	3	7	17	62
Purchase Volume (10,000 shares)	80.1	270.9	419.0	205.2	277.7	234.4	25.5
Sales Volume (10,000 shares)	79.9	269.8	417.9	205.1	277.7	236.6	25.9
Share of Purchase Volume (%)	5.4	20.1	30.0	13.2	14.9	15.2	1.2
Share of Sales Volume (%)	5.6	20.6	30.2	13.2	14.4	15.1	1.0
Number of Holding Shares (10,000 shares)	3,997.1	9,712.9	14,478.4	7,236.1	13,501.2	25,630.2	162,631.7

Share (%)	3.3	10.4	16.0	7.8	14.5	11.5	36.4
Holding Days	50	36	35	35	49	109	6,319
Annual Total Profit and Loss (RMB)	−77,186	−100,877	−177,388	−120,861	−21,162	531,814	1,098,956
Return (%)	−20.53	−9.98	−10.79	−13.20	−1.62	11.22	6.68
Annual Total Profit and Loss (RMB/account)	−2,457	−6,601	−30,443	−164,503	−89,890	13,447,655	23,440,904
Timing Return (RMB/account)	−774	−3,018	−15,558	−80,767	−411,584	−4,176,872	−14,766,355
Stock Selection Return (RMB/account)	−1,532	−2,443	−10,171	−65,269	402,271	18,074,792	38,244,620
Cost of Transaction (RMB/account)	−151	−1,140	−4,714	−18,466	−80,577	−450,265	−37,361

Source: Jones *et al*. (2020).

The primary reason for losses among individual investors with smaller account sizes was an incorrect trading direction. Among these individual investors, those with account values below RMB 3 million frequently adopted a "buy high, sell higher" trading strategy but often failed to achieve their goals. Investors with account values below RMB 10 million tended to buy and sell in directions opposite to future price movements.

2.7 *Insufficient development of the derivatives market*

Since the "3·27" Treasury Bond Futures incident in 1995, China's derivatives market has remained stagnant. The first over-the-counter financial derivative product, bond forwards, was introduced in 2005 and remained active until the bond market reached a certain scale.

After more than a decade of rapid development, China's derivatives market has morphed into a system that includes the interbank market, exchange market, and over-the-counter market. The over-the-counter market for interest rate derivatives has become increasingly diversified and now includes bond forwards, forward rate agreements, and RMB interest rate swaps, as well as credit risk mitigation tools such as credit default swaps (CDS). Exchange-traded financial derivatives mainly include stock index futures and options and government bond futures. In 2010, the China Financial Futures Exchange (CFFEX) introduced its first stock index futures, the CSI 300 Index Futures. In recent years, the variety of exchange-traded options has expanded, and the market's trading volume has increased. On February 9, 2015, the first exchange-traded option, the SSE 50 ETF Option, was listed on the SSE. On December 23, 2019, both the SSE and the SZSE launched the CSI 300 ETF Option, while CFFEX introduced the CSI 300 Index Options. The government bond futures include 2-year, 5-year, and 10-year contracts.

Long-term funds have increasingly entered the market since 2020. In February 2020, the CSRC, together with the Ministry of Finance, PBC, CBIRC, issued an announcement allowing the five major state-owned banks to participate in the first batch of pilot treasury bond futures trading. The pilot was officially launched in April 2020. In July 2020, the CBIRC issued new rules allowing insurers to participate in government bond futures trading. The first batch of seven insurance institutions has all entered the market, and enterprise annuity and occupational annuity funds have also successively participated. The measures make government bond

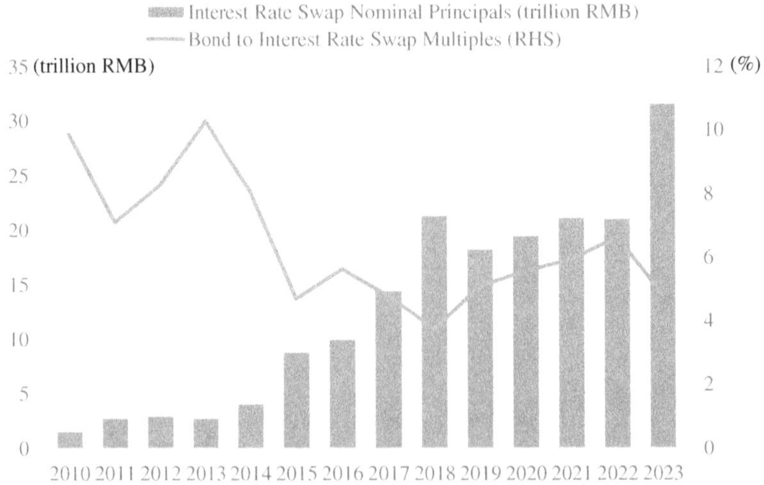

Figure 25. Comparison between interest rate swap nominal principals and bond market.
Notes: Bond to interest rate swap multiple = average bond balance/nominal principal transaction amount of interest rate swap for the year.
Source: The PBC.

futures the future variety with the highest proportion of institutional investors.

Nevertheless, China's derivatives market remains underdeveloped. In 2023, the trading volume of China's interest rate swaps was RMB 31.5 trillion, less than 7% of the outstanding balance of bonds in custody (see Figure 25). By the end of 2023, the size of China's government bond futures positions was approximately RMB 404.9 billion, showing a substantial gap in magnitude when compared with China's government bond market size of approximately RMB 30 trillion (see Figure 26).

China's government bond futures feature high leverage and *T*+0 trading.[8] Although the market size is limited, trading is active, and daily price fluctuations are relatively small (typically approximately 0.1%). However, significant volatility can occur under the influence of news and rumors. Currently, institutional participation dominates the government bond

[8]Government bond futures adopt the margin trading system, which can realize the *T*+0 trading, and there is no limit on the number of open positions; it is the financial product with the highest leverage at present. The minimum margin for 10-year government bond futures is 2%, and theoretically, the leverage can reach 50-fold.

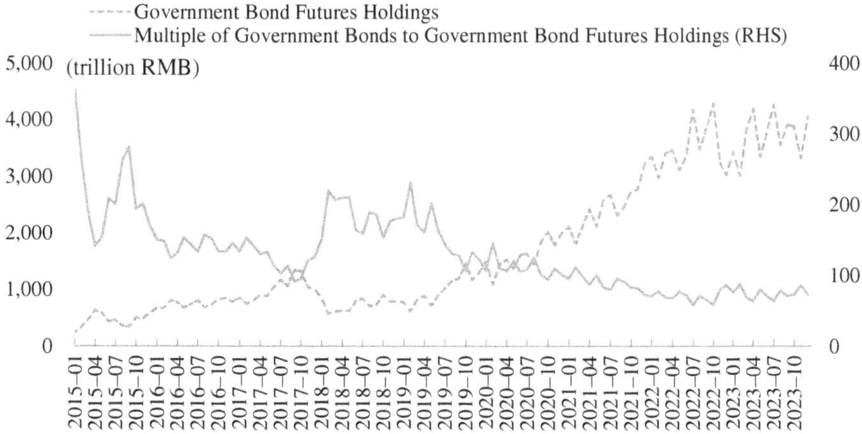

Figure 26. Comparison between government bond futures holdings and the government bond market.

Notes: Multiple government bonds to government bond futures holdings = government bond balance/government bond futures holdings.
Source: CEIC, Wind Economic Database.

futures market, with a diverse range of non-bank institutions involved. Individual investors can also participate in the government bond futures market. Among futures products, government bond futures have the highest proportion of institutional investors. Over time, access has been limited for banks, insurance companies, and other institutions, with securities firms, broadly defined funds (including private equity funds, public funds, securities asset management, and futures asset management), and other institutional investors becoming increasingly dominant. In 2021, institutions accounted for 75.5% of government bond futures trading and 91.4% of positions held (see Figure 27).

At the same time, the financial derivatives market is relatively unbalanced, and its products less diversified. The primary active participants are banks, but the supporting systems require further improvement. Legal uncertainties exist in the single agreement, net termination, and performance guarantee mechanisms, among others. The underdevelopment of the financial derivatives market can be attributed to a historical focus on the financing and investment functions of financial markets, with relatively less consideration for the needs of market participants for hedging and risk mitigation. This is also related to the stage of China's financial

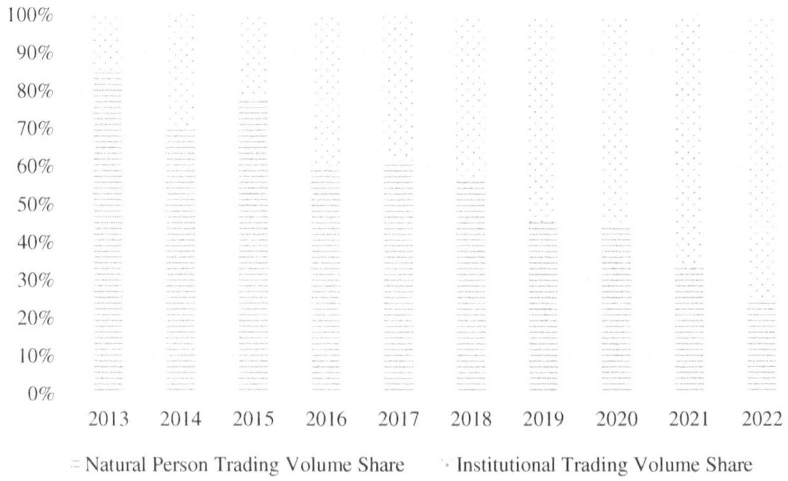

(a) Trading Volume

(b) Holdings

Figure 27. The composition of government bond futures trading holdings and volumes.

Source: CFFEX.

markets and the progressive nature of reforms. Significant progress in foundational product markets, such as interest rates, exchange rates, and credit systems, is a prerequisite for the rapid development of derivatives markets.

On April 20, 2022, the Standing Committee of the 13th National People's Congress passed the *Futures and Derivatives Law*. While it primarily regulates the futures market, it also provides fundamental institutional arrangements for over-the-counter derivatives markets, filling a gap in China's financial legal system. This is conducive to enhancing the legal, market, and international levels of the industry.

On July 4, 2022, the PBC, the Securities and Futures Commission of Hong Kong, and the Hong Kong Monetary Authority issued a joint announcement to promote the interconnectivity of the Hong Kong and mainland interest rate swap markets (referred to as "Swap Connect"). Through the interconnectivity of the financial market infrastructure in both regions, "Swap Connect" enhances the convenience of trading and centralized clearing of RMB interest rate swaps, helping overseas investors manage RMB interest rate risks and promoting the development of onshore interest rate derivative markets. In the early stage, the "Northbound Swap Connect" was introduced, and an expansion to the "Southbound Swap Connect" will be considered in the future. "Swap Connect" was officially launched six months after the announcement.

2.8 *Gold market*

The gold market in China can be divided into an exchange-traded market and an over-the-counter market.[9] The exchange-traded gold transactions primarily take place through the Shanghai Gold Exchange (SGE), the Shanghai Futures Exchange, the Shanghai Stock Exchange, and the Shenzhen Stock Exchange, where contracts for various gold products and services are listed. These products/services include gold spot contracts, gold futures contracts, gold options contracts, and gold ETFs. Over-the-counter gold trading mainly refers to transactions in the interbank and bank counter gold trading markets. In this context, OTC transactions encompass services such as inquiry-based trading, the leasing of gold, account-based gold trading, and gold accumulation services. In recent

[9]Guiyang (2012).

years, there has been a trend of convergence between exchange-traded and over-the-counter markets. On the one hand, exchange-traded markets are characterized by standardized trading processes, transparent transaction procedures, and high liquidity of trading products. To better meet the needs of market participants, exchanges and other exchange trading market entities have been actively combining traditional over-the-counter mechanisms with exchange-traded markets by developing new products. On the other hand, the over-the-counter market is more flexible and dynamic, catering to the diversity of investors' needs. In response to the demand for standardized operation rules and a transparent operation mechanism, aspects of over-the-counter market transactions, such as standardized, systematic, and regulated transaction processes, have gradually transitioned toward the features of exchange-traded markets.

The market-oriented reform of China's gold management system began in 2001. In 2002, the SGE was established, marking the formal establishment of China's gold market.[10] In April 2001, the PBC announced the abolition of the centralized procurement and distribution system for gold, known as "统购统配" (tǒnggòutǒngpèi). This move marked the end of administrative gold management in China. Consequently, the SGE was designed to serve as a financial infrastructure specializing in the trading of precious metals, including gold, and providing related financial services. In November 2001, the SGE began its trial operations. Then, in October 2002, the SGE officially commenced full-scale operations. During this period, the PBC ceased its gold allocation and purchase activities. As a result, China's gold prices became entirely determined by supply and demand. In March 2011, the SGE introduced a system for interbank inquiry-based trading, facilitating large-volume transactions among commercial banks and providing a platform and channel for interbank hedging. In 2013, the SGE launched the first "cross-market, cross-system, cross-asset class" gold ETF product in collaboration with the SSE and the SZSE.

China has been the world's largest gold producer, consumer, and importer for many years. China has maintained its status as the world's largest gold producer for 14 consecutive years since 2007. In 2020, China's gold production (excluding imported raw materials) reached 365.35 tons,

---

[10] Jiao Jinpu (2021).

accounting for over 10% of the world's total gold production.[11] In 2021, gold production is 375.2 tons.[12] On the demand side, China's gold demand surpassed 1,000 tons in 2011, reaching 1,043.9 tons. In 2021, China's actual gold consumption was 1089.7 tons. In 2023, China increased its holdings of gold by 224.88 tons. By the end of 2023, China's gold reserves were 2235.41 tons.

The trading volumes of gold spots, futures, ETFs, and other products vary with fluctuations in gold supply and demand. The cumulative trading volume of all gold products on the SGE was 20,765 tons, with a cumulative trading value of RMB 9.28 trillion. Similarly, the Shanghai Futures Exchange reported a cumulative trading volume of 62,111 tons for all gold varieties, with a total trading value of RMB 23.9 trillion.

2.9 *Opening-up promotes China's financial markets*

Generally speaking, China's financial market has made significant achievements and attracted many global investors. However, structural challenges persist, including a concentrated ownership structure, insufficient liquidity, a relatively low share of structured financing, and relatively underdeveloped derivative instruments. These are interconnected systemic issues at the institutional level. For example, the concentration of ownership can lead to a uniform risk appetite, which is not conducive to improving liquidity levels or the price discovery function. The liquidity premium advantage of standard products over non-standardized products cannot be fully realized. Moreover, the lack of diversity in market participants, especially the high proportion of hold-to-maturity investors, limits the demand for risk hedging through derivative instruments.

The internationalization of financial markets, especially the adoption of internationalization institutional rules, can help reduce the concerns of foreign entities. This, in return, will introduce diverse trading counterparties with different risk appetites than Chinese market participants. With the participation of foreign entities, China's bond market can learn from the experiences and practices of more mature international markets. Specifically, China can explore areas such as market-making systems, derivatives, structured financing, and default handling mechanisms that

[11] British Metal Focus LTD (2021).

[12] *Source*: China Gold Association.

are familiar to foreign participants and can address structural issues. This approach can help foster a virtuous cycle of internal reform and external opening-up in China's financial markets.

3. Progress and Assessment of the Opening-up of Major Financial Submarkets

3.1 *Bond market*

The opening-up of China's bond market began in 2005 when international financial institutions such as the International Finance Corporation (IFC) and the Asian Development Bank (ADB) were first allowed to issue RMB-denominated bonds in the interbank bond market,[13] and the Pan Asia Fund and the Asian Bond Fund (ABF) were also allowed to invest in the interbank bond market.

Following the outbreak of the global financial crisis in 2008, the exchange rates of major currencies, including the US dollar, fluctuated significantly. As a result of efforts to manage exchange rate risks, the demand for cross-border trade settlement in RMB from domestic and foreign enterprises surged, and the cross-border use of RMB increased gradually. In 2010, to meet the demand for the return investment of RMB from abroad as a result of the rapid development of the cross-border RMB settlement business, the PBC permitted foreign central banks or monetary authorities, RMB clearing banks in Hong Kong and Macao, and foreign banks participating in the cross-border trade RMB settlement (i.e., three types of institutions) to invest in the interbank bond market. Upon application to and approval by the PBC, these three types of institutions can participate in bond trading in the interbank market within the approved quotas. With the development of cross-border RMB business, the scope of foreign institutions has been gradually expanded to include sovereign wealth funds, international financial institutions, RMB clearing banks in other regions, and insurance institutions in Hong Kong and Taiwan in China as well as in Singapore. In December 2022, the PBC and the SAFE

[13] On October 9, 2005, the International Finance Corporation (IFC) and the Asian Development Bank (ADB) issued RMB-denominated bonds worth RMB 1.13 billion and RMB 1 billion, respectively, in the national interbank bond market, making them the first foreign issuers in China's bond market.

jointly issued the *Notice on Matters Concerning the Proceeds Management for RMB-Denominated Bonds Issued by Overseas Issuers in China*, unified the fund management rules of "Panda bonds" issued in the interbank bond market and the stock exchange bond market, promoted the integrated management of the RMB and foreign currencies, and further enhanced the convenience for overseas institutions to raise funds in China's bond markets.

Since 2013, with the gradual expansion of the cross-border and international use of the RMB, the international status of the RMB has been significantly enhanced, the opening-up of the bond market has accelerated, and RMB foreign exchange formation has also become more market-oriented.

Various types of issuers, such as international development agencies, overseas nonfinancial enterprises, financial institutions, and foreign governments, have issued RMB-denominated bonds in the interbank bond market. In 2013, Daimler AG issued RMB 5 billion of RMB-denominated debt financing instruments, marking that the channels for overseas nonfinancial enterprises to raise RMB-denominated bond financing had been opened up. In 2015, the Hongkong and Shanghai Banking Corporation Ltd. and the Bank of China (Hong Kong) Ltd., as international commercial banks, were allowed for the first time to issue RMB-denominated bonds in the interbank bond market, becoming another major type of issuer, following international development agencies and overseas nonfinancial enterprises. In 2015, the Province of British Columbia, Canada, and the Republic of Korea completed the registration for issuing RMB-denominated bonds with a value of RMB 9 billion. In 2016, the World Bank issued SDR-denominated bonds amounting to RMB 5 billion, which was strategically significant for expanding the use of SDRs, promoting the internationalization of RMB, and opening up China's financial market. According to the PBC, by the end of August 2023, a total of 434 Panda bonds had been issued by overseas institutions in China's bond markets with a cumulative volume of RMB 740.22 billion. According to the Wind Economic Database, the issuance of Panda bonds in 2023 was RMB 154.47 billion, a year-on-year increase of 81.6%, which accounted for 0.22% of the total issuance in China's bond market (RMB 157.9 trillion) during the same period. Domestic institutions are also making steady progress in issuing bonds abroad.

Meanwhile, the flexibility of foreign issuers in terms of auditing and accounting has significantly increased. In September 2018, the PBC and the Ministry of Finance jointly issued the *Interim Measures for the Administration of Bonds Issued by Overseas Issuers on Interbank Market.*[14] These measures further clarified the qualifications and application procedures for foreign institutions (including foreign governmental institutions issuing bonds in the National Interbank Bond Market of China, international development agencies, financial institutions, and non-financial enterprise legal entities legally registered outside the People's Republic of China) to issue bonds in the interbank bond market and regulated such matters as issuers, agencies, regulators, information disclosure, and accounting standards. Specifically, in terms of information disclosure, foreign issuers were required to declare the accounting standards for financial reporting, and if they did not use the China Accounting Standards for Business Enterprises (CASBE) or equivalent accounting standards for the preparation of disclosed financial reports, they needed to provide supplementary information at the same time[15]; the rules clarifying the auditing of Panda bond issuance by foreign accounting firms for foreign institutions filled regulatory gaps. These were the first systematic administrative measures for Panda bond issuance since China launched Panda bonds in 2005, which further enhanced the coordination and consistency of Panda bond regulation and promoted the relevant system rules to be in line with international standards. The clarification of issuance rules enhanced the transparency of the Panda bond issuance system and further increased the attractiveness of the interbank bond market to international issuers and investors.

The scope of participants and types of investment of foreign institutions investing in China's bond market has been continuously expanded, and the administrative approach has become more market-oriented. In 2013, QFII and RQFII were permitted to operate cash transactions in the

[14] The former *Interim Measures for the Administration of the Issuance of RMB-denominated Bonds by International Development Institutions* was formally abolished.

[15] (1) Major differences between the accounting standards used and the accounting standards for Chinese enterprises and (2) discrepancy reconciliation information adjusted according to Chinese Accounting Standards for Business Enterprises, indicating the amount of financial impact of differences in accounting standards on all important items in the financial statements of foreign institutions.

interbank bond market. In 2015, more favorable policies were introduced for foreign central banks to enter and invest in the interbank market, which simplified the entry process to record filing, removed investment amount restrictions, and expanded the scope of investment to include cash bonds, bond repo, bond lending, bond forwards, interest rate swaps, forward interest rate agreements, and other transactions permitted by the PBC. In 2016, the PBC released Announcement No. 3, which allowed various types of financial institutions to be legally registered and established abroad and the investment products issued by them, as well as medium-to-long-term institutional investors such as pension funds, to invest in the interbank bond market through record filing and independently determine the amount of investment. Thus far, the secondary market of the interbank bond market has been completely open to qualified foreign investors. In terms of the types of investors, both domestic and foreign institutions are subject to the same entry criteria: As long as qualified institutional investors are licensed financial institutions and their products, they can enter the interbank bond market through record-filing, and no administrative approval is needed. Meanwhile, for investment by foreign institutions, neither investment quota nor total investment amount is set for individual institutions, and foreign institutions may decide the amount of investment on their own, which is under the macroprudential management of the PBC. Moreover, there is no restriction on the source of RMB funds for investment in the interbank bond market by foreign institutions, which can be obtained through the RMB cross-border business or the offshore or onshore foreign exchange markets. Only when foreign institutions need to obtain RMB through the onshore foreign exchange market should they handle the procedures of the inward and outward remittance of funds, as well as foreign exchange purchase and settlement in accordance with the relevant provisions on foreign exchange management. In June 2018, China's State Administration of Foreign Exchange (SAFE) launched a new round of reforms on the foreign exchange management system of QFII and RQFII, canceling the restriction on the proportion of remittance of funds from QFII and the relevant lock-up period requirements for QFII and RQFII, allowing QFII and RQFII to engage in foreign exchange hedging so that the management principles of QFII and RQFII could become gradually harmonized, and further facilitating the investment of foreign institutional investors. In 2020, the SAFE relaxed the restriction on foreign exchange risk hedging under the mode of direct investment in the interbank bond market.

As China's bond market has continued to open up, major global bond indices, such as Bloomberg, JP Morgan, and FTSE Russell, have begun including Chinese bonds in their indices. Data from the PBC show that by the end of 2023, the depository balance of foreign institutions in China's bond market stood at RMB 3.72 trillion, accounting for 2.4% of China's bond market depository balance. In terms of the types of securities, foreign institutions held RMB 2.29 trillion of treasury bonds, accounting for 62.4%, and RMB 0.8 trillion of policy financial bonds, accounting for 21.8%. By the end of 2022, a total of 1,071 foreign institutional participants entered the interbank bond market.[16]

Bond Connect, a mutual bond market access scheme between the mainland and Hong Kong, is an initiative for the further opening up of China's interbank bond market. It still complies with the managed opening of capital accounts, the qualification requirements for medium- and long-term institutional investors, and the collection of investment and transaction information. Bond Connect provides a new channel for foreign institutions to access the market conveniently by linking domestic and overseas infrastructures so as to improve the efficiency of entry into the market. In the experience of other countries in opening up their bond markets, foreign investors have been able to either access the markets by opening accounts on a one-by-one basis or invest in the domestic bond markets of these countries through infrastructure connections. Under the former mode, foreign investors face higher requirements and need to have a comprehensive and in-depth understanding of the relevant regulations, systems, and market environment of that country's bond market; under the latter mode, foreign investors can rely on infrastructure connections and multilevel custodianship to conveniently access the global bond market through one entry point, which has become mainstream international practice. The Bond Connect program belongs to the latter mode, which enables international investors to conveniently participate in the mainland bond market without changing their business practices through the connection of the bond market infrastructure in the mainland and Hong Kong on the premise that they effectively comply with the rules and regulations of the mainland market. The Bond Connect program is being implemented in phases under the overall planning and arrangement of the opening up of China's financial market. The PBC and the Hong Kong Monetary Authority jointly announced in June 2017 that the Northbound

[16] *Source*: CCDC Research, *China Bond Market Overview (2022)*.

Bond Connect would be implemented first, and the Southbound Bond Connect would be implemented in September 2021. In terms of trading in the Northbound Bond Connect, the trading of treasury bonds and policy financial bonds has been the most active. As of June 2023, the total amount of mainland bonds held by overseas institutions through Bond Connect exceeded RMB 3.1 trillion. The trading volume of Bond Connect rose from RMB 31 billion in the first month of its opening in 2017 to more than RMB 970 billion in May 2023. The trading volume of Northbound Bond Connect accounts for 70% of the overall trading volume of foreign investors in the mainland interbank bond market. In 2017, 178 overseas institutions participated in Bond Connect, and the number became 822 by the end of 2023.

In May 2022, the PBC, the CSRC, and SAFE jointly issued the *Matters on Further Facilitating Investment in China's Bond Market by Overseas Institutional Investors*, which supported overseas institutional investors in investing in the stock exchange bond market directly or through an interconnectivity mechanism and independently choosing their own trading venues. Overseas institutional investors investing in the interbank bond market may, according to their own actual needs, independently choose bond registration and settlement institutions or domestic custodian banks for bond custody services. This further facilitates foreign institutional investors' investment in China's bond market and harmonizes the cross-border management of funds.

In addition, China is gradually opening up its credit rating market. In March 2018, NAFMII issued the *Rules for the Registration and Evaluation of Credit Rating Agencies of Nonfinancial Enterprise Instruments in the Interbank Bond Market* and the supporting system, accepting applications for registration by overseas rating agencies as overseas legal entities or domestic legal entities and treating them on an equal footing with domestic credit rating agencies. This system is conducive to promoting healthy competition among credit rating agencies and meeting the needs of both domestic and overseas investors. In September 2018, the PBC and the CSRC jointly issued Announcement No. 14 of 2018, which strengthened the harmonized supervision of the credit rating sector in the bond market by gradually harmonizing the qualifications of the rating business in the interbank and stock exchange bond markets. In July 2019, the Office of the Financial Stability and the Development Commission of the State Council announced 11 measures to open up the financial industry.

In terms of credit ratings, foreign agencies were permitted to rate all types of bonds in the interbank and stock exchange bond markets when operating a credit rating business in China. In this context, international credit rating agencies S&P and Fitch formally entered the mainland market as wholly owned companies in January 2019 and May 2020, respectively. In August 2021, the PBC issued Announcement No. 11 of 2021, which canceled the credit rating requirements for the issuance of debt financing instruments on a pilot basis and was conducive to reducing the rating dependence. In August 2021, the PBC, the NDRC, the Ministry of Finance, the China Banking and Insurance Regulatory Commission (CBIRC), and the CSRC jointly issued the *Circular on Promoting the Healthy Development of the Credit Rating Industry in the Bond Market*, which put forward explicit requirements for credit rating agencies in terms of strengthening the development of rating methodology systems, enhancing corporate governance and internal control mechanisms, and improving the disclosure of information. At the same time, this circular also emphasized the optimization of the rating ecosystem and the strict supervision of credit rating agencies, which helped enhance the quality and differentiation of credit ratings and gave a larger role to credit ratings in risk exposure, risk pricing, and certain other aspects. Overall, the supervision of bond market ratings has tended to be harmonized, which helps promote the high-quality development of China's credit rating market.

3.2 *Stock market*

The opening up of China's stock market began in the early 1990s. China's capital account was not convertible at that time, but in order to open up channels for Chinese companies to raise capital overseas and to facilitate foreign investors' investment in the Chinese stock market, in 1991, with the consent of the Stock Market Committee of the State Council, Shanghai and Shenzhen were allowed to issue B shares on a pilot basis. The B-share market was formally established in 1992. B shares are RMB-denominated special shares subscribed and traded in foreign currencies on the SSE and SZSE. B shares are issued by companies incorporated and listed in the mainland and were limited to foreign investment until February 2001, after which, B shares were permitted to be exchanged by domestic citizens.

To further broaden overseas financing channels and enhance the visibility of Chinese enterprises abroad, the Chinese government encouraged domestic enterprises to issue securities abroad. In December 1992, the State Council issued the *Circular on Further Strengthening the Macro-Control of Securities Markets*, which explicitly stated that "several enterprises would be selected for overseas public offerings and listings, which must be implemented under the unified arrangement and with the approval of the Securities Commission". In May and June 1993, the National Economic System Reform Commission issued the *Supplementary Provisions on the Implementation of the Opinions on the Regulation of Joint Stock Limited Companies by Companies Seeking a Listing in Hong Kong* and the *Articles of Association of Companies Seeking a Listing in Hong Kong Prerequisite Clauses* successively, which provided a legal basis for domestic enterprises to seek a listing in Hong Kong. In August 1994, the State Council issued the *Special Provisions of the State Council on Joint Stock Limited Companies Seeking Issuing Shares and Listing Overseas*, which required that if a joint stock-limited company offers shares to overseas investors and is listed abroad, it should, as required by the Securities Commission of the State Council, submit a written application with relevant materials for approval by the commission.

In June 1997, the State Council issued the *Circular of the State Council Concerning Further Strengthening the Administration of Share Issuance and Listing Overseas*, and the CSRC formulated corresponding regulations for domestic enterprises and overseas Chinese-controlled enterprises to list abroad. In August 2002, the SAFE and the CSRC jointly issued the *Notice on Further Improving the Foreign Exchange Management of Overseas Listing*. In December 2012, the CSRC issued the *Supervision Guidelines for Document Filings and Review Procedures in Connection with Overseas Stock Issuance and Listing by Joint Stock Companies*, which further strengthened the supervision of overseas stock offerings and listing applications by domestic companies. To address the regulatory gaps related to the indirect overseas listing of Chinese enterprises, in December 2021, the CSRC released the *Provisions of the State Council on the Administration of Overseas Securities Offerings and Listings by Domestic Companies (Draft for Comment)* and the *Administrative Measures for the Record-Filing of Overseas Securities Offerings and Listings by Domestic Companies (Draft for Comments)*, which for the first time included all forms of arrangements for the overseas listing of domestic enterprises into a comprehensive record-filing supervision system.

In addition, in recent years, China's regulatory authorities have strengthened data security and antimonopoly-related regulations.

Along with the gradual opening up of the capital account, China introduced the QFII and QDII schemes. As a transitional institutional arrangement, QFII and QDII were special channels for the orderly and steady opening up of the securities market in countries and regions where the capital account had not yet been fully opened up. In December 2002, the CSRC and the PBC jointly promulgated the *Interim Measures on the Administration of Domestic Securities Investment by Qualified Foreign Institutional Investors*. The first QFII order was formally issued in July 2003. To further open up the capital account, maintain the RMB exchange rate at a more balanced level, and allow domestic investors to participate in the global market, the QDII system was officially opened up in July 2006, and the SAFE approved a quota of USD 500 million for the Bank of Communications. In recent years, regulators have gradually relaxed the control over qualification and foreign exchange management, and the quota has been continuously increased. In September 2019, the restrictions on the investment quota of QFII and RQFII, as well as on the countries and regions for RQFII pilot programs, were lifted. Since then, foreign institutional investors with appropriate qualifications have been able to remit funds independently and make securities investments in compliance with relevant regulations after completing the registration process, which has significantly facilitated the participation of foreign investors in the domestic financial market. By May 2020, when the SAFE stopped updating data, 295 QFII had been approved, with an investment amount of 116.259 billion USD. As of the end of 2023, 186 QDII had been approved, with an investment amount of USD 165.52 billion.

In recent years, with the steady progress of the internationalization of RMB and the opening up of China's capital account, the opening up of the stock market has accelerated in terms of both depth and breadth. In December 2011, the CSRC, the PBC, and SAFE jointly issued the *Measures for Pilot Domestic Securities Investment Made by RMB Qualified Foreign Institutional Investors of Fund Management Companies and Securities Companies*, which allowed the Hong Kong subsidiaries of qualified fund companies and securities companies to operate RQFII businesses as pilot institutions, with an initial pilot quota of approximately RMB 20 billion. As of the end of May 2020, 230 RQFII had been approved, with an investment amount of RMB 722.992 billion. In

November 2014, the PBC issued the *Notice of the People's Bank of China on Matters concerning the Overseas Securities Investment of RMB Qualified Domestic Institutional Investors*. This notice allowed RMB-qualified domestic institutional investors to invest in RMB-denominated products in overseas financial markets with domestic RMB-denominated funds that they owned or had raised. Unlike the approval-based QDII quota, the RQDII quota is based on the scale of actual fundraising. In June 2018, the PBC and SAFE issued the *Regulations on Foreign Exchange Administration for Domestic Securities Investments by Qualified Foreign Institutional Investors*, canceling the exchange restrictions related to QFII and RQFII.

The two-way flow of capital began opening up in 2014, and this helped China's integration into the international financial market. In April 2014, the State Council formally approved the pilot scheme for the Shanghai-Hong Kong Stock Connect. After half a year of preparation, in November 2014, the CSRC and the Securities and Futures Commission (SFC) of Hong Kong released an announcement to officially launch the Shanghai-Hong Kong Stock Connect. To deepen the financial cooperation between the mainland and Hong Kong, further leverage the geographical advantages of Shenzhen and Hong Kong, and facilitate the close cooperation between the mainland and Hong Kong, the State Council formally approved the *Implementation Plan for the Shenzhen-Hong Kong Stock Connect* in August 2016. In December 2016, the CSRC and the SFC of Hong Kong released an announcement on the official launch of the Shenzhen-Hong Kong Stock Connect. Since then, qualified individual or institutional investors in China have been able to directly trade stocks listed in the Hong Kong market, while foreign investors have been able to directly trade stocks listed in the SSE and the SZSE. In November 2019, the CSRC officially implemented the H-share full circulation program. At present, the Shanghai-Hong Kong Stock Connect and the Shenzhen-Hong Kong Stock Connect operate in a smooth and orderly manner, and each of their parts functions normally, with the inflow of cross-border capital being roughly equivalent to the outflow, realizing conditional and controlled cross-border stock exchanges.

The deepening of cooperation between Hong Kong and the mainland in financial products and services started in 2015 in the fund market. In May 2015, the CSRC and the SFC of Hong Kong issued a joint announcement about having formally signed an "MOU on Regulatory Cooperation" for the mutual recognition of funds arrangements between the mainland and Hong Kong, and the CSRC also issued a set of accompanying rules, the *Interim Provisions on the Administration of Recognized Hong Kong Funds*. In December 2015, the first batch of seven mutually recognized funds were registered at the CSRC and the SFC of Hong Kong. In January 2017, the service platform for the mainland–Hong Kong mutual recognition of funds (MRF) was launched. As a new initiative to open up the capital market, the MRF complements the Shanghai-Hong Kong Stock Connect and the Shenzhen-Hong Kong Stock Connect, thus making the capital market both broader and deeper. As of the end of November 2023, the cumulative net remittance of funds issued and sold on the mainland by Hong Kong funds was RMB 16.9 billion; as of the end of 2022, the cumulative net remittance of funds issued and sold by mainland funds in Hong Kong was RMB 1.03 billion.

Moreover, the Shanghai–London Stock Connect and the China–Japan ETF Connectivity were launched in June 2019. In October 2020, the Shenzhen–Hong Kong ETF scheme was launched. In February 2022, the CSRC amended the *Provisions on the Supervision and Administration of Depository Receipts under the Stock Connect Scheme between Shanghai Stock Exchange and London Stock Exchange (for trial implementation)*, which was renamed the *Provisions on the Supervision and Administration of Depository Receipts under the Stock Connect Scheme between Domestic and Overseas Stock Exchanges*. The amended provisions expanded the scope of application to include qualified companies listed on the SZSE, as well as in Switzerland and Germany, and made arrangements for financing-based Chinese depository receipts (CDRs), which allow the issuers of the underlying offshore securities to raise funds and adopt a market-oriented inquiry mechanism for pricing.

A-shares are integrated into many internationally recognized indices. In June 2017, MSCI announced that it would include A-shares in its Emerging Markets (EM) Index. In June 2018, A-shares were formally integrated into the MSCI EM Index, with the inclusion factor gradually rising to 20%. In June 2019, FTSE Russell included China A-shares in its global equity indices for the first time, with the integration factor gradually increasing to 25%. In September 2019, S&P Dow Jones included A-shares in its Global BMI Index with a 25% factor.

Overall, along with the expanding convertibility of capital accounts, the Chinese stock market has opened up further. In terms of the primary stock market, the establishment of B shares and the listing of domestic enterprises abroad have provided channels for domestic enterprises to raise capital from overseas sources while facilitating the investment of foreign investors in the equity of domestic companies. In the secondary market, QFII and RQFII schemes have been established to facilitate capital inflows; QDII and RQDII schemes have been established to facilitate capital outflows; and the Shanghai–Hong Kong Connect, the Shenzhen–Hong Kong Connect, and the MRF have been established to facilitate two-way flows of capital, which, to a certain extent, can meet the needs of different investors.

However, compared with advanced stock markets, China's stock market still faces gaps in investor protection, the delisting system, and class action. Specifically, it is imperative to impose strict supervision, properly control both the listing and delisting systems, promote a system of the survival of the fittest, effectively protect investor rights, improve market transparency, and enhance the confidence of international investors.

3.3 *Derivatives market*

Prior to 2019, the participation of international investors in the exchange-based trading of derivatives was limited. In May 2011, the CSRC issued the *Guidelines for the Participation of Qualified Foreign Institutional Investors in the Trading of Stock Index Futures*, which allowed QFII to participate in the hedging transactions of stock index futures. The list of over-the-counter options dealers released by the Securities Association of China shows that as of May 2022, UBS Securities (included in the seventh group of the list in November 2020) was the only foreign securities dealer in this list authorized to participate in the domestic over-the-counter options business.

In recent years, the CSRC has gradually expanded the investment scope of QFII to include various types of exchange-traded financial derivatives, accelerating the opening up of the derivatives market. In September 2020, the CSRC, PBC, and SAFE released the *Measures for the Administration of Domestic Securities and Futures Investment by Qualified Foreign Institutional Investors and RMB Qualified Foreign Institutional Investors*. Alongside this, the CSRC released the *Supplementary Rules on the Implementation of the "Measures for the Administration of Domestic Securities and Futures Investment by Qualified*

Foreign Institutional Investors and RMB Qualified Foreign Institutional Investors" (effective from November 1, 2020), which combined the qualifications and rules of QFII and RQFII to lower the requirement for access and facilitate investment operations, expanded the scope of investment, and allowed QFII and RQFII to invest in securities, private investment funds, financial futures, commodity futures, and options listed in the National Equities Exchange and Quotations, as well as to participate in bond repurchases, securities margin trading on stock exchanges, and lending transactions of refinancing securities. In accordance with the above administrative measures, the CSRC issued Announcement No. 24 in October 2021, announcing that QFII is eligible to trade commodity futures, commodity options, and stock index options listed and traded on futures trading venues approved by the State Council or the CSRC and that transactions in stock index options would be limited for the sole purpose of hedging, effective from November 1, 2021. In October 2021, the MSCI China A50 Index Futures were officially launched for trading, providing foreign investors with more diversified risk management tools and further attract foreign long-term funds to A-shares. On September 2, 2022, the Zhengzhou Commodity Exchange; Dalian Commodity Exchange; Shanghai Futures Exchange and its subsidiary, Shanghai International Energy Exchange; and China Financial Futures Exchange released an announcement clarifying that QFII and RQFII were eligible to participate in the transactions of 41 kinds of derivatives, including futures and options. This expansion has helped enhance the international influence and pricing power of commodities. As of August 26, 2022, the customer equities of foreign investors in the domestic futures market amounted to RMB 53.052 billion. Specifically, foreign investors' customer equities in the stock index futures market amounted to RMB 31.755 billion, and their equities in the markets of crude oil futures, iron ore futures, PTA futures, TSR 20, palm oil, international copper, and LSFO futures totaled RMB 21.297 billion.

Although China's legal basis for derivatives is lagging behind market development, there have been breakthroughs in the past two years. The State Council issued the *Provisional Regulation on the Administration of Futures Trading* in June 1999, which was amended in 2007 to the *Regulation on the Administration of Futures Trading* and expanded to include provisions on financial futures, OTC options, and the establishment of futures investor guarantee funds; the 2012 revised version allows foreign investors to participate in the trading of specific futures in China. The *Measures for the Administration of Futures Exchange* and other supporting rules and implementing regulations have been issued successively, effectively regulating the development of China's futures market. However, due to the narrow definition of securities in the *Securities Law* and the lack of a higher-level law on derivatives, the institutional rules are incomplete, and the regulatory standards need to be harmonized. In light of this, in December 2021, the PBC, the CBIRC, the CSRC, and SAFE publicly solicited opinions on the *Guiding Opinions on Promoting the Regulated Development of Derivatives Business (Draft for Opinion)*, which for the first time provided a unified definition and categorization of derivatives and made arrangements for the division of regulatory work in accordance with the responsibilities of the financial management departments. In April 2022, the 34th session of the 13th NPC Standing Committee voted to adopt thc *Futures and Derivatives Law*, which made systematic institutional arrangements for the over-the-counter derivatives market, addressed the fragmented and inconsistent rules and regulatory standards in the derivatives market, and gave full play to the functions of derivatives in deepening the financial market, improving market liquidity, and supporting the national economy.

3.4 *Foreign exchange market*

The opening up of the interbank foreign exchange market began in 2004 when the Hong Kong and Macao branches of the Bank of China successively entered the interbank foreign exchange market. In 2009, with the launch of the business for RMB settlement in cross-border trade, the interbank foreign exchange market was opened up to overseas RMB clearing banks.

In 2015, the PBC permitted foreign central banks (monetary authorities) and other official reserve management institutions, international financial organizations, and sovereign wealth funds to enter China's interbank foreign exchange market through various channels, such as agents and direct connections. These foreign entities were able to operate various kinds of foreign exchange transactions, including spot, forward, swap, and option transactions, with no quota limits. In January 2016, overseas participating banks with a large scale of RMB purchase and sale business, international influence, and geographical representation were allowed to participate in spot, forward, swap, currency swap, and option transactions in the interbank foreign exchange market. In February 2017, to facilitate foreign investors participating in the interbank bond market to control foreign exchange risks, the SAFE allowed interbank market settlement agents qualified for RMB-to-forex derivatives business on behalf of customers to operate foreign exchange derivatives business for foreign investors on the basis of the real demand principle, which was limited to the hedging of foreign exchange risk exposure arising from investing in the interbank bond market with funds remitted from abroad. In July 2017, in order to support the launch of the Bond Connect program, the interbank foreign exchange market expanded the participation of foreign participating banks in the RMB purchase and sale business in Hong Kong in the market, allowing them to automatically obtain the qualification of clearing banks in Hong Kong for the Northbound Bond Connect under the Bond Connect program after becoming members of the interbank foreign exchange market. In January 2018, the CFETS issued the *Announcement on Matters Relating to the Participation of Foreign Banks in Regional Transactions in the Interbank Foreign Exchange Market*, allowing qualified foreign banks to participate in regional transactions in the interbank foreign exchange market. In September 2018, the first batch of Free Trade Accounts (FT Accounts) of Shanghai Free Trade Zone (FTZ) separate accounting units were introduced to participate in interbank foreign currency lending market transactions. Thus far, the interbank foreign exchange market has been opened up to different types of institutions to varying extents, covering all kinds of trading products and significantly increasing the market's level of internationalization. According to the *2023 RMB Internationalization Report* of the PBC, participants in China's domestic interbank foreign exchange (FX) market have been diversified. By the end of 2022, there were 782 members in RMB/FX spot market, 292 in RMB/FX forward market, 283 in RMB/FX swap market, 233 in RMB/FX cross currency swap market, 168 in RMB/FX option market, and 25 in RMB/FX market makers. The influx of foreign investors has diversified the participant base and significantly contributed to the enhancement of market liquidity and market integration. According to the data from the CFETS,[17] by the end of December 2023, 204 foreign institutions

[17]Research Department of China Foreign Exchange Trade System and National Interbank Funding Center (2024).

were participating in the domestic interbank foreign exchange market. In addition, the interbank foreign exchange market has been further opened up through the development of direct trading and regional trading. In 2010, in line with the development of the RMB cross-border trade settlement business, the interbank foreign exchange market launched direct trading between RMB and Malaysian ringgit and between RMB and the Russian ruble, i.e., direct quoted trading between RMB and foreign currencies without calculating from the cross rates between the central parity of RMB against the US dollar. In 2014, the interbank foreign exchange market launched the regional trading of RMB against the Kazakhstani tenge, forming a direct exchange rate without calculating from the cross rates, reducing transaction costs, and improving market transparency. In 2016, in order to support RMB internationalization and the implementation of the Belt & Road Initiative (BRI), the interbank foreign exchange market intensively launched direct trading between the RMB and 11 foreign currencies, including the UAE dirham, South African rand, and Iranian rial. Since then, direct trading between the RMB and relevant foreign currencies has been launched in accordance with the principle of "launching direct trading when ready". In line with the BRI, the CFETS has temporarily waived the transaction fees for 10 direct trading currency pairs, including the Singapore dollar, Russian ruble, Malaysian ringgit, New Zealand dollar, South African rand, Iranian rial, UAE dirham, Polish złoty, Hungarian forint, and Turkish lira, since August 1, 2017. In 2017, regional trading in the interbank market between RMB and Mongolian tugrik and Cambodian riel was launched. In 2020, direct trading between RMB and Singapore dollar, Thai baht, Malaysian ringgit, and Cambodian riel was realized, and the Central Bank of Laos launched direct trading of RMB/kip in the country. At present, the trading currencies in the interbank RMB foreign exchange market cover major international reserve currencies, such as the US dollar, euro, pound sterling, and Japanese yen, as well as emerging market currencies such as the Russian ruble and currencies of countries along the Belt and Road, such as the UAE dirham.

The interbank foreign exchange market has been steadily expanding globally, cooperating with mainstream international institutions, building a community of shared interests, and mapping an orderly layout in the global financial market. In 2015, the CFETS implemented the outcomes of the China–US Strategic Economic Dialogue and the talks between the heads of state of China and Germany and signed cooperation agreements with the Chicago Mercantile Exchange Group and the Deutsche Börse AG, respectively, which clearly stated objectives such as realizing the mutual exchange of financial market infrastructures and exchange rates and other products between China and the US and between China and Europe and the development of RMB-denominated offshore exchange rate spot exchanges and derivatives.

Meanwhile, the interbank foreign exchange market has been actively promoting the strategy of business internationalization, building a global service network, and improving the infrastructure of international financial services. In January 2016, the foreign exchange trading hours of the interbank market were extended to 23:30 Beijing time, covering the European trading sessions and part of the American trading sessions, which facilitates foreign investors. The hours of various market services were also extended accordingly, enhancing the interbank foreign exchange market's ability to provide services to the world. Since 2015, the CFETS has published data on RMB exchange rates in the IMF's Special Data Dissemination Standards (SDDS), as well as real-time RMB reference rates, providing pricing references for international financial organizations, including the IMF. In particular, since December 2015, the CFETS has prepared and released the CFETS RMB exchange rate index, which has wide influence in both the domestic and international markets. In July 2018, the CFETS and Shanghai CFETS-NEX International Money Broking jointly released the Interbank USD Lending Market Sentiment Indicator. In the same month, the foreign currency lending business using foreign currency debt as collateral was launched. In May 2020, the foreign currency repurchase business of sending and receiving messages with foreign currency debt as collateral was launched. In July 2021, the CFETS and Shanghai CFETS-NEX International Money Broking jointly launched the Nikkei Index and improved the Interbank USD Lending Market Sentiment Indicator. In January 2022, the CFETS launched the matching mode for foreign currency lending (C-Lending). In April 2022, the CFETS cooperated with China Central Depository & Clearing Co. Ltd., to launch a system of designated coupons for foreign currency repo, including foreign currency pledged repo and foreign currency buyout repo.

The interbank foreign exchange market provides foreign investors with tools to manage investment risks in China. Currently, foreign institutional investors can settle and sell foreign exchanges on a spot basis through custodians, settlement agents, banks of deposit, or other domestic financial institutions qualified in the settlement and sale of foreign exchange and use foreign exchange derivatives in and outside China to hedge risks. Taking foreign central banks as an example, there are three ways for foreign central banks to enter the interbank foreign exchange market: first, entrusting the PBC to act as an agent; second, participating directly in the interbank foreign exchange market as a member; and third, entrusting the interbank foreign exchange market members to act as agents. Central banks' investments cover all listed products, including spot, forwards, swaps, cross-currency swaps, and options. In December 2023, the turnover of the interbank foreign exchange market amounted to 2.42 trillion USD, accounting for 83.7% of the total turnover in China's foreign exchange market (excluding foreign currency pairs). In 2022, the turnover of China's foreign exchange market reached 34.5 trillion USD, an increase of 43.2% compared to 2017. According to the Bank for International Settlements (BIS), the share of Chinese RMB in global OTC foreign exchange turnover increased to 7% in 2022 (up from 4% in 2019), making the RMB the fifth most traded currency, up from eighth place in 2019.

3.5 *Gold market*

Fueled by growing gold demand and market development, China is swiftly internationalizing its gold market. Shanghai has established itself as the world's third-largest gold trading center, following New York and London (Jiao, 2021, 2022). The process has involved the following measures. First, foreign investors were introduced. In September 2014, the SGE launched the "International Board" for gold within the Shanghai FTZ, allowing overseas investors to trade RMB-denominated precious metals, on both the international and main boards. The number of international members grew from 40 (in 2014) to 103 (in 2023), spanning 12 countries and regions. Second, China established RMB-denominated gold and silver pricing benchmarks, thereby enhancing its pricing influence. In April 2016, the SGE released the world's first RMB-denominated gold benchmark price known as "Shanghai Gold." This benchmark has been widely applied in trading settlements, risk hedging, and more, significantly bolstering the global impact of RMB-denominated gold pricing. In October 2019, the SGE launched the "Shanghai Silver" pricing contract, providing a reference for future RMB silver pricing. Third, ongoing efforts are made to list RMB-denominated precious metal products on overseas trading platforms. In March 2016, the SGE signed a memorandum of cooperation with the Hong Kong Exchanges and Clearing Limited (HKEX) to promote the cross-listing of products enhancing market connectivity. The international board's trading volume increased from RMB 45 billion in 2014 to RMB 2.09 trillion in 2022.

3.6 *Assessment of financial market opening*

3.6.1 *Overall assessment*

China has progressively opened its stock market, bond market, financial derivatives market, foreign exchange market, and gold market to external participation, though the degree of openness varies. Among these, the bond market exhibits a relatively high level of openness, followed by the stock market. In the primary market, although non-residents are currently unable to issue stocks in the domestic stock market, various types of non-residents, including international development organizations, foreign non-financial enterprises, financial institutions, and foreign governments, can issue bonds and raise funds in the interbank market. In the secondary market, the stock market introduced QFII ahead of the bond market in 2002, and this has gradually expanded to include RQFII, Stock Connect, and Bond Connect. The interbank bond market is fully open to QFII, and overseas institutions entering the market follow the same admission criteria as domestic institutions, without quota restrictions, subject only to macroprudential management by the PBC. Foreign investors participating in the interbank bond market can also engage in foreign exchange derivatives trading based on actual demand principles.

Regarding the depth of financial market opening, the usage of RMB in offshore markets has been steadily increasing. Since 2010, offshore RMB markets, with a multicenter layout mainly centered in Hong Kong, have developed diverse RMB products, such as credit, foreign exchange, bonds, funds, and forwards. As of June 2016, the total balance of RMB deposits in major offshore markets reached approximately 1.3 trillion RMB. RMB clearing banks have been established in 14 cities, including New York, London, Frankfurt, Seoul, Paris, Luxembourg, Doha, Toronto, and Sydney. However, there are still price differences between onshore and offshore RMB products and exchange rates, indicating some capital flow controls and limited financial market opening depth. As per the *2023 Renminbi Internationalization Report* by the PBC, by the end of 2022, the

RMB deposit balance in major offshore markets exceeded 1.5 trillion RMB. At the end of September 2023, there were 31 overseas RMB clearing banks designated in 29 countries and regions. In 2022, the volume of RMB clearing made by overseas clearing banks totaled RMB 504.3 trillion, a year-on-year increase of 7.7%.

The number of non-convertible items in China's capital account has gradually decreased, and the convertibility of securities investment has steadily increased, with restrictions mainly concentrating on the primary market. According to the IMF's *Annual Report on Exchange Arrangements and Exchange Restrictions* classification criteria for capital account transactions (7 major categories with 40 items), out of the total 40 items, 39 are fully convertible, mostly convertible, or partially convertible, thus accounting for 97.5% of all transaction items. Non-convertible items mainly pertain to individual cross-border investment and financing. Compared to developed international markets, China's financial market openness remains relatively low, with restrictions on foreign investors' access and capital flows. The market's inclination toward closure remains largely unchanged. There are multiple restrictions on the access of overseas investors and the inflow and outflow of capital. China's market systems, rules, and regulations are not fully aligned with international standards, affecting foreign participation in domestic markets. The proportion of foreign holdings in China's bond market is lower than that in developed bond markets. As of September 2023, foreign holders accounted for approximately 30% of the US government bonds (see Figure 22) and approximately 14% of Japanese government bonds (see Figure 23). China's government bonds are currently held by overseas investors at less than 10% (see Figure 21). Foreign institutions mainly invest in government bonds and policy financial bonds.

China's foreign exchange market is less open than that of developed countries. For instance, in London (see Figure 28), the world's largest forex market, approximately 70% of trading comes from overseas entities, including various participants, such as multinational corporations, investment banks, mutual funds, hedge funds, forex funds, and insurance companies. In contrast, foreign investors in China's interbank forex market account for approximately 10% of participants and less than 1% of trading volume. The participants are homogenous in type, as the commercial institutions include only banks.

Taking the stock market as an example, by the end of 2022, the total market capitalization of companies listed in London was £2.4 trillion, with 57.6% controlled by foreign investors (see Figure 29), a significant increase from 30.7% in 1998. In the US stock market, foreign investors

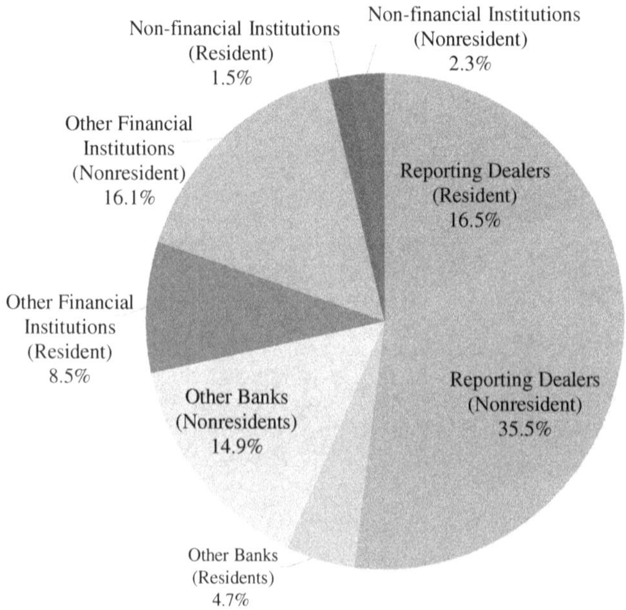

Figure 28. Types of London forex market traders.

Notes: Data as of April 2023.

Source: Foreign Exchange Joint Standing Committee.

also held a 16.7% stake (see Figure 30). Foreign investors consistently held about 30% of the shares in the Japanese stock market. However, in the current A-share market, despite the gradual opening of channels for foreign investment, the combined ownership of QFII, RQFII, Shanghai–Hong Kong Stock Connect, Shenzhen–Hong Kong Stock Connect, and Shanghai–London Stock Connect accounts for less than 5%,[18] which is significantly lower than the figures at international levels.

3.6.2 *Issues in the opening-up of financial markets*

a. Bond Market

While the bond market boasts the highest degree of openness in China's financial system, its breadth and depth still fall short. Notably, differences in rules and regulations between the Chinese market and its international

[18] By the end of the third-quarter of 2023, the total market value of A-shares held by foreign investors was approximately 3.33 trillion yuan, accounting for 4.88% of the value of the circulating A-shares.

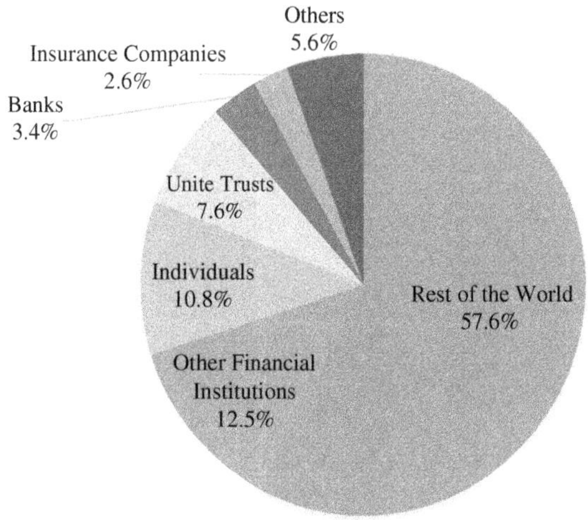

Figure 29. Types of UK stock market holders.

Notes: For better presentation, the smaller four categories of holders are aggregated as "Others", which includes private nonfinancial companies, investment trusts, charities, and the public sectors.
Source: Ownership of UK Quoted Shares: 2022.

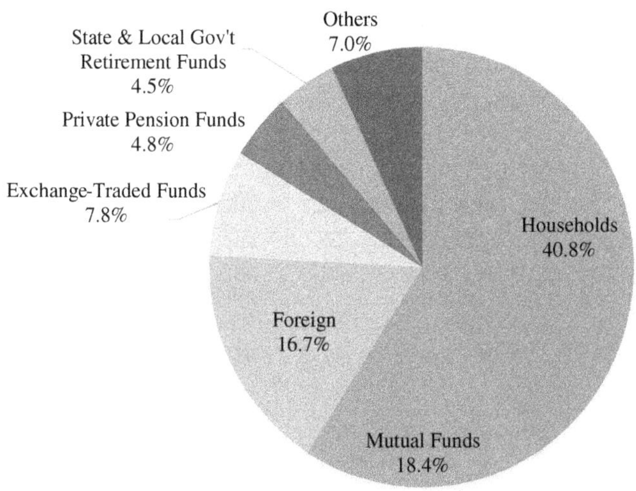

Figure 30. Types of US stock market holders.

Notes: Data as of the end of 2022.
Source: SIFMA 2023 Capital Markets Fact Book.

counterparts hinder the accessibility for overseas issuers and investors. Such issues reveal deeper problems, affecting both local and foreign participants' engagement. Despite being the world's second-largest economy, China lacks the ability to comprehensively reshape global financial market rules. Over the past decade, the country's approach to the bond market has highlighted inadequacies, necessitating a proactive, cooperative stance to align with international standards and adapt to evolving global dynamics.

First, overseas institutions issuing bonds in domestic markets still face numerous constraints due to the application of accounting and audit policies. This increases the issuance costs for bond issuers in the domestic market. According to current regulations, international development organizations and overseas nonfinancial enterprises must prepare financial reports for bond issuance in accordance with Chinese accounting standards or equivalently recognized standards by the Ministry of Finance. Additionally, audit procedures must be conducted by accounting firms qualified in securities and futures auditing in China unless the issuer's country or region has signed an equivalence agreement with the Ministry of Finance for public supervision of registered auditors. Since only Hong Kong currently meets these accounting and audit requirements, issuers in other countries or regions need to reformat financial reports to comply with these standards for domestic bond issuance. This limitation constrains market development.

Another issue lies in China's credit rating industry, which is unable to meet international investor demands. Due to its short history, late development, lack of default rate assessment, and practice of "pricing based on grade and grading based on price," China's credit rating system tends to be overly optimistic and lacks meaningful differentiation. Notably, a significant proportion of Chinese bonds receive high ratings, with over 90% of companies rated AA or higher, far surpassing rates in countries such as the US and Japan. Simultaneously, the proportion of lower-rated enterprises is notably low, resulting in a skewed distribution. As a consequence of the increased number of highly rated firms, differentiation within the same rating level is reduced due to varying risk levels. In the process of bond market opening, international investors allocate assets globally based on their risk control systems aligned with global standards. This misalignment with China's credit rating system, along with lingering doubts about the quality of domestic credit ratings among international investors, might pose obstacles to investing in China's bond market.

A third challenge is the limited variety of foreign exchange and derivative products associated with bond investments, which constrains market openness. Overseas investors lack effective tools to hedge against currency and interest rate risks when investing in RMB-denominated bonds. China's developing derivative market, with its small scale and restricted participant pool, poses technical challenges for foreign institutions. For instance, while overseas investors often employ fixed income, commodities, and currencies (FICC) strategies, China's differing degrees of openness for various products create obstacles in effectively utilizing derivatives and foreign exchange tools to formulate investment strategies.

The fourth hindrance involves international collaboration in financial market infrastructure. Technical complexities for overseas institutions participating in the Chinese market remain unresolved due to fragmented rules and *ad hoc* approaches. Some cases are handled on a case-by-case basis, hampering stable expectations for foreign entities. While the cross-border connectivity of infrastructure[19] has improved in recent years, China's financial market infrastructure still falls short of fully meeting the needs of foreign institutions. In contrast, international electronic trading platforms have evolved over years of market competition, offering powerful features. Overseas investors often use these unified terminals for market updates and trading, whereas domestic terminals lag behind in aspects such as language and user-friendliness. Major global bond markets employ multitier custody arrangements, forming a comprehensive network of custodians that facilitates investors' seamless access to global markets and provides comprehensive services, such as margin trading, information, and research reports. To improve bond market openness, China must become better aligned with international infrastructure.

---

[19] In 2015, the CCDC and the South Korean Central Custodian jointly proposed the China-South Korea Bond Market Connect program. This program, known as the Bond Connect, was launched in 2017 and an important measure for the cross-border interconnection of China's financial infrastructure, providing overseas small- and medium-sized investors with indirect access to the domestic bond market. In November 2018, the CFETS and Bloomberg Inc. were connected through the trading platform to support foreign institutional investors to enter the interbank bond market through direct or indirect market access modes. In 2019, the CCDC was connected to Macau's financial infrastructure agencies.

b. Stock Market

Currently, the investment in securities mainly follows the "pipeline" opening-up mode. For investment, although QFII was introduced into the stock market as early as 2002 and then RQFII, the Shanghai–Hong Kong Stock Connect, the Shenzhen–Hong Kong Stock Connect, and the Shanghai–London Stock Connect were successively adopted, there are still numerous regulatory restrictions, such as those on capital flow, on foreign investors if they intend to invest in the stock market. Overseas long-term funds entering the market through QFII and RQFII are subject to regulation in terms of liquidity management, which discourages long-term investment. Therefore, QFII and RQFII cannot give full play to their positive roles in improving the structure of investors, advocating for the concept of long-term investment value, and enhancing the governance capacity of listed companies. Foreign individual investors can only invest in the underlying stocks of the Shanghai and Shenzhen stock markets through the Shanghai–Hong Kong Stock Connect, Shenzhen–Hong Kong Stock Connect, and Shanghai–London Stock Connect but currently have no access to other direct investment channels.

In terms of financing, the operation of two-way cross-border financing is unbalanced. On the one hand, overseas enterprises have only a few financing channels in China. In terms of the financing of overseas enterprises within China, in March 2018, the CSRC released the *Several Opinions on Launching the Pilot Program for Innovative Enterprises to Offer Stocks or Depositary Receipts within China*, allowing the internet, big data, cloud computing, artificial intelligence, software and integrated circuits, high-end equipment manufacturing, biomedicine, and other high-tech and strategic emerging industries, as well as innovative enterprises above a considerable scale, to offer stocks or depositary receipts in Chinese stock exchanges. In September 2021, the pilot program was further expanded to red-chip enterprises in new-generation information technology, new energy, new materials, new energy vehicles, environmental protection, aerospace, marine equipment, and other high-tech and strategic emerging industries, as well as red-chip enterprises with national strategic significance. In February 2022, the *Provisions on the Supervision and Administration of Depository Receipts under the Stock Connect Scheme between Domestic and Overseas Stock Exchanges* was released by the CSRC to allow overseas enterprises to raise funds in China by issuing Chinese Depositary Receipts (CDRs), which opened up channels for overseas issuers to participate in equity financing in the exchanges. With the lowering of the threshold for the return of red chips, companies such as China Mobile and SMIC have successively returned to the A-shares market. However, companies listed on overseas exchanges need to meet three conditions to return to the A-shares market through CDRs. First, its average market value must be at least RMB 20 billion for 120 trading days before the issuance date. Second, it must have been listed overseas for 3 years. Third, its initial issuance of CDRs must have exceeded 50 million in number, with its market value reaching RMB 500 million. However, CDRs have not been widely adopted thus far.

On the other hand, the overseas financing of Chinese enterprises has faced tough challenges. First, enterprises can raise funds through H-shares, issuing American Depositary Receipts (ADRs) or Global Depositary Receipts (GDRs). At present, the approval mechanism has become stricter. In December 2021, the CSRC released the *Provisions of the State Council on the Administration of Overseas Securities Offerings and Listings by Domestic Companies (Draft for Comment)* and the supporting *Administrative Measures for the Record-Filing of Overseas Securities Offerings and Listings by Domestic Companies (Draft for Comments)*, which for the first time included all forms of arrangements for an overseas listing of domestic enterprises into a comprehensive record-filing supervision system. Second, disputes over Sino-US cooperation on regulation still exist. In August 2022, the CSRC, the Ministry of Finance of China, and the Public Company Accounting Oversight Board (PCAOB) signed an audit supervision cooperation agreement, which marked a significant step in addressing the auditing issues between China and the US. However, the conclusion of the cross-border audit agreement between China and the US has not completely resolved disputes between the two sides, as China emphasizes joint supervision under audit sovereignty, while the US stresses that there should be no limits or restraints. Meanwhile, the number of enterprises seeking listings in Europe through GDRs has increased but is still relatively small.

c. Derivatives Market

Strict control of market risks is an important feature in the opening-up of China's financial derivatives market. As financial derivatives are a double-edged sword, regulatory authorities always prioritize risk prevention, resulting in a slow pace of the opening-up of the financial derivatives market. In recent years, in order to implement relevant requirements on deepening the opening-up of the capital market, the opening-up of the financial derivatives market has sped up, the pace of product innovation has accelerated, and market operation efficiency has gradually improved. The regulatory authorities continue to improve their capacity for market risk monitoring and control and further increase the number of methods for opening-up, which will help promote exploration in the pricing of the domestic financial derivatives market, stimulate innovation in the trading system, strengthen the international influence of the domestic capital market, and attract more overseas funds.

d. Foreign Exchange Market

To some extent, the principle of actual demand limits the further opening-up of the foreign exchange market. At present, the domestic foreign exchange market is under regulation based on actual demand, although no requirement on actual demand has been met in the international market, where there are various participants and less than 10% of the trading volume is driven by real trade. The principle of actual demand requires regulatory authorities to be more cautious when introducing foreign investors into the interbank foreign exchange market. Although institutions such as overseas central banks and clearing banks can enter the market for transactions, overseas investment banks, commercial banks, insurance institutions, pension funds, hedge funds, and large enterprises currently have no access. We can find a similar problem in the types of domestic investors, which mainly include commercial banks, with a relatively small proportion of non-bank financial institutions and non-financial enterprises. The single type and small number of participants lead to similar foreign exchange transactions, fewer proprietary transactions, and strong homogeneity in market demand, reducing the demand for the asset allocation of foreign exchange derivatives. Therefore, there is still an enormous gap in the transaction scale between the domestic market and the international market.

Although dozens of currency pairs have been launched successively in recent years, members are not highly motivated, leading to low transaction volume, insufficient liquidity, and a low proportion of non-USD currencies in RMB transactions. As a result, minor currencies with active transactions mainly include those of neighboring regions or developed economies with frequent economic and trade exchanges with China, while other minor currencies have few transactions.

e. Gold Market

In recent years, China's gold market has grown rapidly. Its core advantages include diversified trading products, well-developed gold and silver pricing benchmarks, and established financial standards for the gold market. Despite the development achievements of China's gold market, the enormous gap between it and well-established gold markets across the world, epitomized by the limited market openness and a relatively small volume of transactions, should also be noted. In terms of opening-up, taking the Shanghai Gold Exchange as an example, there are only a few active foreign members now, with a low degree of integration with international gold markets. In terms of transaction volume, when compared with the London Gold Market, the world's largest spot gold market, the Shanghai Gold Exchange still has a quite small transaction volume.

4. Conforming to the Rules and Practices of the International Market and Promoting the Further Opening-up of China's Financial Market

Finance plays a crucial role in the modern economy. A financial market and institutional system with vitality and international competitiveness that also effectively serves the real economy is the key to the efficient allocation of resources. Since the Reform and Opening-Up began, the basics of a financial market and institutional system adapted to the socialist market economy have been established, making significant contributions to the sustained and sound development of China's economy. However, they have failed to play an effective role in promoting capital formation, optimizing resource allocation, advancing economic transformation, and facilitating structural adjustment. There is still an enormous gap between China and other economies with mature markets, which is reflected in the low proportion of direct financing, particularly inadequate equity financing, and the insufficient development of derivatives.

In the coming years, China, as the world's second largest economy after only the US, will further secure its position, with its economy evolving into a new normal. China will complete its market-oriented reform of interest rates and exchange rates and realize the opening-up of capital accounts. China has further enhanced the international status of the RMB, with its share in the IMF SDR valuation basket increasing from 10.92% in 2015 to 12.28% in 2022. The further opening-up of the financial market is necessary for China to improve its international competitiveness. Given this, China should continue to promote reform and development through opening-up, stress top-level design, and overall arrangement, improve prudent macro management, and build a modern financial market system that is consistent with the open economy of a great power and complete in its variety, reasonable in its structure, efficient in its services, safe and stable, and more inclusive and competitive so as to support the sustainable development of the real economy.

4.1 *For the further opening-up of the financial market, we should improve the macroprudential management framework and promote overall coordination rather than focusing on certain individual aspects*

China should adhere to the principle of gradual progress and develop a road map and timetable for the opening-up of its financial market. In this process of opening-up, China should pay attention to the balance between opening-up, development, and stability. In different stages, China should actively adjust its opening-up strategy, avoid the potential risks brought by opening-up, and improve its prudent macro management framework to avoid risks brought by cross-border capital flow. China should enhance its prudent macro policy framework for foreign debts and cross-border capital flows and upgrade its risk management under convertible conditions. China should consider the matching between assets and liabilities, such as currency and maturity, rationally control the scale of foreign debts, optimize its structure of foreign debts, and monitor foreign debts to prevent foreign debt risks. China should also look into how to restrain the impact of short-term speculative capital through market-oriented means, strengthen the daily monitoring and early warning of risks in investments from foreign investors and large-scale abnormal cross-border capital flows, and urge the institutions involved to perform their monitoring and information reporting duties seriously to prevent illegal transactions and risks from abnormal cross-border capital flows.

The depth and breadth of China's financial market are unlike those of the international market, and the organizational system, management system, restraint mechanism and incentive mechanism of Chinese financial institutions are also different from those of such institutions in developed economies. Therefore, China should compare and analyze the above differences; adjust the sequence for the opening-up of the financial market, financial institutions, and financial services in a timely manner; and promote the coordination and consistency between domestic financial development and the opening-up policy. On the one hand, China should continue to push forward its development through opening-up, adhere to the direction of market-oriented reform, increase the proportion of direct financing, and achieve coordinated development between direct financing and indirect financing, equity financing and debt financing, and basic products and derivatives. On the other hand, it is necessary to further improve the market-oriented restraint mechanism, enhance the robustness and resilience of financial institutions, and strive to build a financial institution system with a reasonable structure, effective competition, and sound governance.

In combination with domestic and international economic and financial development, as well as China's overall foreign debt repayment capability and balance of international payments, and fully considering the real economy's demand for financial services and the impact of the two-way opening up of the financial industry, China should formulate a road map and timetable for the two-way opening up of the financial market and steadily push it forward by building cross-border supervision capacity as the guarantee and ensuring that the policies are introduced after certain conditions are met. Through an orderly financial opening-up strategy that also ensures the long-term benefits of the opening-up of the financial market, the costs and risks of short-term adjustments can be reduced and alleviated so as to realize the dynamic balance and coordination of efficiency and stability. At the present stage, China should further promote the opening-up of the bond market and the stock market on the basis of following the rules and practices of the international market and coordinate the opening-up of the financial derivatives market, the foreign exchange market, and the gold market. Meanwhile, in the process of opening-up, more effort should be made to ensure that the relevant rules are in line with international standards and that they avoid overemphasizing Chinese characteristics.

4.2 *The tax issues related to foreign investors entering China's bond market should be clarified as soon as possible*

In November 2018, the *Notice of the Enterprise Income Tax and Value-Added Tax Policies for Foreign Institutions Investing in the Domestic Bond Market* of the Ministry of Finance and the State Taxation Administration stipulated that from November 7, 2018, to November 6, 2021, the bond interest income of foreign institutions gained by investing in the domestic bond market would be temporarily exempted from corporate income tax and value-added tax. In December 2021, the *Announcement on Extending the Enterprise Income Tax and Value-Added Tax Policies for Foreign Institutions Investing in the Domestic Bond Market* issued by the Ministry of Finance and the State Taxation Administration stipulated that the policy of exempting foreign institutional investors from corporate income tax and value-added tax for investing in the domestic bond market would be extended until the end of 2025 to better facilitate and encourage foreign investors to participate in the interbank bond market. The tax exemption policy has motivated foreign investors to enter the market to a certain extent. However, the tax policy arrangements after the expiration of the policy need to be further clarified.

First, before the tax exemption policy expires, the finance and taxation authorities should clarify the taxation details involved in the bond investment of foreign institutions in a timely manner to attract more foreign institutions to invest in China's bond market. For instance, regulations on whether and how to collect corporate income tax and value-added tax should follow international practices by, for example, formulating a consistent document with clear rules and strong operability and refining the requirements for withholding and remitting taxes of the registry and custody institutions in the interbank bond market.

Second, the issues concerning tax preference provisions in international treaties or tax agreements should be clarified, and the implementation of tax preference policies should be facilitated. For example, the beneficiaries of tax incentives and the application method and process should be clarified.

Third, the exemption of enterprise income tax and value-added tax on the interest income and spread income of foreign investors investing in the issuance of Panda Bonds in China's interbank bond market should be promoted to avoid double taxation and enhance the transparency of the Panda Bond tax policy.

Fourth, the finance and taxation departments should increase the publicity regarding tax policies and create a fairer and more transparent policy environment for foreign institutions to invest in the interbank market.

4.3 *The financial infrastructure construction should take into account China's national conditions and international practices*

The infrastructure arrangements of China's financial market are quite different from those of the international market. The international market usually adopts a multilevel custody system and a relatively developed market maker system. However, China's infrastructure-related institutional arrangements have their own characteristics. Constructed by utilizing the advantages of a latecomer, China's financial infrastructure is relatively centralized, given the basic national conditions that China is still in a market-oriented transition stage and that the corporate governance of market participants needs to be improved. In view of the imperfect corporate governance structure of financial institutions and other participants, which has caused a risk event regarding the misappropriation of customers' bonds, the interbank bond market has established a unified bond custody and settlement platform that meets actual needs. It implements state-level custody with a real-name registration system and has built an electronic trading system for one-on-one inquiry to strengthen centralized information monitoring, prevent the misappropriation of bonds and other irregularities, and provide participants with a transparent and standardized trading platform. The relatively concentrated infrastructure is adapted to the economic and financial development environment in China. It also showed strong superiority during the international financial crisis that broke out in 2008. Even after the crisis, the relevant regulatory reforms have tended to adopt centralized infrastructure.

However, in the process of opening-up, the technical details of the infrastructure arrangements with Chinese characteristics, such as opening an account, securing custody, completing transactions, and reaching settlements, are not quite consistent with the best international practices, which has affected the investment of foreign institutions in the domestic market. For example, from the opening-up of China's bond market in 2005 to the end of 2023, the bonds held by foreign investors amounted to RMB 3.72 trillion, accounting for 2.4% of outstanding bonds in custody in China's bond market, which was not only far lower than the proportion in Western countries but also lower than that of emerging countries such as Malaysia. According to practical experience, although China is the second largest economy in the world, it is not able to completely rewrite the rules of the global financial market system. Therefore, China needs to follow the general trend, take the initiative to change its completely "self-centered" thinking of opening up with an inclusive and cooperative mindset, and actively adapt to international rules. In the future, it will be practical to further promote the opening-up by adopting a single-level custody system for domestic investors and a multilevel custody system for overseas investors in line with international market practices to accommodate the practices and characteristics of various investors.

Through the institutional arrangements of "multilevel custody, nominal holding, centralized trading, and penetrating supervision", the Bond Connect program launched in July 2017 has become a reasonable and effective way to build a safer, more stable, and more open bond market and connect international investors more conveniently based on existing openness. From a macroscopic perspective, implementing the Bond Connect through multilevel custody actually means allocating RMB-denominated bond assets more conveniently and efficiently through internationally accepted arrangements that international investors can understand and accept. This means smoother capital inflow and more diversified debt output, which could promote China's balance of international payments, bolster the smooth deleveraging of the economy and finance, and reduce financing costs, thus strengthening the foundation of financial security to the maximum extent. From the microscopic perspective, the introduction of Chinese banks into the Bond Connect program to implement multilevel custody provides Chinese financial institutions with a historic opportunity to participate in international custody business competition so as to improve the global competitiveness of China and maintain the country's national financial security.

References

British Metal Focus LTD. (2021). *Global Gold Yearbook 2021*. Beijing: China Gold Association.

China Securities Regulatory Commission (CSRC). (2021). China Securities Regulatory Commission Annual Report 2020. Beijing: China Financial & Economics Publishing House.

China Securities Regulatory Commission (CSRC). (2022). Brief Conference Held by the Publicity Department of the Chinese Communist Party on the Reforms and Developments in the Financial Sector since the 18th Party Congress. http://www.csrc.gov.cn/csrc/c100028/c3849994/content.shtml (2022-06-23).

Jones, C.M., Shi, D., Zhang, X., & Zhang, X. (2020). Heterogeneity in retail investors: Evidence from comprehensive account-level trading and holdings data. Working Paper. Available at http://cfrc.pbcsf.tsinghua.edu.cn/__local/9/1F/0B/991FDA10554ABAF7AE4CF152439_565BBE40_17DC16.pdf?e=.pdf.

Jiao Jinpu. (2021). Enhancing China's voice in gold trading and giving full play to the leading role of exchanges in the process of gold market internationalization. *Tsinghua Financial Review*, 10, 20–22.

Jiao Jinpu. (2022). Building a gold market with Chinese characteristics. *China Finance*, 14, 16–18.

People's Bank of China (PBC). (2022). 2022 RMB Internationalization Report. Beijing: People's Bank of China.

Research Department of China Foreign Exchange Trade System and National Interbank Funding Center. (2024). Overview of the overseas RMB market in 2023. https://cj.sina.com.cn/articles/view/6314832590/17864b2ce001016ue5 (2024-01-09).

Shanghai Stock Exchange (SSE). (2021a). Shanghai Stock Exchange Statistical Annual 2021. Beijing: China Financial Publishing House.

Shenzhen Stock Exchange (SZSE). (2021b). *Shenzhen Stock Exchange Fact Book 2021*. Shenzhen: Haitian Publishing House.

Xie Duo. (2014). Comprehensive Knowledge Reader of Interbank Market. Beijing: China Financial Publishing House (in Chinese).

Xu Zhong, Zhang Xuechun, Cao Yuanyuan, Tang Yingwei, & Wan Tailei. (2017). To promote the reform and development of financial markets with opening up. 2017·Jingshan Report (Report 6). Hangzhou: China Finance 40 Forum (in Chinese).

Xu Guiyang. (2012). Research on China's Gold Industry Organization and Development Strategy. Beijing: Economic Management Press.

Part II

Stock Market

Chapter 2

History of the Opening up of China's Stock Market

China's stock market has been developing rapidly since the establishment of the Shanghai Stock Exchange (SSE) and Shenzhen Stock Exchange (SZSE) in 1990. In the initial stage of stock market development, many stock exchanges were set up, leading to issues such as inconsistent trading rules and the disorderly growth of the market. Given this, the State Council decided in April 1992 to retain only the SSE and SZSE and began to rectify various equity trading centers. With the unification of the trading system and operation rules of the SSE and SZSE, a centralized and unified national stock market was gradually established.

The regulatory system has since improved. In October 1992, the Securities Commission of the State Council and the CSRC were formally established. In 1998, the Securities Commission of the State Council was abolished, and its functions were incorporated into the CSRC, thus establishing a unified regulatory system. In addition, the Securities Association of China (SAC), established in August 1991, exercises self-disciplinary administration within the securities industry.

The legal system has been progressively strengthened. The Company Law came into force on July 1, 1994, and was revised in January 2006. The *Securities Law*, which regulates the issuance and trading of stocks in China, came into force on July 1, 1999, and was amended in both January 2006 and March 2020. Significant advancements have also been made in investor protection.

The legal and regulatory framework of the stock market has continued to advance over time, and the administrative intervention of the initial public offering (IPO) mechanism has been strong. In April 1993, to prevent the stock market from overheating, the Securities Commission of the State Council promulgated the *Provisional Regulations on the Administration of Stock Issuance and Trading*, which implemented an approval system with an administrative quota for domestic securities offerings. Companies must be recommended by local governments and industry authorities to be listed. In 1996, "quota management" was replaced by "target management". In 1999, the *Securities Law* clarified the IPO approval system. In March 2001, the China Securities Regulatory Commission (CSRC) abolished the quota and target restrictions in the IPO review and adopted a securities offering review and approval system. The issuer must now apply for an offering and be recommended by its sponsor to the CSRC, who will conduct a preliminary compliance review of the application materials before passing it to the Public Offering Review Committee. In December 2003, the CSRC issued the *Trial Measures on the Sponsor System for the Issuing and Listing of Securities*, officially establishing the sponsor system. The *Securities Law* was amended in October 2005 to formally recognize this system. In October 2008, the CSRC further improved the sponsor system with the amended *Measures for the Administration of Sponsorship Relating to Securities Offering and Listing*, which covers the responsibilities of sponsors according to the arrangements made for the Growth Enterprise Board (GEB).

The CSRC has been reforming the IPO mechanism, transitioning it from an administration-based process to a registration-based one. In June 2019, the SSE formally launched a pilot "Science and Technology Innovation Board" (the STAR Market) using a "registration system", which is similar to those used in Hong Kong, the United Kingdom, and the US. The strict and swift implementation of the delisting procedure for poorly performing firms was also implemented. In 2020, the GEB reformed and piloted the new registration system. Until the pilot program becomes fully functional, the registration system has been extended to other segments of the A-share market in February 2023.

The framework of the delisting process was established by the *Securities Law* of 1999. The revised *Securities Law* and the *Company Law* of 2006 discharged the stock exchange with the authority to suspend, resume, and terminate the listing. In October 2014, the CSRC released the *Opinions on Reforming, Improving and Strictly Implementing the Delisting*

System for Listed Companies, which established a forced delisting system to guard against fraudulent issuance and major information disclosure violations deterring the illegal behaviors of public companies. In July 2018, the CSRC issued the *Decision to Amend the Opinions on Reforming, Improving, and Strictly Implementing the Delisting Rules*. In November 2020, the 16th meeting of the Central Committee for Comprehensively Deepening Reform adopted the *Implementation Plan for Improving the Delisting Mechanism for Listed Companies*, reiterating that improving the delisting mechanism is a necessary institutional arrangement for comprehensively deepening the reform of the capital market.

In April 2005, the CSRC issued the *Notice of Split-Share Structural Reform of Listed Companies* to launch the split-share reform. By the end of 2007, the split-share reform of listed companies in the SSE and SZSE was completed, ending the coexistence of tradable and nontradeable shares of listed companies. As the delisting mechanisms have become better enforced, more firms have been delisted from the exchanges.

After decades of development, China's stock market has undergone comprehensive reform and opening-up, which has included enhanced market legislation and investor protection. Regulators have improved their regulatory efficiency and governance capacity, thus maintaining stability in China's capital markets.

China's multilayered capital market system was established to support diverse types of enterprises in obtaining financing. It primarily includes the Main Board,[1] the Growth Enterprise Board (GEB)[2] (launched on October 23, 2009), the Science and Technology Innovation Board (STAR)[3] (launched on July 22, 2019), the National Equities Exchange and Quotations (NEEQ)[4] (inaugurated on January 16, 2013), the Beijing

[1] The Small-and-Medium Enterprise Board (SMEB) was launched on June 25, 2004; it was originally subordinated under the SZSE and then merged with the Main Board of the SZSE on April 6, 2021.

[2] On April 27, 2020, the 13th meeting of the Central Committee for Comprehensively Deepening Reform adopted the *General Implementation Plan for the Reform of the Growth Enterprise Market and the Pilot Registration System*. On August 24, 2020, the GEB reform and pilot registration system was officially implemented.

[3] On January 28, 2019, the CSRC issued the *Implementation Opinions on Setting up the Science and Technology Innovation Board and the Pilot of Registration-based IPO System on the Shanghai Stock Exchange*.

[4] In July 2012, the State Council approved the establishment of the National Equities Exchange and Quotations (NEEQ). In September 2012, the CSRC issued *Measures for the*

Stock Exchange[5] (launched in September 2021), and the regional equity market.[6] The Main Board is the primary market for stock trading and has strict listing requirements. The GEB provides additional opportunities for small and growth firms to issue stocks publicly and is similar to NASDAQ in the US and to the Alternative Investment Market (AIM) in the United Kingdom. The STAR market is positioned to serve science and technology innovation enterprises that serve the national strategy, make breakthroughs in core technologies, and enjoy wide recognition from the market. The NEEQ, also called the "New Third Board",[7] implemented tiered management (stocks are classified into the "base", "innovation" and "select" tiers) in June 2016. In June 2020, the CSRC issued guidance on the transfer of listings, allowing listed stocks in the selected tier to be transferred to other boards. The BSE was established based on the NEEQ select tier firms and serves as the primary platform for innovation-oriented SMEs, advanced manufacturing, and the modern service industry; it includes a transfer listing function.

According to the Wind Economic Database, by the end of 2023, there were 5,346 companies listed on the SSE and SZSE, with a total

---

Supervision and Administration of Unlisted Public Companies to regulate the transfer and issuance of shares of unlisted public companies. On January 16, 2013, the NEEQ was officially inaugurated. At an executive meeting in June 2013, the State Council decided to speed up the development of multilevel capital market and expand the pilot NEEQ to the whole country. In December 2013, the State Council issued *Decisions on Issues Relating to the National Equities Exchange and Quotations*, setting forth general provisions for the NEEQ. On October 25, 2019, the CSRC launched a comprehensive deepening of the New Third Board reform. In December 2019, the CSRC amended the *Measures for the Supervision and Administration of Non-Exchange-Listed Public Companies*.

[5] The Beijing Stock Exchange (BSE) was incorporated on September 3, 2021, and was the first corporate stock exchange in China approved by the State Council.

[6] In 2013, the State Council incorporated regional equity markets into the multilevel capital market system. In January 2017, the General Office of the State Council issued the *Circular on Regulating and Developing the Regional Equity Markets*, which clarified the legal status of the system. In May 2017, the CSRC issued *Provisional Measures for the Supervision and Administration of Regional Equity Trading Platforms*, established rules on the issuance and transfer of equities, account management, depository and settlement, intermediary services, market self-regulation, and supervision and administration.

[7] The old Third-Board Market was established in 2001 as an alternative trading venue for both firms delisted from or unqualified to be listed on the main board. It is an over-the-counter market dominated by low-quality stocks with little liquidity.

market capitalization of RMB 77.76 trillion. According to the World Federation of Exchanges (WFE), in 2022, China's stock market ranked second in the world after the US, in total market capitalization.

The two-way opening-up of China's capital market has steadily advanced. On the one hand, the B-share pilot was launched in 1991 to attract foreign investors. The QFII and RQFII programs were established in 2002 and 2011, respectively, thus allowing qualified foreign investors to invest in mainland securities. On the other hand, Chinese companies have been allowed to be listed on global capital markets since 1993. The QDII and RQDII programs were launched in 2006 and 2014, respectively, thus allowing qualified domestic institutional investors to invest in overseas financial markets. Since 2014, Shanghai–Hong Kong Stock Connect, Shenzhen–Hong Kong Stock Connect, and Shanghai–London Stock Connect have been gradually established, further widening cross-border investment and financing channels. Since 2015, US-listed Chinese stocks and A-shares have been included in international stock indices. Since 2018, China's financial opening-up has accelerated, and a series of important initiatives have significantly improved the efficiency of the country's securities market.

1. B-Shares

B-shares are RMB-dominated shares traded in USD or HKD, with the B-share system launched in late 1991. B-shares on the SZSE were quoted and settled in Hong Kong dollars, and B-shares on the SSE were quoted and settled in US dollars. Relevant regulations included the *Administrative Measures of Shanghai Municipality for Special Renminbi-denominated Stocks* issued by the PBC and the Shanghai Government in November 1991 and the *Interim Administrative Measures of Shenzhen City for Special Renminbi-denominated stocks* issued by the PBC and the Shenzhen Government in December 1991. In December 1995, the State Council issued the *Provisions on Foreign Capital Stock Listed in China by Joint Stock Limited Companies* while repealing the 1991 *Administrative Measures* and *Interim Measures* as listed above. Accordingly, the Securities Commission of the State Council issued the implementing rules in May 1996.

To a certain extent, the issuance of B-shares alleviated the foreign exchange capital shortage faced by enterprises. However, after 2000, B-shares' fundraising function weakened, and market trading was sluggish due to the increasing availability of foreign funds brought by China's accession to the World Trade Organization (WTO) and overseas listings of Chinese companies. In view of this, the CSRC relaxed the constraints on B-share issuance and financing by implementing the *Interim Methods for Listed Companies' Public Incorporation of Shares* in April 2000, which allowed companies that met certain conditions to publicly issue additional shares, solving the refinancing problem of some B-share companies. In September 2000, the CSRC issued the *Circular on the Issue of the Enterprises of Domestically Listed in Foreign Currencies (B-shares) Listing the B-shares That Are Not Listed Domestically*. The circular stipulated the circulation of foreign non-promoter shares and promoter shares (with a three-year requirement and approval needed) in the B-share market, enhanced the confidence of foreign investors, and promoted the expansion of B-shares. In addition, the CSRC issued the *Notice on Issues Concerning Individual Domestic Residents' Investment in Foreign Currency Stocks Listed in Domestic Stock Markets* in February 2001, allowing domestic residents to invest in B-shares, which enhanced such shares' liquidity.

At the end of 2012, the CSRC launched a pilot scheme for B-share companies to transfer their domestically listed shares in foreign currencies (B-shares) to the Hong Kong Stock Exchange (HKEX) for listing. On December 19, 2012, after approval by the CSRC and a hearing by the HKEX, the China International Marine Container (Group) successfully converted its B-shares to H-shares listed on the HKEX. In May 2014, the *Opinions of the State Council on Further Promoting the Healthy Development of Capital Markets* proposed "steadily exploring B-share market reform". In December 2021, the China Securities Depository and Clearing (CSDC) and SSE issued implementing rules to clarify issues such as asset security, conversion implementation, decision-making, and approval. As of the end of 2021, three B-share companies on the SZSE had converted B-shares to H-shares, and two companies on the SSE had indicated conversion intentions.

By the end of 2023, 85 B-share companies were listed in the SSE and SZSE, including 44 on the SSE and 41 on the SZSE, with a total market capitalization of RMB 0.87 trillion. Of the 86 listed companies, 11 companies are listed solely on B-share market, 74 companies are listed on both B-share and A-share markets, 1 company is listed on both B-share and H-share markets, and 1 company is listed on both B-share, A-share, and H-share markets.

2. Overseas Listing of Chinese Companies

In the early 1990s, China began direct financing in the international capital markets. To strengthen the management of overseas IPOs, the State Council issued the *Circular on Further Strengthening the Macro-Control of the Securities Markets* in December 1992, which required that the transregional issuing of stocks be submitted to the Securities Committee of the State Council for approval. In April 1993, the Securities Commission issued the *Notice of Approving and Forwarding the Report by the China Securities Regulatory Commission on the Problems in the Overseas IPO and Listing by Domestic Enterprises*, which identifies four ways for domestic enterprises to directly or indirectly issue shares and list on foreign exchanges: First, domestic enterprises can directly issue stocks and list abroad with the approval of China's authorities. Second, domestic enterprises can use the name of companies established abroad to issue shares and list abroad. Third, domestic listed companies can list and trade on overseas exchanges. Fourth, domestic listed companies can issue depositary receipts (DRs) or other derivative forms of shares abroad. The notice further reiterated that any enterprise taking the abovementioned approach to overseas IPOs and listings should report to the Securities Commission for prior approval. In August 1994, the State Council issued the *Special Provisions of the State Council on Joint Stock Limited Companies Seeking Issuing Shares and Listing Overseas*, which required companies to submit a written application following the requirements of the Securities Commission of the State Council. In June 1997, the State Council issued the *Circular on Further Strengthening the Administration of Share Issuance and Listing Overseas*, and the CSRC formulated corresponding regulations, forming a regulatory system for domestic enterprises and Chinese-controlled companies incorporated in foreign jurisdictions to list abroad. The original preselection system was abolished, while the new regulatory system emphasized that any company meeting the conditions for overseas listing could apply to the CSRC, which would approve the application according to the established procedures. The thresholds for overseas listing were also set: net assets of at least RMB 400 million, profit after tax of at least RMB 60 million in the past year, and fundraising requirements of at least USD 50 million, based on a reasonable expected P/E ratio. In August 2002, the State Administration of Foreign Exchange (SAFE) and the CSRC jointly issued the *Notice on Further Improving the Foreign Exchange Management of Overseas*

Listing. In December 2012, the CSRC promulgated the *Supervision Guidelines for Document Filings and Review Procedures in Connection with Overseas Stock Issuance and Listing by Joint Stock Companies*, further strengthening the supervisory capacity.

To fill the regulatory gap related to the indirect overseas listing of Chinese companies, the CSRC promulgated the *Provisions of the State Council on the Administration of Overseas Securities Offerings and Listings by Domestic Companies (Draft for Comment)* and *Administrative Measures for the Record-Filing of Overseas Securities Offerings and Listings by Domestic Companies* in December 2021. It unified the regulation framework for all forms of overseas listing into comprehensive filing for the first time. The currency restrictions on raising funds and paying dividends abroad were relaxed to meet the needs of enterprises raising RMB abroad. In December 2021, the National Development and Reform Commission (NDRC) and the Ministry of Commerce issued the *Special Administrative Measures (Negative List) for Foreign Investment Access (2021 Edition)* and the *Special Administrative Measures (Negative List) for Foreign Investment Access in Pilot Free Trade Zones (2021 Edition)*, which concerned the issue of foreign equity participation related to the indirect listing of enterprises through overseas entities and became effective January 1, 2022. For the first time, the two lists stipulated the issuance of shares by domestic enterprises and their listing and trading abroad.

For the spinoff of listed companies, the CSRC has also issued and revised relevant regulations. In July 2004, the CSRC issued the *Circular on Issues Concerning the Standardization on Overseas Listing of Subordinated Enterprises of Domestically Listed Companies*. It allowed A-share listed companies to meet certain conditions to spin off their subsidiaries for overseas listings and made specific provisions to facilitate listed companies to broaden financing channels. In March 2007, the CSRC issued the *Notice on the Centralized Depository and Custody Services of Overseas Listed Companies' Shares That Are Not Listed on Overseas Markets*, which created conditions for the circulation of shares related to spinoffs. In December 2019, the CSRC issued *Several Provisions on the Pilot Program for the Domestic Listing of Spun-off Subsidiaries of Listed Companies*. The provisions piloted separate listings of listed companies' subsidiaries to help expand financing channels, specified qualifications for listed companies to spin off and list their subsidiaries, and tightened oversight in this area. In January 2022, the CSRC published the *Rules for the Spin Off of Listed Companies (For Trial Implementation)*, which revised and integrated the relevant content of the two previous documents, unified the domestic and foreign regulatory requirements, and clarified the conditions for spinoff approval. Articles regarding the prohibition of spinoff listings were also added. For example, the subsidiary's primary business or assets must be the listed company's main business or assets at the time of IPO.

In recent years, China's regulatory authorities have enhanced data security and anti-monopoly regulations, adding additional constraints on Chinese companies' overseas listings. The *Data Security Law* was enacted on September 1, 2021. In July 2021, the Cyberspace Administration of China (CAC) issued the *Measures for Cybersecurity Review (Draft Revision for Comments)*. On February 7, 2021, the Antimonopoly Commission of the State Council issued the *Antimonopoly Guidelines on the Platform Economy*, which applies to all industries, including firms with variable interest entity (VIE) structures. In July 2021, to fully implement the fair competition review system, the State Administration for Market Regulation (SAMR), the NDRC, the Ministry of Finance, the Ministry of Commerce, and the Ministry of Justice issued the *Detailed Rules for the Implementation of the Fair Competition Review System*. The National Antimonopoly Bureau was established on November 18, 2021. Table 1 highlights the diversity of international markets where Chinese companies are listed, with a significant concentration in Hong Kong and the United States. The Hong Kong Stock Exchange (HKEX) leads with 1,244 listed companies and a market capitalization of approximately USD 4.92 trillion, which includes H-shares, red chips, and Chinese private shares. In the United States, Chinese companies are primarily listed on NASDAQ, with 240 companies and a market capitalization of USD 528.33 billion, followed by the New York Stock Exchange with 65 companies and a capitalization of USD 370.02 billion. Other notable exchanges include the Singapore Exchange (60 companies, USD 45.62 billion), the SIX Swiss Exchange (17 companies, USD 84.84 billion), and the Toronto Stock Exchange (13 companies, USD 3.01 billion). Smaller markets such as the London Stock Exchange, Frankfurt Stock Exchange, and Australian Securities Exchange have fewer listings and lower market capitalizations.

2.1 *H-shares*

The government supports the stock listing of domestic companies in Hong Kong, which extends the financing channels of enterprises and promotes the development of Hong Kong's capital market. In the early

Table 1. Major listing exchanges for Chinese stocks by the end of 2023.

Country or Region	Stock Exchange	Number of Listed Companies	Total Market Capitalization (Million USD)
Hong Kong, China	HKEX	1244*	4,917,665.4
United States	NASDAQ	240	528,332.0
	New York Stock Exchange	65	370,016.5
	American Stock Exchange	12	737.9
	Total	317	899,086.3
Singapore	Singapore Exchange	60	45,620.9
Switzerland	SIX Swiss Exchange	17	84,835.3
Canada	Toronto Stock Exchange	13	3,008.7
United Kingdom	London Stock Exchange	8	163,957.4
Germany	Frankfurt Stock Exchange	3	26,777.0
Australia	Australian Securities Exchange	3	400.9
France	Euronext Paris	2	7.4
Korea	Korea Exchange	2	275.4

Note: *Includes H-shares, red chips, and Chinese private shares.
Source: Wind Economic Database.

1990s, many large Chinese SOEs began issuing H-shares while institutional reform was being implemented, as enterprises urgently needed to raise capital for development. At that time, the domestic stock market was immature, and the limited market capacity could not meet the capital needs of SOEs. Hong Kong is geographically close to the mainland and has a similar social economy and cultural traditions, and the Hong Kong stock market is highly open and mature, meaning that it was able to meet enterprises' financing needs and enhance their international reputation. Against this backdrop, a joint working group was established in July 1992 with the approval of the State Council to negotiate the listing of SOEs in Hong Kong. In 1993, the National Reform Commission issued the *Prerequisite Clauses of Companies Seeking a Listing in Hong Kong*. In September 1999, the CSRC issued the *Guidelines for the Approval of and Regulation on Enterprises in Mainland China Applying for Listing on the Hong Kong Growth Enterprise Market*. The guidelines allowed eligible SOEs, collective enterprises, and enterprises with other forms of ownership to be listed on the HKEX's GEM Board after obtaining approval from the CSRC. Since then, the CSRC has continuously optimized the offshore listing review system, including canceling financial audits, removing restrictions on IPO issue prices, streamlining filing documents and review content, and publicizing review concerns and progress. On July 7, 2017, the CSRC announced the improved review and approval system for overseas follow-on offerings; the system allows H-share companies to file for one approval statement covering several issues in a follow-on offering, enabling them to make offerings at the most favorable time to maximize the efficiency of financing. In December 2017, the H-share "full circulation"[8] program was launched. In November 2019, the CSRC announced the full implementation of the H-share "full circulation" reform and issued the *Guidelines for Applying for Full Circulation of Domestic Unlisted Shares of H-Share Listed Companies*. According to the guidelines, eligible H-share companies and companies that intend to apply for an IPO of H-shares can apply for full circulation within the restrictions of laws and regulations, which align the interests of various shareholders of H-share companies and improve corporate governance.

The listing history of domestic enterprises in Hong Kong closely relates to regulatory policies and changing domestic and foreign economic situations. In July 1993, Tsingtao Brewery became the first Chinese firm listed on the HKEX. During 1994 and 1996, the Hong Kong stock market was sluggish, and the number of H-share listings dropped accordingly. In 1997, many domestic enterprises went public in Hong Kong against the backdrop of Hong Kong's return to China. From 1998 to 2000, affected by the Asian financial crisis, the Hong Kong stock market plummeted, and H-shares remained in the doldrums. From 2001 onwards, benefiting from favorable factors (such as China's rapid economic growth, increasing openness, and closer economic and trade cooperation with Hong Kong), the operating performance of H-share enterprises generally

[8] Full circulation refers to the circulation of unlisted domestic shares of H-share-listed companies (including unlisted domestic shares held by domestic shareholders prior to overseas listing, additional unlisted domestic shares issued after overseas listing, and unlisted shares held by foreign shareholders) on the HKEX.

improved, driving up H-share prices. In addition, split-share reform and RMB appreciation have boosted the valuation of domestic companies' shares and enhanced the availability of H-share listing financing. The development of H-shares and the A-share market has laid a solid foundation for stock connects. After the launch of Shanghai–Hong Kong Stock Connect in 2014 and Shenzhen–Hong Kong Stock Connect in 2016, the stock markets' stock liquidity and price discovery function have been markedly enhanced.

According to the Wind Economic Database, by the end of 2023, there were 338 H-share-listed companies, among which 167 were SOEs, accounting for 49.4%; 95 were private enterprises, accounting for 28.1%; and 66 were public enterprises, accounting for 19.5%. As far as industry distribution, there were 117 companies in the manufacturing sector, accounting for 34.6%; 71 companies in the financial sector, accounting for 21%; and the companies in transportation and storage, accounting for 7.7%.

2.2. *Chinese companies listed in Singapore*

Chinese companies listed in Singapore are known as S-chips. In 1994, COSCO Shipping became the first Chinese company to list on the Singapore Exchange (SGX). From 2003 to 2007, the number of S-chips increased significantly, reaching a peak of 34 in 2004. The popularity of the SGX among Chinese companies is mainly due to its high degree of internationalization, low listing threshold and fees, straightforward procedures, and flexible arrangement of transfer boards. Since 2008, the number of IPOs by Chinese companies in Singapore has decreased, and the number of delistings has increased. The main reasons include the following: First, competition intensified from other exchanges, such as the New York Stock Exchange (NYSE), NASDAQ, and HKEX. Second, the reputation of Chinese companies was tarnished by cases of financial fraud and false information disclosure, most notably, by China Printing & Dyeing and Ferro China. The suspension of trading and the involuntary delisting of some S-chips shook investor confidence and deteriorated financing conditions for Chinese companies on the SGX. By the end of 2023, a total number of 184 Chinese companies have been listed in Singapore, of which, 60 are still listed for trading, and 123 have been delisted. The Chinese companies listed in Singapore are mainly from the traditional manufacturing sector.

3. Qualified Domestic and Foreign Institutional Investors

Qualified domestic and foreign institutional investor systems are transitional institutional arrangements implemented in China when capital accounts have not been fully liberalized.

3.1 *QFII and RQFII: Attract foreign capital*

The QFII program was launched in 2002, allowing qualified foreign investors to trade RMB-dominated financial assets in China. In November 2002, the PBC and the CSRC implemented the QFII system on a pilot basis. In May 2003, UBS and Nomura Securities became the first batch of QFIIs. In August 2006, the CSRC, PBC, and SAFE issued the *Measures for the Administration of Domestic Securities Investment by Qualified Foreign Institutional Investors*, and the CSRC issued supporting rules, allowing qualified investors to invest in RMB financial instruments within the approved investment quota. In July 2012, the CSRC issued the *Provisions on Issues Related to Implementation of the Measures for the Administration of Domestic Securities Investments by Qualified Foreign Institutional Investors*, which relaxed restrictions and optimized the QFII system. In March 2013, the PBC issued the *Notice on Relevant Matters Concerning Investment in the Interbank Bond Market by Qualified Foreign Institutional Investors*, allowing QFIIs to invest in the domestic interbank bond market.

A further mechanism of the opening-up of China's capital markets has been the RQFII program launched in 2011. It is a scheme for offshore RMB funds to return to China's domestic financial markets through local securities or fund firms. In December 2011, the CSRC, PBC, and SAFE issued the *Measures for Pilot Domestic Securities Investment by Renminbi Qualified Foreign Institutional Investors That Are Fund-Management Companies or Securities Firms*, which launched the RQFII pilot. The measures stipulate requirements for the pilot institutions' account management, fund remittance, asset allocation, interbank bond market investment, and information reporting. In March 2013, the PBC, CSRC, and SAFE issued the *Measures for the Pilot Program of Making Securities Investments in the Chinese Mainland by RMB Qualified Foreign Institutional Investors* to further expand the scope of the pilot program. In 2016, the PBC and SAFE issued the *Notice of Issues Concerning Domestic*

Securities Investment by RMB Qualified Foreign Institutional Investors to regulate the management of domestic securities investment by RQFIIs, clarifying that the investment quota must be managed by filing or approval and balance management must be implemented. Without approval, it is forbidden to transfer funds between an RQFII deposit account and other accounts.

In recent years, the reform of the QFII and RQFII programs has accelerated. In June 2018, the PBC and the SAFE revised the *Notice of Issues Concerning Domestic Securities Investment by RMB Qualified Foreign Institutional Investors*. The SAFE issued the *Regulations on Foreign Exchange Administration for Domestic Securities Investments by Qualified Foreign Institutional Investors*. These regulations abolished the restrictions on the proportion of QFII fund remittances and the relevant QFII and RQFII lock-in period requirements and allowed QFIIs and RQFIIs to carry out foreign exchange hedging, which further facilitated cross-border securities investment. In September 2019, the SAFE lifted the restrictions on the investment quota of QFIIs and RQFIIs and the pilot countries and regions of RQFIIs, which officially came into effect in May 2020. In September 2020, the CSRC, PBC, and SAFE issued the *Measures for the Administration of Domestic Securities and Futures Investment by Qualified Foreign Institutional Investors and RMB Qualified Foreign Institutional Investors*, and the CSRC simultaneously issued supporting rules (effective November 1, 2020), which unified the qualifications and rules for QFIIs and RQFIIs, lowered the entry threshold, and expanded the investment scope. Specifically, QFIIs and RQFIIs are now allowed to invest in securities listed on the New Third Board, private investment funds, financial futures, commodity futures, and options and are allowed to participate in bond repurchase, securities margin trading on the stock exchange, and securities lending transactions. As of the end of May 2020, when the SAFE stopped updating the list, 295 QFIIs had been approved, with an investment quota of USD 116.259 billion.

3.2 *QDII and RQDII: Invest abroad*

Launched in 2006, the QDII program allows qualified domestic investors to invest in overseas markets. In April 2006, the PBC decided to allow eligible banks, fund companies, and insurance institutions to pool domestic funds and purchase foreign exchanges for overseas financial investment, aiming to deepen the reform of the foreign exchange system, facilitate trade and investment, and promote the balance of payments. In August 2006, HuaAn Fund Management was approved as the first fund company to obtain a QDII quota of USD 500 million. In June 2007, the CSRC issued *Trial Measures for the Administration of Overseas Securities Investment by Qualified Domestic Institutional Investors*, thus implementing the QDII system on a trial basis and setting out the eligibility conditions and approval procedures for domestic institutional investors, overseas investment advisors, asset custody, fund-raising, investment operation, and information disclosure. According to the regulations, QDII qualifications must be approved by the CSRC, the investment quota must be filed with the SAFE, the funds must be entrusted to domestic banks, and QDIIs should entrust overseas investment consultants and securities service institutions with trading securities. In 2007 and 2008, four and five QDII licenses were issued, respectively. However, the development of QDII slowed due to the financial crisis in 2008. By the end of April 2023, 186 QDII institutions received an investment quota of USD 165.52 billion, with investment subjects including banks, bank wealth management subsidiaries, fund companies, securities companies, trust companies, and insurance companies.

The RQDII program, launched in 2014, allows qualified domestic investors to invest in overseas RMB-denominated products using their own RMB funds or RMB funds raised from domestic investors. In November 2014, the PBC issued the *Notice on Matters Concerning the Overseas Securities Investment by RMB Qualified Domestic Institutional Investors*, establishing the RQDII system and stipulating that RMB-qualified investors can use their RMB funds or raised RMB funds from domestic institutions and individuals to invest in RMB-denominated products in overseas financial markets. In late 2015, the PBC suspended the RQDII program due to dramatic fluctuations in the RMB exchange rate. In May 2018, the General Office of the PBC resumed the RQDII program and issued the *Notice on Further Clarifying Matters concerning the Administration of the Overseas Securities Investment of RMB Qualified Domestic Institutional Investors*, which clarifies matters such as macroprudential management and information reporting of RQDII overseas securities investment. Unlike the approval system for QDII quotas, RQDII status is based on the actual fundraising scale.

In addition to accessing the QDII and RQDII programs, domestic investors can invest in foreign markets through Qualified Domestic Limited Partners (QDLP) and Qualified Domestic Investment Enterprises (QDIE).

4. Stock Connect

The Stock Connect established a two-way trading link between China's mainland stock exchanges and overseas stock exchanges. The Stock Connect currently includes Shanghai–Hong Kong Stock Connect, Shenzhen–Hong Kong Stock Connect, and Shanghai–London Stock Connect.

The Stock Connect between China's mainland markets and HKEX was launched in November 2014 between the SSE and HKEX (Shanghai–Hong Kong Stock Connect) and was extended in late 2016 to encompass the Shenzhen–Hong Kong Stock Connect. The stock connects allow qualified mainland China investors to access eligible Hong Kong shares (Southbound) and Hong Kong and overseas investors to trade eligible A-shares (Northbound), subject to a certain daily quota. In April 2014, the CSRC and the Hong Kong Securities and Futures Commission (SFC) issued a joint announcement approving the SSE, HKEX, China Securities Depository and Clearing Corporation Limited (CSDC), and Hong Kong Securities Clearing Company Limited (HKSCC) to administrate the Shanghai–Hong Kong Stock Connect system. In June 2014, the CSRC issued *Provisions on Shanghai–Hong Kong Stock Connect Pilot Program*, which defined the business scope, foreign ownership ratio, method of clearing and delivery, settlement of currency and related issues, and requirements regarding investors' protection and supervision. In November 2014, Shanghai–Hong Kong Stock Connect was officially launched. In August 2016, the CSRC and the Hong Kong SFC issued a joint announcement approving the establishment of Shenzhen–Hong Kong Stock Connect. In September 2016, the CSRC issued *Provisions on the Program of Mutual Stock Market Access between Mainland and Hong Kong* to regulate activities related to the interoperability mechanism for trading in the mainland and Hong Kong stock markets. In December 2016, Shenzhen–Hong Kong Stock Connect was officially launched. The Northbound Investor ID Model was formally launched for Shanghai–Hong Kong Stock Connect in September 2018 and for Shenzhen–Hong Kong Stock Connect in January 2020.[9] In June 2022, the CSRC and

---

[9]However, the lack of restrictions on investors participating in the Shanghai Stock Connect and Shenzhen Stock Connect, coupled with the lower financing costs and higher leverage in Hong Kong, has created space for investors to engage in policy arbitrage. Sometimes, mainland investors open securities accounts in Hong Kong and trade A-shares through the

Hong Kong SFC jointly announced that ETFs would be included in the Stock Connect program starting July 4, 2022. According to CSRC, by the end of 2022, there were 83 ETFs for northbound ETF Connect, with a scale of RMB 721.731 billion; there were 5 ETFs for southbound ETF Connect, with a scale of RMB 169.58 billion. In August 2022, the trading calendar for the Stock Connect was optimized, allowing previously closed trading days due to settlement issues to be open, reducing non-tradable days by half. In December 2022, the CSRC and the Hong Kong SFC issued a joint announcement agreeing to expand the scope of the Stock Connect further.

Some restrictions are imposed on Shanghai–Hong Kong Stock Connect and Shenzhen–Hong Kong Stock Connect arrangements, such as investment targets, quotas, and investor qualifications. The investment targets include the stocks of "A+H" companies and the constituent stocks of specific stock indices, such as the SSE 180 Index and SSE 380 Index for Shanghai Stock Connect, the SZSE Composite Index and SZSE Small/Mid Cap Innovation Index for Shenzhen Stock Connect, and the Hang Seng Composite LargeCap Index and Hang Seng Composite MidCap Index for Hong Kong Stock Connect. The aggregate quota for Shanghai–Hong Kong Stock Connect was RMB 550 billion at its launch (including a quota of RMB 300 billion for Shanghai Stock Connect and RMB 250 billion for Hong Kong Stock Connect), with a daily quota of RMB 13 billion for Shanghai Stock Connect and RMB 1 billion for Hong Kong Stock Connect. The aggregate quota was lifted in August 2016, while the daily quota for Hong Kong Stock Connect was increased. There is no limit on the aggregate amount of Shenzhen–Hong Kong Stock Connect, and the daily quota is the same as that of Shanghai–Hong Kong Stock Connect at its launch. Institutional investors can participate in Shanghai–Hong Kong Stock Connect and Shenzhen–Hong Kong Stock Connect, while individual investors participating in Hong Kong Stock Connect must have a securities and capital account balance of not less than RMB 500,000. The investment quota and scope of the stock connects have gradually expanded. In October 2019, stocks of companies

---

Shanghai Stock Connect and Shenzhen Stock Connects as a "fake" foreign investment. In June 2022, the CSRC issued the *Decision to Amend the Several Provisions on the Mainland-Hong Kong Mutual Stock Market Access Mechanism*, which came into effect on July 25, 2022, and clarifies that investors in the Shanghai Stock Connect and Shenzhen Stock Connect cannot include mainland investors. The decision filled this regulatory gap.

with different voting rights structures were included in Hong Kong Stock Connect for the first time. In February 2021, STAR Market-listed shares that are constituent stocks of the SSE 180 Index or the SSE 380 Index or are the A-shares of "A+H" companies became eligible northbound stocks.

According to the Wind Economic Database, as of the end of 2023, the cumulative net purchases of northbound stocks reached RMB 1.8 trillion, and the cumulative net purchases of southbound stocks reached RMB 2.9 trillion. According to CSRC Annual Report 2022, by the end of 2022, the Northbound investors had a net purchase of RMB 90.02 billion in A-shares, with a trading amount of RMB 23.28 trillion, accounting for 5.2% of the A-share trading volume. The Northbound investors hold a circulating market value of 2.24 trillion yuan in A-shares, accounting for 3.27% of the total. The Southbound investors had a net purchase of HKD 335.89 billion in Hong Kong stocks, with a trading amount of HKD 6.23 trillion, accounting for 11.77% of the total trading volume of Hong Kong stocks. The Southbound investors hold HKD 2 trillion in Hong Kong stocks, accounting for 6.27% of the total market value of Hong Kong stocks.

Shanghai–London Stock Connect was launched in 2019. It allows eligible companies listed in each market to issue, on the other exchange, a depository receipt (DR)[10] that can be traded under local rules. In October 2018, the CSRC issued *Provisions on the Supervision and Administration of Depository Receipts under the Stock Connect Scheme between the Shanghai Stock Exchange and London Stock Exchange (for trial implementation)* to regulate issuance, trading, cross-border conversion, and information disclosure. In June 2019, the CSRC and the UK Financial Conduct Authority (FCA) issued a joint announcement approving the SSE and the London Stock Exchange (LSE) to develop the Shanghai–London Stock Connect. This Stock Connect is a two-way arrangement between the SSE and the LSE, comprising both eastbound and westbound capital flow. Eastbound refers to the issuance of China Depositary Receipts (CDRs) by LSE-listed companies on the SSE, while westbound refers to the issuance of Global Depositary Receipts (GDRs) by SSE-listed companies on the LSE. SSE-listed companies can issue

[10]A depository receipt is a certificate issued by a depository bank; it represents underlying shares in a foreign company and is traded on a local stock exchange.

GDRs with newly issued shares as underlying securities, meaning they can raise funds in the LSE. The depositary receipts and underlying shares are interconvertible. In June 2019, Huatai Securities issued the first GDR listed for trading on the LSE through Shanghai–London Stock Connect. In 2020, Pacific Insurance, Yangtze Power, and SDIC Power Holdings issued GDRs on the London Stock Exchange via the Stock Connect. In February 2022, the regulator revised the above regulatory provision under the title *Provisions on the Supervision and Administration of Depository Receipts under the Stock Connect Scheme between Domestic and Overseas Stock Exchanges* to strengthen the stock connection scheme. The scope of the depository receipt business was expanded to cover the SZSE and overseas markets, including those in London, Germany, and Switzerland. Subsequently, Mingyang Smart Energy Group Limited listed GDRs on the LSE, and some A-share listed companies, including heavy machinery manufacturer Sany Heavy Industry, Lepu Medical Technology, and battery maker Gotion High-Tech, announced plans to issue GDRs on the Swiss Stock Exchange (SIX). In 2022, 10 companies issued GDR in the UK and Switzerland, raising a total of USD 3.894 billion.

The exchange-traded fund (ETF) connection is another connection channel. In June 2019, the Japan Exchange Group (JPX) and the SSE launched Japan–China ETF Connectivity, enabling the listing of feeder ETFs of ETFs investing in Japanese or Chinese assets. In January 2021, JPX and the SZSE agreed to establish a similar scheme. In October 2020, the CSRC and Hong Kong SFC officially launched ETF Connect, which allows Hong Kong and overseas investors to trade eligible ETFs listed in the mainland via Hong Kong securities firms, and reciprocally, mainland investors can trade Hong Kong-listed eligible ETFs through local brokerages. According to HKEX, by the end of 2023, 8 ETFs had been launched in the mainland and Hong Kong ETF Connect, and Southbound ETF average daily turnover reached HKD 2.7 billion in 2023, up 196.5% from 2022 and representing 8.6% of total Southbound turnover. According to the CSRC, by the end of 2022, the investment of southbound ETFs was about RMB 8.601 billion, and the stock size of northbound ETFs was about RMB 153 million. Under the China–Japan ETF Connect, 11 ETFs are listed on the SSE, SZSE, and Tokyo Stock Exchange. In addition, the SZSE and Singapore Exchange Limited (SGX) jointly launched SZSE-SGX ETF Connect in 2022.

5. Inclusion in International Indices

On November 13, 2015, MSCI announced the official inclusion of 14 US-listed Chinese stocks into its global benchmark index system; these stocks included Alibaba, Baidu, Ctrip, JD.com, NetEase, New Oriental Education, Qihoo, Qunar Cayman Islands, Soufun Holdings, Tal Education, Vipshop Holdings, Youku Tudou, YY, and 58.com, which accounted for a weighting of approximately 13.5% in the MSCI China Index as of the first trading day in December 2015.

As China's financial liberalization has advanced, A-shares have been added to international indices, with their overall inclusion factor rising. The MSCI included A-shares in the MSCI Emerging Markets Index, with an inclusion factor of 5% in June 2018, and the inclusion factor increased to 20% in three steps in May, August, and November 2019. In June 2019, FTSE Russell officially included A-shares in its global stock index series, with an inclusion factor of 5%, and later increased this to 15% in September 2019. In that same month, S&P Dow Jones Indices made a one-time inclusion of A-shares in its Global Broad Market Index (BMI), with an inclusion factor of 25%. According to the CSRC Annual Report 2019, foreign investors in that year had a net purchase of A-shares worth RMB 294.722 billion (including through the QFII, RQFII, the Shanghai–Hong Kong Stock Connect, and the Shenzhen–Hong Kong Stock Connect systems).

The inclusion of US-listed Chinese stocks and A-shares in international indices indicates their increasing attractiveness to foreign investors and promotes capital allocation to relevant RMB assets. This inclusion in renowned international indices can also activate secondary market trading, enhance stock liquidity, and facilitate Chinese companies' access to offshore financing.

6. Assessment of the Opening-up of the Stock Market

China's stock market opening-up has proceeded in tandem with the progress of exchange rate regime reform and capital account convertibility, which has substantially improved over the last four decades. In the primary market, the issuance of B-shares and the presence of overseas listing companies have provided a channel for domestic enterprises to raise funds abroad, facilitating foreign investors' investment in China's stock market. In the secondary market, the QFII and RQFII mechanisms facilitate capital inflows, QDII and RQDII mechanisms facilitate capital outflows, and the stock connects facilitate two-way capital flows, meeting the needs of different investors.

The opening-up has promoted China's stock market reform, strengthened the corporate governance of listed companies, and enhanced stock market effectiveness. For example, to enable the inclusion of A-shares in the MSCI index, the CSRC has introduced relevant rules to regulate trade suspension and the resumption of listed companies and strengthen information disclosure, which has in turn improved market efficiency and helped protect investors' rights and interests. The relevant initiatives have also consolidated the foundation for MSCI to increase the inclusion factor of A-shares and for A-shares to be included in other international stock indices.

Nevertheless, there are issues in China's stock market. First, the scale of two-way primary market issuance is relatively small. The influence of B-shares is weak, and few overseas issuers seek a listing in mainland stock exchanges. Second, although foreign ownership of A-shares has risen in recent years, it is still far below that of developed countries such as the United Kingdom and the US. China's stock market is dominated by retail investors, with a high turnover ratio and a significant herding effect. In the first half of 2022, when the market was highly volatile, the net inflow of foreign capital through the stock connects was RMB 71.8 billion, which is small compared with the daily turnover of approximately a trillion. Given this, more emphasis should be placed on further improving institutional arrangements and expanding the investment targets of the stock connects.

Meanwhile, the two-way opening-up has brought international capital flows, which may magnify financial market volatility. Large-scale capital inflows in a short period may lead to stock price bubbles, while large-scale capital outflows may cause sharp stock price declines and exchange rate depreciation. The risks related to highly volatile capital flows may be contagious to local financial markets through liquidity and investor sentiment channels or even trigger systemic risks. In this regard, regulators should strengthen the integrated supervision of foreign accounts, including QFII and RQFII accounts, Stock Connect accounts,

Free Trade Zone (FTZ) accounts, and interbank bond market accounts, and further improve the macroprudential regulatory framework for cross-border capital flows.

Reference

China Securities Regulatory Commission (CSRC). (2021). *Thirty Years of China's Capital Market*. Beijing: China Financial Publishing House (in Chinese).

Chapter 3

History of US Listings by Chinese Companies

1. Background

US–China financial relations set the background for US listings by Chinese companies. The US–China financial relationship has evolved with the two countries' political and economic relationships. In recent years, the US economic strategy toward China has gradually shifted focus from trade to financial issues. The asymmetry in interdependence is a critical feature of US–China economic and financial relations. China is still in a relatively disadvantaged position, although it has made progress in capital account convertibility and achieved remarkable results in financial market opening-up.

1.1 *Currency*

The US dollar and its financial strength forms the core of the US' power. The US dollar is central in the international monetary and financial system. RMB internationalization has progressed rapidly in recent years, and its status as an international currency has been established, though challenging the US dollar remains difficult.

1.1.1 *Payment function*

The US dollar is the most important currency for trade and foreign exchange settlement. According to data released in January 2024 by the Society for Worldwide Interbank Financial Telecommunications (SWIFT), the US dollar ranks first as a global payment's currency, with a share of 47.54%, and the RMB ranks forth, with a share of 4.14%. However, compared to its ranking several years ago, the RMB has made progress, even surpassing the Japanese yen.

The cross-border use of the RMB has grown steadily and reached a new high in terms of its share in the total cross-border settlement in domestic and foreign currencies in 2022. Since 2009, policies for cross-border RMB use have continuously improved. In 2022, the total amount of cross-border RMB settlement was RMB 42.1 trillion, a year-over-year increase of 15.1%. The total amount of the cross-border RMB settlement of trade in goods reached RMB 7.9 trillion, a year-over-year increase of 37.2%, accounting for 18.2% of the total cross-border settlement in goods trade. Cross-border RMB settlement of trade in services totaled RMB 1.2 trillion, a year-over-year increase of 14.8%, accounting for 25.7% of total cross-border trade in services.

1.1.2 *Pricing function*

The US dollar is the most important pricing currency in global trade. In recent years, the role of the RMB as a pricing currency has improved. China is the largest buyer and consumer of various bulk commodities and has promoted the use of RMB for commodity pricing. In April 2016, the Shanghai Gold Exchange (SGE) launched Shanghai Gold, the first RMB-denominated benchmark price for commodities in China, followed by the RMB-denominated silver benchmark price three years later. In March 2018, the Shanghai International Energy Exchange launched crude oil futures contracts, the first RMB-denominated futures that foreign traders could directly buy and sell. Foreign traders can use RMB or USD as a margin when investing in certain futures contracts. The trading of the seven specified varieties of futures listed in China, namely, crude oil, iron ore, purified terephthalic acid (PTA), TSR 20, low-sulfur fuel oil, international copper, and palm oil, had developed steadily and now plays a role in providing benchmarks for pricing and settlement of commodity trading in RMB. By the end of 2021, overseas investors remitted total funds inward equivalent to RMB 124.50 billion as margin and total funds outward equivalent to RMB 125.31 billion, within which, the RMB accounted for 69.1% and 81.3%, respectively. In the first nine months of 2023, cross-border RMB settlement for major commodities amounted to RMB 1.5 trillion.

1.1.3 *Reserve function*

The US dollar remains the dominant reserve currency, although the function of the RMB as a reserve currency has improved. The Currency Composition of Official Foreign Exchange Reserves (COFER) data released by the International Monetary Fund (IMF) showed that the US dollar reserve share reached 54.6% in the third quarter of 2023, and the RMB reserve share was 2.2% (ranking fifth in the world). In May 2022, the IMF Executive Board concluded its quinquennial SDR valuation review and announced the new amounts for the five currencies (the US dollar, euro, yen, British pound, and RMB[1]) that determined the value of the SDR during the new valuation period that runs from August 1, 2022, until July 31, 2027. The weights assigned were 43.38% for the US dollar, 29.31% for the euro, 12.28% for the Chinese RMB, 7.59% for the Japanese yen, and 7.44% for the pound sterling. According to the *2023 RMB Internationalization Report* released by the People's Bank of China, more than 80 foreign central banks or monetary authorities have held RMB reserves.

The currency structure and asset structure of China's foreign exchange reserves are dominated by the US dollar and USD-denominated assets. The share of USD-denominated assets in China's foreign exchange reserves reached 79% in 1995 and then declined, remaining at 58% in 2015, much higher than those for the euro, yen, and other emerging market currencies. The asset structure of China's foreign exchange reserves is dominated by USD-denominated assets, including US treasury bonds. According to the US Ministry of Finance, China's holdings of US treasury bonds increased sharply from USD 71.4 billion in March 2000 to USD 1.314 trillion in July 2011, peaked at USD 1.316 trillion in November 2013, and then decreased to approximately USD 0.782 trillion in November 2023. In addition, the currency structure of China's external

[1]As of October 1, 2016, the IMF added the Chinese renminbi (RMB) to the basket of currencies that make up the SDR.

liabilities is also dominated by the US dollar. By September 2023, China recorded RMB 17.104 trillion in outstanding external debt denominated in domestic and foreign currencies. For currency structures, the outstanding external debt in domestic currency totaled RMB 7696.9 billion, accounting for 45%; the outstanding external debt in foreign currencies (including SDR allocation) totaled RMB 9407.1 billion, accounting for 55%. In the outstanding registered external debt in foreign currencies, the USD debt accounted for 84%, the Euro debt accounted for 7%, the HKD debt accounted for 4%, the JPY debt accounted for 2%, and the SDR and other foreign currency-denominated external debt accounted for 3%.

1.2 *Exchange rate and monetary policy*

The US dollar has long been the benchmark currency for the RMB exchange rate. China had a fixed exchange rate regime when economic reform started in 1978. From January 1, 1994, to July 20, 2005, the Chinese government introduced a managed floating exchange rate system. From July 21, 2005, the RMB shifted toward a newly managed floating exchange rate regime based on market supply and demand with reference to a basket of currencies. The US dollar remains the most important reference currency in the basket of currencies. The exchange rate regime helps expand exports while reinforcing the US dollar's status as the benchmark currency. To enhance the market orientation and benchmark status of central parity, the PBC adjusted the quotation of the central parity of RMB against the US dollar, which is also known as the "811" exchange rate reform. Effective from August 11, 2015, the quotes of central parity that market makers report to China's Foreign Exchange Trade System (CFETS) daily before the market opens should refer to the closing rate of the interbank foreign exchange market on the previous day, in conjunction with demand and supply conditions in the foreign exchange market and exchange rate movement of the major currencies.[2] This adjustment makes the RMB more flexible against the US dollar.

Since 2003, the US has urged China to widen the range of RMB fluctuations and adopt a more flexible RMB exchange rate regime. Since 2010, the US has accused China of manipulating the RMB exchange rate

[2] PBC (2015).

to obtain a large trade surplus, which it claims has caused significant losses to US jobs and the US economy. On August 6, 2019, the US Department of the Treasury labeled China a "currency manipulator". However, on August 9, 2019, the IMF released the Article IV Consultation Report and reiterated that China's current account surplus shrank in 2018 and that China's external position was broadly in line with medium-term fundamentals. In January 2020, the US Department of the Treasury released the semiannual *Report on Macroeconomic and Foreign Exchange Policies of Major Trading Partners of the United States*, removing its "currency manipulator" labeling of China.

The monetary policies of China have little influence on the US economy. The US conducts monetary policy based on its own domestic economic and financial situation and can fully pursue its monetary policy targets, including promoting maximum employment and stable prices. However, US monetary policy (especially quantitative easing) has spillover effects on China through capital flows, exchange rates, financial markets, and other channels. First, a global liquidity glut raises bulk commodity prices, which creates imported inflationary pressures on China. Second, hot money flows exacerbate China's exchange rate and asset price, to maintain financial stability. Third, if the US dollar depreciates, and China's holdings of US assets shrink in valuation. Fourth, as US monetary policy changes, China's monetary policy may face multiple constraints, such as the China–US interest rate differential, capital outflow, and exchange rate depreciation.

1.3 *Financial markets*

Most of China's foreign financial assets are allocated in the US financial market due to its superior safety, liquidity, and profitability. Between 2004 and 2015, more than 50% of China's foreign financial assets were invested in the US financial market; the scale increased from USD 340.972 billion in 2004 to USD 1,844.02 billion in 2015 and has decreased to USD 1.47 trillion in June 2022. In addition, China's purchases of US bonds have increased significantly since 2000 and have shown a downward trend since 2016. As of November 2023, China was the second largest foreign holder of US treasury bonds, totaling approximately USD 0.78 trillion, second only to Japan (which holds approximately USD 1.13 trillion) and accounting for 10% of total foreign holdings of US

Figure 1. US holdings of Chinese securities.

Source: Wind Economic Database, CEIC.

treasury bonds. In contrast, US portfolio investment in China has increased in recent years but still accounts for less than 2% of the country's foreign holdings (Figure 1).

For financing, is the most important foreign financial market for Chinese companies to list and raise capital. By the end of 2023, 317 Chinese companies were listed in the US stock market, including 240 on the NASDAQ exchange, 65 on the NYSE, and 12 on the AMEX, with a the total market capitalization of USD 899.1 billion. In contrast, the US barely relies on the Chinese financial market for financing, and no US companies are listed in China's mainland stock markets.

1.4 *Financial infrastructure*

The US has been a leading players in establishing the post-World War II global monetary and financial system, thus having unparalleled advantages in financial market infrastructure, including payment systems, central securities depositories, securities settlement systems, central counterparties, and trade repositories. The payment system, essential for international trade, investment, and financing, is a potential tool for the US to sanction other countries.

The core of the current international payment system comprises SWIFT and the Clearing House Interbank Payment System (CHIPS), both established under the leadership of developed countries, including the US. SWIFT provides global network messaging services supporting corresponding banking and financial market utilities. It is not a payment or settlement system. SWIFT provides messaging services not only in US dollars but also in euro, JPY, and RMB. SWIFT is not a US-controlled entity and is not subject to the jurisdiction of the US government. SWIFT shareholders elect a Board of 25 independent directors that governs the company and oversees management. SWIFT's board composition is designed to reflect the usage of SWIFT messaging services. Although the US has only two seats on the board, the US dollar accounts for over 40% of SWIFT services, and the chairperson of SWIFT has long been American. CHIPS is the largest cross-border US dollar funds transfer system, established and operated by the New York Clearing House, fully controlled by the US government. Once CHIPS shuts down a bank's clearing channel following an executive order, the bank itself and the banks it served can no longer process cross-border dollar payments and settlements. In other words, the US controls CHIPS and can broadly restrict the operation of SWIFT.

In recent years, the US' approach of using the US dollar and payment system as a foreign policy tool to punish opponents has generated widespread concern. In 2008, the US cut off the US dollar payment channel for Iran's international oil transactions. In March 2012, SWIFT disconnected all Iranian financial institutions from cross-border messaging services, cutting off almost all Iranian funds from international financial markets, resulting in fuel shortages, material scarcity, soaring inflation, and mass marches and strikes. After the outbreak of the Russia–Ukraine conflict in February 2022, Western countries imposed sanctions on Russia, including freezing USD 300 billion of the Russian central bank's foreign exchange reserves, banning Russian institutions from trading through the US and EU systems, excluding major sanctioned Russian banks from participating in SWIFT, and freezing the assets of Russia's largest banks in Europe and the US.

China built the RMB Cross-Border Interbank Payment System (CIPS) to facilitate the clearing and settlement of cross-border RMB payments and to support the RMB's global use. CIPS is a real-time gross settlement (RTGS) system that provides both onshore and offshore banks a central location for clearing RMB payments and is directly linked to the China National Advanced Payment System (CNAPS). In October 2015, CIPS

Phase I was successfully launched. In March 2018, CIPS Phase II was put into operation, with operating hours covering the working hours of all time zones around the world and better meeting the RMB business needs of global users. In recent years, the RMB cross-border clearing system has been continuously improved. By the end of 2022, 1,360 domestic and foreign institutions were linked with CIPS, with 77 direct participants (an increase of 56 institutions from the initial launch of CIPS in October 2015) and 1,283 indirect participants (an increase of nearly sixfold from the initial launch of CIPS). From its launch to the end of 2022, CIPS processed 1525.5 million transactions, amounting to RMB 301.3 trillion, for various participants.

However, CIPS still relies on the SWIFT messaging system for some transactions. Once a bank is excluded from SWIFT, not only is the information system of the bank's USD payment cut off, but the transaction information of other currencies is also disrupted. In this case, the bank loses the messaging function with most global banks and fails to serve international transactions.

1.5 *Financial rule-making*

Asymmetry also exists in the interdependence between the US and China regarding global financial rulemaking. The US has advantages in its allies and the institutions and norms established after World War II. Most existing international financial rules are decided by and in favor of the US.

In recent years, the US has been requesting that China expand its financial openness. On January 15, 2020, the US and China signed the Phase One Economic and Trade Agreement in Washington, D.C. The financial services chapter covers six areas: banking services, credit rating services, electronic payment services, financial asset management (distressed debt) services, insurance services, securities, fund management, and futures services. China committed to relaxing restrictions on access to the financial sector; easing restrictions on the shareholding ratio and business scope of foreign investors in the sectors of insurance, securities, fund management, and futures; and optimizing specific regulatory rules. Overall, the agreement on financial services reached between China and the US is consistent with China's strategy of expanding the financial opening-up in a proactive and orderly manner in recent years. The agreement will enhance the competitiveness and resilience of China's financial system, strengthen cooperation between China and the US in the financial sector, and help maintain and promote Sino-US relations. China and the US should respect each other and cooperate for a win–win situation.

In September 2023, China and the United States established an Economic Working Group and a Financial Working Group to enhance dialogue on economic and financial topics. The Economic Working Group is led by vice-ministerial officials from China's Ministry of Finance and the US Treasury Department, while the Financial Working Group is led by vice-ministerial officials from the PBC and the US Treasury Department. The working groups are ongoing channels for both countries to discuss macroeconomic issues, financial policies, and cooperative approaches on shared challenges.

2. The History of US-Listed Chinese Stocks

2.1 *Overview of the US stock market*

The main stock markets in the US include the New York Stock Exchange (NYSE), National Association of Securities Dealers Automated Quotations (NASDAQ), and American Stock Exchange (AMEX).[3] In February 2006, NASDAQ grouped listed companies into three tiers based on market cap: the Capital Market, Global Market, and Global Select Market.

The Over-the-Counter Bulletin Board (OTCBB) is an electronic interdealer quotation system for over-the-counter (OTC) securities. It was launched in 1990 after the Penny Stock Reform Act of 1990 stipulated that the SEC must develop an electronic quotation system for stocks that could not be listed on one of the major exchanges. Since the end of June 2000, OTCBB companies have been required to file financial reports with the SEC.

Companies may transfer from the OTCBB to the NYSE, NASDAQ, or AMEX if they meet the applicable financial and regulatory requirements. Meanwhile, companies delisted from the NYSE, NASDAQ, or AMEX may apply for listing on the OTCBB. Some Chinese enterprises have successfully transferred from the OTCBB to the major US stock markets. For

[3] In 1998, NASDAQ and AMEX merged to form the NASDAQ-AMEX Group, but the two remained separate stock markets.

example, in December 2004, Sinovac Biotech, a leading provider of biopharmaceutical products in China, successfully transferred to AMEX.

2.2 *Overview of US-listed chinese stocks*

As China has continued to advance its opening-up and adjusts domestic and foreign regulatory policies, US-listed Chinese stocks have evolved through five stages. Figure 2 demonstrates the listing and delisting trends of Chinese stocks in the US stock market. Figure 3 illustrates the NASDAQ Golden Dragon China Index trend, a proxy for the valuation of Chinese stocks.

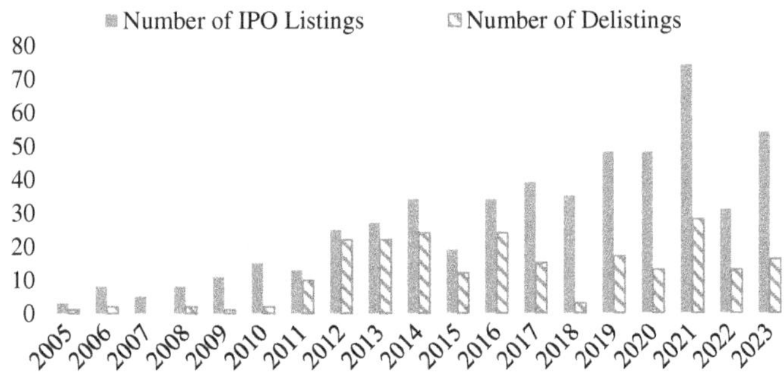

Figure 2. Listing and delisting of Chinese stocks in the US (2005–2023).
Source: Wind Economic Database.

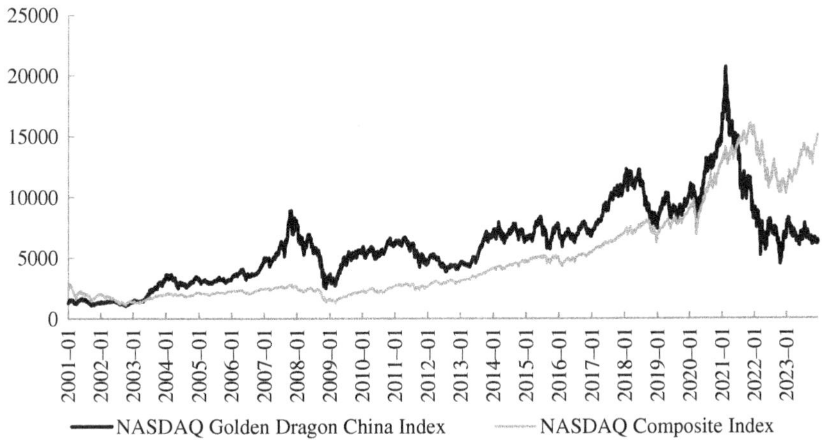

Figure 3. NASDAQ Golden Dragon China index.
Source: Bloomberg, Wind Economic Database.

The first stage is the exploration stage, which covers the period before 2005. In the early 1990s, a number of Chinese enterprises began to raise funds from the international capital market. In this stage, the Chinese government actively explored ways to reform SOEs, participate in international capital markets, and encourage large SOEs in important industries such as energy, electricity, and communications to be listed in the US stock markets. China Natural Resources, PetroChina, and China Sinopec were listed in the US in March 1995, April 2000, and October 2000, respectively. China Mobile, China Unicom, and China Telecom were listed on the NYSE in 1997, 2000, and 2002, respectively. Meanwhile, private companies also went public in the US. Brilliance Auto was listed on the NYSE in 1992. Sina, NetEase, and Sohu were listed on the NASDAQ in April, June, and July 2000, respectively.

The second stage is characterized by a surge in listings and covers the period from 2005 to 2010. As China's economy developed rapidly and the opening-up continued to advance, enterprises' demand to obtain financing from overseas markets increased dramatically, and there was precedent for choosing the US stock market. At the same time, foreign investors were optimistic about China's economy and were eager to invest in Chinese enterprises. The number of Chinese stocks listed in the US and the amount of financing have since increased significantly. Baidu, New Oriental Education and Tomorrow Advancing Life were listed in the US in 2005, 2006, and 2010, respectively. This phase of the US listing boom exposed some problems, including financial fraud, related party transactions, and information disclosure violations by some companies. The data show that most Chinese stocks listed between 2005 and 2010 have since been delisted from the US stock markets.

In 2010, Muddy Waters began short-selling Chinese stocks in response to financial fraud and other problems. As a wave of short selling shook investor confidence, the valuation of Chinese stocks dropped dramatically. Under these circumstances, Chinese companies faced increased challenges in going public in the US and are less enthusiastic about doing so. From 2010 to 2014, 45 Chinese stocks were delisted from the US Chinese stocks, and this pattern did not reverse until 2014, when Alibaba, JD. COM, Weibo, and other industry leaders were listed in the US.

The fourth stage the second surge in the listing of Chinese companies, from 2015 to 2020 (especially after 2018). Important events in this phase include the fluctuation of the RMB exchange rate in 2015 and the escalating economic and trade tensions between China and the US in 2018. However, the listing of Chinese companies in the US was not significantly affected. Chinese companies actively seek listing in the US, facing a rebound in the valuation of Chinese stocks and difficulty for some new economy startups to list domestically. It was not until 2020 that financial fraud, such as that of Luckin Coffee, once again shook investor confidence in Chinese stocks.

The fifth stage, since 2021, features high uncertainty and a decreased number of listings of Chinese companies in the US. In November 2020 and June 2021, two US presidents (Trump and Biden) issued executive orders prohibiting US Americans from trading in the securities of military-related Chinese companies, and index providers such as MSCI, FTSE Russell, and S&P Dow Jones have since successively removed related Chinese securities from their indices, thereby heightening the impact of political factors on Chinese stocks. In December 2020, the US Holding Foreign Companies Accountable Act (HFCAA) came into effect, prohibiting companies that fail to comply with the audit requirements of the Public Company Accounting Oversight Board (PCAOB) for three consecutive years from trading on US stock exchanges. Since March 2022, the SEC has maintained a provisional list and a conclusive list of issuers identified under the HFCAA.[4] In addition, the main factors constraining Chinese companies from listing in the US include the tightening of China's regulations on overseas listings, antimonopoly and data security, and uncertainty about regulatory cooperation between the US and China.

As of the end of 2023, there were 317 listed Chinese stocks in the US, with a total market capitalization of approximately USD 899.1 billion. The number of stocks and their market capitalization are equivalent to 5.9% and 8.2% of A-shares, respectively. There have been approximately 457 Chinese stocks listed in the US, of which 140 stocks have been delisted, accounting for approximately one-third of the total.

2.3 *US-listed Chinese stocks seek listing on other exchanges*

In recent years, affected by events such as the financial fraud of Luckin Coffee, the delisting of DiDi, the removal of certain Chinese stocks from some international stock indices, the HFCAA, and the provisional list, the valuations of Chinese stocks listed in the US have largely shrunk, and

[4] https://www.sec.gov/hfcaa.

many US-listed Chinese stocks are seeking listing on mainland China stock markets, HKEX, or other overseas exchanges.

2.3.1 *Listing on mainland China stock markets*

In 2018, China started to allow companies in the internet, big data, cloud computing, artificial intelligence, software and integrated circuits, high-end equipment manufacturing, and biomedical industries to issue shares or depositary receipts in the mainland stock market on a pilot basis. In September 2021, the CSRC issued the *Announcement on Expanding the Scope of the Pilot Program for Domestic Listing of Red Chip Enterprises*, which allows red chip enterprises in high-tech industries and strategic emerging industries[5] that meet certain requirements to be listed on the domestic main board, the STAR market and the GEB. In March 2022, the CSRC issued the *Notice on Launching the Pilot Program of Innovative Enterprises Domestically Issuing Stocks or Depository Receipts*, which allows pilot enterprises to apply for the issuance of China depositary receipts (CDR) for listing. The program provides a dual-track system distinguishing companies not yet listed and distinguished from red-chip enterprises already listed outside mainland China. It also differentiates between red-chip enterprises that have been listed overseas and innovative enterprises that are not yet listed overseas and sets differentiated standards for market capitalization and operating income to support the listing of innovative enterprises in A-shares.

2.3.2 *Listing on HKEX*

In April 2018, the HKEX issued a revised version of the Main Board Listing Rules, which lowered the listing threshold to allow the listing of eligible prerevenue biotech companies that are unable to meet the current Main Board financial requirements and companies with a weighted voting right structure and specified qualifying criteria for new concessionary secondary listings. Chinese companies listed in the US, such as JD.com,

[5]This includes industries such as new-generation information technology, new energy, new materials, new energy vehicles, green environmental protection, aerospace, and marine equipment. In addition, red-chip enterprises with national strategic significance are not subject to the aforementioned industry restrictions.

Baidu, and NetEase, have obtained secondary listing on the HKEX. To further optimize and simplify the procedures for overseas issuers to list in Hong Kong, HKEX published the *Consultation Paper on the Listing Regime for Overseas Issuers* on March 31, 2021, and the consultation summary was released on November 19. The amended listing rules and new guidance took effect on January 1, 2022. The new rules provided additional flexibility by expanding the secondary listing regime for overseas-listed Greater China companies from traditional sectors without weighted voting rights (WVR) structures and allowing companies to have dual primary listings on HKEX and maintain their existing WVR and VIE structures. The new rules clarified various routes for converting a secondary listing to a primary listing and facilitated the listing of more companies on HKEX. As of mid-May 2023, 29 US-listed Chinese companies have been listed on HKEX.

2.3.3 *Listing on other overseas exchanges*

In February 2022, the CSRC revised *Provisions on the Supervision and Administration of Depository Receipts under the Stock Connect Scheme between Domestic and Overseas Stock Exchanges*, which broadened the options for domestic listed companies to issue GDRs abroad through the stock connect mechanism, with listing destinations including London, Switzerland, and Germany. The issuance of GDRs by A-share listed companies helps raise foreign capital and attracts medium- and long-term investors. In May 2022, NIO NextEV Limited became the first company to list on the main board of the SGX through an introductory listing, which also made it the first company to simultaneously list in the US, Hong Kong, and Singapore. It did not issue new shares or raise capital, and its SGX-listed shares are fungible with the NYSE-listed shares.

3. Legal and Regulatory Framework for US-Listed Chinese Stocks

3.1 *China's legal provisions on the overseas listing of domestic enterprises*

3.1.1 *Direct listing*

In August 1994, the State Council issued the *Special Provisions of the State Council on Joint Stock Limited Companies Seeking Issuing Shares and Listing Overseas*, which required that a joint stock company raising shares from overseas investors and listing abroad report to the Securities Commission of the State Council for approval. For the implementation rules, the CSRC issued the *Circular on the Issues Concerning Companies Applying for Overseas Listing* in 1999. The circular emphasized that SOEs, collective enterprises, and enterprises of other ownership forms that have been restructured and reformed into joint stock companies and meet the conditions for overseas listing may apply to the CSRC for overseas listing. The CSRC will approve the application according to the procedures following the law. The circular also set the thresholds for overseas listing: net assets of at least RMB 400 million, profit after tax of at least RMB 60 million in the previous year, and fundraising target of at least USD 50 million based on a reasonable expected P/E ratio (collectively known as the "456 requirement"). In November 1999, the CSRC issued *Guidelines for the Approval of and Regulation on Enterprises in Mainland China Applying for Listing on the Hong Kong Growth Enterprise Market*, which did not set any financial constraints in terms of assets or profitability, meaning that small and medium-sized domestic enterprises could apply for listing on the Hong Kong GEM. In general, direct overseas listing has high thresholds, and the approval of the CSRC is difficult to obtain due to the restrictions of relevant regulations, particularly the national industrial policy and the policy on the utilization of foreign capital Xiao, Gang (2020).

In December 2021, the CSRC published *Provisions of the State Council on the Administration of Overseas Securities Offerings and Listings by Domestic Companies (Draft for Comment)* and *Administrative Measures for the Record-Filing of Overseas Securities Offerings and Listings by Domestic Companies (Draft for Comments)*, unifying all forms of overseas listing arrangements for domestic enterprises. In December 2021, the NDRC and the Ministry of Commerce issued *Special Administrative Measures (Negative List) for Foreign Investment Access (2021 Edition)* and the *Special Administrative Measures (Negative List) for Foreign Investment Access in Pilot Free Trade Zones (2021 Edition)*, effective January 1, 2022. For the first time, the two lists stipulated the issuance of shares by domestic enterprises and their listing and trading outside China.

3.1.2 *Red chip companies*

A red chip company is incorporated outside mainland China, with its main business and assets in mainland China, and listed on the HKEX or other overseas stock markets. Red chip companies are substantially owned, directly or indirectly, by mainland China state entities. Red chip companies are primarily incorporated in jurisdictions such as the British Virgin Islands (BVI),[6] the Cayman Islands, and Hong Kong. Hong Kong and the US are the principal places of listing. Red chip companies are subject to the laws and regulations of their incorporation location, place of listing, and mainland China, where the assets and business are located. A major benefit is that they can bypass the regulations of China regarding direct listing and achieve indirect listing outside mainland China.

The red chip model is regulated by various legal provisions, including the *Securities Law*, regulations on the overseas listing of red chip companies, and regulations on foreign investment and foreign exchange management. China's regulatory approach to red chip companies has alternated between "strict-loose-strict" phases.

The first "strict" phase was before 2000, during which time the listing of domestic enterprises was regulated in a covert manner. In 1993, the State Council issued the *Circular Concerning Suspending the Purchase of Overseas Enterprises and Further Strengthening the Administration of Overseas Investment*. In 1997, the State Council issued the *Circular on Further Strengthening the Administration of Overseas Stock Offering and Listing*, which clarified that overseas listing through any channels should be reported to the CSRC for approval and filing, thus covering the activities red chip companies. The Securities Law implemented on July 1, 1999, stipulated that official approval must be obtained for "domestic enterprises to issue securities directly or indirectly abroad or to list and trade securities abroad". To regulate the indirect overseas listing and prevent the loss of state-owned assets, the CSRC issued the *Circular on Issues Concerning Stock Issuance and Public Offering Abroad of Overseas Corporations, which Involve Domestic Equity ("Circular 72")* in 2000, which required the relevant companies to provide a legal opinion from a Chinese lawyer. Then, the CSRC reviewed the document and issued a "No Objection Letter". Additional requirements were imposed on the qualifications of the law firms engaged in relevant business.

The second "loose" phase occurred between 2001 to 2005. In early 2002, the State Council announced a list of administrative approval items to be canceled, including the "No Objection Letter" required by the

[6]For example, China Unicom set up a BVI company.

CSRC. On April 1, 2003, the CSRC announced the cancellation of the letter. In March 2003, the former Ministry of Foreign Trade and Economic Cooperation (now the Ministry of Commerce), the State Administration of Taxation (SAT), the State Administration for Industry and Commerce (SAIC), and SAFE issued the *Trial Regulations for Acquisition of Domestic Enterprises by Foreign Investors*, which relaxed some restrictions. In January 2004, the State Council published *Several Opinions on Promoting the Reform, Liberalization and Stable Development of the Capital Market*, aiming to actively use the overseas capital market and support qualified mainland enterprises in issuing securities abroad. In January 2005, the SAFE issued the *Notice on Issues Concerning Improvement in the Administration of Foreign Exchange in Connection with Mergers and Acquisitions by Foreign Investors* ("*Circular 11*"), which set strict approval requirements for the establishment of companies abroad by individuals and the acquisition of domestic assets by foreign companies, the latter of which required approval by the Ministry of Commerce, the NDRC and the SAFE. In April 2005, the SAFE issued the *Notice on Relevant Issues of Registration of Overseas Investments Contributed by Domestic Individual Residents and Foreign Exchange Registration of Merger or Acquisition with Foreign Investments* ("*Circular 29*"), which refined relevant approval procedures. However, in October 2005, the SAFE issued the *Notice on Relevant Issues concerning Foreign Exchange Administration for Domestic Residents to Engage in Financing and in Return Investment via Overseas Special Purpose Companies* ("*Circular 75*"), which explicitly allowed domestic residents (including legal persons and natural persons) to establish an overseas financing platform in the form of a special purpose vehicle (SPV).[7] The circular allows domestic residents to transfer the raised funds back to China for use according to declared plans and enables them to pay profits, dividends, and other payments to the SPV according to the corresponding procedures. *Circular 75* was implemented on November 1, 2005, replaced *Circular 11* and *Circular 29*, facilitating the overseas listing of Chinese enterprises.

The new "strict" phase commenced in 2006. In August 2006, six central government departments, including the Ministry of Commerce, the

[7]SPV refers to an offshore company controlled directly or indirectly by a domestic company or a natural person for the purpose of realizing an offshore listing with interest in the domestic company.

CSRC, and the SAFE, jointly issued and implemented the *Regulations for Acquisition of Domestic Enterprises by Foreign Investors* ("*Circular 10*"), which set a new administrative license for domestic enterprises to list overseas indirectly by holding companies abroad. According to the regulations, the SPV's overseas listing must be approved by the CSRC, and the SPV's merger and acquisition of domestic companies in the form of share exchange for overseas listing should be approved by the Ministry of Commerce. Funds financed by the SPV's overseas listing should be transferred back to China following the declared plan submitted to the SAFE, such as providing financing to domestic companies, setting up new foreign-invested enterprises in China, and merging with and acquiring domestic enterprises. The complexity of relevant procedures and stricter requirements on the use of funds have public through the red chip channel.

In July 2014, the SAFE issued the *Notice on Issues Concerning Foreign Exchange Administration of the Overseas Investment and Financing and the Round-tripping Investment Made by Domestic Residents through Special-Purpose Companies* ("*Circular 37*") to replace *Circular 75*. *Circular 37* made revisions in various aspects, including the scope of supervision, the scope of SPV, domestic residents' overseas investment, financing and domestic investment, registration procedures, and penalties. The circular added a prohibition clause stipulating that SPVs should not endanger China's national sovereignty, security, or public interests.

3.1.3 *Variable interest entity (VIE) model*

To raise money on overseas stock exchanges, many Chinese companies are structured as VIEs. With the VIE model, a China-based operating company establishes an offshore shell company in another jurisdiction, such as the Cayman Islands, and the operating company and the shell company enter into service and other contracts. Then, the shell company issues shares on an overseas exchange (mostly US stock exchanges). The VIE model establishes control through contractual agreements, designating the shell company as the primary financial beneficiary of the operating company. While the shell company has no equity ownership in the China-based operating company, it can consolidate the operating company into its financial statements for accounting purposes. The foreign-listed shell company may establish a foreign investment enterprise in China as a bridge between domestic and foreign markets and a channel for the remittance of funds.

The Congressional Research Service[8] estimates that two-thirds of all Chinese companies listed in the US, including Alibaba, Baidu, and Tencent, use a VIE structure. The complexity of the VIE structure and inadequate information disclosure can easily lead to negative interpretations and trigger mistrust and even class action lawsuits. Typical VIE risk events include Alipay's unilateral termination of its VIE structure in 2011 to obtain a third-party payment license and New Oriental Education's simplification of the equity structure of its domestic entity in 2012.

China's regulatory policy did not explicitly allow or prohibit the offshore listing of companies with a VIE structure until December 2021, when the CSRC issued *Provisions of the State Council on the Administration of Overseas Securities Offerings and Listings by Domestic Companies (Draft for Comment)* and *Administrative Measures for the Record-Filing of Overseas Securities Offerings and Listings by Domestic Companies (Draft for Comments)*, which unified the filing management for direct and indirect offshore listing by domestic enterprises. The provisions did not preclude enterprises with VIE structures that meet the compliance requirements from list abroad.

By the end of 2023, 168 of the 317 Chinese companies listed in the US had a VIE structure, with most of these companies listed post-2010 (Figure 4).

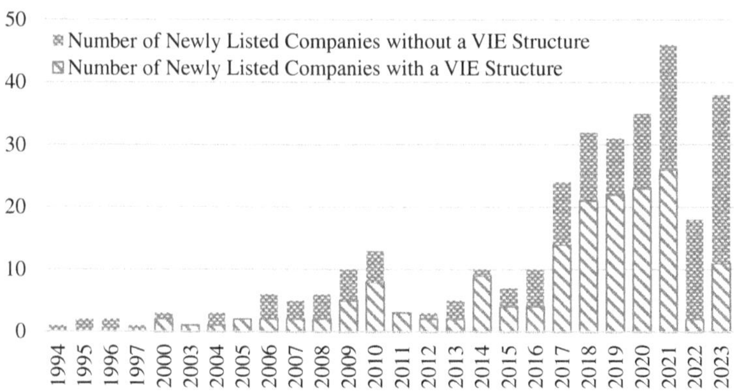

Figure 4. US-listed Chinese companies with and without a VIE structure.

Source: Wind Economic Database.

[8]Congressional Research Service (2021).

3.2 *US regulatory rules on Chinese stocks*

To be listed on the US stock market, a Chinese company must comply with listing-related regulations, meet the listing requirements of stock exchanges, and adhere to the relevant regulations and information disclosure requirements during the listing period.

3.2.1 *Listing-related regulatory policies*

The SEC and the Commodity Futures Trading Commission (CFTC) are the primary federal regulators for US capital markets, and the SEC is the authority that enforces federal securities laws. State and local securities regulators cooperate with federal agencies to fulfill their regulatory responsibilities. Other industry self-regulatory organizations have been established by statutes with different regulatory powers. Examples include the Financial Industry Regulatory Authority (FINRA), the Municipal Securities Rulemaking Board (MSRB), and the National Futures Association (NFA). The National Association of Securities Dealers (NASD) is the leading self-regulatory body of the securities market. Related laws include the *Securities Act of 1933*, *Securities Exchange Act of 1934*, *Public Utility Holding Company Act of 1935*, *Investment Company Act of 1940*, *Securities Investor Protection Act of 1970*, *Bankruptcy Reform Act of 1978*, *Public Company Accounting Reform and Investor Protection Act of 2002* (*Sarbanes-Oxley Act of 2002)*, and *Dodd-Frank Wall Street Reform and Consumer Protection Act of 2010.*

According to securities laws, shares may be issued and securities may be sold in the US market only if registered with the SEC or qualified for an exemption from registration. For registration with the SEC, the company files numerous disclosure documents with the SEC, including information on its production and operations, audited financial statements, and compliance with regulatory requirements, including continuous information disclosure. Companies may also qualify for exemption from registration of the public offering. The US regulations governing exemptions from registration include *Regulation A* for small public companies, *Regulation D* for private placements, *Regulation D* for private placement, *Regulation CF* for crowdfunding, *Regulation S* for offshore offerings, *Regulation 144A* to identify qualified institutional buyers, and *Regulation 147* and *Regulation 147A*, which apply to internal offerings. Most exemptions are based on *Regulation D.*

In recent years, new regulations have been implemented to relax the financing requirements. In April 2012, President Obama signed the *Jumpstart Our Business Startups Act (JOBSAct)*, which provides a dedicated IPO ramp-up system for startups by relaxing corporate financing restrictions. *Regulation A+* came into effect, raising the revenue threshold of companies registered for issuance under *Regulation A* from USD 5 million to USD 50 million. Different disclosure requirements, investment regulations, and preferential registration requirements apply to companies with revenues below and above USD 20 million.

After the Enron scandal, the Sarbanes–Oxley Act was implemented to improve the accuracy and reliability of corporate disclosures in financial statements and other documents. An entity must consolidate a special purpose entity (SPE) or VIE if it is controlled by the entity (primary beneficiary). The aim is to avoid the problem of off-balance sheet financing through SPEs and concealing off-balance sheet liabilities like those exposed in the Enron scandal.[9] In June 2009, the Financial Accounting Standards Board (FASB) mandated an analysis to determine whether a VIE can be consolidated, including whether the company has control over the VIE operating activities or is obligated to bear (or receive) the losses (or profits) of the VIE. In July 2021, SEC Chairperson Gary Gensler issued a statement requesting additional disclosures regarding the relationship between China-based operating companies and offshore shell companies.

3.2.2 *Information disclosure requirements during listing*

Securities regulators in developed countries such as Europe and the US enforce strict information disclosure requirements for listed companies. US securities regulatory laws and regulations emphasize full information disclosure, and shareholders must be informed in a timely manner of any activities in operations that may affect corporate performance and shareholders' rights and interests. Under the Sarbanes–Oxley Act and other laws and regulations, listed companies must disclose information fully and accurately, as any omissions, errors, or misrepresentations could lead

[9]The consolidation of VIEs is required in the generally accepted accounting principles (GAAP) in the US, while the Chinese GAAP, IFRS and Hong Kong GAAP do not allow the consolidation of VIEs. From a financial accounting perspective, it is difficult for companies with a VIE structure to be listed in mainland China or Hong Kong.

to shareholder litigation.[10] In August 2000, the SEC adopted *Regulation Fair Disclosure*, which prohibits selective disclosure of information by securities issuers. In addition, relevant laws and regulations prohibit market manipulation, insider trading, and other securities fraud.

The SEC regulates stock market disclosures, including financial disclosures and nonfinancial disclosures. In addition to the *Securities Act of 1933*, the *Securities Exchange Act of 1934*, and other relevant laws and regulations, the SEC has established various rules for information disclosure in the securities market. Among them, *Regulation S-K* covers matters related to the disclosure of nonfinancial information of listed companies. *Regulation S-T* applies if the nonfinancial reports provided by companies are in an electronic format. *Regulation S-X* stipulates the content and format for the financial information disclosure of listed companies. *Regulation C* specifies details for companies in preparing a registration statement. Listed companies must file appropriate reporting forms with the SEC. In addition, listed companies are required to comply with stock exchange regulations.

In July 2002, the Sarbanes–Oxley Act came into effect, stipulating the responsibility of senior managers for the reliability of a company's financial information and clarifying the mandatory requirements for the company's internal controls. Under the act, the CEOs and CFOs of companies with significant issues in information disclosure face fines of up to USD 5 million and imprisonment for up to 20 years.

3.2.3 *Rules of delisting*

Listed companies may voluntarily or involuntarily delist from US stock markets. A US-listed Chinese company may voluntarily delist by repurchasing ADRs from investors through the depositary bank or converting the ADRs into common stock for investors. However, due to tax, regulatory, and other factors, investors rarely convert to common stock. The termination of ADRs may be due to the company's strategy or its failure to meet the requirements of the regulators or exchanges. Procedurally,

---

[10]China.com filed a class action lawsuit in the US in 2001. Since then, a number of US-listed Chinese companies, including NetEase, China Life Insurance, UTStarcom, Sina, Giant Network, Luckin Coffee, DiDi, and Alibaba, have faced class action lawsuits.

regulators and exchanges allow listed companies to explain and defend themselves in case of involuntary delisting. For example, NYSE listing rules contain "Continued Listing" and "Procedure for Delisting" provisions. As per the requirements of the *Securities Exchange Act of 1934* and related rules, a listed company must complete Form 25 to delist from the US stock market and must notify investors in writing 30 days in advance. It is worth noting that delisting of ADRs does not relieve Chinese companies of their obligations, as investors can choose to continue to hold stocks. Under US SEC rules, delisted companies are still required to provide quarterly financial reports if there are 300 or more investors. If the post-delisting regulations are not obeyed, the SEC can impose heavy fines, force the company to forfeit its assets abroad, and permanently bar the company from access to the US market.

The rules related to the termination of a deposit agreement, cancelation of DRs, and delivery of the underlying shares are also specified in the deposit agreement between the issuer and the depositary bank. Generally, the deposit agreement provides a 90-day notice period for the issuer to notify the depositary bank. During this period, shareholders may inform the depositary bank of the explicit decision to surrender the DRs or deliver the amount of deposited securities represented by the DRs. If any DR remains outstanding after the termination of the deposit agreement, the custodian bank may continue to collect dividends and other distributions pertaining to deposited securities. Six months after the termination date of the deposit agreement, the depositary bank may sell the DRs held under the depositary agreement.

3.3 *Cross-border regulatory cooperation*

3.3.1 *China's provisions on cross-border regulatory cooperation*

In 1994, the State Council issued the *Special Provisions Concerning the Floatation and Listing Abroad of Stocks by Limited Stock Companies*, granting the CSRC authority to enter into memoranda of understanding with foreign securities supervision and management organizations to exercise cooperative supervision and management. Following its amendment in 2005, the *Securities Law* clarifies that the securities regulatory authorities under the State Council may establish cooperation mechanisms with the securities regulatory authorities of other countries or regions to implement cross-border supervision. The *Securities Law* (amended in 2019 and implemented on March 1, 2020) further clarifies the basic principles and specific requirements for cross-border securities supervision cooperation. Article 177 stipulates that "the securities regulatory authority of the State Council may establish supervision and administration cooperative mechanisms with the securities regulatory authorities of other countries or regions. The securities regulatory authorities of other countries or regions shall not directly carry out investigation and evidence collection within the territory of the People's Republic of China. Without the consent of the securities regulatory authority under the State Council and the relevant authorities under the State Council, no entity or individual shall provide documents or materials related to securities business activities to other countries or regions without authorization".

In October 2009, the CSRC, the National Administration of State Secrets Protection, and the State Archives Administration issued the *Provisions on Strengthening the Relevant Confidentiality and Archives Management Work Relating to the Overseas Issuance of Securities and Listing*. According to the provisions, in listing securities abroad, securities companies and securities service institutions should store their files generated in mainland China within the PRC, and on-site inspections should be conducted mainly by Chinese regulators. In April 2022, the CSRC launched a public consultation for revising the *Provisions on Strengthening Confidentiality and Archives Administration for Overseas Securities Offering and Listing* to clarify the responsibility for corporate information security that applies to direct and indirect overseas listing. The revision clarified that investigations and evidence collection or inspections of foreign regulators in China should be conducted through cross-border regulatory cooperation mechanisms, and the CSRC and relevant authorities should provide the necessary assistance in accordance with bilateral and multilateral cooperation mechanisms.

For cross-border securities regulatory cooperation, China signed both multilateral and bilateral memoranda of understanding. First, the CSRC joined the International Organization of Securities Commissions (IOSCO) in 1995. IOSCO established the *Multilateral Memorandum of Understanding Concerning Consultation and Cooperation and the Exchange of Information* in 2002 and updated and strengthened it in 2017 with the enforcement powers of the signatories strengthened. The relevant provisions form the framework for cross-border regulatory cooperation in securities under the multilateral approach. The CSRC joined the aforementioned multilateral memorandum at the 32nd annual meeting of IOSCO in India in April 2007.

Second, the CSRC also signed bilateral memoranda of understanding. In June 1993, the CSRC, SSE, SZSE, Hong Kong SFC, and HKEX signed the *Memorandum of Understanding on Regulatory Cooperation*, the first memorandum of understanding on regulatory cooperation the CSRC signed. In April 1994, the CSRC and US SEC signed the *Memorandum of Understanding Regarding Cooperation, Consultation and the Provision of Technical Assistance*. On this basis, the CSRC and the US SEC signed a cooperation framework outlining the terms of reference. By the end of 2020, the CSRC signed bilateral memoranda of understanding with the securities and futures regulators from 66 countries and regions, including the US, the United Kingdom, Japan, and Australia.

3.3.2 *US practice of cross-border regulatory cooperation regarding Chinese stocks*

Under the Sarbanes–Oxley Act of 2022, all accounting firms providing audit services to US public companies must be registered with the PCAOB, which has the authority to monitor accounting firms' compliance. In December 2020, the HFCAA came into effect, prohibiting companies from being listed in the US if they fail to comply with PCAOB audit requirements for three consecutive years. Section F(2) of the HFCAA and the SEC's implementing rules (effective January 10, 2022) require US-listed Chinese companies to provide relevant agencies with the required information beginning in fiscal year 2021. In June 2021, the US Senate passed a draft of the *Accelerating Holding Foreign Companies Accountable Act* (AHFCAA), which required foreign companies to comply with PCAOB audits within two consecutive years instead of three.

The US primarily employs a bilateral approach to cross-border regulatory cooperation in securities. The SEC has entered into more than 75 formal cooperation agreements with foreign governments and law enforcement agencies.

3.3.3 *Progress in US–China regulatory cooperation*

Chinese and US regulators have engaged in technical cooperation in auditing for many years. On May 7, 2013, the CSRC and the China

Ministry of Finance signed a memorandum of understanding with the PCAOB on enforcement cooperation, establishing a cooperation mechanism for providing audit work papers to the PCAOB. The memorandum allows Chinese accounting firms registered with the PCAOB to provide audit work papers to the US when their operations in the US involve cases requiring such access; the PCAOB may request that the CSRC and China Ministry of Finance provide the audit work papers falling under a certain scope and follow the relevant procedures, provided that doing so does not violate the *Law of the People's Republic of China on Guarding State Secrets* and *Archives Law of the People's Republic of China*. In July 2015, the China Ministry of Finance released the *Interim Provisions on the Audits Conducted by Accounting Firms Concerning the Overseas Listings of Domestic Companies*, which enhanced the implementation of the aforementioned memorandum. In 2016, the CSRC, China Ministry of Finance, and the PCAOB signed a memorandum of cooperation to conduct pilot inspections. In July 2013, China provided the PCAOB with the first audit work paper. By the end of 2020, 17 audit work papers of overseas listed companies had been provided to the SEC and PCAOB.

On August 26, 2022, the CSRC, China Ministry of Finance, and the PCAOB signed a Statement of Protocol (SOP) Agreement. This was an important step in resolving audit issues between the US and China following the implementation of the HFCAA. However, the agreement did not fully resolve the controversy between the two sides. On the one hand, a statement from the CSRC emphasized equality as the key principle of cooperation, required that the PCAOB obtain documents through Chinese regulators, and stressed both coregulation under audit sovereignty and the security of sensitive data. On the other hand, the PCAOB statement said the agreement "includes three provisions that, if abided by, would grant the PCAOB complete access", emphasizing the authenticity of audit materials and the absence of restrictions and limitations on review. SEC Chairperson Gary Gensler argued that "this agreement will be meaningful only if the PCAOB can inspect and investigate completely audit firms in China". This statement indicates that the focus of the dispute between the two sides is shifting to the implementation of the agreement. On December 15, 2022, the PCAOB announced that it was able, in 2022, to inspect and investigate completely issuer audit engagements of PCAOB-registered public accounting firms headquartered in China and Hong Kong. In the future, the PCAOB will continue to inspect the audit firms of US-listed Chinese companies.

4. Impact of the HFCAA

On May 20, 2020, the US Senate passed the HFCAA, which was subsequently signed into law. The act prohibits companies that fail to comply with the audit requirements of the PCAOB for three consecutive years from trading on US stock exchanges. It also mandates that listed companies disclose whether they are owned or controlled by a foreign government. The act may have a short-term impact and not result in the massive delisting of US-listed Chinese stocks. China should focus on minimizing political factors and deepen its cooperation with the US on auditing and regulatory matters. In addition, efforts should be made to crack down on financial fraud by listed companies, facilitate financial transactions by overseas investors, and strengthen cooperation with markets such as Hong Kong, Singapore, and London.

4.1 *Status of US-listed Chinese stocks*

Listing in the US enhances corporate image, improves capital and technology, and expands the US market. Meanwhile, US-listed Chinese stocks have benefited US financial services institutions and investors. Chinese companies started to list in the US in 1992. By the end of February 2020, 156 Chinese companies had been listed across the three major US exchanges, with a total market capitalization of approximately USD 1.2 trillion.[11] Most US-listed Chinese companies are from five major industries, including e-commerce, telecom services, information technology, energy, and finance, and are representative of innovation, efficiency, and good governance among Chinese companies. Chinese companies have generated gains for US investors and contributed significant profits to US exchanges and investment banks. Another category of beneficiaries is the shorting agencies represented by Muddy Waters, who target weak Chinese companies that have possibly engaged in financial fraud, accelerating the delisting of some companies.

The number of listings and delistings of Chinese companies (Figure 5) is closely related to the Sino-US political and economic relationship. In 2010, 42 Chinese stocks were delisted. Investors' trust in Chinese stocks

---

[11] Excluding Chinese offshore companies registered in Hong Kong and other countries or regions.

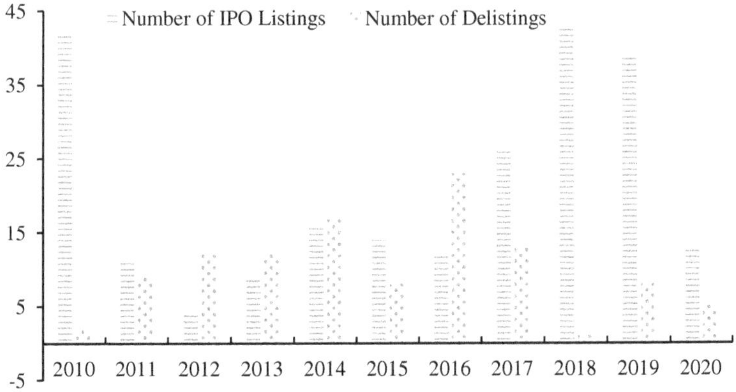

Figure 5. Listing and delisting of Chinese stocks in the US (2010–2020).

Note: The data are up to date as of May 22, 2020.
Source: Wind Economic Database.

was depressed for several years. From 2015 to 2017, the listing of Alibaba and other high-quality companies in the US quelled market doubts. Since 2019, Sino-US relations have deteriorated, and the listing of Chinese companies in the US has become less attractive.

The direct cost of delisting is not high for Chinese companies, but the indirect losses should not be underestimated. The US delisting rules are well-defined, and the procedure is standardized. The general process is as follows: After the company proposes a privatization call, the majority shareholders vote on the price of a stock buyback and then the company pays the attorney and financial consulting fees for the buyback. The cost of delisting is not high, considering the current low valuation of Chinese stocks. In recent years, the delisting of Chinese stocks has not resulted in market volatility or class action lawsuits in the US However, the indirect costs of delisting, including the loss of the US financing platform, goodwill, technology, and market, could prove to be considerable.

4.2 *China–US audit and regulatory cooperation is a win–win solution*

The technical differences between China and the US regarding the audit work papers of listed companies stem from a conflict between laws. The *Sarbanes–Oxley Act of 2002* grants the PCAOB the authority to review audit work papers. However, according to China's *Securities Law* and the *Provisions on Strengthening Confidentiality and Archives Administration for Overseas Securities Offering and Listing*, auditors must not move abroad documents and records related to audit work conducted in China, and the audit reports of multinational enterprises related to their operations in China should be kept in China.

The SEC has signed over 75 formal cooperation agreements with various governments and law enforcement agencies. The PCAOB has conducted inspections of PCAOB-registered audit firms in 50 countries outside the US. As of April 2020, accounting firms in mainland China, Hong Kong, France, and Belgium are not covered by PCAOB inspections and investigations, which affects 224 public companies that together have a market capitalization of USD 1.8 trillion.

The Chinese and US regulators have been cooperating on auditing for years. China has not prohibited US-listed Chinese companies from being inspected and submitting relevant materials to US securities regulators but emphasizes that overseas securities regulatory agencies need to obtain audit work papers through a request to China's regulators. On May 7, 2013, the CSRC, China Ministry of Finance, and PCAOB signed a memorandum of understanding on enforcement cooperation. According to the memorandum, under the premise of not violating the *Law of the People's Republic of China on Guarding State Secrets* and *Archives Law of the People's Republic of China,* the PCAOB can request that the CSRC and China Ministry of Finance provide audit work papers falling under a particular scope after completing the relevant procedures. In July 2015, the China Ministry of Finance announced the *Interim Provisions on the Audits Conducted by Accounting Firms Concerning the Overseas Listings of Domestic Companies*, which enhanced the implementation of the abovementioned memorandum. In October 2019, the US and China reached a consensus on accessing the audit work papers of companies listed in the US audited by Hong Kong accounting firms and stored in mainland China.

However, US regulators cannot fully implement audit investigations of US-listed Chinese companies. First, the SEC has long negotiated with the Chinese regulatory authorities regarding audit supervision matters and did not enter an applicable agreement. This means that the SEC cannot exercise the same authority as the PCAOB, such as demanding direct access to information and audit work papers, in the process of investigating the financial fraud of cross-border listed companies.

Second, the PCAOB only has access to the audit work papers of Chinese companies found guilty of misconduct through a request to the CSRC and cannot directly talk to auditors.

The CSRC provided the PCAOB with the first audit work paper in July 2013. By 2015, it had provided the audit work papers of four Chinese companies to the US. In August 2016, the PCAOB announced that it would successively access the audit work papers of the auditors for Alibaba (PWC) and Baidu (Ernst & Young). As of May 2022, the CSRC has provided the SEC and PCAOB with relevant audit work papers of approximately one dozen US-listed Chinese companies.

4.3 *Heterogeneous impacts and responses of US-listed Chinese companies*

A three-year transition period for implementing the HFCAA, and the short-term impact on Chinese stocks may be limited. The massive delisting of Chinese companies is unlikely, and the cost of Chinese stock delisting will be mainly borne by US exchanges, investment banks, and other financial service institutions. The biggest losers of Chinese stock delisting are the three major exchanges in the US since each stock listed on the exchanges brings in millions of dollars in registration, management, and transaction fees. Investment banks also bear the losses from reduced underwriting, consulting, and related incomes. Shareholders and investors in the US also lose investment income. It is reported that ETFs in the US had not their holdings of Chinese stocks as of May 27, 2020, the market's perception that the bill will not massive delisting of Chinese stocks. Since other countries and regions are unlikely to follow the US' approach, the US may not force many Chinese stocks to delist due to political concerns.

Overall, US-listed Chinese stocks will face higher compliance costs and delisting risks, but the HFCAA will cause heterogeneous impacts on Chinese stocks of different quality and sizes. High-quality Chinese stocks (such as Baidu, Alibaba, and Tencent), whose investors are primarily large institutional investors with solid lobbying power, are likely to be less affected in the future than other stocks. Low-quality and low-capitalization Chinese stocks are more likely to be delisted. It is reported that NASDAQ will introduce new rules to restrict listings of IPO amounts less than USD 25 million. If so, a quarter of the currently listed Chinese stocks do not meet the requirements, and such small IPOs will not be realized. Even without the bill and the new NASDAQ rules, Chinese stocks are characterized by frequent delisting. Some Chinese companies have long been short-selling targets due to suspicions of regulatory arbitrage or financial statement problems.

Chinese companies can choose to list and delist in multiple locations, and some companies are actively preparing for new US companies to be listed in the US stock market. Large and prestigious companies, especially those listed in the US before December 15, 2017, can easily choose multiple listings. Alibaba is already listed in Hong Kong (at a listing cost of HKD 765 million), and more than 30 Chinese stocks, such as those of JD.com, meet the criteria for listing in Hong Kong, and their valuation in Hong Kong is likely to exceed that in the US. The best option for some small companies with high growth potential may be to voluntarily delist from the US market and seek A-share or H-share listings. Moreover, some companies may choose to buy back shares from the US market and increase the supply of their shares on the Hong Kong market. Alternatively, through stock swaps, US investors' shares can be gradually transferred to Hong Kong for trading, thus achieving delisting from the US and listing on the Hong Kong market. In addition, seeking listing in the US, some companies are establishing new US companies based on businesses outside the US and China. These companies are divesting Chinese assets and technology while preserving benefits from the US market, capital, and technology.

4.4 *China should strengthen its audit cooperation with the US and advance onshore market development*

The HFCAA the politicization of the audit issue, related to the needs of US electoral politics. It is a lose–lose situation for China and the US, with the US potentially bearing a greater share of the resulting costs. A fundamental solution for China to turn crisis into opportunity is to downplay political factors, strengthen audit cooperation, and promote the vigorous development of the onshore market.

First, China should strengthen its audit cooperation with the US. The Luckin Coffee financial fraud case has ignited the fuse of the HFCAA, and China's current disclosure requirements provide some companies with opportunities for regulatory arbitrage. Chinese companies could consider hiring the affiliates of Big 4 accounting firms in the US or providing electronic access to the SEC and PCAOB for some audit work papers with the approval of the CSRC. The CSRC should strengthen its technical cooperation with the SEC and PCAOB. Since the PCAOB does not request that audit work papers be transferred offshore, the SEC could consider inviting the PCAOB to conduct on-site audits in China and should provide the PCAOB with access to the required audit work papers without violating Chinese laws.

Second, China should crack down on the financial fraud by listed companies and accounting firms. China should substantially increase the cost of financial fraud and consider matching the US penalties for financial fraud by listed companies and audit fraud by accounting firms to restore investors' trust in Chinese stocks and the Chinese stock market. As long as auditing firms can maintain high audit quality, fraudulent overseas listings can be significantly reduced.

Third, China should promote A-share market development to attract overseas investors. Previously, the main reason for the overseas listing of Chinese companies was the immaturity and underdevelopment of the A-share market, but China's stock market is currently the second largest in the world and can meet the financing needs of overseas listed Chinese stocks. The HFCAA should be treated as an opportunity. By seizing this opportunity, China can improve its domestic regulation and corporate governance, accelerate the launch of an International Board (allowing overseas companies to issue RMB-denominated shares), speed up the introduction of the IPO registration system, and further facilitate overseas investment. In particular, policies can be introduced to facilitate foreign investment institutions' purchasing of A-shares included in international stock indices.

Fourth, the Chinese stock market should emphasize stock index inclusion effects and strengthen cooperation with other markets. Including Chinese stocks in an index would bring an automatic inflow of funds from all ETFs associated with the index, particularly indices compiled by renowned index providers, such as MSCI and S&P. As long as China's economy remains stable, stock indices may still include Chinese stocks to reflect investment opportunities, guiding foreign capital flow to China. In addition, China should actively expand and strengthen its cooperation with markets such as Hong Kong, Singapore, London, and Frankfurt to provide a better regulatory and cooperative environment for the overseas listings of Chinese companies.

5. Analysis of US-Listed Chinese Stock Events

5.1 *Analysis of Chinese stocks' price plunge in July 2021*

In July 2021, China tightened its regulatory policies for the platform economy and private education industry, and the prices of US-listed Chinese stocks plunged accordingly. Investors have formed new expectations of Chinese stocks, which are still attractive to international investors in the medium and long term. This event reflects Chinese companies' lack of market communication and a lack of policy communication among government departments and between the government and the market. China urgently needs to take action to improve the market communication of policies. First, a mechanism for comprehensive policy impact assessment should be introduced. Second, the language of investors should be used in external communications. Third, the role of industry associations and professionals in guiding investors to form reasonable expectations of industry-related policies should be optimized.

5.1.1 *The price plunge is a short-term market fluctuation*

In July 2021, the market interpreted China's regulatory initiatives on the platform economy and private education sector as unanticipated policy shocks, significantly increasing the risk premium for Chinese stocks. In July, the prices of US-listed Chinese stock fell 20.0% (unweighted arithmetic average), with US-listed Chinese stocks in the education sector falling 41.2% on average in July. Chinese companies such as Keep, Ximalaya, and LinkDoc Technology terminated their listing process in the US Meanwhile, S&P Dow Jones decided to remove 25 Chinese companies from its index starting on August 2, as FTSE Russell had done with another 20 Chinese companies starting on July 28. On July 30, the SEC warned of risks in emerging markets, including China, which would further delay the listing of Chinese stocks in the US.

The recent plunge in Chinese stock prices is a short-term market fluctuation, and Chinese stocks are still attractive to international investors. Listing Chinese stocks in the US benefits the US exchanges, financial institutions, and investors, who will not rashly give up their interests. Technically, the price adjustment of Chinese stocks is due to the following factors: first, a pullback from the high valuation, driven by policies such as the quantitative easing of the Federal Reserve and investors in the US stock market; second, the industry policy adjustment, which triggered investors' concerns about policy uncertainty; third, uncertainty about the deterioration of geopolitical relations between China and the US and the strengthening of financial sanctions by the US; and fourth, revisions of market expectations caused by the COVID-19 pandemic. Except for the education sector, investment institutions generally believe that the adjustment in Chinese stock prices is a short-term event-based shock, not a trend reversal triggered by changes in fundamentals. The investment management firm Bridgewater Associates estimates that the decline in Chinese technology company stock prices is more prominent than the best estimates of deterioration in cash flow fundamentals; as much as 10% of the 31% decline in prices can be attributed to rising equity risk premiums in China, making the stock price decline a buying opportunity.

5.1.2 *The price plunge reflects a severe lack of market communications*

The primary reason for the price fluctuation is inadequate and untimely communication with investors (especially international investors) by Chinese companies and the government, resulting in the overinterpretation and misinterpretation of the regulatory policies that amplify market impacts.

Chinese companies and industries have provided inadequate market communication. First, insufficient information disclosure about VIE structures has triggered widespread distrust of Chinese companies among international investors. The PCAOB requires companies to disclose a range of potential business risks. US investors have long acquiesced in the practice of Chinese companies using VIE structures, but inadequate information disclosure can easily lead to negative interpretations. One US researcher complained that Chinese companies use complex structures to hide risks and avoid regulation.[12] On July 30, 2021, SEC Chairperson Gary Gensler issued a statement calling for increased disclosure regarding the relationship between China-based operating companies and offshore shell companies.

Second, the inadequate information disclosure of regulatory actions has triggered class action lawsuits. On July 4, 2021, several US Wall

---

[12]Congressional Research Service, April 2021, US Capital Markets and China Issues for Congress.

Street firms launched a class action investigation into DiDi, arguing that DiDi's positive statements about its business and prospects were materially misleading and lacked a reasonable basis. In fact, DiDi came under cybersecurity scrutiny on July 2 after representatives were interviewed by relevant authorities in March and May about issues such as passenger safety, the percentage of draw between drivers and the platform, and arbitrary adjustments to pricing rules. Previously, Alibaba, Baidu, Pinduoduo, Sina, and Weibo have all been subject to class action lawsuits by US shareholders for failing to disclose regulatory investigations, with the highest compensation being paid by Alibaba (USD 250 million).

Third, insufficient market communication from companies causes overseas investors to underestimate policy impacts. In recent years, China has emphasized new development concepts such as common prosperity and has introduced several regulatory initiatives in the private education sector since 2018. The "double reduction" policy has attributes consistent with the initiatives, and laws and regulations seeking to reinforce the separation of off-profit and not-for-profit schools have been implemented.[13] Among Chinese securities firms, CITIC Securities has been voicing concerns about policy risks in the private education sector since February 2021. However, most international investors are not aware of the timing of possible policy changes. Listed companies (and investment banks) thus failed to promptly alert investors due to concerns about their interests. International investors' lack of understanding of China's education sector and high sensitivity to policy adjustments led to the overinterpretation of the "double reduction" policy. Analysts from financial institutions such as Goldman Sachs and JP Morgan, internationally recognized for analyzing Chinese companies, do not understand the related market and policies.

The government's communication with market participants was also inadequate. First, *ex ante* regulatory measures were not conducted in a timely manner. Didi submitted an application for a New York listing in

[13] *The Law of the People's Republic of China on the Promotion of Private Education (Revised in 2018)* stipulates that for-profit education groups may not control not-for-profit private schools through merger and acquisition, franchising or contractual control. On April 7, 2021, the State Council issued the revised *Implementing Regulations of the Law of the People's Republic of China on the Promotion of Private Education (effective September 1, 2021)*, which addresses areas of industry disorder such as the overcapitalization and overcommercialization of private education that has emerged in recent years. On June 15, the Department of Supervision of Off-Campus Education was officially established, ushering in the normalized supervision of the private education sector.

April 2021 and became listed on June 30. The MSCI announced the inclusion of DiDi ADR in the MSCI China All Share Index, which became effective on July 15. If the regulators had conducted a cybersecurity review of DiDi earlier, investors would have been able to price it more accurately and may have felt differently. It was not until July 10 that the State Internet Information Office (SIIO) added the SEC to the national cybersecurity review work mechanism, according to the release of the *Measures for Cybersecurity Review (Draft Revision for Comments)*. Second, *ex post* communication is not timely and has limited influence. On August 1, 2021, the CSRC website released news about the CSRC spokesperson answering a reporter's question regarding the SEC's statement on additional disclosure requirements for China-based companies seeking to list on the US securities market lacking detailed measures.

5.1.3 *Policy suggestions*

As China deepens its opening up, sectoral policies increasingly impact both domestic and international markets. The intensive introduction of policies and regulations in different sectors may cause negative synergy, thus worsening enterprises' domestic and foreign market environment. In the current geopolitical climate, it is easy to trigger cross-market and cross-border risks and even escalate risks from economic to political concerns. To this end, the government should introduce a comprehensive policy impact assessment mechanism to address the issues (how to interpret policies and who should do so) and improve the market communication of policies.

First, a comprehensive policy assessment mechanism should be introduced. Policies may have widespread impacts on employment, social capital and competition, financial markets, and stability. Assessment before implementation is necessary. The Financial Stability and Development Commission (FSDC) should take the lead in making a comprehensive market impact assessment of sectoral policies involving financial institutions and listed companies. The State Administration of Market Supervision (SAMR) should be in charge of assessing anti-monopoly policies.

Second, market communication should be strengthened. China's regulatory rules and industries have unique characteristics, and the Chinese government must use the market's language to communicate with international investors. Companies should emphasize compliance with laws and regulations, social responsibility, and improved corporate governance. Chinese companies preparing for overseas listing and those already listed should provide timely and adequate information disclosures.

In the future, the government should reassert that the "disorderly expansion of capital" must be regulated, that stronger law enforcement for anti-monopoly is conducive to fair competition, and that China's policy is to practice the new development concept and enhance social equality. The Bridgewater report pointed out that platform and technology companies have enjoyed "digital exceptionalism" (minimal-to-no regulation) for nearly 20 years. It has led to issues such as financial stability, fair competition, data security, and privacy. While policymakers around the world are revisiting "digital exceptionalism", China is acting much swiftly than its developed-world counterparts.

Third, industry associations and professionals should improve external communication and guide investors in forming reasonable expectations. Hampered by language and negative publicity, international investors have difficulty understanding China's regulatory dynamics. While it is costly for companies to communicate with investors about industry-level policy changes, industry associations can significantly improve communication efficiency through regular and as-needed industry policy interpretations. In addition, there should be more interpretation by professionals who genuinely understand each policy. Otherwise, the discourse of policy interpretation and assessment in China will automatically be in the hands of nonprofessionals or even populists.

5.2 *US concerns about Chinese stocks*

In recent years, the US has been highly concerned about the risks posed by Chinese stocks to US investors and national security. In the current geopolitical environment, the US government will continue to be vigilant on Chinese stocks raising capital in the US capital market.

Financial ties between the US and China have expanded significantly over the past few years. As of December 2020, US investors held USD 100 billion in Chinese debt and USD 1.1 trillion in Chinese equities, while Chinese investors held USD 1.4 trillion in US debt and USD 720 billion in US equities. As of May 2021, 248 Chinese companies are listed in the US, with a total market capitalization of USD 2.1 trillion. In the first half of 2021, Chinese companies accounted for 50% of foreign IPO financing in the US and 15% of total IPO financing in the US stock market.

In addition, Chinese companies can attract US capital through venture capital, private equity, and private placement.

The US policymakers believe that listing and fundraising Chinese companies in the US may bring risks to the state and investors' rights and interests. First, the Chinese government's control of companies may threaten the US economy and national security. The US has provided capital for China's strategic and emerging industries, improved Chinese capital markets, and facilitated the growth of Chinese companies as global leaders and competitors. In particular, US investors have inadvertently funded Chinese military-related companies, which may threaten US national security and foreign policy. The ongoing mix of US and Chinese capital through venture capital, private equity, and private placement makes it difficult to distinguish whether financial transactions are used to support strategic purposes and makes it more challenging to assess US financial and economic exposure to China. Second, the behaviors of Chinese companies may impair investors' rights and interests. The US financial industry is not equipped to identify, understand, and act in response to the market and reputational risks posed by China's rapid integration into global capital markets. The behavior of some Chinese companies may hamper US investors from making sound investment decisions; such behavior includes inadequate transparency and information reliability (such as using VIE structures) and financial fraud. The SEC's existing disclosure requirements cannot sufficiently address the ensuing risks.

The US intends to expand the use of capital market sanctions. While sanctions are not a panacea, the US can effectively use them in narrow and targeted ways. Excessive disclosure requirements may increase the due diligence and disclosure burden on companies, reduce the attractiveness of US financial markets, and discourage Chinese companies from investing and operating in the US. In contrast, targeted sanctions are effective in protecting US investors and national security. Certain disciplinary measures, such as delisting and imposing new disclosure requirements on Chinese companies, are believed to be necessary.

First, different sanctions implementation authorities should be allowed to cross debar entities for the same act of misconduct. Maximum impact and effectiveness could be achieved by aligning US economic and financial sanction programs with similar policy objectives and introducing cross-debarment authorities. For example, a Chinese company that is blocked from exporting US technology components under the Entity List due to its involvement in developing state surveillance systems should also be prevented from raising capital in US markets. Such cross-debarment would enhance the consistency of sanction programs, promote information sharing and coordinated investigations, and amplify the impact of sanctions.

Second, the identification and regulation of Chinese firms with state and military ties should be enhanced. The US may examine China's role beyond US stock exchange listings to cover private equity, debt financing, and private placements. Other investment options may emerge when the US government increases oversight and scrutiny over Chinese firms listed on US exchanges. In this regard, the US may constantly monitor and analyze the operating, investment, and financing strategies of Chinese companies in strategic and emerging technology sectors. Chinese companies that cannot be listed in the US stock market may also be prohibited from accessing US capital markets through other means.

Third, stock market-related regulatory measures should be upgraded. The US may strengthen disclosure requirements to account for ownership, shareholding, state ties, complex corporate structures, and limited legal recourse. Doing so may require all Chinese companies to issue timely updates on major changes and provide separate unconsolidated financial statements for VIEs. The SEC may be required to give regular alerts on Chinese investments.

5.3 *Some Chinese stocks included in the provisional delisting list*

On March 8, 2022, the SEC added five US-listed Chinese companies to a provisional list of issuers identified under the HFCAA. Since companies on the list face possible delisting from US stock exchanges, the event triggered a plunge in Chinese stock prices. While some market analysts took it as a warning for China not to intervene in sanctions against Russia, our analysis of the relevant laws and regulations shows that the SEC's action was not directed by the US Congress or the government and did not alter the regulatory rules for Chinese stocks, although it worsened market sentiment. In the future, if the audit inspection issue can be appropriately resolved, the Chinese stocks still listed in the US market will align with the common interests of China and the US and will help enhance China's corporate governance.

5.3.1 *There is no need to over-interpret geopolitical reasoning and implications*

A group of five Chinese companies were the first to file annual reports[14]; thus, they were first provisionally identified and then moved to a conclusive list in 15 business days if they did not appeal their identification as being incorrect.

The SEC's actions must be comply with the law but are not directed by the US Congress or government, and there is no need to overinterpret its geopolitical reasoning and implications. The HFCAA (effective December 2020) and Section F(2) of the SEC's interim final rules (effective January 10, 2022) require US-listed Chinese companies to provide the PCAOB with certain information, such as audit work papers, beginning in 2021. As required, the SEC evaluates US-listed Chinese companies annually, generally after the release of their annual reports. It is expected that at least some of the remaining US-listed Chinese companies will also be added to the provisional list after the release of their annual reports.

The SEC's actions severely impact market sentiment, as concerns about Chinese stock delisting are compounded by geopolitical risks. Chinese stocks have faced selling pressure, and stock prices have plummeted. From March 9 to March 11, 2022, the NASDAQ Golden Dragon China Index dropped 19.2%, which meant that it was down 34.0% from the end of 2021 and 62.2% from 2020. In the same three-day period in 2022, Alibaba's stock price was down 14.1% from and Baidu's was down 17.5%.

A plunge in Chinese stock prices hurts both US investors and Chinese companies. Currently, there are 280 Chinese stocks listed in the US, and the total market value is currently less than a trillion dollars, down more than two-thirds from its peak. US investors and investment banks bear the largest loss from the plunge in Chinese stock prices. In the worst-case scenario, Chinese stocks will be delisted, and roughly half of the related losses will be borne by US investors, stock exchanges, and investment banks. Some Chinese companies can seek listings in Hong Kong. However, given that the Hong Kong stock market is not the same size as

[14] The annual reports were announced on the following dates: BeiGene (February 28), Yum China Holdings (February 28), Zai Lab Limited (March 1), ACM Research (March 1), and HUTCHMED (China) Limited (March 3).

that in the US in terms of liquidity and global influence, the valuation of Chinese stocks may be lower. Some companies that do not meet the listing requirements in Hong Kong will be privatized according to the procedures. If the cross-default clauses of bonds and derivatives are not triggered, the delisting from the US will have controllable impacts on Chinese companies in the short term.

5.3.2 *Main reasons for sluggish stock prices since 2021*

Since 2021, US-listed Chinese stock prices have fallen sharply, declining far more than during the 2008 financial crisis and the 2018 US–China trade conflict and deviating from economic fundamentals and US stock market trends. In 2021, the NASDAQ Golden Dragon China Index fell 42.7%, while the NASDAQ Composite Index rose 21.4%. The main reasons for this include the following.

First, US regulatory crackdowns affect investor sentiment. In the past two years, the US government and Congress have tightened regulations on US-listed Chinese stocks. Investors, especially US investment institutions, have strict investment rules and are extremely sensitive to US policy adjustments. In November 2020 and June 2021, Trump and Biden, respectively, issued executive orders prohibiting US Americans from trading in the securities of military-related Chinese companies. MSCI and other index providers removed the stocks and bonds of these companies from their indices. These events had transitory effects on stock prices. In December 2020, the HFCAA took effect, prohibiting companies that have failed to comply with PCAOB audit requirements for three consecutive years from trading on US stock exchanges. On June 22, 2021, the US Senate passed a draft of the AHFCAA, which required foreign companies to comply with PCAOB audit requirements within two consecutive years instead of three. If the act had been implemented, US-listed Chinese companies would have faced delisting in early 2023 (after the disclosure of 2022 annual reports).

Second, China's domestic policy adjustment lacks comprehensive evaluation and market communication. In the first half of 2021, China tightened regulatory policies on the platform economy and the private education sector. However, due to the lack of communication, investors overinterpreted and overreacted to the policy changes, resulting in a 20% drop in the share prices of US-listed Chinese stocks in July 2021. A series of laws and regulations were introduced from April to July. However, different government departments lacked comprehensive policy assessment before the more intensive introduction of policies, forming a negative synergy of policies. At the same time, the government did not communicate well with the market.

Third, Chinese companies had insufficient communication with the market. Inadequate information disclosure about the VIE structure has sparked widespread mistrust of Chinese companies among international investors. The Congressional Research Service estimates that two-thirds of all Chinese companies listed in the US, including Alibaba, Baidu, and Tencent, use a VIE structure. The VIE structure was originally designed to address China's investment restrictions; however, insufficient information disclosure can lead to negative interpretations and concerns among international investors. Some Chinese companies do not pay enough attention to adequate and timely communication with investors (especially international investors), resulting in overinterpretation or misinterpretation and amplifying the market impact of regulatory policies.

5.3.3 *Strengthening financial relationships serves the common interests of China and the US*

While there are no geopolitical reasons or implications for the SEC actions described above, Chinese stocks will probably face US political pressure. The SEC is expected to add more US-listed Chinese companies to the provisional and conclusive lists. Even if US-listed Chinese companies meet audit requirements, the US may use other technical issues to suppress US-listed Chinese companies. If the audit work paper issue goes unresolved, some or even most Chinese stocks will probably be delisted within two to three years.

Maintaining and strengthening financial relationships serves the common interests of China and the US. The Hong Kong stock market is not in the same league as that of the US in terms of liquidity, corporate reputation, and corporate governance, and the devaluation of the Hong Kong dollar negatively impacts the valuation of Chinese stocks. In this regard, China needs to continue advancing its financial opening up and strengthening its financial cooperation with the US. First, an international board of the Shanghai stock market should be established to increase China's leverage in addressing possible financial crackdowns in the future.

Second, overseas Chinese financial institutions should be encouraged to launch financial products based on China's treasury bonds to attract European pension funds and various US investors. Third, communications with international investors should be promoted. That is, China's economic and financial policies and situation should be communicated clearly and in a language that international investors can easily understand, comments on US financial media should be released, and international investors should be provided with a more objective perspective on Chinese stocks than they have at present.

6. Impacts of the US Presidential Executive Orders and Stock Index Exclusion

Since the end of 2020, two US presidents have issued executive orders prohibiting US Americans from trading in the securities of military-related Chinese companies. Accordingly, index providers such as MSCI, FTSE Russell, and S&P Dow Jones have successively removed the stocks and bonds of related Chinese companies from their indices. Our analysis shows that the executive orders significantly negatively impact US-listed Chinese stock prices, while the impacts of index exclusion were transitory. In terms of parties' responses, some companies resorted to legal action or initiated A-share or H-share listings, index providers continued to expand coverage of Chinese companies, and index ETFs listed in the US that track Chinese companies were adjusted. In the future, China should facilitate and accelerate the inclusion of Chinese corporate securities in important domestic and international indices, attract different international investors, and enhance the variety and stability of China's corporate financing sources.

6.1 *US presidential executive orders and stock index exclusion*

6.1.1 *Executive order signed by Trump*

On November 12, 2020, President Trump signed Executive Order 13959, which prohibited US persons from trading in the publicly traded securities of CCMCs beginning January 11, 2021, and complete divestment was requested by November 11 of that year. Now, if a company is added to the CCMC list, US persons are required to stop trading its shares within 60 days of such determination and to divest within 365 days. The CCMC list is determined by the US Department of Defense and Department of Treasury and includes 44 entities.

Trump's restrictions on CCMC companies were provisional actions with a strong political purpose and have faced difficulties in implementation. First, their subject identification is ambiguous. The military-related companies restricted by the executive order cover closely related entities, but the US Department of Treasury's OFAC has not clarified how to identify the affiliates of the companies on the list. Second, Xiaomi Group and Luokung Technology, previously on the CCMC list, challenged US government authority by winning a suit against the US Department of Defense. The overlay of other issues has caused the OFAC to repeatedly delay the executive order's effective dates.[15]

6.1.2 *Executive order signed by Biden*

On June 3, 2021, President Biden issued Executive Order 14032, which Trump's Executive Order 13959 and imposed similar restrictions on investments in 59 CMICs. Among the 59 companies, 26 were previously listed as CCMCs or are still subsidiaries of previously listed CCMCs, and aerospace companies accounted for the majority of the other 33 companies added. Executive Order 14032 does not materially change the applicable prohibitions. The restrictions on the CMICs took effect on August 2, 2021, and the restrictions on any entity identified in the future as a CMIC will take effect 60 days after its identification and addition to the Non-SDN CMIC (NS-CMIC) list. US persons will have 365 days from the effective date to divest any CMIC securities.

Biden's executive order and related documents clarified some previously ambiguous issues. First, only entities whose names exactly match those on the NS-CMIC list are subject to the prohibitions in the executive

[15]On January 8, 2021, the OFAC issued General License 1 (GL-1), postponing the effective date to January 28, 2021. On January 27, the OFAC issued GL-1A, which superseded and replaced GL-1, postponing the effective date to May 27, 2021. On May 18, 2021, the OFAC issued GL-1B, which superseded GL-1A, again postponing the effective date to June 11, 2021.

order.[16] Second, the CMIC list is issued by the OFAC, reducing the likelihood that the Biden administration will face judicial action for its order. Third, US persons are not prohibited from providing investment advisory, investment management, or similar services to a non-US person, including a foreign entity or foreign fund, in connection with a non-US person's purchase or sale of a covered security.[17] Fourth, the executive order does not prohibit US persons from engaging in any activities with companies listed on the NS-CMIC list. The prohibitions apply only to certain purchases or sales of publicly traded securities but do not apply to activity that is unrelated to such securities or to the purchase or sale of goods or services with respect to subsidiaries of such entities.[18]

6.1.3 *Stock indices remove some Chinese companies*

After the signing of Trump's executive order, US investors and institutions stopped trading Chinese stocks almost within a week, which also forced several index providers, such as FTSE Russell, S&P Dow Jones, and MSCI, to announce the removal of A-shares, H-shares, and Chinese stocks of CCMC listed companies from the relevant index products from December 2020 to March 2021 (Figure 6).

Index providers remove securities from Chinese companies in response to regulation and investor behavior in order to maintain the effectiveness of index products. Equity indices make periodic or occasional reviews and adjust constituent stocks. Companies that are no longer eligible for index inclusion, that is, those with liquidation or bankruptcy risks, may be deleted from stock indices. Index providers announce adjustments of component stocks in advance so that market participants can develop stable expectations.[19]

In general, index inclusion pushes up stock prices, increases stock liquidity, enhances stock price informativeness, and strengthens companies' external governance mechanisms, creating the so-called index inclusion effect. A stock's inclusion in an index is usually associated with

[16] https://home.treasury.gov/policy-issues/financial-sanctions/faqs/899.

[17] https://home.treasury.gov/policy-issues/financial-sanctions/faqs/902.

[18] https://home.treasury.gov/policy-issues/financial-sanctions/faqs/905.

[19] For example, in February 2020, the MSCI ACWI Index added six Chinese companies, including Luckin Coffee, and removed three Chinese companies, including the Midea Group. In May 2020, it removed Luckin Coffee and a number of other constituents.

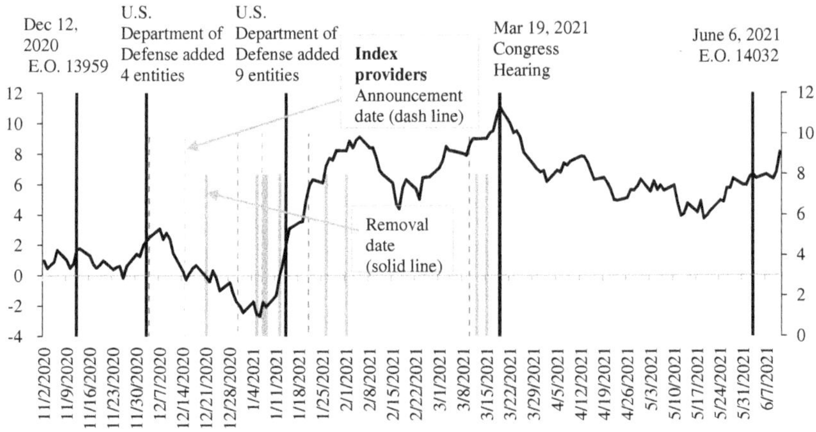

Figure 6. Key events related to the presidential executive orders.

Note: The black line is the moving average of the past 22 trading days of the average daily returns of the stocks of Chinese companies covered by Trump's executive order. The average is taken from across each company's A-shares, H-shares, and ADRs and then across stocks.

positive excess returns, while a stock's removal from an index is associated with negative excess returns. However, the effects of index inclusion and exclusion from the index are asymmetric, and the latter is believed to be smaller.

Index Inclusion Effect and Empirical Evidence

Index inclusion promotes stock price and trading volume, stock price informativeness, stock liquidity, and corporate governance. Demand theory suggests that the increased (or decreased) demand and liquidity of index-tracking investors create positive (negative) abnormal returns (Harris & Gurel, 1986; Afego, 2017). Information theory suggests that the index inclusion (exclusion) of stocks conveys positive (negative) information about the prospects or valuation, which affects the price (Amihud & Mendelson, 1986; Chen *et al*., 2004).

1. The impact of index exclusion is less than that of index inclusion

First, the effects of index removal on stock liquidity, analyst coverage, and other relevant variables are generally less significant than those of index inclusion. Empirical evidence is provided by Chen *et al*. (2004) on the S&P

500, Daya *et al.* (2012) on the FTSE 100, and Biktimirov & Xu (2019) on the Dow Jones Industrial Average.

Second, price informativeness declines after exclusion. Index inclusion increases stock liquidity, trading volume, and investor attention to the stock, thus increasing the pricing efficiency of the stock. However, there is no significant change in the pricing efficiency of stocks that are removed from indices (Daya *et al.*, 2012; Liu, 2020).

Third, the systematic risk of individual stocks also changes after exclusion. Index inclusion increases the covariance between stock and market returns and the beta of stock price returns (Vijh, 1994). However, the beta of stocks removed from indices usually remains unchanged (Kot *et al.*, 2015).

Fourth, corporate governance mechanisms take effect after exclusion. Index inclusion promotes external governance with enhanced scrutiny from analysts, institutional investors, and the media. Internal governance mechanisms are correspondingly enhanced (Li & Tan, 2015). However, no relevant evidence shows that index removal leads to a decrease in corporate governance.

There may be reverse causality between index adjustment and firm profitability changes. Studies have shown that firms' profitability decreases before being removed from the index and increases afterward. Evidence has been documented for the S&P 500 (Chan *et al.*, 2013) and for the Hang Seng Index (Kot *et al.*, 2015).

2. The index inclusion effect decreases with time

The increasing stringency of global financial regulation and the consequent increase in corporate transparency has reduced information asymmetry in financial markets, changes in liquidity associated with index inclusion and removal, and a more rapid retracing of share price aftershocks (Kamal, 2014). Evidence has been documented for major indices, such as the S&P 500 (Kamal *et al.*, 2012), the FTSE 100 (Soe & Dash, 2008), and the Russell 2000 (Petajisto, 2011).

3. The impacts vary with stocks and stock indices

If no perfect substitutes exist for the stocks included in the index (imperfect substitutes hypothesis), the index inclusion effect is permanent (Shleifer, 1986). The temporary reaction around index changes is caused by index fund managers who rebalance their portfolios (Harris & Gurel, 1986; Vespro, 2006). In addition, the magnitude of the index inclusion effect is related to the constituent selection criteria (Petajisto, 2008).

According to Biden's executive order, index providers may add or remove relevant stocks. For companies removed from the list, FTSE Russell announced on June 9, 2021, that six Chinese companies would be re-added to the indices starting on June 21. Index providers have not yet announced whether the relevant securities for the new companies on the list will be removed.

6.2 *The impacts of the executive orders are significantly negative, while the impacts of index exclusion are transitory*

The executive order restrictions have caused a decrease in QFII funds investing in China, US funds investing in Hong Kong, and the automatic inflow of funds from all ETFs associated with the index. In terms of the market reaction, within a few weeks of Trump's executive order announcement, US institutions and investors stopped trading the relevant stocks, and the companies' share prices on the CCMC list fell sharply. However, investors from Europe and Asia, especially mainland China, purchased stocks at low prices and drove up share prices. Overall, share price fluctuations were relatively minor.

To quantify the impacts, we conducted an event study based on stock market data.[20] We split the NS-CMIC list into the "Trump List", which has been classified as a CCMC, and the "Biden New List". As shown in Figure 7, the stock returns of the sample companies dropped before the issuance of Trump's executive order. The executive orders amplified the price declines of the Trump List stocks, while the Biden New List stocks returned to normal afterward. Biden's executive order harmed the stock prices of all companies on the CMIC list, but the influence was smaller than that of Trump's executive order. In addition, the political nature of the executive orders negatively impacted the stock prices of all US-listed Chinese companies (Figure 8).

The impacts of the executive orders on individual stocks were heterogeneous, with different effects on the A-shares and H-shares of the same company (Figure 9). The impact of Biden's executive order was

[20] Event studies measure the impact of an event by examining the abnormal return (AR) of stock prices before and after the event. We use the MSCI China Index as the market index and 210 trading days as the estimation window. The results are presented with a cumulative average abnormal return (CAR) curve, which is the average of CAR of individual stocks during the event window.

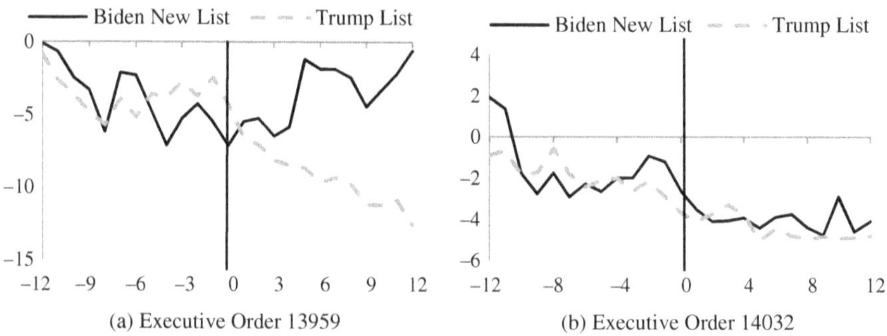

Figure 7. Event analysis of executive orders on CMIC stocks.[21]

Note: The horizontal axis indicates the time window (in trading days), with 0 denoting the announcement dates of the executive orders.

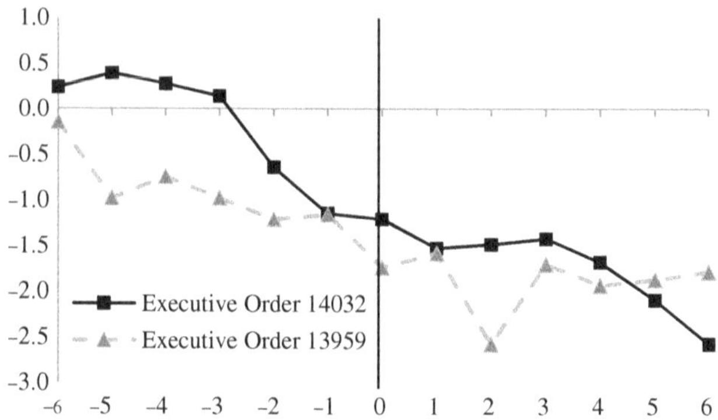

Figure 8. Event study of the executive orders for US-listed Chinese stocks.

Note: The sample includes 213 stocks of Chinese companies listed in the US no later than 2019.

generally smaller, as risks reflected in Trump's executive order were already priced in.

The index exclusion of the stocks of companies on the CCMC list showed transitory negative impacts, returning to normal after approximately ten trading days (Figure 10). The index exclusion also demonstrated a negative spillover effect on other military-related Chinese

[21]There are 36 listed companies (42 stocks, including A-shares and H-shares) among the 59 companies covered by Executive Order 14032. Excluding Aerospace Communications, which will be delisted from A-shares in January 2021, and SMIC and Shaanxi Zhongtian Rocket Technology, which have few observations, the sample includes 39 stocks (29 A-shares and 10 H-shares) of 35 listed companies.

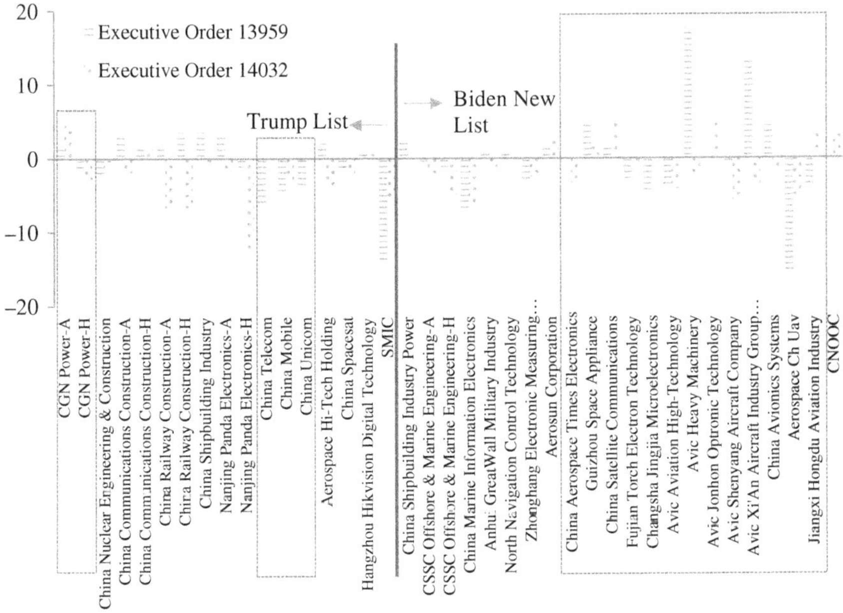

Figure 9. Cumulative abnormal returns (CAR) of executive orders.

Note: For comparison, a six-day event window is chosen for both the Biden and Trump executive orders.

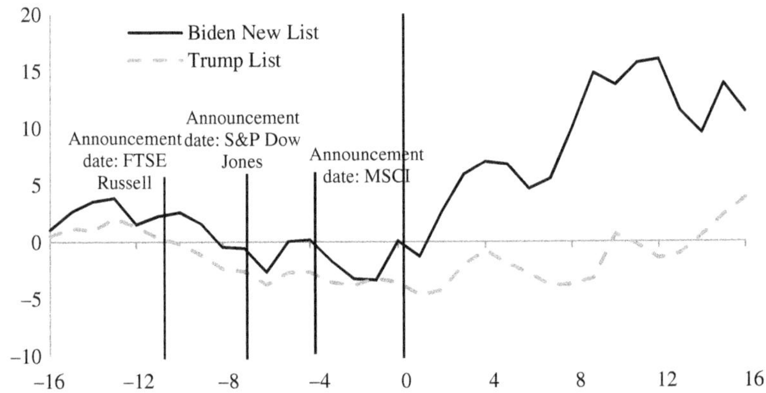

Figure 10. Event analysis of the index removal of Chinese stocks.

Note: The sample includes 213 stocks of US-listed Chinese companies (listed before 2019). The event date is December 21, 2020, when the first batch of stocks was removed from the indices. The selected event window is 16 trading days, covering the announcement dates of the index providers.

companies (the Biden New List), but these stocks soon realized positive abnormal returns.

Overall, the event study shows that the political concerns brought about by the executive orders had significant negative impacts on Chinese stocks, including the companies on the list and other US-listed Chinese stocks. In contrast, the index exclusion, accompanied by the executive orders, had a transitory impact on stock prices.

6.3 *Responses of companies, index providers, and investors*

6.3.1 *Some companies took legal action or sought A-share or H-share listings*

Xiaomi Group and Luokung Technology were successfully removed from the CCMC list after they won suits against the US Department of Defense.

As required by the executive order, US stock exchanges have initiated delisting procedures for CCMC-listed companies, including China Unicom, China Mobile, China Telecom, Semiconductor Manufacturing International, and China Railway Construction. The stock index exclusion and mandatory delisting were mainly driven by political factors. Biden's executive order did not prohibit US persons from doing business (the purchase or sale of goods or services) with companies on the CMIC list.[22] Meanwhile, there has been no deterioration in fundamentals such as operating performance, and the dividends of China's development and corporate growth remain substantial. Some companies have sought a listing or secondary listing in the A-share and Hong Kong stock markets, benefiting mainland and Hong Kong investors and reinforcing the influence of the Chinese capital market and government.

6.3.2 *Index providers continue to expand coverage of Chinese companies*

Since November 2015, international stock and bond indices have successively included securities of Chinese companies, which benefits the

[22] Since August 2018, the US has been imposing restrictions on Chinese technology companies, such as an entity list and a blacklist. Chinese companies subject to restrictions have restructured their businesses to varying degrees.

cross-border business and financing of Chinese companies and is a sign of the internationalization of the Chinese capital market. The MSCI has taken the lead in including US-listed Chinese stocks in the MSCI Emerging Markets Index and MSCI China Index, and index providers such as S&P and FTSE have also included stocks of Chinese companies (including US-listed Chinese stocks, A-shares, H-shares) in the indices.

The index inclusion of Chinese stocks is necessary due to the increasing importance of the Chinese market.[23] The removal of representative companies goes against the original intention of index providers. In the past few months, while removing the securities of companies on the CCMC list, international index providers have further expanded the coverage of Chinese companies, reflecting investors' optimal balance of exposure to China's stock opportunities. For example, MSCI announced on April 28, 2021, that it had launched 20 thematic indices reflecting long-term structural changes in China's technology, environment, society, and lifestyle; these are the first suite of country-specific thematic indices.

6.3.3 *Index ETFs listed in the US that track Chinese companies have been adjusted*

According to ETFDB data, the total scale of the top 52 index ETFs listed in the US that invest in Chinese securities is over USD 29.06 billion. Among them, 20 ETFs track MSCI indices, but more than half track the newly launched thematic indices. In addition, the scale of index ETFs tracking stock indices published by China and other international index providers, such as the CSI 300 and indices published by the CICC, cannot be neglected. Overall, many index ETFs listed in the US that track Chinese companies are not among the current indices that remove Chinese companies.

6.4 *Policy implications*

Capital market restrictions on China may remain a focus of the Biden administration's sanctions policy. On the one hand, due to the Biden

[23] Orzano (2020) finds that one year after the inclusion of Chinese A-shares, the A-shares have increased the returns and reduced the volatility of S&P Dow Jones emerging market indices.

administration's thorough review and modification procedures, it is unlikely that Chinese companies can be removed from the CMIC list through lawsuits, which Xiaomi Group and Luokung Technology were previously successful in. On the other hand, the Biden administration is not entirely blocking the channels of foreign investment in the listed companies but only prohibits trading in publicly traded securities.

In the future, China should facilitate and accelerate the inclusion of Chinese corporate securities in important domestic and international indices. The enhanced availability of financing at the macro level will reduce the crowding-out effect on financing for sanctioned companies, which is particularly important in the face of adverse external shocks. It is also important for China to advance its capital market reform and opening-up to attract international investors, maintain economic and financial stability, and enhance the diversity and stability of China's corporate financing sources.

References

Afego, P.N. (2017). Effects of changes in stock index compositions: A literature survey. *International Review of Financial Analysis*, 52, 228–239.

Amihud, Y. & Mendelson, H. (1986). Asset pricing and the bid-ask spread. *Journal of Financial Economics*, 17(2), 223–249.

Biktimirov, E.N. & Xu, Y. (2019). Market reactions to changes in the Dow Jones industrial average index. *International Journal of Managerial Finance*, 15(5), 792–812.

Chan, K., Kot, H.W., & Tang, G.Y. (2013). A comprehensive long-term analysis of S&P 500 index additions and deletions. *Journal of Banking & Finance*, 37(12), 4920–4930.

Chen, H., Noronha, G., & Singal, V. (2004). The price response to S&P 500 index additions and deletions: Evidence of asymmetry and a new explanation. *The Journal of Finance*, 59(4), 1901–1930.

Congressional Research Service. (September 2, 2021). US capital markets and China: Issues for congress. https://crsreports.congress.gov/product/pdf/IF/IF11803/2.

Daya, W., Mazouz, K., & Freeman, M. (2012). Information efficiency changes following FTSE 100 index revisions. *Journal of International Financial Markets, Institutions and Money*, 22(4), 1054–1069.

Harris, L. & Gurel, E. (1986). Price and volume effects associated with changes in the S&P 500 list: New evidence for the existence of price pressures. *The Journal of Finance*, 41(4), 815–829.

Kamal, R. (2014). New evidence from S&P 500 index deletions. *The International Journal of Business and Finance Research*, 8(2), 1–10.

Kamal, R., Lawrence, E.R., McCabe, G., & Prakash, A.J. (2012). Additions to S&P 500 index: Not so informative any more. *Managerial Finance*, 38(4), 380–402.

Kot, H.W., Leung, H.K., & Tang, G.Y. (2015). The long-term performance of index additions and deletions: Evidence from the Hang Seng Index. *International Review of Financial Analysis*, 42, 407–420.

Li, X. & Tan, T.K. (2015). Governance changes for firms added to the S&P 500. *The International Journal of Business and Finance Research*, 9(4), 21–35.

Liu, S. (2020). S&P 500 affiliation and stock price informativeness. *Journal of Behavioral Finance*, 21(3), 219–232.

Orzano, M. (2020). China A-share inclusion — An update one year later. https://www.spglobal.com/en/research-insights/market-insights/china-a-share-inclusion-an-update-one-year-later (2020-09-26).

Petajisto, A. (2008). Selection of an optimal index rule for an index fund. Available at SSRN 1264698.

Petajisto, A. (2011). The index premium and its hidden cost for index funds. *Journal of Empirical Finance*, 18(2), 271–288.

Shleifer, A. (1986). Do demand curves for stocks slope down? *The Journal of Finance*, 41(3), 579–590.

Soe, A.M. & Dash, S. (2008). The shrinking index effect: A global perspective. Available at SSRN 1568122.

The People's Bank of China (PBC). (August 11, 2015). PBC announcement on improving quotation of the central parity of RMB against US dollar. http://www.pbc.gov.cn/english/130721/2941603/index.html.

Vespro, C. (2006). Stock price and volume effects associated with compositional changes in European stock indices. *European Financial Management*, 12(1), 103–127.

Vijh, A.M. (1994). S&P 500 trading strategies and stock betas. *Review of Financial Studies*, 7(1), 215–251.

Xiao, Gang. (2020). Changes in China's Capital Market. Beijing: CITIC Press Group (in Chinese).

Chapter 4

AH Premium: A Macro Perspective*

Macro factors have played an important role in explaining the A-share and H-share price differences of cross-listed companies (AH premium), especially the surge of AH premium index after 2015. Over the period of 2007 and 2019, the impacts of USD index shocks dominate the overall changes of AH premium on individual equity basis. Moreover, USD index can explain about 50–70% of the changes of the AH premium index, and the investors' expectation of Chinese economy can add another 10% of the explanatory power. After the initiation of Shanghai-Hong Kong Stock Connect (SH Connect) in November 2014, the AH premium index jumped from 115.8 to 126.4 but with significant decline in its variance. If we segregate the impacts of USD index, the AH premium index average only increased 2.7 ppt from 98.8 to 101.5. Furthermore, after the initiation of SH Connect, the prices of cross-listed shares have been more responsive to exchange rate information. Over a longer term, SH Connect may have reduced the impacts of USD index while increased the impacts of effective prices on equity prices. The above findings demonstrate that hedging for foreign exchange risks is the main reason for investment in H-shares of mainland firms, and as a result, enhancing RMB foreign exchange rate flexibility is the core component as well as a pre-condition for financial market opening in China. Besides, when the

*This chapter was originally published as Xuechun, Z., Yandong, J., & Tingting, L. (2020). The impacts of the US dollar index and the investors' expectations on the AH Premium – a macro perspective. *China Economic Journal*, **13(3)**, 249–269. https://doi.org/10.1080/17538963.2020.1804709. Reproduced with kind permission from Taylor & Francis.

market conditions permit, policymakers and regulators should consider a pilot program allowing investors to arbitrage those shares with AH premium in a reasonable range. This may further reduce AH premium, and enable the share prices convergence in the long run.

The modern equity market in China was established in the early 1990s and has become the second largest equity market in the world. The Chinese equity market is also fairly open but not fully integrated into international financial markets. There are hundreds of Chinese companies listed abroad, some of which are cross-listed in China and other countries and regions. Two peculiar facts related to the share prices of cross-listed companies in China (A-share) and Hong Kong (H-share) include relatively higher A-share prices and the surge of AH premium after improved market connectivity in late 2014.

In theory, expected cash flow determines the fundamental price of a listed company, so the equity prices of a company in different markets should be the same after adjusting for the foreign exchange differences. In practice, the prices of a cross-listed company may vary given different market risks (currency, governance structure, laws and regulations, liquidity, tax arrangement, and the like) and market forces (investor demands and sentiments). In general, the cross-listed stocks between advanced markets pose similar prices; and between advanced and emerging markets, stocks in advanced markets carry higher prices. The situation in China is different. The share prices of the same company in RMB (A-share) are not only higher than the shares in US dollar (B-share) but also higher than the shares listed in Hong Kong (H-share) and in the US (ADR). Since 2007, Hang Seng China AH Premium Index (HSAHP)[1] averaged 120, indicating an average of 20% A-share premium over H-share. On individual equity level, AH premium of cross-listed shares has been averaging above 40%, and some close to 200% over the years.

According to the Law of One Price, the prices of the same commodity or asset in different markets should be similar if the commodity or asset can be traded between markets. That is, the share prices of the

[1]Hang Seng China AH Premium Index (HSAHP) of the Hong Kong Hang Seng Index Service Company was first published on July 9, 2007 to track the price difference of cross-listed A-shares and H-shares. HSAHP is average premium (or discount) of A-shares and H-shares in the index weighted by their respective capitalization in circulation. The higher the index, the higher the premium of A-share over that of H-share. In September 2017, it was renamed as Hang Seng Stock Connect China AH Premium Index. For simplicity, this chapter uses HSAHP.

same company listed in Shanghai/Shenzhen and Hong Kong should be similar if cross-market arbitrage can be conducted. Further, if the connectivity of the markets has increased with the introduction of Shanghai-Hong Kong Connect (November 2014) and Shenzhen-Hong Kong Connect (December 2016) (hereafter SH Connect to include both[2]), the share prices should converge. However, data tell a different story. After December 2014, AH premium increased from 115 to 128 (Figure 1), and factors lead to the jump have generated heated discussions among market analysts but not many academicians yet.

This chapter provides a systematic analysis of the differences between mainland and Hong Kong's securities markets using a sample of 95 cross-listed equities. Specifically, this chapter examines the formulation of the AH premium index and conducts empirical studies of the impacts of US dollar (USD) index and investors' expectation of Chinese economy on AH premium, taking into consideration the foreign exchange mechanisms of RMB and HK dollar (HKD). Furthermore, this chapter explores how SH Connect affects the impacts of USD index and price discovery efficiency of HK and mainland markets.

This chapter has four sections: The first section reviews the transaction mechanism of A-shares and H-shares under SH Connect, as well as views of market entities. The second section summarizes the related literature on cross-listed equity share price differences, including those related to AH premium. The third section conducts empirical studies on the impacts of macro factors on AH premium and A-share and H-share prices, as well as how SH Connect affects market efficiency and the impacts of USD index and fundamental prices. The fourth section is conclusions and policy suggestions.

So far, most studies on AH premium have examined the issue using micro-level variables (Bailey, 1994; Hu & Xiaokun, 2008; Nishimura *et al*., 2018). Moreover, there has been no in-depth study specifically on the surge of AH premium after 2015 and the reason for the surge (Hui & Chan, 2018; Bai & Chow, 2017; see Table 1 for details). The paper contributes to the existing literature in the following areas. First, this chapter examines AH premium from a macro perspective. Second, this chapter studies how SH Connect affects market efficiency as well as the impacts of foreign exchange rate and fundamental prices. Third, this chapter assumes the same effective price of the A-shares and

[2]In this chapter, we use SH Connect to include both Shanghai–Hong Kong Stock Connect and Shenzhen-Hong Kong Stock Connect because they share the same designs, and differ only in the starting dates.

H-shares of a cross-listed company and provides feasible policy options for Chinese equity markets to integrate into the international financial markets. Fourth, this chapter extends the data of similar studies to the end of 2019.

1. Preliminary Analysis of SH Connect and AH Premium

The rules and regulations of equity market in China, especially those related to information disclosure, are not fully in line with best practices in advanced markets, and some tools for price discovery and risk management are still lacking. Besides, given the shortages of institutional investors, individual investors have caused high turnover ratio and short investment period.

Even with many constraints, the equity markets in China have been enhancing and expanding their openness. In the early 1990s, companies were allowed to cross-list in mainland and Hong Kong exchanges. In the following years, more measures have been introduced, including B-shares denominated in US dollar (USD, 2001), Qualified Foreign Institutional Investors (QFII, 2002), and Qualified Domestic Institutional Investors (QDII, 2006). SH Connect (2014 for Shanghai and 2016 for Shenzhen) allows mainland and HK investors to invest in selected equities listed in the other markets, which is a landmark event for the openness of the Chinese equity markets.

SH Connect is a technical connection between Shanghai Stock Exchange, Shenzhen Stock Exchange, and Stock Exchange of Hong Kong Ltd. to provide investors of the mainland[3] and Hong Kong with more investment opportunities. SH Connect adopts order routing technology and cross-border settlement arrangement, and transactions are settled in RMB in both markets. That is, mainland investors can buy and sell HK dollar-denominated equities in Hong Kong with RMB, and Hong Kong investors can transact equities in mainland markets, quoted and settled in RMB. Regulators have set the daily quota of SH Connect,[4] although the

[3]An eligible mainland individual investor needs an aggregate balance of more than RMB 500,000 in his/her securities and cash accounts.

[4]The Northbound Daily Quota is set at RMB 52 billion, and the Southbound Daily Quota is RMB 42 billion.

daily transaction volume has been lower than 10% of the quota in most trading days.

AH premium has existed for years. Since 2007, A-share prices have averaged around 20% over those of cross-listed H-shares, and at individual equity level, the premium can surpass 100%. Figure 1 shows that between 2007 and 2009, the AH premium index was highly volatile with a minimum of less than 110 and a maximum of more than 200. The volatility reflected the market uncertainties during the Global Financial Crisis. In a relatively peaceful period from 2010 to June 2014, the AH premium index fluctuated between 95 and 115. After mid-2014, the premium index has increased from a low point to about 130, with an average of 126.4. The drastic surge in AH premium has attracted much attention from market entities. Many of their analytic reports view investor structure, market structure, and transaction mechanisms of the mainland and Hong Kong as factors affecting the market effectiveness in the price discovery and correction and in turn, AH premium.[5]

1.1 *Different investor structure and thereby different investment preferences and turnover ratios*

In the mainland, overseas investors (2.7%) and institutional investors (20%) are far less important than those in Hong Kong where the two types of investors accounted for more than 46% and 60%, respectively. In terms of transaction volume, institutional investors count for 50% of HK, while in the mainland, the figure is 15%. Most market analysts agree that individual investors of A-shares lack capacities to assess the fundamentals of companies listed and are more sensitive to stimulus policy measures than the fundamentals of the listed companies. As a result, they are more sentiment-driven and generate herding behavior in their frequent trading. In comparison, investors in Hong Kong equity market are more rational. They pay more attention to the fundamentals, profitability, and dividend payout of the listed companies. That is, they prefer stable and profitable companies and are not interested in high-risk short-term speculation.

Data support the above-mentioned investment preference. Investors in Hong Kong prefer large companies, especially leaders of industries. The top 20 most traded shares through SH Connect are mainly finance and

[5] Information from reports of various securities firms.

consumption related, and those shares with net buy-in of more than RMB 1 billion are all industry leaders. Besides, AH premium is notably positively related to the daily turnover of A-shares, with the higher turnovers of a company, the higher the AH premium.

1.2 *Direct transaction costs are moderate and opportunity costs may be substantial*

Although transaction costs under SH Connect are small at around 0.7% of the transaction value,[6] the opportunity costs can be large. The latter include foreign exchange conversion cost, dividend tax, and the like. Regarding the foreign exchange conversion, the ChinaClear settles the transaction in the net and exchanges the net to HKD, so the conversion costs are shared by all investors. Under this arrangement, individual investors can enjoy whole-sale price (foreign exchange rate). Regarding the dividend tax, under SH Connect, mainland investors need to pay 20% of the dividend tax (exempt if holding the H-share for more than 12 months), and Hong Kong investors 10%. Nevertheless, for long-term investors, it seems that dividend tax is not a determinant factor.

No consensuses have been reached regarding the impacts of foreign exchange rates and interest rates on AH premium. Yiu (2016) views foreign exchange rate as a key factor. "Some mainlanders have been buying H-shares via the stock connect as they are worried about the devaluation of the yuan. But these investors are not doing arbitrage, they are only trying to hedge against the falling currency". However, most institutions hold the view that both A-shares and H-shares are quoted in RMB, so changes in RMB foreign exchange rates should not affect the share prices of neither markets except for the psychological impact on the investors. The interest rates in Hong Kong have been lower than those in the mainland, not supportive of long-term AH premium. That is, mainland

[6]The transaction costs include stamp duties (0.1% of the transaction value), transaction levy (0.0027% of the transaction value, for both sides), transaction fee (0.0005% of the transaction value, for both sides), cost for using the system (HKD0.5 per transaction, for both sides), stock settlement fee (0.002% of the transaction value, for both sides, with a minimum of HKD2 and a maximum of HKD100), portfolio fee (an annual fee of 0.008% of capitalization for equity below HKD50 billion), commission (vary for different securities firms), and the like.

investors do not buy H-shares because of lower interest rates in Hong Kong as the interest rate gap does not change the relative prices of A-shares and H-shares.

1.3 *Different transaction regulations lead to different market liquidity and prevent arbitrage*

Transaction rules in Hong Kong are all in line with international practices and are considered more efficient in price discovery, transaction, as well as liquidity and risk management. Rules in Hong Kong on IPO, repo, and delisting are more flexible in seasoned and rights issues. Mainland markets adopt $T+1$, meaning that the investors can only sell the shares they purchased on the next trading day. In Hong Kong, such a constraint does not hold under the $T+0$ rule, which enables short sales and improves market liquidity. Moreover, Hong Kong allows for more structured products and derivatives, but in the mainland, net shorting is prohibited. Besides, the mainland has different rules about trading hours, daily price limits (daily fluctuation limit is capped at 10%), and margin trading, and some rules have partly prevented arbitrage between the two markets. As a result, investors under SH Connect can't conduct cross-market sell of their equities purchased, prohibiting arbitrage as well as profit opportunities.

As for why AH premium has not gone down as expected after the introduction of SH Connect, the market analysts argue that A and H markets remained independent and investors will continue to select shares that will bring them higher returns in the future. SH Connect is still in the primary stage, and the share prices moved by their own market logic. Many market analysts agree that over the long run, AH premium will converge with mainland markets becoming more mature and the connection between the markets deepening. To reduce AH premium, arbitrage is regarded as the most effective means.

2. Literature Review

Research papers on cross-listed equities are mainly based on the Law of One Price, and a majority of them use micro-level variables to examine the share price differences. That is, in effective and highly integrated markets, the prices of a cross-listed company should be affected by similar common factors, and their share prices should be similar after adjusting for foreign exchange rates. Various hypotheses are used to prove the Law of One Price, including information asymmetry hypothesis, demand divergence hypothesis, liquidity hypothesis, and risk preference divergence hypothesis. Most studies assume that the investors of cross-listed companies face the same fundamental prices (or implicit efficient prices) which are determined by endogenous factors related to these companies (Schreiber & Schwartz, 1986). Based on this assumption, exogenous factors such as foreign exchange risks, legal, tax, and investor sentiment are assessed. However, Eichler (2011) argues that the Law of One Price does not apply to China with capital or investment control. Arquette *et al.* (2008) also note that the mainland's market rules have prevented investors from arbitrage and generated very high AH premium. However, this argument does not hold in practice. Arbitrage can only be conducted when the prices of different markets converge, so it is difficult to realize even between developed markets. Since the timing of the convergence is uncertain, the arbitrage entities have to face tremendous uncertainties. Given their limited investment term, few investors can wait for the prices to converge.

Most studies on price difference between A-share and B/H-share (and ADR) test difference hypotheses to prove the Law of One Price. These hypotheses mainly use micro-level data to explain differences in the prices of cross-listed shares. It is generally agreed that information asymmetry is prominent in the Chinese equity markets. Foreign investors have more difficulties in obtaining reliable information about the Chinese economy and listed companies because of different accounting standards, legal and regulatory frameworks, as well as information evaluation and transmission mechanisms. Information asymmetry hypothesis has strong explanatory power for AB and AH premium (Chakravarty *et al.*, 1998; Chan *et al.*, 2008; Hu & Xiaokun, 2008). Sun & Tong (2000) use the size of the listed company as the information asymmetric indicator and find it powerful in explaining the AB and AH premium. This is because large companies have a higher public profile, so their degree of information asymmetry is lower than that of smaller companies.

Liquidity hypothesis indicates that share prices are higher in a more liquid market. Chen *et al.* (2001) note that short of liquidity is an important reason for AB premium, and this applies to AH premium as well (Wang & Jiang, 2004). Hu & Xiaokun (2008) also find that both liquidity hypothesis and information asymmetry hypothesis hold in AH premium analysis. Risk preference hypothesis states that, in general, share price premium can attract cross-border fund flow; however, the shares with investment constraints will suffer from lower prices. In China, the opposite holds; A-share prices are higher. This is because mainland investors have limited investment opportunities and lower return expectations, and they are more willing to take risks (Ma, 1996; Eun & Sabherwal, 2001).

More research papers have focused on factors such as investor structure, market structure, transaction rules, and market efficiency in examining long-term A-share premium. Among others, investor structure difference is considered a direct cause and has received most of the attention. Researchers find that mainland investors have lower equity demand elasticity (Bailey, 1994) and higher share price elasticity (Liu, 2004) and pay more attention to short-term capital gain (Song & Wu, 2008). Besides, mainland investors prioritize capital gain (Song & Wu, 2008). Yeh *et al.* (2002) find that the lagged AB premium can explain part of A and B share prices and their volatility based on data from January 1995 to November 1997. When AB premium increases, returns on A-share would increase and on B-share decline. Besides, investor sentiment is also explored in the studies of AH premium (Wang & Jiang, 2004; Arquette *et al.*, 2008; Burdekin & Redfern, 2009).

Meso-level reasons for share price differences include market supply (Chan & Kwok, 2005), systemic risk premium (Li *et al.*, 2006), and spillover effects of international investment to equity market (Nishimura *et al.*, 2018). Chan & Kwok (2005) analyze the supply constraint on share prices during the 1991–2000 period and find that AB and AH premiums of different companies are negatively related to their A-share supply and positively related to B/H supply. This means that AB and AH premiums mainly come from limited supply of A-shares. Li *et al.* (2006) construct a two-factor risk premium model of the mainland and Hong Kong equity markets, which can well explain the returns of shares of 13 cross-listed companies between 1997 and 2003. This chapter finds that AH premium is positively related to savings interest rates of mainland and HK, meaning that risk premium from market segregation is important to the share price difference. This chapter also finds that in the Asian Financial Crisis period, the performance of market indexes could better explain AH premium. Nishimura *et al.* (2018) constructed a spillover impact index and found that the spillover impact was higher for the cross-listed shares in the matured Hong Kong market, causing AH premium.

The impacts of macro-level factors are sometimes more significant than those of other factors. Chen *et al.* (2001) found that B-share prices are more closely related to indicators such as macroeconomic performance, foreign exchange rate, and foreign reserve than A-shares. This means that foreign investors are more sensitive to these macro indicators, while domestic investors focus more on factors other than economic fundamentals. Fong *et al.* (2007) examined AH premium from April 2000 to February 2007 and found that market segregation had affected fund allocation efficiency. Among others, both micro- and meso-level factors (market liquidity, share supply, risk level, and market conditions) and macro factors (RMB appreciation expectation and monetary expansion) have played a role in determining AH premium, but macro factors may be more important.

Of all macro variables, foreign exchange rate is the focus. Early studies examine the price differences between local market shares (including A-shares) and ADR (Bailey *et al.*, 2000; Gramming *et al.*, 2005). These studies note that as ADR is denominated in US dollar, depreciation of local currencies means relatively lower returns of ADR. Eichler (2011) studies the panel data of 22 A-ADR premium and 52 AH premium between December 1998 and February 2009. He found that the premiums reflect RMB to US dollar exchange expectations, and the premiums are better than random walk and previous period foreign exchange rates in projecting the current term exchange rate. He also found that investors' RMB appreciation expectation rises when RMB over appreciation expectation subdues, Sino-US inflation differences shrink, China's relative productivity enhances, Sino-US interest rate gap narrows, China's domestic credit to GDP ratio reduces, and China's sovereign debt yield declines. His findings about the investors' foreign exchange rate expectations are also in line with foreign exchange rate theories. Arquette *et al.* (2008) examined A-ADR and AH premiums between 1998 and 2006 and found that 40% of A-ADR premium changes can be explained by RMB non-deliverable forwards. This means that investors have included foreign exchange rate risks when pricing ADR and H-shares.

SH Connect was introduced in late 2014, and the surging AH premium after 2015 has confused many. Yet, few academic studies have explored this issue in depth, although a few studies have examined the changes in market connectivity and the impact of fund flow on AH premium (Table 1). First, SH Connect has brought about fund flow between the two markets, and yet, such flow is not meaningful in explaining the changes in AH premium (Burdekin & Siklos, 2018;

Table 1. Impacts of SH connect on AH premium: List of studies.

	Paper	Data, Obs. Period and Methods	Main Conclusions
1	Hui & Chan (2018)	AH premiums (April 2, 2012–June 30, 2016) Method: Linear regression	Reasons for AH premium jump: (1) mainland market not mature; (2) mainland market's transactions behavior. Mainland markets dominate in affecting share prices and AH premium.
2	Bai & Chow (2017)	Several stock indexes (June 21, 2006–April 5, 2016) Method: Event study	Mainland and Hong Kong markets are in different development stages, and impacts of SH Connect differ from mainland and Hong Kong investors over short- and medium term. In short term, the impact is positive.
3	Huo & Ahmed (2017)	High-frequency data of Shanghai Composite Index, Hang Sheng Index (July 2, 2014–August 8, 2015) Method: GARCH	After SH Connect, (1) the cointegration between two indexes is significant; and (2) the spillover effect of Shanghai market on Hong Kong is much larger and faster than the reverse impacts.
4	Ma *et al.* (2019)	Shanghai Composite Index, Shenzhen Composite Index, Hang Sheng Index, S&P 500 Index (January 1, 2013–December 4, 2016 Method: DCC, ADCC, and GO-GARCH	Segregated the market co-movement due to market liberalization and other factors, and found that in the short-term, SH Connect has not enhanced the market connection as measured by the co-movement of equity prices. However, the correlation of two market indexes has increased after SH Connect.
5	Burdekin & Siklos (2018)	AH premium between 2015 and 2017	Impacts of south- and north-bound capital flow on AH premium are insignificant.
6	Lin (2017)	Shanghai Composite Index, Hang Sheng Index before and after introduction of Shanghai-SH Connect	In terms of spillover effects of shocks, Hong Kong to Shanghai transmission exists pre- and post-SH Connect. In terms of volatility transmissions, the impacts are two-way prior to SH Connect, but insignificant afterward.

(*Continued*)

Table 1. (*Continued*)

	Paper	Data, Obs. Period and Methods	Main Conclusions
7	Cao & Zhou (2019)	Price changes and transactions of 79 cross-listed shares from January 2014 to May 2017	In a bear market, AH premium changes in different directions. Besides, the mainland markets have strong transmission on Hong Kong market, while there exists two-year conduction effects.
8	Lu *et al.* (2018)	AH premium between 2013 and 2016	Main reasons for increased AH premiums: most funds flow the mainland. In the observation period, information of cross-listed companies did not affect fund flow, as the EM market investors need longer "learning process" after entering newly opened markets. Six months after SH Connect, mainland investors investment in Hong Kong shares has reduced AH premium to the level of the first 6 months after SH Connect.

Note: SH Connect in the table all means Shanghai-Hong Kong Connect.

Lu *et al.*, 2018). Second, there has not been any consensus on whether SH Connect has enhanced the co-movement of the two markets (Ma *et al.*, 2019), although there is evidence that the relationship between the indices of the two markets has strengthened (Huo & Ahmed, 2017; Ma *et al.*, 2019). Third, the rise of AH premium after 2015 is the result of the different development stages of the two markets (Hui & Chan, 2018; Bai & Chow, 2017).

3. Empirical Analysis

The objectives of the empirical studies are three folds: (1) to explore whether foreign exchange rate and investors' expectation of Chinese economy can affect AH premium; (2) to assess the impacts of foreign exchange rates on the AH premium index as well as individual shares; and (3) to identify how foreign exchange rates affect the pricing of A-shares and H-shares. We start with the formulation of HSAHP, and examine the impact of USD index and forwarded GDP growth rate on the AH premium index. Then, we identify and assess the impacts of foreign exchange rate on AH premium index and individual equity prices using cointegration regression, and we can then obtain the AH Premium index segregating USD index impacts. In the end, we construct a simple price discovery model to examine the impacts of foreign exchange rates and fundamental prices on the A-share and H-share prices. This model can also help to identify the permanent shocks of USD index on A-share and H-share prices.

3.1 *Preliminary analysis of AH premium (HSAHP)*

AH premium is normally proxied by HSAHP, an index of weighted average of the cross-listed A-share and H-share price differences based on the capitalization of A-share and H-shares in circulation:

$$\mathrm{HSAHP}_t = \frac{\sum_{i=1}^{n}\left[(\mathrm{IS}_i^A \times \mathrm{FAF}_i^A + \mathrm{IS}_i^H \times \mathrm{FAF}_i^H)\times P_{i,t}^A \times \frac{1}{\mathrm{FX}_t^A}\right]}{\sum_{i=1}^{n}\left[(\mathrm{IS}_i^A \times \mathrm{FAF}_i^A + \mathrm{IS}_i^H \times \mathrm{FAF}_i^H)\times P_{i,t}^H \times \frac{1}{\mathrm{FX}_t^H}\right]}\times 100.$$

where i means individual stocks, j means location of the market, $P_{i,t}^j$ are the corresponding prices of A-share and H-shares, IS_t^j are the shares issued by the firms in mainland and Hong Kong markets, FAF_t^j are the free float-adjusted coefficient, and FX_t^j are RMB to USD and HK dollar (HKD) to USD rates.

The above formula shows that HSAHP is compiled with the market capitalization converted into USD. The higher the HSAHP, the higher the A-share price related to H-share price, and *vice versa*. Most previous empirical studies have used this formula and converted the share prices into either RMB or USD or HKD.

Simple statistics in Table 2 show that HSAHP averaged 115.8 during the period of January 2007 and November 2014 and 126.4 from December 2014 to December 2019, a drastic surge of 10.6 ppt. However, the difference between maximum and minimum reduced from 123.1 to 50.6, and standard deviation reduced from 22.9 to 7.7, indicating much enhanced stability.

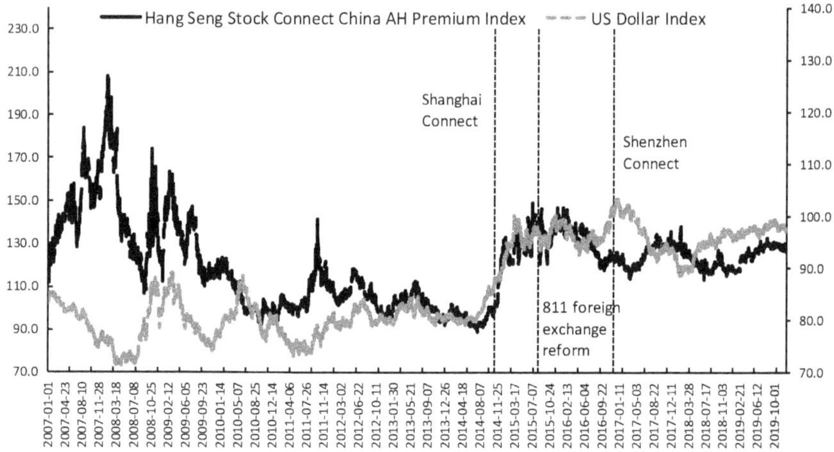

Figure 1. HSAHP and USD index.

Source: Wind Economic Database.

In theory, if both RMB and HKD float freely against USD, then the changes of HSAHP are not affected by foreign exchange rates. However, if the two currencies have different foreign exchange rate arrangements, the story should be different. In fact, RMB adopts a managed floating mechanism against USD, while HK dollar is pegged to USD under a currency board arrangement. In the HSAHP formula, when USD index changes, the HKD exchange rate (FX_t^H) remains stable while RMB exchange rate (FX_t^A) fluctuates. This means that regardless of which currency we use in the A and H premium calculation, USD value will directly affect HSAHP.

This is obvious in USD index and HSAHP over the past 12 years (Figure 1). The correlation is especially clear after 2010 as the changes in the two indexes follow similar trend with USD index leading the changes. Note that we have also tried RMB to USD and RMB to HKD rates in the model but found that UDS index has the strongest explanatory power. This indicates that investors pay more attention to USD foreign exchange rate and that the enhanced flexibility of RMB foreign exchange arrangement is needed to attract investors' attention.

3.2 *Single equation analysis*

We explore the relationship between AH premium and USD index using HSAHP and individual equity prices. For HSAHP, we first examine the

Table 2. Pre- and post-SH Connect HSAHP.

	HSAHP			HSAHP w/o USD Index		
	Average	**Range**	**Std. Dev.**	**Average**	**Range**	**Std. Dev.**
2007.07.09–2014.11.04	115.8	123.1	22.9	98.8	92.2	22.2
2014.11.05–2019.12.31	126.4	50.6	7.7	101.5	23.8	7.6
Changes	10.6	**−72.5**	**−15.2**	2.7	**−68.3**	**−14.6**

Source: Wind Economic Database.

cointegration of HSAHP and USD index and identify the short- and long-term impacts of US dollar value on AH premium. For individual equities, we design a panel cointegration regression using the 95 cross-listed shares data. Considering the events such as SH Connect, Foreign Exchange Reform dated August 11, 2015, as well as equity market turbulence in 2015, we select various periods for detailed estimation. Besides, we introduce a few macro variables such as the investors' expectation of the Chinese economy to distinguish the impacts of foreign exchange rate and other factors on the prices of cross-listed shares in the two markets.

3.2.1 *Data description*

This section uses daily data of HSAHP and USD index from July 9, 2007 to December 20, 2019. For individual equities, we select the 95 cross-listed equity prices over the same period. The exchange rates in use are the daily closing prices of RMB to US dollar rate and of the HKD to US dollar rate. To examine the impacts of SH Connect[7] and of the 2015 equity market volatility, we separate the sample into two periods, from July 2007 to November 2014, and from December 2014 to December 2019, and add a dummy variable for 2015.

3.2.2 *Cointegration between HSAHP and USD index*

To study the relationship between HSAHP and USD index, we conduct a single equation test and estimate their cointegration. Using ARDL, we have the following long-term cointegration in different observation periods:

[7] Shanghai-HK Connect started in November 2014, prior to the introduction of Shenzhen-HK Connect started (December 2016).

$$\begin{aligned}
&\text{All sample period:} && \text{HSAHP}_t = 0.76 \cdot \text{USindex}_t + c,\\
&\text{Pre-SH Connect:} && \text{HSAHP}_t = 1.22 \cdot \text{USindex}_t + c,\\
&\text{Post-SH Connect:} && \text{HSAHP}_t = 0.0748 \cdot \text{USindex}_t + c.
\end{aligned}$$

where HSAHP_t is the Hang Sheng AH Premium index and USindex_t is the USD index. The result shows that the two variables have long-term cointegration. On the whole, the cointegration is significant, and the parameters are positive. This means that when USD appreciates, A-share prices are less affected as most investors are domestic. However, for investors in Hong Kong, the mainland firms' attractiveness is reduced with their declined corresponding assets and cash flow in USD. As a result, HSAHP goes up. Comparing with the period post-SH Connect, the cointegration is stronger in the pre-SH Connect period. Moreover, the degrees of fitting of the ECM equations in two different periods are both above 70%. Next, we add investors' expectation of Chinese economy (E_t) in the cointegration assessment, approximated by the GDP growth rate in one period after.[8] It is noteworthy and also unique that foreign investment in Chinese firms listed in Hong Kong reflects investors' expectations of the Chinese economy. Given different investor structures in mainland and Hong Kong markets, such a proposition still holds even with relatively high AH premium. This is clearly reflected in the following results based on the monthly data from July 2007 and December 2019:

$$\begin{aligned}
&\text{All sample period:} && \text{HSAHP}_t = 0.58 \cdot \text{USindex}_t + 0.13 \cdot E_t + c\\
&\text{Pre-SH Connect:} && \text{HSAHP}_t = 0.84 \cdot \text{USindex}_t + 0.21 \cdot E_t + c\\
&\text{Post-SH Connect:} && \text{HSAHP}_t = 0.23 \cdot \text{USindex}_t + 0.02 \cdot E_t + c
\end{aligned}$$

On the whole, the cointegration remains significantly positive between the two variables, taking into consideration investor expectations of the Chinese economy, with similar degrees of correlation. Moreover, the equation poses an overall R-square of higher than 80%, indicating the expectations of the Chinese economy are an important variable in understanding the changes of AH premiums, although less important than USD index. The two variables can explain most of the changes in AH premium index.

[8] We get the monthly GDP year-on-year growth by interpolating the quarterly real GDP year-on-year growth.

3.2.3 *Cointegration relationship between individual equity prices and USD index*

(i) AH premium versus USD index

To examine whether individual share prices are affected by USD index, we conduct panel cointegration test and cointegration regression using A-share and H-share prices of the cross-listed 95 companies over the period of 2007 and 2019[9]:

$$\begin{aligned} &\text{All sample period:} && AH_{i,t} = 1.39 \cdot \text{USindex}_t + c_i, \\ &\text{Pre-SH Connect:} && AH_{i,t} = 1.87 \cdot \text{USindex}_t + c_i, \\ &\text{Post-SH Connect:} && AH_{i,t} = 0.22 \cdot \text{USindex}_t + c_i. \end{aligned}$$

where $AH_{i,t} = 100*(P^A_{i,t}/P^H_{i,t})$ is the premium of A-share over H-share prices, USindex_t is the USD index, and c_i the individual differences of different shares. The three equations carry strong explanatory power of 67%, 70%, and 80%, respectively. It seems that the estimation results of the individual share prices share the same direction as those of the index (HSAHP). In the long run, USD index has significant positive impacts on the individual share price premiums, and the impacts moderated after the introduction of SH Connect. Meanwhile, we note that the coefficient of the cointegration reduced, but the overall explanatory power of the cointegration surged from 70% to 80% after the introduction of SH Connect (Table A1).

(ii) AH prices versus USD index

The changes in prices are the reasons for changes in price premiums. To further study the pricing difference between mainland and Hong Kong markets, we examine the long-term relationship between USD index, A-share prices, and H-share prices in an effort to examine the long-term impacts of USD index on A-share and H-share prices. Based on the cointegration regression of panel data, the long-term relationships of A-share and H-share prices and US index are as follows:

$$\begin{aligned} &\text{All sample period:} && P^A_{i,t} = 1.25 \cdot P^H_{i,t} + 0.06 \cdot \text{USIndex}_t + c_i, \\ &\text{Pre-SH Connect:} && P^A_{i,t} = 1.45 \cdot P^H_{i,t} + 0.22 \cdot \text{USIndex}_t + c_i, \\ &\text{Post-SH Connect:} && P^A_{i,t} = 1.36 \cdot P^H_{i,t} + 0.01 \cdot \text{USIndex}_t + c_i. \end{aligned}$$

[9] Of which, H-share prices are converted into RMB, and both A- and H-share prices are panel unit root tested.

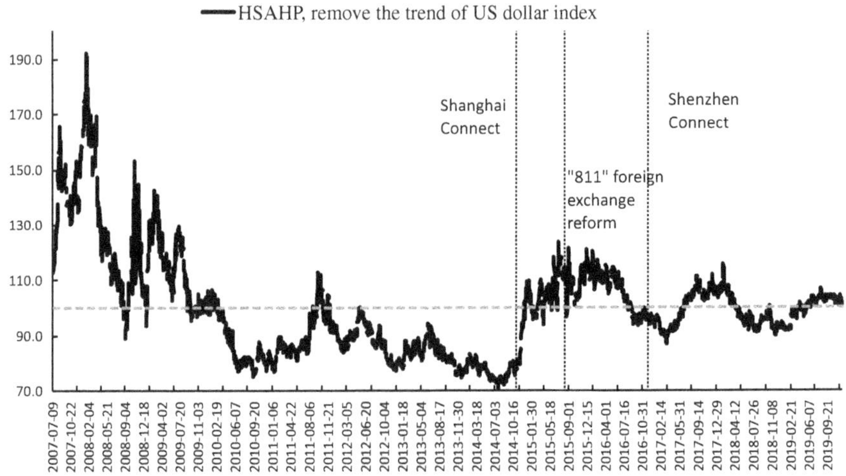

Figure 2. HSAHP without USD index impacts.

Source: Wind Economic Database.

where $P^A_{i,t}$ and $P^H_{i,t}$ are the RMB prices of A-shares and H-shares. The results prove a long-term cointegration among the trends of A-share, H-share, and USD index, and their common trend affects the share prices.

3.2.4 *AH premium index after segregating USD index impact*

The above analysis demonstrates that USD index positively affects the AH premium. We then remove the impacts of USD index using cointegration regression between indexes (Figure 2). It is clear that after segregating the impacts of USD index, the average AH premium increases by 2.7 ppt (from 98.8 to 101.5) after the introduction of SH Connect, compared to a 10.6 ppt increase in the original data. Furthermore, the range of the AH premium reduces from 92.2 to 28.8, and the standard deviation shrinks from 22.6 to 7.6, indicating enhanced stability. This further illustrates that the efficiency of A-share market has improved with enhanced market connectivity after the introduction of SH Connect.

3.3 *Multiple equation analysis based on the price discovery model*

In theory, the cross-listed company is the issuer of both its A-shares and H-shares, and its net assets and cash flow determine the shares' fundamental price (or effective price). To explore how foreign exchange rate affects the pricing of A-share and H-share, we design a simple price discovery model and estimate under a VECM framework.

3.3.1 *A simple price discovery model*

We introduce a simple price discovery model for the cross-listed company. In the model, we assume the issuer of the A-shares and H-shares are the same, so the share prices should not diverge notably from their fundamental price. However, as the shares are traded in different currencies, the fundamental price and the foreign exchange rate of the denominated currency will be the two main factors in the changes in the share prices.

We assume m_t and e_t are the fundamental price and foreign exchange variables, respectively. Both can't be observed, and both are determined by two unrelated shocks, fundamental price shock (η_t^m) and effective foreign exchange rate shock (η_t^e):

$$e_t = e_{t-1} + \eta_t^e + \lambda_t^m, \tag{1}$$

$$m_t = m_{t-1} + \eta_t^m + \rho\eta_t^e. \tag{2}$$

where $\eta_t^P = (\eta_t^e, \eta_t^m)'$, $E(\eta_t^P) = 0$, standard deviation matrix $\mathrm{Var}(\eta_t^P)$ is diagonal, and $\mathrm{Var}(\eta_t^e) = \zeta_e^2$, $\mathrm{Var}(\eta_t^m) = \zeta_m^2$, and e_t is the foreign exchange rate of local currency to foreign currency. Equations (1) and (2) accommodate non-zero contemporaneous correlation between the common factors. This correlation is driven by the parameters λ and ρ as in (3):

$$\mathrm{Var}\left([\Delta e_t, \Delta m_t]'\right) = \begin{pmatrix} \varsigma_e^2 + \lambda^2\varsigma_m^2 & \rho_e^2 + \lambda^2\varsigma_m^2 \\ \rho_e^2 + \lambda^2\varsigma_m^2 & \varsigma_m^2 + \rho^2\varsigma_e^2 \end{pmatrix}. \tag{3}$$

where $\Delta e_t = e_t - e_{t-1}$ and $\Delta m_t = m_t - m_{t-1}$.

Next, we set the changing process of the share prices. Because the markets are not fully effective, and they differ significantly, the prices of A-shares and H-shares in the markets may not correspond to the prices set in equations (1) and (2), although they converge over the long run. In the short run, factors such as market liquidity, information asymmetry, and microstructure (transaction mechanisms, shorting mechanisms, etc.) differences can affect the converging level. In theory, the share prices should move around the fundamental prices and market microstructure. Here, we assume η_t^T as the temporary shock and will not create sustained impacts on prices. We also assume that the price vector P_t as 3×1 observed variable vector consisting of foreign exchange rate index (w_t) and the share prices of two markets ($p_{i,t}$). The price vector subjects to the following conditions:

$$w_t = w_{t-1} + \gamma_1(m_t - m_{t-1}) + \dot{\gamma}_1(e_t - w_{t-1}) + b_1\eta_t^T, \tag{4}$$

$$p_{2,t} = p_{2,t-1} + \gamma_2(m_t - p_{2,t-1}) + \dot{\gamma}_2(e_t - w_{t-1}) + b_2\eta_t^T, \tag{5}$$

$$p_{3,t}^* = p_{3,t-1}^* + \gamma_3(m_t - p_{3,t-1}) + \dot{\gamma}_3(e_t - w_{t-1}) + b_3\eta_t^T. \tag{6}$$

where $p_{2,t}$ is the A-share price, $p_{3,t}$ is the H-share price, b_1, b_2, b_3 are 1×2 vectors, respectively, and η_t^T is the 2×1 vector. Equations (4)–(6) are measurement equations of the foreign exchange rates, A-share prices, and H-share prices, respectively. All prices are affected by both fundamental prices and foreign exchange rate, and $p_{3,t}^*$ is the foreign exchange transaction prices (H-share prices in HKD):

$$p_{3,t}^* = p_{3,t} - w_t. \tag{7}$$

Based on the above specifications, the changes in A-share and H-share prices are the function of two independent common shocks $\eta_t^P = (\eta_t^P, \eta_t^m)'$. We can then re-write equations (4)–(6) in the VMA form:

$$\Delta P_t = d_0\eta_t + d_1\eta_{t-1} + d_2\eta_{t-2} + \cdots = \sum_{i=0}^{\infty} d_i\eta_{t-i}. \tag{8}$$

where $\Delta P_t = (\Delta w_t, \Delta p_{2,t}, \Delta p_{3,t}^*)$.

Through equations (4)–(6), we can obtain the current term impacts and accumulated impacts $D = d_0 + d_1 + d_2 + \cdots = \sum_{i=0}^{\infty} d_i$. And using iterations, we can get d_0 and D as follows:

$$d_0 = \begin{pmatrix} \dot{\gamma}_1 + \gamma_1\rho & \dot{\gamma}_1\lambda + \gamma_1 & b_1 \\ \dot{\gamma}_2 + \gamma_2\rho & \dot{\gamma}_2\lambda + \gamma_2 & b_2 \\ \dot{\gamma}_3 + \gamma_3\rho & \dot{\gamma}_3\lambda + \gamma_3 & b_3 \end{pmatrix}, \tag{9}$$

$$D = \begin{pmatrix} 1 & \lambda & 0 \\ \rho & 1 & 0 \\ \rho - 1 & 1 - \lambda & 0 \end{pmatrix}. \tag{10}$$

Note that although the two shocks are independent, the current term fundamental price and foreign exchange rate are correlated. The reason for assuming the two common shocks are correlated is that foreign exchange rate and fundamental price may be correlated, which is the base for this empirical study. Exchange rate fluctuation may affect firms' fundamental prices in a variety of channels including future cash flow, and discount rate (or cost of shares) that investors use to calculate present value (Minton & Schrand, 1999). Changes in fundamental price will also affect foreign exchange rate and capital cost expectation. Moreover, such changes can further alter foreign exchange rate by influencing cross-border capital flows and capital costs.

We can call d_0 the current term impact matrix and D the accumulated impacts on observed prices given shocks to the latent common factors. Based on our assumptions, d_0 reflects the price discovery capacity of different markets, and D is the long-term impacts, where ρ and $\rho - 1$ denote respective impacts on A-share and H-share prices. These two matrices contain almost all the parameters involved in the structural equation and are the keys to analyzing the impacts of exchange rate.

3.3.2 *Identification of common shocks*

The above simple price discovery model is to estimate d_0, D and the structure parameters λ and ρ in the cointegration, and then to obtain cointegration vector. There are many ways to estimate the structure of VECM containing cointegration, this chapter adopts the two-step method provided by Gonzalo & Granger (1995) and Warne (1993). Assume the A-share and H-share price equations can be expressed in the following vector error correction model (VECM):

$$\Delta P_t = \xi_1 \Delta P_{t-1} + \xi_2 \Delta P_{t-2} + \cdots + \xi_l \Delta P_{t-l} + \zeta + \xi_0 P_{t-1} + \varepsilon_t. \tag{11}$$

where $\Delta P_t = (\Delta w_t, \Delta p_{2,t}, \Delta p^*_{3,t})$, $\xi_0 = \alpha\beta'$, α is the error correction matrix, β is the cointegration vector, and ε_t is the zero mean White Noise Process.

VECM can be expressed in VMA form, i.e., the simplified form:

$$\Delta P_t = \varepsilon_t + \varphi_1 \varepsilon_{t-1} + \varphi_2 \varepsilon_{t-2} + \cdots = \phi(L)\varepsilon_t. \tag{12}$$

Based on equations (4)–(6), we can further acquire the following structural VECM:

$$\Delta P_t = d_0 \eta_t + d_1 \eta_{t-1} + d_2 \eta_{t-2} + \cdots = \sum_{i=0}^{\infty} d_i \eta_{t-i}. \tag{13}$$

We intend to impose sufficient constraints over the simplified equation (12) to obtain the structural equation. First, we estimate the reduced form equation through the ADSL model, get the cointegration relation, and calibrate the cointegration coefficient β in the structural formula based on the estimated relation. Next, based on the cointegration relationship, we can further estimate the error correction coefficient α and the dynamic adjustment parameters. Due to the limited number of variables, we use the Cholesky decomposition. At the same time, we conduct initial analysis and stability tests by altering the orders of A-share and H-share.

3.3.3 *Results*

The above price discovery model enables us to examine the index-level data from a macro perspective.[10] We select Hang Seng Stock Connect China AH (AHXA) and Hang Seng Stock Connect China AH Index (AHXH)[11] as the observed variables. All variables are monthly data from July 2007 to December 2019, and the indexes including USD index are also monthly averages of their daily values.

Based on our estimation of the reduced form, we can obtain the structural parameters according to the identification conditions. In the empirical studies, we also separate the sample period into two, pre- and post-SH Connect, and the estimated results of the first two rows of d_0 and D[12] are in Tables 3–5.

The estimation shows that shocks of foreign exchange rate and of fundamental prices are negatively related, that is, ρ and λ are both negative. This means that a rise in USD index can cause a decline in fundamental price, and *vice versa*.

From the mutual impacts of two permanent shocks, the impacts of USD index shock on fundamental prices are notably more significant than

[10]We did not assess all 95 cross-listed A- and H-shares on individual basis because they have different time series, and on an individual level, the prices of A and H-share may not have cointegration relationship with USD index.

[11]AHXA and AHXH are the A-share and H-share price indexes, respectively, for cross-listed companies, denominated in local currencies, and published by Hong Kong Hang Seng Index Service Company. For details: https://www.hsi.com.hk/eng/indexes/all-indexes/chinaah.

[12]Equations (9) and (10) demonstrate that the first two rows of matrices d_0 and D correspond to the permanent shock of foreign exchange rate and fundamental prices. Here, we also show the first two rows of the two matrices.

Table 3. Estimation of structural model: 2007.07–2019.12.

	Current Impacts d_0		Accumulative Impacts D		β	
	η_t^e	η_t^m	η_t^e	η_t^m		
FX index w_t	1.21	0.05	0.97	**−0.11**	0	−1
	(0.026)	(0.014)	(0.004)	(0.007)		
A-share $p_{2,t}$	0.18	0.88	**−0.52**	0.97	0	1
	(0.05)	(0.021)	(0.036)	(0.004)		
H-share $p_{3,t}$	−1.20	0.89	−1.49	1.08	1	0
	(0.07)	(0.022)	(0.033)	(0.004)		

Note: Numbers in the parenthesis are standard deviations.

Table 4. Estimation of structural model: 2007.07–2014.11.

Pre-SH Connect	Current Impacts d_0		Accumulative Impacts D		β	
	η_t^e	η_t^m	η_t^e	η_t^m		
FX index w_t	1.34	0.01	0.97	**−0.09**	0	−1
	(0.028)	(0.037)	(0.023)	(0.025)		
A-share $p_{2,t}$	0.19	0.84	**−0.64**	0.97	0	1
	(0.027)	(0.059)	(0.037)	(0.023)		
H-share $p_{3,t}$	−0.82	0.74	−1.68	1.07	1	0
	(0.044)	(0.063)	(0.045)	(0.023)		

Note: Numbers in the parenthesis are standard deviations.

Table 5. Estimation of structural model: 2014.12–2019.12.

Post-SH Connect	Current Impacts d_0		Accumulative Impacts D		β	
	η_t^e	η_t^m	η_t^e	η_t^m		
FX index w_t	1.30	0.01	0.97	**−0.15**	0	−1
	(0.029)	(0.049)	(0.023)	(0.047)		
A-share $p_{2,t}$	0.31	0.78	**−0.45**	0.97	0	1
	(0.042)	(0.058)	(0.024)	(0.033)		
H-share $p_{3,t}$	−1.10	0.81	−1.47	1.16	1	0
	(0.021)	(0.055)	(0.012)	(0.064)		

Note: Numbers in the parenthesis are standard deviations.

the reversed impacts as the absolute value of ρ is 3–6 times that of λ. We also note that prior to SH Connect, ρ is −0.64 and afterward, −0.45; correspondingly, λ reduced from −0.09 to −0.15. This means that prior to SH Connect, the impacts of US dollar value on the fundamental prices are relatively larger than the reversed impacts. After the initiation of SH Connect, the impacts of USD index moderated, while the impacts of fundamental prices enhanced. However, over the observed 12-year period, the impacts of USD index shocks dominate the direction of the AH premium and are much larger than those of the fundamental price changes. This coincides with the results of the single equation.

Regarding the impacts on A-share and H-share prices, USD index shocks are much stronger on H-share prices than A-share prices over the long run. That is, H-share prices are more closely related to USD index, which may be related to the currency board arrangement. In the short run, H-share prices respond much faster and adjust to a higher degree to the changes in USD index. At the same time, the impacts of fundamental price shocks are similar to A-share and H-share prices. This means that in terms of price discovery capacity, H-share prices are stronger in identifying changes in foreign exchange rate and are similar to that of A-share prices in identifying changes in fundamental prices.

Overall, the price discovery model shows that over the long run, USD index shock has significant negative impacts on both A-share and H-share prices, while in the short run, the direction of the impacts is unclear. In addition, the impacts of USD index shock on A-share and H-share prices can be enhanced through its shocks on the fundamental prices, with stronger impacts on H-share prices than A-share prices. This is the very reason that AH premium is more affected by USD index overtime. Besides, with the introduction of SH Connect, the price discovery capacity of both mainland and Hong Kong markets has improved. However, due to different foreign exchange arrangements of the two markets, their capabilities in discovering fundamental prices are similar. Yet, there are significant differences in the impact of foreign exchange on share pricing, mostly due to the different foreign exchange arrangements of the two markets.

4. Conclusions and Policy Implications

Investors in H-shares of the cross-listed companies aim at sharing the performances of the targeted companies and managing foreign exchange risks, both are highly related to China's macroeconomic performance.

Naturally, they concern not only the companies' cash flow but also foreign exchange rate and the future of Chinese economy. As a result, macro factors play an important role in determining the H-share price and AH premium of cross-listed companies. Given the currency board arrangement in Hong Kong, mainland investors in H-shares shoulder the risks of HKD, and in turn, USD. This is equivalent to investing in H-shares plus USD foreign exchange forward. And the returns of H-share investors depend on the performances of both H-share and USD. Similarly, overseas' A-share investment has an RMB forward embedded.

We find, not surprisingly, that these two macro factors can explain the changes in AH premium overtime, including the sudden rise in AH premium after the introduction of SH Connect in late 2014. During the period of 2007 and 2019, the impacts of USD index shocks dominated the overall changes of AH premium on individual equity basis, and there exists a long-term cointegration relationship among the trends of A-share, H-share, and USD index. Specifically, USD index can explain about 50–70% of the changes in AH premium index, and the investors' expectation of the Chinese economy can add another 10% of the explanatory power. AH premium index's jump since late 2014 coincides with the surge of USD index during the period; and if we segregate the impacts of USD index, the AH premium index stability has significantly enhanced.

As investors of cross-listed firms face the same net assets and cash flow, the fundamental prices of the same shares in different markets are the same. As such, the adjustments of share prices and fundamental prices to USD index may be able to reflect the impacts of SH Connect. We find that SH Connect has improved the ability of price discovery of both A-share and H-share markets, especially share prices' response to exchange rate information. Prior to December 2014, the impacts of USD index on the fundamental prices were larger than the impacts of fundamental prices on USD index. Afterward, the impacts of USD index were moderated, while the impacts of fundamental prices were enhanced. That is, SH Connect may have reduced the relative impacts of USD index versus fundamental prices on both A-share and H-share prices.

A few distinctive policy implications can be drawn from the above empirical findings. First, enhancing RMB foreign exchange rate flexibility is the pre-condition for financial market opening in China and the core component of RMB internationalization. Second, enhanced market connectivity is useful for price discovery, and SH Connect can help the convergence of the share prices of cross-listed firms. Assuming the fundamental prices of these cross-listed firms are identical, AH premium will go down with further opening of the mainland securities markets, with the improved market rules and more matured investor structure. Third, for policymakers and regulators, a pilot program for arbitrage can also be considered. When the market is not volatile, certain shares with AH premium within a reasonable range (i.e., 5%–10%) can be allowed to arbitrage between the two markets. These may further reduce AH premium. Such a pilot can be expanded with the development of mainland's financial markets and the enhanced RMB foreign exchange rate flexibility. Ultimately, this will facilitate the future integration of Chinese financial markets into the international markets.

Future research can explore the fundamental price of equities and the reasonable price differences of cross-listed shares, as well as their respective determinants. With the same fundamental price, the share prices of a cross-listed company should converge if we control external factors such as market rules, governance structure, and foreign exchange rate arrangements. However, even if the market is highly effective and capital can flow freely, the differences in share prices of the cross-listed companies may still exist. If we can identify a reasonable price difference range, regulators can then design mechanisms to facilitate price converge.

Appendix

Table A1. Individual equity prices and USD index.

Dependent Variable	AH Premium			A Prices		
	Full Sample	**Before**	**After**	**Full Sample**	**Before**	**After**
D(AH(−1))	−0.021	−0.023	−0.015			
	(0.006)	(0.006)	(0.007)			
D(AH(−1))	−0.037	−0.024	−0.054			
	(0.005)	(0.005)	(0.006)			
D(AH(−1))	−0.023	−0.033	−0.006			
	(0.004)	(0.005)	(0.005)			
D(A(−1))				0.012	−0.01	0.025
				(0.006)	(0.007)	(0.008)
D(A(−2))				−0.056	−0.029	−0.072
				(0.006)	(0.004)	(0.007)
D(A(−3))				0.0066	0.013	0.021
				(0.004)	(0.004)	(0.004)

Table A1. (*Continued*)

Dependent Variable	AH Premium			A Prices		
	Full Sample	**Before**	**After**	**Full Sample**	**Before**	**After**
D(H)				0.880	0.648	1.086
				(0.004)	(0.033)	(0.005)
D(H(−1))				0.089	0.07	0.091
				(0.014)	(0.012)	(0.012)
D(H(−2))				0.056		0.081
				(0.015)		(0.014)
D(H(−3))				0.032		
				(0.010)		
D(USindex)	0.095	0.322	−0.259	−0.0065	−0.028	−0.002
	(0.054)	(0.010)	(0.056)	(0.003)	(0.009)	(0.003)
D(USindex(−1))	0.593	0.871		0.0061	−0.029	0.013
	(0.068)	(0.010)		(0.003)	(0.010)	(0.003)
D(USindex(−2))	0.361	0.424		0.024		0.024
	(0.040)	(0.070)		(0.003)		(0.004)
D(USindex(−3))	0.180	0.385		−0.006		
	(0.040)	(0.007)		(0.003)		
C	0.698	1.969	4.07	−0.036	−0.089	0.050
	(0.011)	(0.01)	(0.041)	(0.005)	(0.010)	(0.008)
COINTEQ	**−0.013**	**−0.016**	**−0.023**	**−0.01**	**−0.012**	**−0.018**
	(0.002)	(0.001)	(0.003)	(0.0007)	(0.0008)	(0.002)

Notes: Standard errors are reported in parentheses. It should be noted that the purpose of single equation analysis is to make a preliminary analysis of the relationship between the AH premium and the US dollar index, so as to carry out the estimation and analysis of the structural model. The direct correlation between A-H stock price and US dollar index is very strong. In our preliminary analysis, macro factors, such as Exchange, may be more important than some micro factors which usually be used to explain the AH price premium. Therefore, we do not control the mic factors in the model estimating, such as information, demand, risk preference, and liquidity.

References

Arquette, G.C., Brown, W.O., & Burdekin, R.C.K. (2008). US ADR and Hong Kong H-share discounts of Shanghai-listed firms. *Journal of Banking and Finance*, 32(9), 1916–1927.

Bai, Ye & Darien Yan Pang Chow. (2017). Shanghai-Hong Kong stock connect: An analysis of Chinese partial stock market liberalization impact on the local and foreign markets. *Journal of International Financial Markets, Institutions & Money*, 50, 182–203.

Bailey, W. (1994). Risk and return on China's new stock markets: Some preliminary evidence. *Pacific-Basin Finance Journal*, 2(2), 243–260.

Bailey, W., Chung, Y.P., & Kang, J.K. (1999). Foreign ownership restrictions and equity price premiums: What drives the demand for cross-border investments? *Journal of Financial and Quantitative Analysis*, 34(4), 489–511.

Burdekin, R.C.K. & Redfern, L. (2009). Sentiment effects on Chinese share prices and savings deposits: The post-2003 experience. *China Economic Review*, 20(2), 246–261.

Burdekin, R.C.K. & Siklos, P.L. (2018). Quantifying the impact of the November 2014 Shanghai-Hong Kong stock connect. *International Review of Economics and Finance*, 57, 156–163.

Cao, Guangxi, & Ling Zhou. (2019). Asymmetric risk transmission effect of cross-listing stocks between Mainland and Hong Kong stock markets based on MF-DCCA method. *Physica A: Statistical Mechanics and its Applications*, 526, 120741.

Chakravarty, S., Sarkar, A., & Lifan Wu. (1998). Information asymmetry, market segmentation and the pricing of cross-listed shares: Theory and evidence from Chinese A and B shares. *Journal of International Financial Markets, Institutions & Money*, 8(3), 325–356.

Chan, Kalok & Johnny K.H. Kwok. (2005). Market segmentation and share price premium: Evidence from Chinese stock markets. *Journal of Emerging Market Finance*, 4(1), 43–61.

Chan, Kalok, Menkveld, A.J., & Zhishu Yang. (2008). Information asymmetry and asset prices: Evidence from the China foreign share discount. *The Journal of Finance*, 63(1), 159–196.

Chen, G.M., Bong-Soo Lee, & Oliver Rui. (2001). Foreign ownership restrictions and market segmentation in China's stock markets. *Journal of Financial Research*, 24(1), 133–155.

Eichler, S. (2011). Exchange rate expectations and the pricing of Chinese cross-listed stocks. *Journal of Banking and Finance*, 35(2), 443–455.

Eun, C.S. & Sabherwal, S. (2003). Cross-border listings and price discovery: Evidence from US-listed Canadian stocks. *The Journal of Finance*, 58(2), 549–575.

Fong, T, Wong, A., & Yong, I. (2007). Share price disparity in Chinese stock markets. HKMA Working Paper 11/2007.

Gonzalo, J., & Granger, C. (1995). Estimation of common long-memory components in cointegrated systems', *Journal of Business & Economic Statistics*, 13(1), 27–35.

Gramming, J., Melvin, M., & Schlag, C. (2005). Internationally cross-listed stock prices during overlapping trading hours: Price discovery and exchange rate effects. *Journal of Empirical Finance*, 12(1), 139–164.

Hu, Zhanghong & Wang, Xiaokun. (2008). Empirical study on the stock price difference between A shares and H shares of listed companies in China. *Economic Research*, 4, 119–131 (in Chinese).

Hui, Eddie C.M. & Ka Kwan Kevin Chan. (2018). Does the Shanghai–Hong Kong stock connect significantly affect the A-H premium of the stocks? *Physica A: Statistical Mechanics and Its Applications*, 492, 207–214.

Huo, Rui & Ahmed, A.D. (2017). Return and volatility spillovers effects: Evaluating the impact of Shanghai-Hong Kong stock connect. *Economic Modelling*, 61, 260–272.

Li, Yuming, Daying Yan, & Joe Greco. (2006). Market segmentation and price differentials between A shares and H shares in the Chinese stock markets. *Journal of Multinational Financial Management*, 16(3), 232–248.

Lin, Wensheng. (2017). Modeling volatility linkages between Shanghai and Hong Kong stock markets before and after the connect program. *Economic Modelling*, 67, 346–354.

Liu, Xin. (2004). Quantitative research on the relationship between information asymmetry and H-share discount. *Financial Research*, 30(4), 39–49 (in Chinese).

Lu, Yao, Shi, Xinzheng, Yang, Bohan, & Zhang, Yeqing. (2018). Shanghai-Hong Kong stock connect implementation, capital flow and A-H share premium. *Journal of Economics*, 5(1), 38–63 (in Chinese).

Ma, Xianghai. (1996). Capital controls, market segmentation and stock prices: Evidence from the Chinese stock market. *Pacific-Basin Finance Journal*, 4(2), 219–239.

Ma Rufei, Chengtao Deng, Huan Cai, & Pengxiang Zhai. (2019). Does Shanghai-Hong Kong stock connect drive market comovement between Shanghai and Hong Kong: A new evidence. *North American Journal of Economics and Finance*, 50, 100980.

Minton, B.A. & Schrand, C. (1999). The impact of cash flow volatility on discretionary investment and the costs of debt and equity financing. *Journal of Financial Economics* (Elsevier), 54(3), 423–460.

Nishimura, Y., Tsutsui, Y., & Hirayama, K. (2018). Do international investors cause stock market spillovers? Comparing responses of cross-listed stocks between accessible and inaccessible markets. *Economic Modelling*, 69, 237–248.

Schreiber, P.S. & Schwartz, R.A. (1986). Price discovery in securities markets. *Journal of Portfolio Management*, 12(4), 43.

Song, Jun & Wu, Chongfeng. (2008). International investors' value preference for Chinese stock assets: Evidence from the discount rates of A-H shares and A-B shares. *Financial Research*, 3, 103–116 (in Chinese).

Sun, Q. & Tong, W.H.S. (2000). The effect of market segmentation on stock prices: The China syndrome. *Journal of Banking and Finance*, 24(12), 1875–1902.

Tian, Ying & Wang, Yanming. (2009). Empirical research on market segmentation theory in China's A-share and B-share markets. *International Economic and Trade Exploration*, 9, 58–62 (in Chinese).

Wang, S.S. & Jiang, L. (2004). Location of trade, ownership restrictions, and market illiquidity: Examining Chinese A-and H-shares. *Journal of Banking and Finance*, 28(6), 1273–1297.

Warne, A. (1993). A Common Trends Model: Identification, Estimation and Inference (Anonymous Translator). Stockholm: Institute for International Economic Studies.

Xianfeng Jiang & Frank Packer. (2017). Credit ratings of domestic and global agencies: What drives the differences in China and how are they priced? BIS Working Paper.

Yang, Kun, Yu Wei, & Jianmin He. (2019). Dependence and risk spillovers between Mainland China and London stock markets before and after the stock connect programs. *Physica A: Statistical Mechanics and Its Applications*, 526, 120883.

Yeh, Yin-Hua, Tsun-siou Lee, & Jen-fu Pen. (2002). Stock returns and volatility under market segmentation: The case of Chinese A and B shares. *Review of Quantitative Finance and Accounting*, 18(3), 239–257.

Yiu, Enoch. (2016). Price gap between A and H shares expected to remain, even with the arrival of Shenzhen-Hong Kong trading link. *South China Morning Post*.

Chapter 5

A-H and A-ADR Premiums

This chapter explores the micro-, meso-, and macro-level determinants of the A-H and A-ADR premiums using share price data from cross-listed companies over 2002–2020. During the period, the 9 pairs of shares listed in all three markets averaged an A-ADR premium of around 30% and an A-H premium of 34%, while the weighted average A-H premium of 116 pairs was 35%. Both types of premiums surged after the introduction of Shanghai–Hong Kong Stock Connect (SH Connect) in November 2014. Our empirical analyses find that micro factors weigh much more heavily in explaining both types of premium and that dividend ratio and financial openness are the two most important determinants. In addition, individual share liquidity is important for A-ADR premium, and market sentiment has a significant impact on A-H premium.

To test the policy impacts of foreign exchange rate reform and financial openness, we construct a two-stage two-country model and prove that in certain scenarios, both can help reduce price differences. These results hold when we simulate the impacts of these two policy changes on premiums in a more generalized scenario using numerical analysis. Our empirical analyses also confirm the results of the model. First, after the foreign exchange rate reform, international investors are more adaptive to RMB's foreign exchange rate volatility. This is reflected in the enhanced effectiveness of onshore foreign exchange rates and moderated impacts of the US dollar index in explaining both types of premiums, and the reduced explanatory power of expected onshore foreign exchange rate in A-ADR changes. Second, SH Connect has increased the price discovery capacity of the A-share market, and the surge of premiums after December 2014 can be attributed to systematic changes in factors, such as the US dollar index and market sentiment.

The above findings have multiple policy implications for promoting the price discovery capacity of A-shares and the resource allocation of capital markets in China. On the micro-level, setting appropriate dividend ratios can help reduce A-ADR and A-H premiums. The meso-level measures include expanding the short-sale pilot program and developing long-term institutional investors to reduce speculative transactions. The macro-level policies may hold the key for further integration of China and the international financial market. Related measures include enhancing the RMB foreign exchange rate flexibility and China's capital account convertibility.

1. Introduction

China's equity market marked its 30th anniversary in 2020 and is already the second largest in the world in terms of capitalization. In its early years of development, the Chinese equity market suffered from limited financing capacity; even today, its governance structure, information disclosure, and transaction rules are not yet in line with the best practices. These shortcomings have forced some Chinese companies to list abroad or to cross-list on two or more exchanges to attract overseas funds, to enhance corporate governance and international reputation, and to expand their international market. Cross-listing also enables international investors to diversify their investment options and to hold shares of high-quality companies in emerging markets (EM) with less convertible capital accounts (SEC, 2012[1]). EM investors can also hedge their domestic assets with shares in developed markets (Auguste *et al.*, 2006).

Academics are particularly interested in the share price differences of the cross-listed firms. As a general rule, the stocks cross-listed between advanced markets share similar prices, while between advanced and emerging markets, stocks in advanced markets carry higher prices (Jithendranathan *et al.*, 2000; Bae *et al.*, 2008; Stigler *et al.*, 2010). China does not follow this rule. First, the share prices in the A-share market have been higher than the share prices in Hong Kong (H-share) and the

[1] SEC (2012).

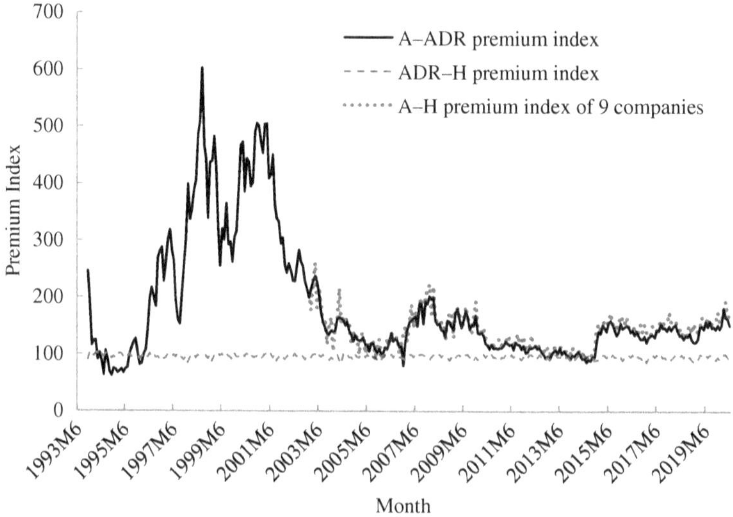

Figure 1. A-H, A-ADR, and ADR-H premiums.

Note: ADR-H premium index is based on 15 Chinese stocks cross-listed in the main boards of the US and Hong Kong; A-ADR and A-H premium indices are based on nine Chinese stocks listed in China, Hong Kong, and the US; all are a capitalization-weighted average of monthly share price data.

American Depository Receipts (ADRs) in the United States. Second, after the introduction of Shanghai–Hong Kong Connect (November 2014) and Shenzhen–Hong Kong Connect (December 2016) (hereafter, SH Connect, to include both), the connectivity of the markets has increased, yet both the A-H premium and A-ADR premium have surged (Zhang *et al.*, 2020).

In Figure 1, monthly A-ADR and A-H premium indices are calculated using a similar formula to that of the HSAHP, an index of the weighted average of the cross-listed A-share and H-share price differences based on the capitalization in circulation.[2] During the period from January 2002 to June 2020, the A-ADR premium index averaged around 142.0 and the A-H premium index around 143.4 for the 9 companies listed in the

[2]We construct an A-ADR premium index and an AH premium index by applying the formula of the Hang Seng China AH Premium Index (total market value of the constituent stocks using their A-share prices against that using their H-share prices). Considering that ADR conversion ratio varies across stocks and time, we convert A- and H-shares in circulation into ADR shares, and A-share and H-share prices are also converted into US dollar per ADR share.

three markets. Since H and ADR are fungible, the weighted premiums of H-shares are less than 1% of those of ADRs; as such, this chapter focuses on A-ADR and A-H premiums and their causes.

The evolution of different premiums can be divided into four periods. In period 1 (1993–2003), A-ADR premium rates had an extremely high average of 263.5. In this period, the Chinese market was in its primary stage of development; good companies were highly valued domestically but received limited attention when listed overseas. In period 2 (2004–2009), the A-ADR premium index shrank to 144.4, while the A-H premium index of the 9 companies was 149.0. During this period, the strong Chinese economy and rapid opening up lifted the enthusiasm of overseas investors of Chinese companies and, in turn, these companies' evaluation in the US markets. Chinese equity markets also went through drastic reform and expansion, both of which promoted the valuation of cross-listed companies. In period 3 (2010–2014), the A-ADR premium index further reduced to 108.7, while the A-H premium index of the same 9 companies was 116.7. Notably, the listing of Alibaba, Jingdong, and other high-quality Chinese companies in the US after 2013 energized the overall ADR prices. In period 4 (2015–June 2020), the A-ADR premium index expanded to 143.2, and the A-H premium index of the 9 listed companies was 153.9. The reasons for such changes may include, among others, the introduction of SH Connect in November 2014, the recovery of A-shares from the market volatility experienced in 2015, the effects of the pandemic that broke out in 2020, the Luckin Coffee incident, and geopolitical tensions between China and the US.

This chapter compares A-ADR and A-H premiums using a sample of 9 China–Hong Kong–US cross-listed equities and 116 China–Hong Kong cross-listed equities from January 2002 to June 2020. We analyze the

---

$$\text{A-ADR Premium Index}_{i,t} = \frac{\sum_{i=1}^{9} \text{Implied ADR Price of A-share}_{i,t} \cdot \text{Stocks in Circulation}_{i,t} / \text{ADR Conversion Ratio}_{i,t}}{\sum_{i=1}^{9} \text{ADR Price}_{i,t} \cdot \text{Stocks in Circulation}_{i,t} / \text{ADR Conversion Ratio}_{i,t}}$$

$$\text{A-H Premium Index}_{i,t} = \frac{\sum_{i=1}^{9} \text{A-Share Price}_{i,t} \cdot \text{Stocks in Circulation}_{i,t}}{\sum_{i=1}^{9} \text{H-Share Price}_{i,t} \cdot (\text{HKD/RMB Exchange Rate})_{t} \cdot \text{Stocks in Circulation}_{i,t}}$$

where i denotes individual stocks, t denotes date, and Implied ADR Price of A-share$_{i,t}$ = [Price in Renminbi$_{i,t}$/(Renminbi/USD spot exchange rate)$_t$] ADR Conversion ratio$_{i,t}$.

micro-, meso-, and macro-level factors in determining the premiums. To examine the policy impacts of foreign exchange rate reform and financial openness, we construct a two-period two-country model and prove that in certain scenarios, both policies can help reduce price differences. Further, we simulate the impacts of these two policy changes on premiums in a more generalized scenario using numerical analysis. Our empirical analyses confirm the results of the model with the quantitative impacts of macro-level factors such as financial openness and the US dollar index, meso-level factors (market sentiments), and micro-level factors (dividend ratio, speculative incentives, liquidity of individual shares, information asymmetry).

This chapter contributes to the existing literature in four areas. First, it constructs a model to explore foreign exchange rate expectations, financial openness, information asymmetry, and short selling on the share price differences. Most previous theoretical models conduct qualitative analysis of one factor in a framework of infinite periods (Greenwood *et al.*, 2018; Eichler *et al.*, 2009; Stulz & Wasserfallen, 1995; Chen *et al.*, 2002). These models are mainly based on the Gordon Growth Formula and target issues related to dividend payment and speculation incentives as well as heterogeneity (Mei *et al.*, 2009), making it difficult to examine multiple factors including policy impacts in a single framework. Second, it investigates the systematic jump of A-H and A-ADR premiums using individual share prices and tests the effectiveness of financial openness and foreign exchange rates in reducing share price differences. Previously, only Zhang *et al.* (2020) noted the surge in the Hang Sheng A-H premium index after the introduction of SH Connect and examined the issue from a macro perspective. Third, this chapter examines the relative importance of different factors in explaining the share price differences, and our models are much more powerful than most previous empirical studies using individual share prices. Fourth, it extends the data of similar studies to mid-2020 with a more careful selection of samples and added stability tests. Specifically, we exclude shares in the US OTC market as used in the work of Arquette *et al.* (2008) to ensure the effectiveness of the empirical tests. Moreover, we include a large sample of A-H share premium to add stability to our tests and extra implications to the empirical results.

This chapter is organized into five sections. Following this introductory section, Section 2 reviews the literature on cross-listed equity share price differences. Section 3 constructs a two-period two-country model to evaluate the impacts of foreign exchange rate expectations and financial opening on the price differences. Section 4 conducts empirical analysis of A-ADR and A-H premiums and explores the reasons for their changes. Section 5 concludes with policy suggestions.

2. Literature Review

According to the law of one price, the prices of the same commodity or asset in different markets should be similar if the commodity or asset can be transacted between markets. If the markets are segregated, price differences will remain (Lamont & Thaler, 2003). With regard to the share prices of cross-listed firms, the price differences may stem from micro-level factors such as an individual share's liquidity, information asymmetry, and supply; meso-level factors such as transaction rules and market liquidity; and macro-level factors such as capital control and foreign exchange.

2.1 *Impacts of micro-level factors on premiums*

Micro-level factors such as share liquidity, information asymmetry, and share supply affect share price premiums through different channels. Chan *et al.* (2008) and Atanasova & Li (2018) find that liquidity affects ADR and their respective home country share prices; the latter study regards the transmission mechanism as including institutional transactions and the holding costs of the equity. Amihud (2002) considers that prices of illiquid shares consist of a liquidity premium compensation component, while Amihud *et al.* (2015) further note the evidence of significant positive illiquid return premium in the global equity markets.

Several empirical studies prove the information asymmetry hypothesis, that is, the less the information differs, the lower the share price premium (Hu & Wang, 2008; Chen & Zhou, 2009; Chen & Tan, 2013; Pascual *et al.*, 2006; Chen & Choi, 2012; Frijns & Zwinkels, 2018). Sun & Tong (2000) use market capitalization of listed companies to measure information asymmetry and find this indicator has strong explanatory power in explaining A-B and A-H premiums. The rationale is that large companies have lower information asymmetry, owing to their high profile and larger amount of public information. Beckmann *et al.* (2015) find that information asymmetry caused the misvaluation of 482 ADRs from

33 countries from 1995 to 2012. Lu *et al.* (2018) argue that the main cause of the rising A-H premium after the introduction of SH Connect is information asymmetry. In addition, a recent study by Wu *et al.* (2020) points out that the relative supply of share can explain 53% of A-H premium, as such an increase in the Chinese equity supply will result in a reduction of A-H premium.

2.2 *Impacts of meso-level factors on premiums*

Meso-level factors include transaction rules and investor structure. The rules in Hong Kong and the US normally represent the best international practices, but some rules in China do not. In general, the US and Hong Kong exchanges have strict requirements and procedures for listing and delisting, mechanisms for information disclosure, and corporate governance. In comparison, Chinese equity markets suffer from limited market tools and less efficient transaction rules, especially information disclosure requirements. Moreover, the A-share market is dominated by individual investors with strong speculative incentives as shown in its high turnover ratio and short investment terms. For example, overseas investors and institutional investors account for 3% and 20% respectively in the A-share market, far below the percentages of such investors in the H-share market (46% and 60%, respectively) and US market (16% and 62.4%, respectively).

The institutional set-ups have helped the US and Hong Kong equity markets in price discovery, share transactions, and risk management. The rules in Hong Kong and the US on initial public offerings, repos, and delisting are more flexible in seasoned and rights issues. This makes their market liquidity theoretically better than that of the Chinese market. For example, Chinese markets have adopted $T+1$, meaning that investors can sell the shares they purchased on or after the next trading day. In Hong Kong and the US, there is no such constraint under the $T+0$ rule, which enables short selling. $T+0$ can improve market liquidity but has higher requirements for the risk management of investors. Moreover, Hong Kong allows more structured products and derivatives, but in the mainland, net shorting is prohibited. Further, the mainland has different rules on trading hours, daily price limits (daily fluctuation limit is capped at 10%), and margin trading, and some rules have partly prevented arbitrage between the two markets.

Several studies note that allowing for short sale can reduce share price premium. Huang *et al.* (2015) found that the relaxation of short sale constraints helped reduce A-H premium for 57 cross-listed companies during the period from 2009 to 2013. Blau *et al.* (2012) point out that ADR of one country is more prone to shorting if that country prohibits short selling as ADR may be under more frequent temporary misvaluation.

Many studies confirm the impacts of US market sentiments on ADR price and ADR premium (Grossmann *et al.*, 2007; Chan *et al.*, 2008; Chen & Zhou, 2009; Wu & Chen, 2015; Wu *et al.*, 2017). In addition, both Kadiyala & Kadiyala (2004) and Arquette *et al.* (2008) found that company sentiment and market sentiment (both measured by P/E ratio) have significant impacts on A-ADR premium.

2.3 *Impacts of macro-level factors on premiums*

On the macro-level, China, Hong Kong, and the US markets differ in terms of capital flow and foreign exchange rate arrangements. Capital accounts are convertible in Hong Kong and the US but not in China where there are constraints regarding the primary equity market and individual investment abroad. Moreover, the US dollar is the major reserve currency, and the HK dollar is pegged to it under a currency board arrangement, while RMB follows a managed floating arrangement with reference to a currency basket. China has made efforts to enhance the flexibility of the RMB foreign exchange rate, and on August 11, 2015, the foreign exchange rate market makers started to make quotations to the China Foreign Exchange Transaction Center using the previous day's closure rate. This enables the foreign exchange rate to better reflect the market demand and supply. Another landmark event happened in August 2019 when the US dollar to RMB exchange rate surpassed 7; subsequently, RMB flexibility has notably improved. Since 7 is no longer the ceiling for RMB to US dollar rate, flexibility of the RMB foreign exchange rate and, in turn, China's monetary policy have been substantially enhanced.

Many studies have confirmed the impacts of foreign exchange rates on share price premium. RMB foreign exchange rate devaluation expectation (or US dollar appreciation expectation) is frequently used as a determinant for the expansion of A-H and A-ADR premiums (Grammig *et al.*, 2005; Arquette *et al.*, 2008; Eichler *et al.*, 2009; Eichler, 2011; Grossmann *et al.*, 2017). Specifically, Arquette *et al.* (2008) found that the foreign exchange expectation can explain 40% of A-H and A-ADR premium changes. Li & Wu (2016) identified foreign exchange rate arrangement changes as able to affect share price premium, although to a lesser degree.

Financial openness affects share price premium via different pricing mechanisms due to market segregation (Hietala, 1989; Baruch *et al.*, 2007; Gagnon & Karolyi, 2010; Goldstein *et al.*, 2014; Greenwood *et al.*, 2018; Ding *et al.*, 2020). Hu & Wang (2008) found that A-H premium is mainly caused by market segregation and China's capital control. Using Argentina and Venezuela data from the early 2000s, Auguste *et al.* (2006) found that capital outflow control can enlarge home country share prices over ADR premium by affecting domestic demand. However, some other studies do not concur with these findings on the impacts of capital control and find instead that share price premium is mainly a result of transaction costs and market liquidity (Rabinovitch *et al.*, 2003).

In recent years, the impacts of SH Connect on A-H premium have received much attention. Chan & Kwok (2015) and Nishimura *et al.* (2018) found that SH Connect has enhanced the price discovery capacity of A-shares and H-shares. Zhang *et al.* (2020) analyzed the systematic increase of A-H premium index after 2015 and found that the US dollar index and the investors' expectations of the Chinese economy can explain such increases. Earlier studies focus more on the impacts of SH Connect on capital flow and market connectivity. Burdekin & Siklos (2018) and Lu *et al.* (2018) provide evidence that impacts of capital flow through SH Connect on A-H premium are insignificant. Although following the introduction of SH Connect, the relationship between the indices of the two markets (Huo *et al.*, 2018; Ma *et al.*, 2019) and the correlations of individual share prices (Chan & Kwok, 2015) has been enhanced, the connectivity of the two markets has not (Ma *et al.*, 2019).

3. Model

Our model refers to existing theoretical studies on asset prices and price disparity. Most of these focus on the impact of a single factor or conduct qualitative analysis in an economic framework of infinite period. First, the impact of financial openness on asset prices and price disparity is based on the market segmentation theory. Relevant studies include Errunza & Losq (1985, 1989), Alexander *et al.* (1987), Domowitz *et al.* (1997), Baruch *et al.* (2007), Greenwood *et al.* (2018), and Pavlidis & Vasilopoulos

(2020). Second, the impact of exchange rate expectations on price disparity is straightforward in theory, and we refer to the empirical study of Eichler (2011). Third, studies on the impacts of information asymmetry or information friction on asset prices and price disparity are mainly based on the framework of Grossman & Stiglitz (1980). We assume that domestic investors have the information advantage as in Stulz & Wasserfallen (1995). Fourth, existing theoretical studies of the impact of short sale constraints on asset prices are mainly based on the framework of Miller (1977) and Harrison & Kreps (1978). Among these studies, many (e.g., Chen *et al*., 2002) have introduced investors' heterogeneous expectations, and we follow suit in our model. In addition, some studies discuss the influence of multiple factors on asset prices and price disparity in one framework; for example, Diamond & Verrecchia (1987) and Hong & Stein (2003) consider the roles of information friction and short sale constraints. We refer to these studies to extend our model.

This chapter explores the impacts of financial openness, foreign exchange rate expectation, information friction, and short sale constraints on the price disparity of cross-listed shares in one model. To avoid the computational complexity of quantitative analysis in an economic framework with infinite periods, we consider an open economy with two periods. Specifically, we assume domestic firms can issue equities (hereinafter called risky assets) in both home and foreign capital markets. That is, a Chinese firm can issue shares in China (A-share), Hong Kong (H-share), and the US (ADR). Owing to different institutional set-ups and consequent market segregation, the share prices of one firm in different markets are not necessarily equal, meaning that the law of one price may not hold. For simplification purposes, we standardize the quantity of risky assets in home and foreign markets as 1. We also assume an infinite number of investors in both markets, where a domestic investor is denoted by $i \in [0,1]$ and a foreign investor $j \in [0,1]$, and the sum of each type of investor equals 1.

3.1 *Structure of the model*

3.1.1 *Domestic investors*

Assume that the utility function of a domestic investor i is constant absolute risk aversion (CARA) preference, then

$$U_i = \mathbb{E}_i\left[-\exp(-\gamma \widetilde{W}_i)\right],$$

where $\mathbb{E}_i$ is the expectation operator of investor *i*, $\widetilde{W}_i$ represents wealth in the 2nd period, and γ represents the degree of risk aversion. In the model, a domestic investor can invest in risk-free and risky assets in the home market. The demands for these two assets are B_i and D_i, respectively. X_i is the demand for the risky asset issued by domestic firms in the foreign market. The nominal prices of the risky assets in the home and foreign markets are q and q^*, respectively. Exchange rates in periods 1 and 2 are denoted as e_0 and e_1, representing the amount of foreign currency that can be exchanged by 1 unit of home currency. Higher e_0 or e_1 means appreciation of home currency in the period. After normalizing the exchange rate in the first period to one, we obtain the budget constraint in period 1:

$$W = qD_i + q^*X_i + B_i.$$

The value of the risky asset in both markets is $\tilde{v}$ in home currency (i.e. RMB) in period 2, so the return for investors in the domestic market is $\tilde{v}D_i$. Each unit of the risky asset issued by a domestic firm in the foreign market is worth $e_1\tilde{v}$ in period 2. Since domestic investors only care about their investment return in home currency, the return from the risky asset in foreign markets equals to $\tilde{v}$ in home currency. In this case, investors are not subject to exchange rate risk when investing across markets. After normalizing the return of the risk-free asset to one, the wealth in period 2 can be expressed as

$$\widetilde{W}_i = \tilde{v}(D_i + X_i) + B_i = W + (\tilde{v} - q)D_i + (\tilde{v} - q^*)X_i.$$

Assume the value of the risky asset $\tilde{v}$ is determined by

$$\tilde{v} = v + \varepsilon_v,$$

where ε_v is normally distributed, i.e., $\varepsilon_v \sim \mathcal{N}(0,\sigma_v)$. After substituting B_i into the utility function, we simplify the optimization problem of investor *i* as choosing D_i and X_i to maximize U_i. Therefore, we can obtain the demands for risky assets in home and foreign markets:

$$D_i = \frac{\mathbb{E}_i[\tilde{v}] - q}{\gamma \mathbb{V}_i[\tilde{v}]}, \tag{1}$$

$$X_i = \frac{\mathbb{E}_i[\tilde{v}] - q^*}{\gamma \mathbb{V}_i[\tilde{v}]}, \tag{2}$$

where $\mathbb{V}_i[\tilde{v}]$ stands for the subjective variance of $\tilde{v}$ resulting from the information or beliefs biases of investor *i*.

3.1.2 *Foreign investors*

The utility function of foreign investor *j* follows CARA preference:

$$U_j^* = \mathbb{E}_j[-\exp(-\gamma^* \widetilde{W}_j^*)],$$

where $\widetilde{W}_j^*$ is investor *j*'s wealth in the second period and γ^* is the degree of risk aversion. We assume $\gamma^* = \gamma$ as the impacts of risk aversion on price disparity are beyond the scope of this chapter. Foreign investor *j* begins with an endowment of W^* in period 1, which can be invested in both the risk-free and risky assets issued by domestic firms in the foreign market. Demands for these two assets are B_j^* and D_j^*, respectively. The price of the risky asset is q^*. Investor *j* can also buy risky assets issued by domestic firms in the domestic market, whose demand is represented by X_j^*. Therefore, the budget constraint for *j* is

$$W^* = q^* D_j^* + qX_j^* + B_j^*.$$

Now, we standardize the return of the risk-free asset as 1 and express the wealth of investor *j* in the 2nd period as

$$\widetilde{W}_j^* = \tilde{v}^*(D_j^* + X_j^*) + B_j^* = W^* + (\tilde{v}^* - q^*)D_j^* + (\tilde{v}^* - q)X_j^*,$$

where $\tilde{v}^*$ is the return of 1 unit of domestic risk assets of the foreign investor. Since the foreign investor shares a similar optimization preference with the domestic investor, demands for his/her risky assets are

$$D_j^* = \frac{\mathbb{E}_j[\tilde{v}^*] - q^*}{\gamma \mathbb{V}_j[\tilde{v}^*]}, \tag{3}$$

$$X_j^* = \frac{\mathbb{E}_j[\tilde{v}^*] - q}{\gamma \mathbb{V}_j[\tilde{v}^*]}. \tag{4}$$

Assume the exchange rate in period 2 is

$$e_1 = e + \varepsilon_e,$$

where $e \in [e_L, e_H]$ is the unconditional expected value ($\mathbb{E}[e_1] = e$) and $_e$ follows a normal distribution, $\varepsilon_e \sim \mathcal{N}(0, \sigma_e)$. Although one unit of the domestic asset in both markets has the same value $\tilde{v}$, the foreign investor needs to adjust it by exchange rate $\tilde{e}$:

$$\tilde{v}^* = e_1 \tilde{v}.$$

An increase in e_1 (appreciation of domestic currency) will increase the returns of the risky asset in the foreign market for foreign investors. Thus, the domestic currency appreciation expectation will raise demand for the risky asset in the foreign market.

3.1.3 *Market clearing*

Assume that financial markets are not fully open, and only a domestic investor $i \in [0, \theta]$ and a foreign investor $j \in [0, \theta^*]$ can invest in both markets. We only consider the case with symmetric market openness, $\theta^* = \theta$. Then the market clearing conditions for risky assets in the domestic and foreign markets are

$$\int_0^1 D_i di + \int_0^\theta X_j^* dj = 1, \tag{5}$$

$$\int_0^1 D_j^* di + \int_0^\theta X_j dj = 1. \tag{6}$$

Here, θ can be the degree of openness in capital markets, where θ = 0 means completely closed, and $\theta = 1$, completely open. As informational frictions are not factored in, there is no need to take noise trade into account for market clearing conditions. Given data constraints in China, we assume that policies such as SH Connect, QFII, and RQFII can affect θ. We can also use quantitative constraints as a measure of financial openness. For example, assume all investors can participate in both markets, but investments by domestic and foreign investors are subject to some limits such that $X_i \leq \bar{X}$ and $X_j^* \leq \bar{X}^*$. Then, larger $\bar{X}$ or $\bar{X}^*$ stand for fewer capital flow restrictions and a higher degree of openness.

In this chapter, we denote the aggregate trading volume in the domestic market by foreign investors as X^* and the aggregate trading volume in the foreign market by domestic investors as X^*. Then we can have $X^* = \int_0^\theta X_j^* dj$ and $X = \int_0^\theta X_i di$. When constraints on trading restrictions are binding, then $\bar{X}^* = \int_0^\theta X_j^* dj$ and $X^* = \int_0^\theta X_i di$. That is, an increase in θ has the same meaning as an increase in $\bar{X}$ and $\bar{X}^*$ in the quantity constraint model. Although these two methods have the same properties in describing the extent of market openness, for numerical analysis, it is simpler to use the value of θ as the degree of openness in capital markets.

3.2 *Characteristics of equilibrium price and price disparity*

Assume all investors carry rational expectations and face the same information, that is, $\mathbb{E}_i(\cdot) = \mathbb{E}_j(\cdot) = \mathbb{E}(\cdot)$ and $\mathbb{V}_i(\cdot) = \mathbb{V}_j(\cdot) = \mathbb{V}(\cdot)$. After substituting the demand equations (1) and (4) into the domestic market clearing condition (5) and substituting demand equations (2) and (3) into the foreign market clearing condition (6), we can obtain price equations for risky assets in both markets:

$$q = \varphi \mathbb{E}[\tilde{v}] + (1-\varphi)\mathbb{E}[\tilde{v}^*] - \gamma\varphi \mathbb{V}[\tilde{v}], \tag{7}$$

$$q^* = \varphi^* \mathbb{E}[\tilde{v}^*] + (1-\varphi^*)\mathbb{E}[\tilde{v}] - \gamma\varphi^* \mathbb{V}[\tilde{v}^*], \tag{8}$$

where

$$\varphi = \frac{\mathbb{V}[\tilde{v}^*]}{\mathbb{V}[\tilde{v}^*] + \theta\mathbb{V}[\tilde{v}]} = \frac{v^2\sigma_e + \sigma_v(e^2+\sigma_e)}{v^2\sigma_e + \sigma_v(e^2+\sigma_e) + \theta\sigma_v},$$

$$\varphi^* = \frac{\mathbb{V}[\tilde{v}]}{\mathbb{V}[\tilde{v}] + \theta\mathbb{V}[\tilde{v}^*]} = \frac{1-\varphi}{1-\varphi+\varphi\theta^2}.$$

Hence, $\frac{\partial\varphi}{\partial e} = \frac{2\theta\sigma_v^2 e}{(v^2\sigma_e + \sigma_v(e^2+\sigma_e)+\theta\sigma_v)^2} > 0$ and $\frac{\partial\varphi^*}{\partial e} = -\frac{\theta^2}{(1-\varphi+\varphi\theta^2)^2}\frac{\partial\varphi}{\partial e} < 0$. That is, the appreciation expectation of the domestic currency will affect the weight of pricing and, in turn, the prices in the two markets. We define price disparity function as $\Gamma = q - q^*$, from which we can obtain the following price disparity function:

$$\Gamma = \frac{\varphi(1-\varphi)(1-\theta^2)}{1-\varphi+\varphi\theta^2}(\mathbb{E}[\tilde{v}] - \mathbb{E}[\tilde{v}^*]) + \gamma\frac{1-\varphi}{1-\varphi+\varphi\theta^2}\mathbb{V}[\tilde{v}^*] - \gamma\varphi\mathbb{V}[\tilde{v}].$$

From $\varphi = \frac{\mathbb{V}[\tilde{v}^*]}{\mathbb{V}[\tilde{v}^*]+\theta\mathbb{V}[\tilde{v}]}$, we can obtain $\mathbb{V}[\tilde{v}^*] = \frac{\varphi}{1-\varphi}\theta\mathbb{V}[\tilde{v}]$ and then substitute it in the price disparity functions:

$$\Gamma = \frac{\varphi(1-\varphi)(1-\theta^2)}{1-\varphi(1-\theta^2)} v(1-e) + \gamma\left(\frac{\theta}{1-\varphi(1-\theta^2)} - 1\right)\varphi\sigma_v. \tag{9}$$

Note that price disparity can also be denoted as $\tilde{\Gamma} = \frac{q-q^*}{q^*} = \frac{q}{q^*} - 1$. Since having the same properties in the form of differences and ratios will complicate calculations, and given that Γ and $\tilde{\Gamma}$ share similar monotonic properties, we use $\Gamma = q - q^*$ as the price disparity function in our model.

3.2.1 *Impacts of exchange rate expectation on price disparity*

To study the relationship between expectations on exchange rate and price disparity, we first examine two extreme cases, in which $\theta = 0$ and $\theta = 1$, and then $0 < \theta < 1$.

Assumption 1. $\gamma < \bar{\gamma}$, where $\bar{\gamma} = \frac{v}{2\sigma_v e_H}$.
Under Assumption 1, $\gamma < \frac{v}{2\sigma_v e}$ always holds. Since σ_v is smaller than v, $\bar{\gamma}$ is still relatively larger even when e_H is large. This makes $\gamma < \bar{\gamma}$ a reasonable assumption.

Proposition 1. *When $\theta = 0$, the greater the expected depreciation of domestic currency (smaller e), the larger the price disparity; the higher the expected appreciation in domestic currency (larger e), the smaller the price disparity. That is, when $\theta = 0$, then $\frac{\partial \Gamma}{\partial e} < 0$. When $\theta = 1$, then $\Gamma = 0$, and the law of one price holds.*

Proof. When $\theta = 0$, then $\varphi^* = \varphi = 1$, and the price disparity $\Gamma = v(1 - e) + \gamma[v^2\sigma_e + \sigma_v(e^2 + \sigma_e) - \sigma_v]$. As a result, we have $\frac{\partial \Gamma}{\partial e} = 2\gamma\sigma_v e - v$. Also, Assumption 1, that $\gamma < \bar{\gamma}$, can yield $\frac{\partial \Gamma}{\partial e} < 0$. When $\theta = 1$, $\varphi^* = 1 - \varphi$. After substituting $\varphi^* = 1 - \varphi$ into the price disparity function, it can be shown that $\Gamma = 0$, which means that $\frac{\partial \Gamma}{\partial e} = 0$. ■

In a closed economy, $\varphi^* = \varphi = 1$ means that the exchange rate does not affect the asset prices in the domestic market (q) but does affect the price disparity by influencing the price in the foreign market (q^*). With complete financial openness, the price disparity means arbitrage opportunities, while the free flow of capital will make the market arbitrage opportunities disappear. Then, the law of one price prevails, and the change of exchange rate will not affect the price disparity.

In the case that $0 < \theta < 1$, numerical analysis is needed to assess the effects of the expected exchange rate on price disparity.

3.2.2 *Effects of capital market financial openness on price disparity*

In a financial market that is fully open ($\theta = 1$ and $\varphi^* = 1 - \varphi$), price disparity $\Gamma = 0$ always holds. Hence, without considering distortions from information, expectations, and market microstructures, the law of one price always holds in an open market. In a closed financial market (e.g., $e = 1$), price disparity is $\Gamma = \gamma\sigma_e(v^2 + \sigma_v)$. Intuitively, with the opening up of a financial market, the price disparity will decline.

To simplify the analysis of the relationship between market openness and price disparity, we remove the effects of exchange rate expectations by setting $\mathbb{E}[e_1] = e_0$.

Proposition 2. *If* $\mathbb{E}[e_1] = e_0$, *the larger the extent of capital market openness (larger θ), the smaller the asset price disparity, i.e.,* $\frac{\partial\Gamma}{\partial\theta} < 0$. (The proof is in Appendix A1.)

Hence, in the case of $e \neq 1$, numerical analysis is also needed to assess the effects of financial openness on price disparity. The above discussions demonstrate that in general, expected appreciation of domestic currency and enhanced openness of financial markets can reduce price discrepancy. More specific situations require numerical analysis and simulation (Appendix A2).

3.3 *Model extensions*

3.3.1 *Effects of information frictions*

To examine the impacts of information frictions on price differences, we assume that there exists noise trade in domestic and foreign markets with trading volumes of N and N^*, respectively. Both are normally distributed, $N \sim \mathcal{N}(0,\sigma_N)$ and $N^* \sim \mathcal{N}(0,\sigma_N^*)$. Assume that both domestic and foreign investors receive private signals about $\tilde{v}$ (denoted by s and s^*, respectively), which are determined as follows:

$$s = \tilde{v} + \varepsilon,$$

$$s^* = \tilde{v} + \varepsilon^*,$$

where $\varepsilon \sim \mathcal{N}(0,1/\tau_\varepsilon)$ and $\varepsilon^* \sim \mathcal{N}(0,1/\tau_\varepsilon^*)$, and τ_ε and τ_ε^* are the accuracy of private signals for domestic investors and foreign investors, respectively.

Assume $\varepsilon = \sqrt{\kappa \varepsilon^*}$, we then have $\tau_\varepsilon^* = \kappa \tau_\varepsilon$ $(0 < \kappa \leq 1)$. Hence, a higher κ means less information asymmetry between two countries. Given that foreign investors receive poorer signals, they may learn from public information, such as asset prices q and q^*. To reduce the computation complexity from learning mechanisms of foreign investors, we assume that the size of noise trade is large enough and that $1/\sigma_N$ and $1/\sigma_N^*$ are close to 0. Then, we can have $\mathbb{E}[\tilde{v}|s] \simeq \mathbb{E}[\tilde{v}|s, q, q^*]$ and $\mathbb{E}[\tilde{v}^*|s^*] \simeq \mathbb{E}[\tilde{v}^*|s^*, q, q^*]$, which means that noise trade invalidates public signals. According to Bayes' theorem, the introduction of information frictions will cause expectations of domestic investors to have the following properties:

$$\mathbb{E}_i[\tilde{v}] = \mathbb{E}[\tilde{v}|s] = v + \lambda(s - v),$$

$$\mathbb{V}_i[\tilde{v}] = \mathbb{V}[\tilde{v}|s] = \frac{1}{\tau_v + \tau_\varepsilon},$$

where $\lambda = \frac{\tau_\varepsilon}{\tau_v + \tau_\varepsilon}$ and $\tau_v = 1/\sigma_v$. As this section focuses on the effects of information frictions, we hold the exchange rate in the second period constant, i.e., $e_1 = e_0$. Then, the expectations of foreign investors are characterized by

$$\mathbb{E}_j[\tilde{v}^*] = \mathbb{E}[\tilde{v}^*|s^*] = v + \lambda^*(s^* - v),$$

$$\mathbb{V}_j[\tilde{v}^*] = \mathbb{V}[\tilde{v}^*|s^*] = \frac{1}{\tau_v + \tau_\varepsilon^*} = \frac{1}{\tau_v + \kappa\tau_\varepsilon}.,$$

where $\lambda^* = \frac{\tau_\varepsilon^*}{\tau_v + \tau_\varepsilon^*} = \frac{\kappa\tau_\varepsilon}{\tau_v + \kappa\tau_\varepsilon}$. In the presence of noise traders, the market clearing conditions become

$$\int_0^1 D_i di + \int_0^\theta X_j^* dj + N = 1,$$

$$\int_0^1 D_j^* dj + \int_0^\theta X_i di + N^* = 1.$$

As such, the price functions can be written as

$$q = \varphi\mathbb{E}[\tilde{v}|s] + (1 - \varphi)\mathbb{E}[\tilde{v}^*|s^*] - \gamma(1 - N)\varphi\mathbb{V}[\tilde{v}|s],$$

$$q^* = \varphi^*\mathbb{E}[\tilde{v}^*|s^*] + (1 - \varphi^*)\mathbb{E}[\tilde{v}^*|s^*] - \gamma(1 - N^*)\varphi^*\mathbb{V}[\tilde{v}^*|s^*],$$

where $\varphi = \frac{\mathbb{V}[\tilde{v}^* | s^*]}{\mathbb{V}[\tilde{v}^* | s^*] + \theta \mathbb{V}[\tilde{v} | s]}$ and $\varphi^* = \frac{\mathbb{V}[\tilde{v} | s]}{\mathbb{V}[\tilde{v} | s] + \theta \mathbb{V}[\tilde{v}^* | s^*]}$. We can finally obtain the following price disparity function:

$$\Gamma = \frac{\varphi(1-\varphi)(1-\theta^2)}{1-\varphi+\varphi\theta^2}(\lambda(s-v) - \lambda^*(s^*-v)) + \gamma\frac{1-\varphi}{1-\varphi+\varphi\theta^2}\frac{1-N}{\tau_v+\kappa\tau_\varepsilon} - \gamma\varphi\frac{1-N^*}{\tau_v+\tau_\varepsilon},$$

where $\varphi = \frac{\tau_v+\tau_\varepsilon}{\tau_v+\tau_\varepsilon+\theta(\tau_v+\kappa\tau_\varepsilon)}$. Since noise trade is random, it only matters in the short run; in the long run, the expected price discrepancy can be written as

$$\begin{aligned}\mathbb{E}[\Gamma] &= \gamma\frac{1-\varphi}{1-\varphi+\varphi\theta^2}\frac{1}{\tau_v+\kappa\tau_\varepsilon} - \gamma\varphi\frac{1}{\tau_v+\tau_c} \\ &= \gamma\frac{(1-\theta)(1-\kappa)}{\tau_v+\kappa\tau_\varepsilon+\theta(\tau_v+\tau_\varepsilon)}\frac{\tau_\varepsilon}{\tau_v+\tau_\varepsilon+\theta(\tau_v+\kappa\tau_\varepsilon)}.\end{aligned}$$

Proposition 3. *The degree of information asymmetry is positively correlated with the expected price discrepancy, i.e.,* $\frac{\partial \mathbb{E}[\Gamma]}{\partial \kappa} < 0$.

Proof. Based on the formula of $\mathbb{E}[\Gamma]$, we can have $\frac{\partial \mathbb{E}[\Gamma]}{\partial \kappa} = -\frac{\mathbb{E}[\Gamma]}{1-\kappa}\{1 + \frac{(1+\theta)^2\tau_v + (1+2\theta\kappa+\theta^2)\tau_\varepsilon}{\gamma(1-\theta)}\mathbb{E}[\Gamma]\}$. Since $\mathbb{E}[\Gamma] > 0$, $\frac{\partial \mathbb{E}[\Gamma]}{\partial \kappa} < 0$. Hence, as the degree of asymmetric information becomes less severe, the expected price discrepancy decreases. ■

When financial markets are completely open, $\theta = 1$, so $\mathbb{E}[] = 0$. Hence, even with information asymmetry, the law of one price still holds.

3.3.2 *Heterogeneous expectations and short sale constraints*

In order to investigate the relationship between short sale constraints and asset price discrepancy, we assume that investors have heterogeneous expectations on asset prices. Using the DSSW model in the work of De Long *et al.* (1990), we assume that the expectations of domestic and foreign investors have the following properties:

$$\mathbb{E}_i[\tilde{v}] = v + \eta_i,$$
$$\mathbb{E}_j[\tilde{v}^*] = v^* + \eta_j^*,$$

where η_i and η_j^* represent distortions caused by irrational expectations with normal distributions, $\eta_i \sim \mathcal{N}(0, \sigma_\eta)$ and $\eta_j^* \sim \mathcal{N}(0, \sigma_\eta^*)$.

If $\eta_i > 0$, then domestic investors are more optimistic toward future returns of assets; if $\eta_j^* > 0$, then foreign investors are more optimistic, and vice versa. According to the DSSW model, this kind of expectation will not distort variance, i.e., $\mathbb{V}_i[\tilde{v}] = \mathbb{V}[\tilde{v}]$ and $\mathbb{V}_j[\tilde{v}^*] = \mathbb{V}[\tilde{v}^*]$. It has been proved that this form of expectation is equivalent to having a distorted factor in expectations, which makes expectation irrational (Hansen & Sargent, 2008; Jurado, 2016).

Without short sale constraints, demands from domestic investors in an open economy are the same as those in the previous section. Under the assumption of a fully open market, price functions can be derived as

$$q = \varphi \int_0^1 \mathbb{E}_i[\tilde{v}]di + (1-\varphi)\int_0^1 \mathbb{E}_j[\tilde{v}^*]dj - \gamma\varphi\mathbb{V}[\tilde{v}],$$
$$q^* = \varphi^* \int_0^1 \mathbb{E}_j[\tilde{v}^*]dj + (1-\varphi^*)\int_0^1 \mathbb{E}_i[\tilde{v}]di - \gamma^*\varphi^*\mathbb{V}[\tilde{v}^*].$$

Since η_i and j_i are both normally distributed, then $\int_0^1 \mathbb{E}_i[\tilde{v}] = \mathbb{E}[\tilde{v}]$ and $\int_0^1 \mathbb{E}_j[\tilde{v}^*]dj = \mathbb{E}[\tilde{v}^*]$. Intuitively, even though every individual investor has irrational expectations, average expectations can still be rational when all investors can participate. In this case, the price functions are the same as in the previous part with rational expectations. However, when there are short sale constraints in the domestic market, the demands of domestic and foreign investors are different:

$$D_i = \max\left\{0, \frac{\mathbb{E}_i[\tilde{v}] - q}{\gamma\mathbb{V}[\tilde{v}]}\right\}, \quad X_i = \frac{\mathbb{E}_i[\tilde{v}] - q^*}{\gamma\mathbb{V}[\tilde{v}]},$$
$$D_j^* = \frac{\mathbb{E}_j[\tilde{v}^*] - q^*}{\gamma^*\mathbb{V}[\tilde{v}^*]}, \quad X_j^* = \max\left\{0, \frac{\mathbb{E}_j[\tilde{v}^*] - q}{\gamma^*\mathbb{V}[\tilde{v}^*]}\right\}.$$

Since the foreign market does not limit short selling, its asset price q^* does not vary; only asset price in the domestic market affects changes in price discrepancy. Therefore, there exist $\bar{\eta} = q - v$ and $\bar{\eta}^* = q - ev$ such that when $\eta_i \leq \bar{\eta}$, foreign investments by domestic investors are 0; when $\eta_j^* \leq \bar{\eta}^*$, domestic investments by foreign investors are 0. Then, we can derive the following market clearing conditions:

$$\int_0^1 \frac{\mathbb{E}_i[\tilde{v}|\eta_i > \bar{\eta}] - q}{\gamma \mathbb{V}[\tilde{v}]} di + \int_0^1 \frac{\mathbb{E}_j[\tilde{v}^*|\eta_j^* > \bar{\eta}^*] - q}{\gamma^* \mathbb{V}[\tilde{v}^*]} dj = 1.$$

Therefore,

$$\int_0^1 \frac{\mathbb{E}_i[\tilde{v}] - q}{\gamma \mathbb{V}[\tilde{v}]} di + \int_0^1 \frac{\mathbb{E}_j[\tilde{v}^*] - q}{\gamma^* \mathbb{V}[\tilde{v}^*]} dj = 1 - D_\eta - X_\eta,$$

where $D_\eta = \int_0^1 \frac{q - \mathbb{E}_i[\tilde{v}|\eta_i \leq \bar{\eta}]}{\gamma \mathbb{V}[\tilde{v}]} di$, $X_\eta = \int_0^1 \frac{q - \mathbb{E}_j[\tilde{v}^*|\eta_j^* \leq \bar{\eta}^*]}{\gamma^* \mathbb{V}[\tilde{v}^*]} dj$. Then the price function is the following:

$$q = \bar{q} + \gamma\varphi(D_\eta + X_\eta)\mathbb{V}[\tilde{v}],$$

where $\bar{q} = \varphi \int_0^1 \mathbb{E}_i[\tilde{v}]di + (1-\varphi)\int_0^1 \mathbb{E}_j[\tilde{v}^*]dj - \gamma\varphi\mathbb{V}[\tilde{v}]$ is the asset price without restrictions on short sales.

Proposition 4. *Under heterogeneous expectations, the price in the domestic market with short sale constraints is higher than that without restrictions. That is,* $q > \bar{q}$.

Proof. From $\bar{\eta} = q - v$ and $\mathbb{E}_i[\tilde{v}|\eta_i \leq \bar{\eta}] \leq v + \bar{\eta}$, we can have $\mathbb{E}_i[\tilde{v}|\eta_i \leq \bar{\eta}] \leq v + \eta_i \leq v + \bar{\eta} = q$, which is equivalent to $\mathbb{E}_i[\tilde{v}|\eta_i \leq \bar{\eta}] \leq q.$. Therefore, we can have $\int_0^1 \{q - \mathbb{E}_i[\tilde{v}|\eta_i \leq \bar{\eta}]\}di > 0$, from which we can obtain $D_n > 0$. Similarly, it can be proven that $X_n > 0$. From $D_n > 0$ and $X_n > 0$, we obtain $q > \bar{q}$. ■

The above analysis demonstrates that short sale constraints will increase asset prices in the domestic market by $\gamma\varphi(D_\eta + X_\eta)\mathbb{V}[\tilde{v}]$. Since short sale constraints in the domestic market do not affect the asset prices in the foreign market q^*, the conclusion from Proposition 4 implies that relaxing short sale constraints will reduce price disparity. The above analysis shows that the law of one price always holds in a fully open market, regardless of information asymmetry. However, if we consider heterogeneous expectations by investors and short sale constraints in the domestic market, price discrepancy still exists. In conclusion, relaxing short sale constraints will narrow down price disparity in a fully open market.

4. Empirical Analysis

4.1 *Methodology and data*

Following Arquette *et al*. (2008), we define the ADR premiums of A-share and H-share firms as

$$\text{A-ADR Premium}_{i,t} = \frac{\text{Implied ADR Price of A-share}_{i,t} - \text{ADR Price}_{i,t}}{\text{Implied ADR Price of A-share}_{i,t}},$$

where i denotes individual stocks, t denotes date, Implied ADR Price of A-share$_{i,t}$ = [Price in Renminbi/(Renminbi/USD spot exchange rate)] · ADR Conversion ratio, and we consider offshore and onshore Renminbi/USD exchange rate. The A-share versus H-share premium is defined as

$$\text{A-H Premium}_{i,t} = \frac{\text{A-share Price}_{i,t} - \text{H-share Price}_{i,t} \cdot (\text{HKD/Renminbi exchange exchange rate})_t}{\text{A-share Price}_{i,t}}.$$

We follow Arquette *et al*. (2008), Beckmann *et al*. (2015), and Grossmann & Ngo (2020) to set up the ADR premiums determinant model:

$$\begin{aligned}\text{A-ADR Premium}_{i,t} = {} & \alpha_0 + \alpha_1 \text{ Expected Exchange Rate Change}_t \\ & + \alpha_2 \text{ Market Sentiment}_t + \alpha_3 \text{ Dividend Yield}_{i,t} \\ & + \alpha_4 \text{ Illiquidity}_{i,t} + \alpha_5 \text{ Speculative Motive}_{i,t} \\ & + \alpha_6 \text{ Information Asymmetry}_{i,t} + \varepsilon_{i,t},\end{aligned} \tag{10}$$

where i denotes the individual stocks and t denotes the date. The determinant models for A-H premium are set similarly, while definitions of some explanatory variables are appropriately adjusted. The definitions of explanatory variables and the related influence mechanism on the price premiums are presented as follows.

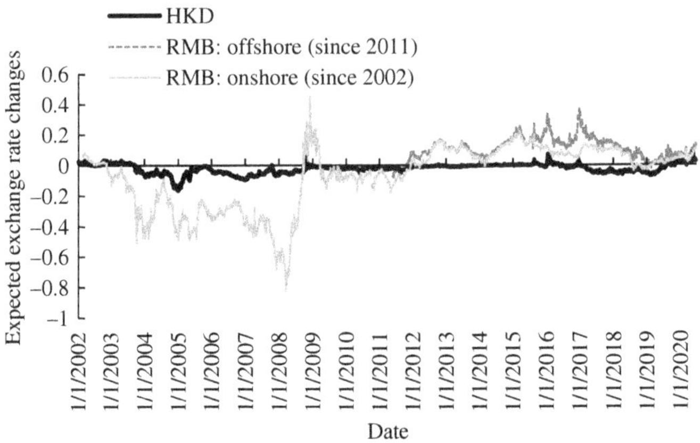

Figure 2. Expected exchange rate changes of renminbi and Hong Kong dollar.

Expected Exchange Rate Change$_t$ is a macro-level indicator of the predicted change in exchange rates implied by forward contract rates. Specifically, expected exchange rate changes of CNY (or CNH, offshore exchange rate) and HKD versus USD are defined as the corresponding forward rates minus spot exchange rates. The decline of Expected Exchange Rate Change$_t$ indicates expected appreciation of the local currency versus the US dollar. Figure 2 shows the trends based on 1 year forward (adopted from Arquette *et al*., 2008), while forward rates with a duration of 1 month, 3 months, or 6 months share a similar trend. The expected depreciation of offshore Renminbi exchange rate during 2015 and 2017 is significantly stronger than that of onshore exchange rate. As there are no forward exchange rates between the Hong Kong dollar and Renminbi, this variable is not included in the determinant analysis of A-H premium, and the influence of the exchange rate on A-H premium is mainly illustrated by the US dollar index.

Market Sentiment$_t$ is a variable at the stock market level, the ratio of price-to-sales ratios of stock indices (domestic market versus the US stock market, or mainland versus Hong Kong stock market). The price-to-sales ratio is used instead of the price-earning ratio, considering that some stocks have negative PE ratios (Arquette *et al*., 2008). For stock market indices, we choose the Shanghai A-Share Index, Hang Seng China Enterprises Index, and S&P 500 Index, respectively.

Dividend Yield$_{i,t}$ is an indicator for individual stocks, the dividend yield of A-share in the past 12 months. For A-H premium analysis, this variable is defined as a ratio of the dividend yield of A-share versus H-share in the past 12 months.

$\text{Illiquidity}_{i,t}$ is an indicator proposed by Amihud (2002) to measure stock level illiquidity. A higher value means more illiquidity, as one dollar of trading volume generates a larger price impact (absolute value of stock returns). Specifically, the illiquidity of stock *i* in month *t* is defined as

$$\text{Illiquidity}_{i,k} = \frac{1}{N_{i,t}} \sum_{d=1}^{N_{i,t}} \frac{|r_{i,d,k}|}{\text{Dvol}_{i,d,k}},$$

where $|r_{i,d,k}|$ is the absolute value of return on stock *i* on day *t* during month *k*, $Dvol_{i,d,k}$ is the trading volume in million US dollars of stock, and $N_{i,t}$ is the number of trading days (with non-zero trading volume) during month *k*. For the analysis of A-H premium, the ratio of this illiquidity indicator between A- and H-shares is used. Since the illiquidity indicator has a monthly frequency, it is replicated for each day in the same month, thus converted into daily data.

We follow Mei *et al*. (2009) to define a proxy for speculative motives, $\text{Speculative Motive}_{i,t}$; that is,

$$\tau_{it}^{A} = \ln(1 + \text{turnover}_{it}^{A}), \tau_{it}^{H} = \ln(1 + \text{turnover}_{it}^{H}),$$

where turnover_{it}^{A}, turnover_{it}^{H} are turnover rates of A-share and H-share, respectively. Mei *et al*. (2009) show that the speculative component in A-share prices is positively related to the turnover rate. Since turnover series of ADRs are not available, we employ τ_{it}^{A} as the proxy for speculative motive in A-ADR premium analysis. For A-H premium analysis, the speculative indicator is defined as τ_{it}^{A} minus τ_{it}^{H}.

$\text{Information Asymmetry}_{i,t}$ is a proxy of the standard deviation of stock prices within a month, as in the works of Beckmann *et al*. (2015) and Grossmann & Ngo (2020). Since multiple stock markets are involved, we use the ratio of the standard deviations between ADR and A-share for ADR premium analysis and use the ratio between A-share and H-share in the A-H premium analysis.

Several policy-related variables are also included in the empirical analysis, including financial openness and reform of stock market trading rules. Given that existing indices of China's capital account openness have few observations or barely change (such as the Chinn-Ito index and the capital account openness index released by the IMF), we introduce two financial openness measures *Openness1* and *Openness2* (annual data), where *Openness1* is the ratio of overseas assets and liabilities to GDP ratio, and *Openness2* is the ratio of overseas assets and liabilities (excluding foreign exchange reserves) to GDP. When analyzing the A-H premium, we consider Shanghai (Shenzhen)–Hong Kong Stock Connect as an important mechanism for financial openness and set dummy variables $D_{\text{SH Connect}}$ accordingly.

The relaxation of short sale constraints on A-share was a milestone of stock market reform in mainland China. The reform was implemented gradually applied to different stocks on different dates, as listed in Table A1 for our sample stocks. We define a policy dummy $D_{\text{short-sell}}$ according to the dates for individual stocks.

Our sample covers all cross-listed stocks in the US, mainland China, and Hong Kong stock exchanges (cross-listed stocks in the OTC market are excluded). Specifically, there are 9 A-ADR stock pairs (listed in the three markets) and 116 A-H stock pairs (Main Board and Small and Medium Enterprise Board in China's stock market), according to data accessed at the end of June 2020. The information and listing dates of the 9 companies are provided in Table A1, while the corresponding details for other A-H cross-listed companies are omitted for the sake of concision but are available upon request. The full sample period runs from February 1993 to June 2020 but is automatically restricted to January 2002 onward, due to the availability of forward exchange rates.

Data on individual stocks are retrieved from Wind Economic Database; these include daily stock prices, trading volumes, price-to-sale ratios, and dividend yields. From the same database, we also obtain price-to-sales ratios of stock market indices, including the S&P 500, Hang Seng China Enterprises Index, and Shanghai A-share Index. Some other series are extracted from DataStream, including spot exchange rate of CNY (and CNH) versus the US dollar, and CNY (and CNH) forward contract rates (with a duration of 1 year) versus USD. The financial openness indicators are constructed by the authors based on data from China's National Bureau of Statistics and State Administration of Foreign Exchange. Our sample constitutes unbalanced panel data.

Table 1 summarizes the descriptive statistics of selected variables. A-ADR premium averages around 30% and A-H premiums 35% for the whole sample. For the explanatory variables, the expected offshore RMB exchange rate depreciation is stronger than that of the onshore exchange rate. The price-to-sales ratio of A-shares is higher than that of ADRs, and

Table 1. Summary statistics for selected variables (January 2002–June 2020).

	Obs.	Mean	Std. Dev.	Min	Max
Panel A: Mainland China–US ADR Sample (9 A–ADR Stock Pairs)					
A-ADR premium (offshore RMB exchange rate, %)	21,933	29.362	19.572	–35.475	76.956
A-ADR premium (onshore RMB exchange rate, %)	35,768	34.900	21.702	–48.630	85.049
Expected exchange rate change (offshore)	2,375	0.110	0.070	–0.081	0.370
Expected exchange rate change (onshore)	4,604	–0.077	0.204	–0.827	0.452
Market sentiment (relative price-to-sales ratio)	4,741	1.100	0.616	0.430	3.580
Dividend yield	37,505	1.745	1.829	0.000	14.144
Illiquidity indicator	37,368	0.158	0.353	0.002	4.982
Speculative motive	34,895	0.555	0.542	0.000	4.091
Information asymmetry	37,368	1.300	0.639	0.133	8.855
Panel B: Mainland China–Hong Kong sample (116 A-H stock pairs)					
A-H premium (%)	273,214	35.009	25.828	–68.317	92.409
A-H premium (%, the 9 companies)	32,909	33.923	21.291	–30.948	85.447
Market sentiment (A-H)	4,565	0.702	0.216	0.248	1.383
Dividend yield (A-H)	246,756	0.657	0.389	0.000	13.829
Illiquidity Indicator (A-H)	297,571	1.238	6.541	0.000	476.513
Speculative motive (A-H)	273,410	0.243	0.590	–3.401	4.285
Information asymmetry (A-H)	299,504	1.028	1.303	0.000	123.212
Natural logarithm of market capitalization (in millions RMB)	302,574	6.128	1.607	1.782	11.223
Panel C: Other Variables					
The US dollar index (JP Morgan)	4,826	109.422	9.899	92.279	132.947

Notes: (1) A-ADR premium (offshore RMB exchange rate) is based on offshore RMB versus USD exchange rate (CNH); the CNH data start on April 30, 2012, retrieved through the Wind Economic database from ICAP. A-ADR premium (onshore RMB exchange rate) is calculated with onshore RMB versus USD exchange rate, which is published by the China Foreign Exchange Trade System and dates back to January 2, 1981.

(2) "9 A–ADR stock pairs" means the 9 companies are cross-listed in the US, mainland China, and Hong Kong markets.

information asymmetry is more severe for ADRs than for H-shares. Given factors related to the composition of investors, A-shares carry weaker liquidity, and stronger speculative motives than H-shares. According to unit root tests of variables (Table A2), the time series and panel data are all stable hence can be used for our empirical analysis.

4.2 *Determinants analysis of A-ADR premium*

Table 2 presents the impacts of explanatory variables on A-ADR premium based on equation (10),[3] and the following observations are noteworthy. First, Expected Exchange Rate Change_t has a positive impact on the A-ADR premium, or alternatively, the premium shrinks as investors anticipate RMB appreciation (decline of Expected Exchange Rate Change_t). That is, RMB appreciation increases the value of the underlying asset of the listed companies and thereby reduces A-ADR premium. This is consistent with the results in our theoretical model and with the study by Arquette *et al.* (2008) which examines ADR and Hong Kong H-share discounts versus A-share during 1998–2006. The impact of Expected Exchange Rate Change_t remains both statistically and economically significant as we add more explanatory variables.

Second, the higher Market Sentiment_t the domestic market (mainland China) has, the higher the A-share price relative to ADR (higher A-ADR premium), which is consistent with Arquette *et al.* (2008).

Third, shares with higher dividend payment (Dividend $\text{Yield}_{i,t}$) are more attractive to US investors (due to favorable capital gain tax arrangement or lower holding costs) and produce higher ADR prices, thereby generating lower A-ADR premium. This is in line with the reasoning in the works of Arquette *et al.* (2008) and Grossmann & Ngo (2020).

Fourth, illiquid shares include a liquidity compensation component in their prices (Amihud, 2002). Consequently, those illiquid A-shares are less attractive to ADR investors and worsen the liquidity condition of corresponding ADRs. This can add to the A-ADR premium.

---

[3]VIF (Variance Inflation Factor) statistics indicate no severe multicollinearity in our empirical analysis. For models in Table 2, VIF values of all variables are less than 3 and the mean VIF value of the model is less than 2. For models of AH premiums, the mean values of VIFs are less than 3 and only the VIF value of dummy variable $D_{\text{SH Connect}}$ is around 5, indicating mild collinearity. For this reason, we adopt variable *Openness*1 instead of $D_{\text{SH Connect}}$ in the optimal model for AH premium.

Table 2. Determinants of A-ADR premium (onshore exchange rate).

Variables	(1)	(2)	(3)	(4)	(5)	(6)
Expected Exchange Rate Change$_t$	22.612***	17.049***	20.331***	17.352***	22.222***	24.324***
(onshore exchange rate)	(0.583)	(0.564)	(0.595)	(0.654)	(0.593)	(0.614)
Market Sentiment$_t$	12.077***	15.115***	15.528***	15.104***	12.880***	13.376***
	(0.183)	(0.182)	(0.183)	(0.182)	(0.200)	(0.203)
Dividend Yield$_{i,t}$	–3.841***	–3.936***	–3.933***	–3.938***	–4.015***	–4.006***
	(0.053)	(0.051)	(0.051)	(0.051)	(0.050)	(0.050)
Illiquidity$_{i,t}$	16.032***	14.042***	12.656***	13.927***	11.014***	10.194***
	(0.287)	(0.276)	(0.287)	(0.303)	(0.297)	(0.303)
Speculative Motive$_{i,t}$	7.162***	5.901***	6.218***	5.905***	4.699***	5.039***
	(0.195)	(0.187)	(0.187)	(0.187)	(0.191)	(0.193)
Information Asymmetry$_{i,t}$	4.417***	3.703***	3.621***	3.693***	3.335***	3.303***
	(0.145)	(0.139)	(0.139)	(0.139)	(0.138)	(0.138)
US dollar Index$_t$		60.663***	44.227***	60.016***	65.297***	52.307***
		(1.030)	(1.426)	(1.249)	(1.035)	(1.455)
Openness1			–26.559***			–20.388***
			(1.600)			(1.609)
Openness2				–1.286		
				(1.405)		
$D_{\text{Short-sell}}$					–7.368***	–6.775***
					(0.284)	(0.288)
Constant	17.092***	–268.526***	–165.200***	–264.212***	–281.699***	–201.321***
	(0.316)	(4.857)	(7.885)	(6.769)	(4.836)	(7.970)
Observations	34,132	34,132	34,132	34,132	34,132	34,132
Adj-R^2	0.413	0.467	0.471	0.467	0.477	0.480

Note: Standard errors in parentheses, *** $p<0.01$, ** $p<0.05$, * $p<0.1$.

Fifth, information asymmetry of underlying stocks (Information $\text{Asymmetry}_{i,t}$) is positively related to the A-ADR premium. This is because information asymmetry hampers price discovery and is associated with persistent ADR mispricing, as documented in Beckmann *et al.* (2015).

Sixth, the US dollar index (US dollar Index_t) is positively related to A-ADR premium, which is consistent with the evidence in the work of Zhang *et al.* (2020) regarding the A-H premium index. Introduction of the US dollar Index_t variable weakens the influence of Expected Exchange Rate Change_t and adds to the explanatory power of the model.

Consistent with the propositions in our theoretical models, the policy variables have the predicted signs and significant coefficients, and add to the explanatory power of the estimation model. Specifically, financial openness significantly narrows A-ADR premium, as seen from both indicators *Openness1* and *Openness2*. The introduction of these two financial openness indicators strengthen the positive impact of expected exchange rate changes and weaken the impact of the US dollar index. This may reflect the coordinated advancement of Chinese financial opening and exchange rate reform progress.

The relaxation of short sale constraints on A-shares significantly narrows the A-ADR premium, which confirms our theoretical results. The transmission mechanisms could be two-fold. First, the easing of constraints adds A-share stock liquidity, strengthens the impact of dividend yield, and weakens the impacts of speculative motive and information asymmetry (as displayed in column (5), Table 2), thus facilitates price discovery in the domestic market. Second, it helps moderate the deviation of ADR prices' from its fundamental value, which is an opposite effect to that of a prohibition on short selling as stated in Blau *et al.* (2012).

As onshore and offshore Renminbi exchange markets are segregated, we also analyze A-ADR premiums using offshore Renminbi/US dollar exchange rate. Table 3 shows that the explanatory variables share the same signs as those in Table 2, with the exception of the expected foreign exchange rate, where the sign changes after adding the US dollar index. Such a change is probably due to the collinearity between these two variables; therefore, we omit the US dollar index in the following estimations. The magnitude of the effect of the expected offshore exchange rate on A-ADR premium is smaller than that of the onshore exchange rate. The coefficient of expected offshore exchange rate change is 10.970

Table 3. Determinants of A-ADR premium (Offshore exchange rate).

Variables	**(1)**	**(2)**	**(3)**	**(4)**	**(5)**	**(6)**
Expected Exchange Rate Change$_t$	10.970***	–30.916***	15.040***	46.374***	16.910***	23.390***
(offshore exchange rate)	(1.737)	(1.501)	(1.473)	(1.608)	(1.772)	(1.489)
Market Sentiment$_t$	11.809***	39.695***	26.068***	24.088***	6.788***	19.385***
	(0.689)	(0.639)	(0.605)	(0.631)	(0.762)	(0.654)
Dividend Yield$_{i,t}$	–2.807***	–2.860***	–2.921***	–2.899***	–2.815***	–2.935***
	(0.059)	(0.049)	(0.050)	(0.052)	(0.059)	(0.049)
Illiquidity$_{i,t}$	50.330***	82.099***	72.309***	63.786***	38.570***	56.416***
	(1.405)	(1.207)	(1.216)	(1.255)	(1.602)	(1.359)
Speculative Motive$_{i,t}$	14.477***	12.272***	12.863***	14.221***	14.283***	12.560***
	(0.307)	(0.255)	(0.261)	(0.271)	(0.305)	(0.257)
Information Asymmetry$_{i,t}$	4.428***	3.271***	5.052***	5.133***	4.316***	4.908***
	(0.197)	(0.163)	(0.167)	(0.175)	(0.196)	(0.165)
US Dollar Index$_t$		113.881***				
		(1.187)				
Openness1			–161.496***			–164.917***
			(1.831)			(1.809)
Openness2				–174.415***		
				(2.344)		
$D_{Short\text{-}sell}$					–8.113***	–11.285***
					(0.541)	(0.456)
Constant	11.419***	–538.910***	160.210***	170.166***	22.613***	178.933***
	(0.623)	(5.762)	(1.768)	(2.204)	(0.971)	(1.898)
Observations	19,812	19,812	19,812	19,812	19,812	19,812
Adj-R^2	0.315	0.532	0.508	0.465	0.323	0.523

(column (1) in Table 3), and its standard deviation is 0.0696, hence a one-standard increase in expected offshore exchange rate leads to an increment in A-ADR premium of about 0.764 percentage points. The influence is smaller than that of onshore exchange rate, where a one-standard deviation in expected onshore exchange rate change leads to a change in A-ADR premium of about 4.617 percentage points. This reflects the fact that onshore Renminbi exchange rate was not liberalized in its early years, and investors tend to be more sensitive to its fluctuation than to that of offshore exchange rate.

4.3 *Determinants analysis of A-H premium*

Drawing on the rich dataset of 116 A-H stock pairs, we analyze the effects of explanatory variables on A-H premium, in order to provide additional insights and check similarities with A-ADR premium determinants. A concern with the whole sample regressions is that the relationship of interest may be disturbed by omitted company characteristics; to reduce this concern, we control for firm capitalization in our estimations. Results of the whole sample and a subsample of the 9 companies (cross-listed in three markets) are presented in Table 4. The interpretation of the estimation coefficient signs and significance are parallel to those of A-ADR premium. Financial openness and removal of short sale constraints again appear to narrow the A-share and H-share price gaps. However, the magnitudes of these influences differ across variables. A one-standard deviation variation in market sentiment causes an adjustment to A-H premium of 6.481 percentage points, which is smaller than the 7.270 percentage points of A-ADR premium, reflecting higher sensitivity of ADR investors with respect to market fluctuations. A one-standard deviation changes in information indicators leads to an adjustment to A-H premium of 0.889 percentage points, much smaller than the impact on A-ADR premium (about 7.584 percentage points); this difference could be attributed to a lower level (and larger marginal effect) of information asymmetry between the A and H markets than between the A and ADR markets. Compared with the whole sample, the A-H premiums of the 9 companies are more sensitive to market sentiment, financial openness, and enabling of short selling. Moreover, these 9 companies are less sensitive to dividend yield as a one-standard-deviation rise of dividend yield can reduce

Table 4. Determinants of A-H premium.

	All 116 Companies				The 9 Companies			
Variables	**(1)**	**(2)**	**(3)**	**(4)**	**(5)**	**(6)**	**(7)**	**(8)**
US dollar Index$_t$	12.560***	–7.075***	23.521***	9.123***	–14.276***	–39.147***	21.032***	–4.220***
	(0.357)	(0.519)	(0.746)	(0.553)	(1.012)	(1.363)	(1.924)	(1.437)
Market	25.521***	28.388***	27.371***	29.904***	28.885***	32.639***	35.369***	37.558***
Sentiment$_t$	(0.193)	(0.199)	(0.222)	(0.198)	(0.458)	(0.474)	(0.545)	(0.459)
Dividend Yield$_{i,t}$	–34.971***	–34.198***	–34.825***	–32.540***	–28.984***	–28.011***	–27.661***	–22.174***
	(0.095)	(0.096)	(0.096)	(0.097)	(0.248)	(0.248)	(0.254)	(0.258)
Illiquidity$_{i,t}$	–0.008*	–0.012**	–0.011**	–0.036***	–0.708***	–0.793***	–0.825***	–1.067***
	(0.005)	(0.005)	(0.005)	(0.005)	(0.035)	(0.035)	(0.035)	(0.034)
Speculative	0.262***	0.537***	0.233***	–0.462***	0.041	0.329	–0.578***	–1.956***
Motive$_{i,t}$	(0.061)	(0.061)	(0.061)	(0.062)	(0.204)	(0.202)	(0.205)	(0.197)
Information	0.634***	0.590***	0.698***	0.650***	–1.480***	–1.504***	–1.014***	–1.649***
Asymmetry$_{i,t}$	(0.040)	(0.039)	(0.040)	(0.039)	(0.177)	(0.175)	(0.177)	(0.167)
ln(capitalization)	–5.597***	–5.598***	–5.574***	–5.014***	–2.681***	–2.595***	–2.646***	–2.400***
	(0.024)	(0.024)	(0.024)	(0.025)	(0.071)	(0.070)	(0.071)	(0.067)
Openness1		–34.395***		–29.616***		–41.930***		–26.406***
		(0.662)		(0.657)		(1.560)		(1.511)
$D_{\text{SH Connect}}$			–2.612***				–8.737***	
			(0.156)				(0.406)	
$D_{\text{Short-sell}}$				–6.496***				–12.614***
				(0.083)				(0.222)
Constant	12.644***	136.490***	–39.270***	53.719***	120.806***	275.339***	–47.375***	95.470***
	(1.655)	(2.897)	(3.514)	(3.052)	(4.746)	(7.421)	(9.127)	(7.749)
Observations	243,484	243,484	243,484	243,484	31,857	31,857	31,857	31,857
Adj-R^2	0.601	0.605	0.601	0.615	0.452	0.464	0.460	0.514

A-H premiums by 8.251 percentage points, as compared to 12.427 percentage points for the whole sample of 116 companies.

In addition to *Openness1*, we also consider SH Connect as an important milestone for financial openness and investigate its influence on A-H premium. Table 4 shows that the dummy variable $D_{\text{SH Connect}}$ has negative and significant impacts on A-H premium (more economically significant for the 9 companies), implying that SH Connect has improved price parity in the two stock markets. This adds to the findings of existing studies, which explain the jump in the A-H premium index in December 2014 as mainly driven by systematic shifts in the US dollar index, market sentiment, and other factors (Nishimura *et al.*, 2018; Chan & Kwok, 2015).[4]

4.4 *Exchange rate reform affects the sensitivity of A-ADR and A-H premium on exchange rates*

Comparing the influences of onshore and offshore RMB exchange rates on A-ADR price premiums prior to and after the related reforms can shed light on the effectiveness of these reforms. As demonstrated in Table 5, the impact of onshore RMB exchange rate on A-ADR premium has significantly increased while that of the US dollar has decreased since the "8.11 reform" (as compared with column (2) in Table 2), and the impacts of onshore and offshore rates have been further enhanced since the market quoted RMB exchange rate dropped below 7. This has illustrated the effectiveness of financial opening and exchange rate reform policies.[5] First, the financial opening policies have strengthened the linkage

[4]The shifts could be confirmed through *t*-test and standard deviation comparison of the explanatory factors around December 2014 (the introduction of SH-connect). Results are omitted here for concision but available upon request.

[5]We confirm this conclusion with rolling window estimations. A window of 36 months is adopted for estimating the A-ADR premium determinant model with variables including expected exchange rate changes, US dollar index, and Openness1. Only significant coefficients of the three variables are retained. The results show that expected changes of onshore exchange rate exerts larger impacts on A-ADR premium after August 2015 and the second half of 2019, roughly consistent with the timing of the "811 reform" and RMB exchange rate dropping below "7". Meanwhile, the influence of the dollar index weakened significantly. In addition, the role of financial opening in narrowing A-ADR premium was

Table 5. Effectiveness of exchange rate reform as seen from A-ADR premium.

Variables	August 11, 2015 (the "811 Reform")–June 30, 2020		August 5, 2019 (RMB Exchange Drops Below "7")–June 30, 2020	
	(1)	(2)	(3)	(4)
Expected Exchange Rate Change$_t$ (onshore exchange rate)	35.602*** (3.417)		81.865*** (8.332)	
Expected Exchange Rate Change$_t$ (offshore exchange rate)		3.754 (2.452)		76.410*** (7.998)
Market Sentiment$_t$	4.065*** (1.509)	6.245*** (1.671)	75.834*** (6.941)	96.444*** (6.176)
Dividend Yield$_{i,t}$	–1.863*** (0.052)	–1.888*** (0.053)	–1.538*** (0.068)	–1.522*** (0.070)
Illiquidity$_{i,t}$	71.460*** (2.513)	73.496*** (2.534)	69.174*** (2.842)	70.808*** (2.903)
Speculative Motive$_{i,t}$	7.332*** (0.360)	7.418*** (0.365)	–13.923*** (0.987)	–13.410*** (1.001)
Information Asymmetry$_{i,t}$	2.750*** (0.176)	3.333*** (0.173)	–1.165*** (0.244)	–0.510** (0.240)
US dollar Index$_t$	52.862*** (4.063)		76.055*** (9.343)	
Constant	–229.292*** (19.671)	23.547*** (0.917)	–366.300*** (43.349)	–12.200*** (3.032)
Observations	10,610	10,610	1,962	1,962
Adj-R^2	0.250	0.231	0.415	0.382

between A-shares and ADR, and RMB/USD exchange rates as an important market-based rate exert greater impacts on the ADR prices. Second, since the "8.11 reform", floating flexibility of onshore RMB exchange rates has been gradually enhanced, together with the investors' adaptability to its changes. Third, since the exchange rate dropped below the

relatively stable before 2010 became most significant during 2013–2014 but has been weakened since 2017.

Table 6. Sensitivity of A-H premium to the US dollar: Before and after exchange rate reform.

	All 116 Companies		The 9 Companies	
Variables	**(1)**	**(2)**	**(3)**	**(4)**
US Dollar Index$_t$	14.865***	–59.088***	4.430**	–53.916***
	(0.677)	(1.498)	(1.756)	(3.019)
Market Sentiment$_t$	25.648***	8.941***	30.956***	16.171***
	(0.195)	(0.329)	(0.483)	(0.649)
Dividend Yield$_{i,t}$	–34.962***	–48.811***	–28.520***	–53.634***
	(0.095)	(0.163)	(0.250)	(0.408)
Illiquidity$_{i,t}$	–0.009*	–0.068***	–0.740***	–0.019
	(0.005)	(0.004)	(0.035)	(0.060)
Speculative Motive$_{i,t}$	0.236***	0.277***	–0.568***	–1.570***
	(0.062)	(0.075)	(0.209)	(0.284)
Information Asymmetry$_{i,t}$	0.637***	2.454***	–1.640***	–0.173
	(0.040)	(0.073)	(0.177)	(0.209)
ln(capitalization)	–5.592***	–3.386***	–2.689***	–0.437***
	(0.024)	(0.029)	(0.071)	(0.070)
$D_{811\ Reform}$ · US Dollar Index$_t$	–0.111***		–0.984***	
	(0.028)		(0.076)	
$D_{Exchange\ Rate\ Below\ 7}$ · US dollar Index$_t$		0.738***		0.639***
		(0.023)		(0.049)
Constant	–542.392***	167.179***	33.217***	318.354***
	(10.642)	(25.907)	(8.228)	(14.538)
Observations	243,484	102,491	31,857	10,306
Adj-R^2	0.601	0.674	0.455	0.676

Note: $D_{811\ Reform}$ is a dummy for dates since August 11, 2015 (the "811 reform"), $D_{Exchange\ Rate\ Below\ 7}$ is a dummy for dates since August 5, 2019, when the market quoted RMB exchange rate dropped below 7. For columns (2) and (4), the sample period is restricted to August 11, 2015–June 30, 2020.

psychologically important level of 7, investors are more sensitive to signals of exchange rate volatilities.

The effectiveness of RMB exchange rate reform is also confirmed by the sensitivity of A-H premium to the US Dollar (Table 6). Since the "8.11 Reform", the A-H premiums have become less sensitive to the US dollar index, implying that investors in Hong Kong are more adaptive to fluctuations in RMB/HKD exchange rate.[6] However, its influence on the whole sample is smaller than on the 9 companies, which might reflect investors' heterogeneous requirements on exchange rate premium for different stocks.[7] Although the sensitivity of A-H premium on the US dollar index increased after the RMB/USD exchange rate dropped below 7 in August 2019, for the 9 companies, the magnitude is around two-thirds of the influence of the "8.11 Reform", implying that the effects of market connection mechanism and the exchange rate reform are generally solid.

4.5 *Relative importance of factors in explaining cross-market price premiums*

Following Harmon & Walker (1995), Shea (1997), and Artavanis *et al.* (2015), we calculate partial R^2 to illustrate which variables are incrementally important. Based on an optimal model, partial R^2 of a variable x is calculated by removing it and keeping all other variables, then comparing the error sum of squares (SSE) of the reduced model and optimal model.[8] A higher value of partial R^2 means the variable is incrementally more important.

Overall, micro-level factors are more important than macro-level and meso-level factors in determining A-share price premium. Table 7 shows that four factors are relatively more important than others in explaining A-ADR premium, namely, dividend yield, financial openness, speculative motive, and illiquidity indicator. This implies that the abnormal A-share premium versus ADR (as compared with ADR premium in other

[6]Rolling window estimations show that the influence of US dollar index on AH premium fluctuates widely over time. It was significantly enhanced after the global financial crisis but weakened significantly around the launch of Shanghai-Hong Kong Stock Connect. Financial opening reduced AH premium significantly before 2017, while since 2017, its influence has been weakened.

[7]In general, equities in counter-cyclical sectors are less sensitive to foreign exchange rate changes.

[8]The proportion of variation explained by x that cannot be explained by the other factors (denoted as group A) is given by $R^2_{x|A} = \frac{\mathbf{SSR}(x|A)}{\mathbf{SSE}(A)} = \frac{\mathbf{SSE}(A)-\mathbf{SSE}(A,x)}{\mathbf{SSE}(A)}$. Partial r-squares do not necessary add up to R^2 of the optimal model.

Table 7. Partial R^2 of main explanatory variables.

Variables		A-ADR Premium				A-H Premium	
		Onshore Exchange Rate		Offshore Exchange Rate			
		Since August 2005	Since "811" Reform	Since August 2005	Since "811" Reform	All 116 Companies	The 9 Companies
Macro-level	Expected exchange rate change	0.044	0.001	0.042	0.002	—	—
	US dollar index	0.020	0.001	—	—	0.000	0.005
	Capital account openness	**0.067**	**0.074**	**0.329**	**0.096**	**0.259**	**0.281**
Meso-level	Market sentiment	0.120	0.002	0.048	0.005	**0.030**	**0.116**
	Removal of short sale constraints	0.035	—	0.032	—	**0.031**	**0.127**
Micro-level	Dividend yield	**0.183**	**0.114**	**0.166**	**0.116**	**0.386**	**0.159**
	Illiquidity indicator	**0.029**	**0.060**	**0.075**	**0.062**	0.016	0.012
	Speculative motive	0.041	0.038	0.165	0.105	0.007	0.000
	Information asymmetry	0.025	0.014	0.035	0.011	0.002	0.009

Note: Due to data availability of *Openness1*, this table covers only the sample period between 2014 and 2019.

economies) is mainly caused by China's institutional and market-specific features. The orderly opening-up of financial markets, strong speculative motives of A-share investors, and illiquidity of individual stocks all contribute to the price premium. For A-ADR premium based on offshore exchange rate, investors care most about financial openness. For A-H premium, dividend ratio and financial openness contribute the most, while market sentiment and the relaxation of short sale constraints are more important than speculative motive and illiquidity indicator and other factors, whose partial R^2 are less than 0.02. Meso-level factors are incrementally more important for explaining A-H premium than for A-ADR premium, possibly resulting from the more severe cross-market herding behavior in A-H markets than in A-ADR markets.

Moreover, after the “8.11 Reform”, the partial R^2 of expected exchange rate change (both onshore and offshore exchange rates) declines from over 0.04 to less than 0.002; its ranking also drops significantly. This re-confirms our views that the effect of the exchange rate reform is solid and that foreign investors are more adaptive to fluctuations in RMB exchange rates.

5. Conclusions and Policy Implications

This chapter explores the micro-, meso-, and macro-level determinants of the significant A-H and A-ADR premiums over the period 2002–2020. The empirical analyses find that the most important determinants of the two types of premium are micro-level factors (dividend yield, share liquidity, speculative incentive of investors, information asymmetry, etc.), followed by macro- (expected foreign exchange rate changes, and financial openness) and meso-level (market sentiment) factors. The following findings are noteworthy. First, dividend ratio is the most decisive in premium determination, meaning that international investors pay most attention to fundamentals. Second, market sentiment is incrementally more important for explaining A-H premium than A-ADR premium, reflecting the fact that irrational cross-market herding behavior is stronger between the A and H markets than between the A and ADR markets. Third, over the observed period overseas investors are more sensitive to China’s financial market openness and more adaptive to RMB foreign exchange rate volatility.

The relative importance of determinants for the premiums also illustrates that the Chinese equity market still lacks investor rationality and a degree of financial openness. For example, the high A-ADR premium mainly comes from insufficient market openness, speculative incentives, and lack of liquidity. Empirical analysis of A-H premium also confirms that financial openness and market sentiment are important in determining A-H premiums.

The empirical results manifest the impacts of foreign exchange rate reform and financial openness policies. For example, impacts of expectations of onshore foreign exchange rate on A-ADR premium have been much enhanced since the “8.11 Reform”, while the impacts of the US dollar index have been moderated. Both confirm the effectiveness of the

RMB foreign exchange rate reform. Meanwhile, the reduced relative importance of expected (onshore) foreign exchange rates in determining premiums also reflects that overseas investors are more adaptive to foreign exchange rate volatilities in China. These results based on individual share prices confirm the conclusion of Zhang *et al.* (2020) that the systematic rise of the A-H premium after late 2014 can be attributable to the US dollar index, while the introduction of SH Connect has enhanced the price discovery capacity of A-shares.

The empirical findings show that certain policy measures can help enhance the price discovery capacity of the Chinese equity market and thereby reduce A-ADR and A-H premiums. These measures include, among others, enhancing RMB foreign exchange rate flexibility and stabilizing foreign exchange rate expectation; improving transaction rules in line with international best practices; enhancing market connectivity and financial market openness; developing long-term institutional investors to reduce speculative transactions; and setting reasonable dividend ratios to increase the investment value of A-shares as well as ADR and H-shares.

It would be valuable for future research to explore the impacts of geopolitics on premiums of cross-listed shares as more Chinese companies may be forced to shift from the US exchanges to the Hong Kong Exchange. In particular, if the pricing mechanism of cross-listed shares can generate cross-market externalities, then the cross-listed shares may carry a higher value than single-market listed shares. This will make cross-listing a preferred option for many companies.

Appendix A1. Proof of Proposition 2

Proposition 2. *If* $\mathbb{E}[e_1] = e_0$, *i.e.,* $e = 1$, *the larger the extent of capital market openness (larger* θ*), the smaller the asset price disparity, i.e.,* $\frac{\partial \Gamma}{\partial \theta} < 0$.

Proof. If $e = 1$, then

$$\Gamma = \gamma\left(\frac{\theta}{1-\varphi(1-\theta^2)} - 1\right)\varphi\sigma_v,$$

where $\varphi = \frac{v^2\sigma_e + \sigma_v(1+\sigma_e)}{v^2\sigma_e + \sigma_v(1+\sigma_e) + \theta\sigma_v}$, $\frac{\partial\varphi}{\partial\theta} = -\frac{\varphi(1-\varphi)}{\theta} < 0$. We thus obtain

$$\frac{\partial\Gamma}{\partial\theta}=\gamma\sigma_v\left[\left(\frac{\theta}{(1-\varphi+\varphi\theta^2)^2}-1\right)\frac{\partial\varphi}{\partial\theta}+\frac{\varphi(1-\varphi-\varphi\theta^2)}{(1-\varphi+\varphi\theta^2)^2}\right]$$

$$=\gamma\sigma_v\frac{\varphi}{\theta(1-\varphi+\varphi\theta^2)^2}\left[(1-\varphi)(1-\varphi+\varphi\theta^2)^2-\varphi\theta^3\right]$$

$$=\gamma\sigma_v\frac{\varphi}{(1-\varphi+\varphi\theta^2)^2}\left[\frac{\sigma_v(1-\varphi+\varphi\theta^2)^2}{v^2\sigma_e+\sigma_v(1+\sigma_e)+\theta\sigma_v}-\varphi\theta^2\right]$$

$$=\gamma\sigma_v\frac{\varphi\theta^2}{(1-\varphi+\varphi\theta^2)^2}\left[\frac{\sigma_v}{v^2\sigma_e+\sigma_v(1+\sigma_e)+\theta\sigma_v}\left(\frac{\sigma_v}{v^2\sigma_e+\sigma_v(1+\sigma_e)+\theta\sigma_v}+\varphi\theta\right)^2-\varphi\right]$$

$$=\gamma\sigma_v\frac{\varphi^2\theta^2}{(1-\varphi+\varphi\theta^2)^2}\left[\frac{\sigma_v}{v^2\sigma_e+\sigma_v(1+\sigma_e)}\left(\frac{\theta v^2\sigma_e+\theta\sigma_v(1+\sigma_e)+\sigma_v}{v^2\sigma_e+\sigma_v(1+\sigma_e)+\theta\sigma_v}\right)^2-1\right]$$

$$=-\gamma\sigma_v\frac{\varphi^2\theta^2}{(1-\varphi+\varphi\theta^2)^2}\frac{\sigma_v(v^2+\sigma_v)\sigma_e}{v^2\sigma_e+\sigma_v(1+\sigma_e)}\left[\left(\frac{\theta v^2\sigma_e+\theta\sigma_v(1+\sigma_e)+\sigma_v}{v^2\sigma_e+\sigma_v(1+\sigma_e)+\theta\sigma_v}+1\right)\frac{1-\theta}{v^2\sigma_e+\sigma_v(1+\sigma_e)+\theta\sigma_v}+1\right]$$

$$=-\gamma\sigma_v\frac{\varphi^2\theta^2}{(1-\varphi+\varphi\theta^2)^2}\frac{\sigma_v(v^2+\sigma_v)\sigma_e}{v^2\sigma_e+\sigma_v(1+\sigma_e)}\left[\left(\frac{\theta v^2\sigma_e+\theta\sigma_v(1+\sigma_e)+\sigma_v}{v^2\sigma_e+\sigma_v(1+\sigma_e)}\varphi+1\right)\frac{1-\theta}{v^2\sigma_e+\sigma_v(1+\sigma_e)}\varphi+1\right].$$

Therefore, we can obtain $\frac{\partial\Gamma}{\partial\theta}<0$. ■

Appendix A2. Numerical Analysis of the Model

This chapter shows that RMB appreciation expectation and enhanced financial market openness in China can reduce A-ADR and A-H premiums. Figure A1 illustrates the features of premium in a more general scenario using numerical analysis. It shows that the higher the expected appreciation of domestic currency (e) and the openness of financial market (θ), the lower the premium. Moreover, higher openness of financial market reduces marginal impacts of foreign exchange rate expectation on premium.

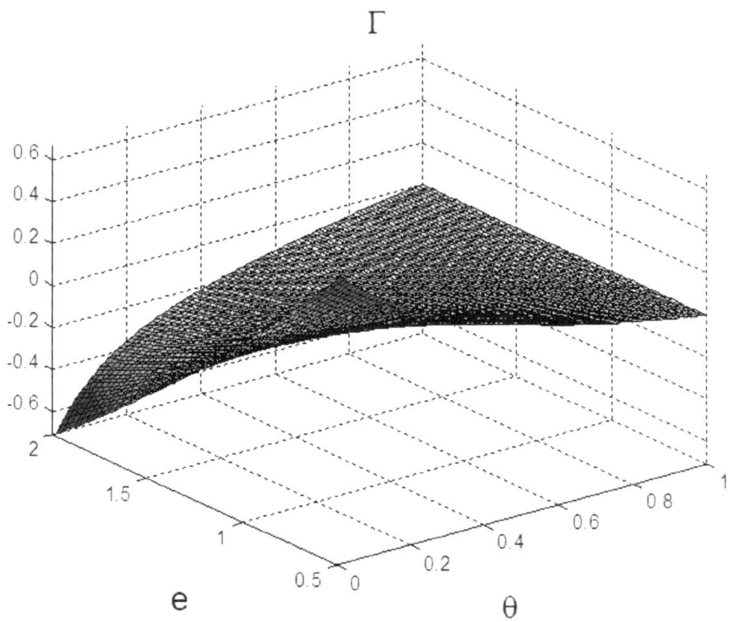

Figure A1. Impacts of exchange rate expectation and financial market openness on share price premium.

Note: $\gamma = 1$, $\nu = 1.2$, $\sigma_e = 0.1$, $\sigma_v = 0.1$.

Table A1. The 9 companies included in the sample.

		H-share		ADR		A-share		
Order	Name	Ticker	Listing Date	Ticker	ADR Effective Date	Ticker	Listing Date	Short-sell Effective Date
1	Sinopec Shanghai Petrochemical	0338	1993/7/26	SHI	1993/7/26	600688	1993/11/8	2013/9/16
2	Guangshen Railway	0525	1996/5/14	GSH	1996/5/14	601333	2006/12/22	2013/1/31
3	China Eastern Airlines	0670	1997/2/5	CEA	1997/2/4	600115	1997/11/5	2011/12/5
4	China Southern Airlines	1055	1997/7/31	ZNH	1997/7/30	600029	2003/7/25	2011/12/5
5	Huaneng Power International	0902	1998/1/21	HNP	1994/10/5	600011	2001/12/6	2013/1/31
6	PetroChina	0857	2000/4/7	PTR	2000/4/6	601857	2007/11/5	2010/3/31
7	China Petroleum & Chemical	0386	2000/10/19	SNP	2000/10/18	600028	2001/8/8	2010/3/31
8	Aluminum Corporation of China	2600	2001/12/12	ACH	2001/12/11	601600	2007/4/30	2010/3/31
9	China Life Insurance	2628	2003/12/18	LFC	2003/12/17	601628	2007/1/9	2010/3/31

Table A2. Unit root tests (January 2002–June 2020).

Time Series

Variables	Dickey–Fuller Statistics	*p*-value
ln(the US dollar index)	−16.318	0.000
Expected exchange rate change (offshore)	−9.959	0.000
Expected exchange rate change (onshore)	−14.227	0.000
Market sentiment (A-ADR)	−13.614	0.000
Market sentiment (A-H)	−2.759	0.064

Panel Data

Variables	Fisher Statistics	*p*-value	Im–Pesaran–Shin Statistics	*p*-value
A-ADR premium (offshore RMB exchange rate, %)	−0.265	0.605	−4.245	0.000
A-ADR premium (onshore RMB exchange rate, %)	2.149	0.016	−5.679	0.000
Dividend yield (A-share)	10.832	0.000	−9.278	0.000
Illiquidity Indicator (A-share)	18.930	0.000	−16.140	0.000
Speculative motive (A-share)	83.574	0.000	−34.914	0.000
Information asymmetry (A-ADR)	26.546	0.000	−20.489	0.000
A-H premium (%)	34.007	0.000	−21.499	0.000
Dividend yield (A-H)	52.477	0.000	—	—
Illiquidity Indicator (A-H)	109.280	0.000	−73.554	0.000
Speculative motive (A-H)	264.617	0.000	−120.000	0.000
Information asymmetry (A-H)	80.880	0.000	−77.850	0.000
ln(market capitalization)	4.497	0.000	−5.965	0.000

Note: In unit root tests of panel data, the listed Fisher statistic is modified inv. chi-squared. The null hypothesis Ho: all panels contain unit roots. For the Fisher-type unit-root test, Ha: at least one panel is stationary. For the Im–Pesaran–Shin unit-root test, Ha: some panels are stationary.

References

Alexander, G.J., Eun, C.S., & Janakiramanan, S. (1987). Asset pricing and dual listing on foreign capital markets: A note. *The Journal of Finance*, 42(1), 151–158.

Amihud, Y. (2002). Illiquidity and stock returns: Cross-section and time-series effects. *Journal of Financial Markets*, 5(1), 31–56.

Amihud, Y., Hameed, A., Kang, W., & Zhang, H. (2015). The illiquidity premium: International evidence. *Journal of Financial Economics*, 117(2), 350–368.

Arquette, G.C., Brown Jr, W.O., & Burdekin, R.C. (2008). US ADR and Hong Kong H-share discounts of Shanghai-listed firms. *Journal of Banking & Finance*, 32(9), 1916–1927.

Artavanis, N.T., Morse, A., & Tsoutsoura, M. (2015). Tax evasion across industries: Soft credit evidence from Greece. NBER Working Paper 21552.

Atanasova, C. & Li, M. (2018). Multi-market trading and liquidity: Evidence from cross-listed companies. *Journal of International Financial Markets, Institutions and Money*, 53, 117–138.

Auguste, S., Dominguez, K.M., Kamil, H., & Tesar, L.L. (2006). Cross-border trading as a mechanism for implicit capital flight: ADRs and the Argentine crisis. *Journal of Monetary Economics*, 53(7), 1259–1295.

Bae, S.C., Kwon, T.H., & Li, M. (2008). Foreign exchange rate exposure and risk premium in international investments: Evidence from American depositary receipts. *Journal of Multinational Financial Management*, 18(2), 165–179.

Baruch, S., Andrew Karolyi, G., & Lemmon, M.L. (2007). Multimarket trading and liquidity: Theory and evidence. *The Journal of Finance*, 62(5), 2169–2200.

Beckmann, K.S., Ngo, T., & Wang, D. (2015). The informational content of ADR mispricing. *Journal of Multinational Finance Management*, 32–33, 1–14.

Blau, B.M., Van Ness, R.A., & Warr, R.S. (2012). Short selling of ADRs and foreign market short-sale constraints. *Journal of Banking & Finance*, 36(3), 886–897.

Burdekin, R.C. & Siklos, P.L. (2018). Quantifying the impact of the November 2014 Shanghai-Hong Kong stock connect. *International Review of Economics & Finance*, 57, 156–163.

Chan, M.K. & Kwok, S.S. (2015). Capital account liberalization and dynamic price discovery: Evidence from Chinese cross-listed stocks. *Applied Economics*, 48(6), 517–535.

Chan, K., Menkveld, A.J., & Yang, Z. (2008). Information asymmetry and asset prices: Evidence from the China foreign share discount. *The Journal of Finance*, 63(1), 159–196.

Chen, H. & Choi, P.M.S. (2012). Does information vault Niagara Falls? Cross-listed trading in New York and Toronto. *Journal of Empirical Finance*, 19(2), 175–199.

Chen, X.S. & Tan, J.Q. (2013). Difference of price discovery abilities among cross-listings and the measurement of the trade-related information (in Chinese). *Chinese Journal of Management Science*, 21(2), 9–16.

Chen, X.S. & Zhou, A.M. (2009). Cross-sectional research on the contributions to the price discovery process of the cross-listings (in Chinese). *Chinese Journal of Management Science*, 17(2), 21–28.

Chen, J., Hong, H., & Stein, J.C. (2002). Breadth of ownership and stock returns. *Journal of Financial Economics*, 66(2–3), 171–205.

De Long, J.B., Shleifer, A., Summers, L.H., & Waldmann, R. (1990). Noise trader risk in financial markets. *Journal of Political Economy*, 98(4), 703–738.

Diamond, D.W. & Verrecchia, R.E. (1987). Constraints on short-selling and asset price adjustment to private information. *Journal of Financial Economics*, 18(2), 277–311.

Ding, H., Jin, Y., Koedijk, K.G., & Wang, Y. (2020). Valuation effect of capital account liberalization: Evidence from the Chinese stock market. *Journal of International Money and Finance*, 107, 1–8.

Domowitz, I., Glen, J., & Madhavan, A. (1997). Market segmentation and stock prices: Evidence from an emerging market. *The Journal of Finance*, 52(3), 1059–1085.

Eichler, S. (2011). Exchange rate expectations and the pricing of Chinese cross-listed stocks. *Journal of Banking & Finance*, 35(2), 443–455.

Eichler, S., Karmann, A., & Maltritz, D. (2009). The ADR shadow exchange rate as an early warning indicator for currency crises. *Journal of Banking & Finance*, 33(11), 1983–1995.

Errunza, V. & Losq, E. (1985). International asset pricing under mild segmentation: Theory and test. *The Journal of Finance*, 40(1), 105–124.

Errunza, V. & Losq, E. (1989). Capital flow controls, international asset pricing, and investors' welfare: A multi-country framework. *The Journal of Finance*, 44(4), 1025–1037.

Frijns, B. & Zwinkels, R.C. (2018). Time-varying arbitrage and dynamic price discovery. *Journal of Economic Dynamics and Control*, 91, 485–502.

Gagnon, L. & Karolyi, G.A. (2010). Multi-market trading and arbitrage. *Journal of Financial Economics*, 97(1), 53–80.

Goldstein, I., Li, Y., & Yang, L. (2014). Speculation and hedging in segmented markets. *The Review of Financial Studies*, 27(3), 881–922.

Grammig, J., Melvin, M., & Schlag, C. (2005). Internationally cross-listed stock prices during overlapping trading hours: Price discovery and exchange rate effects. *Journal of Empirical Finance*, 12(1), 139–164.

Greenwood, R., Hanson, S.G., & Liao, G.Y. (2018). Asset price dynamics in partially segmented markets. *The Review of Financial Studies*, 31(9), 3307–3343.

Grossmann, A. & Ngo, T. (2020). Economic policy uncertainty and ADR mispricing. *Journal of Multinational Financial Management*, 55, 1–19.

Grossmann, A., Ngo, T., & Simpson, M.W. (2017). The asymmetric impact of currency purchasing power imparities on ADR mispricing. *Journal of Multinational Financial Management*, 42, 74–94.

Grossmann, A., Ozuna, T., & Simpson, M. W. (2007). ADR mispricing: Do costly arbitrage and consumer sentiment explain the price deviation? *Journal of International Financial Markets, Institutions and Money*, 17(4), 361–371.

Grossman, S.J. & Stiglitz, J.E. (1980). On the impossibility of informationally efficient markets. *The American Economic Review*, 70(3), 393–408.

Hansen, L.P. & Sargent, T.J. (2008). *Robustness*. Princeton: Princeton University Press.

Harmon, C. & Walker, I. (1995). Estimates of the economic return to schooling for the United Kingdom. *The American Economic Review*, 85(5), 1278–1286.

Harrison, J.M. & Kreps, D.M. (1978). Speculative investor behavior in a stock market with heterogeneous expectations. *The Quarterly Journal of Economics*, 92(2), 323–336.

Hietala, P.T. (1989). Asset pricing in partially segmented markets: Evidence from the Finnish market. *The Journal of Finance*, 44(3), 697–718.

Hong, H. & Stein, J.C. (2003). Differences of opinion, short-sales constraints, and market crashes. *The Review of Financial Studies*, 16(2), 487–525.

Hu, Z.H. & Wang, X.K. (2008). The empirical study on Chinese A-H share premium (in Chinese). *Economic Research Journal*, 2008(4), 119–131.

Huang, Y.Q., Hu, N.F., & Li, H.J. (2015). Does securities margin trading in China decrease A-H share price difference? (in Chinese). *Review of Investment Studies*, 34(9), 76–89.

Huo, W., Fu, C., Huang, Y., & Zheng, S.X. (2018). The valuation of ADR IPOs. *Journal of International Financial Markets, Institutions and Money*, 53, 215–226.

Jithendranathan, T., Nirmalanandan, T.R., & Tandon, K. (2000). Barriers to international investing and market segmentation: Evidence from Indian GDR market. *Pacific-Basin Finance Journal*, 8(3–4), 399–417.

Jurado, K. (2016). Advance information and distorted beliefs in macroeconomic and financial fluctuations. Society for Economic Dynamics 2016 Working Papers No. 154.

Kadiyala, P. & Kadiyala, P. (2004). ADRs as leading indicators of exchange rates. *Emerging Markets Review*, 5(1), 83–107.

Lamont, O.A. & Thaler, R.H. (2003). Anomalies: The law of one price in financial markets. *Journal of Economic Perspectives*, 17(4), 191–202.

Li, Y. & Wu, F.F. (2016). Stock price disparities and fluctuations in exchange rates: The case of the A- and H-shares of Chinese companies (in Chinese). *Journal of International Trade*, 2016(2), 134–144.

Lu, Y., Shi, X.Z., Yang, B.H., & Zhang, Y.Q. (2018). Shanghai-Hong Kong stock connection, capital flows and A-H premium (in Chinese). *China Journal of Economics*, 5(1), 38–63.

Ma, R., Deng, C., Cai, H., & Zhai, P. (2019). Does Shanghai-Hong Kong Stock Connect drive market comovement between Shanghai and Hong Kong: A new evidence. *The North American Journal of Economics and Finance*, 50, 1–13.

Mei, J., Scheinkman, J., & Xiong, W. (2009). Speculative trading and stock prices: Evidence from Chinese A-B share premia. *Annals of Economics and Finance*, 10(2), 225–255.

Miller, E.M. (1977). Risk, uncertainty, and divergence of opinion. *The Journal of Finance*, 32(4), 1151–1168.

Nishimura, Y., Tsutsui, Y., & Hirayama, K. (2018). Do international investors cause stock market spillovers? Comparing responses of cross-listed stocks between accessible and inaccessible markets. *Economic Modelling*, 69, 237–248.

Pascual, R., Pascual-Fuster, B., & Climent, F. (2006). Cross-listing, price discovery and the informativeness of the trading process. *Journal of Financial Markets*, 9(2), 144–161.

Pavlidis, E.G. & Vasilopoulos, K. (2020). Speculative bubbles in segmented markets: Evidence from Chinese cross-listed stocks. *Journal of International Money and Finance*, 109, 1–24.

Rabinovitch, R., Silva, A.C., & Susmel, R. (2003). Returns on ADRs and arbitrage in emerging markets. *Emerging Markets Review*, 4(3), 225–247.

SEC. (August 2012). Investor Bulletin: American Depository Receipts.

Shea, J. (1997). Instrument relevance in multivariate linear models: A simple measure. *Review of Economics and Statistics*, 79(2), 348–352.

Stigler, M., Shah, A., & Patnaik, I. (2010). Understanding the ADR premium under market segmentation. National Institute of Public Finance and Policy Working Paper.

Stulz, R.M. & Wasserfallen, W. (1995). Foreign equity investment restrictions, capital flight, and shareholder wealth maximization: Theory and evidence. *The Review of Financial Studies*, 8(4), 1019–1057.

Sun, Q. & Tong, W.H. (2000). The effect of market segmentation on stock prices: The China syndrome. *Journal of Banking & Finance*, 24(12), 1875–1902.

Wu, C. & Chen, K. (2015). Return transmissions between ADRs and A-shares of dual-listed Chinese firms. *Managerial Finance*, 41(5), 465–479.

Wu, Q., Hao, Y., & Lu, J. (2017). Investor sentiment, idiosyncratic risk, and mispricing of American Depository Receipt. *Journal of International Financial Markets, Institutions and Money*, 51, 1–14.

Wu, J., Lin, J., Yang, Z., & Dong, L. (2020). Effects of cross-border capital flows on stock returns of dual-listed firms in mainland China and Hong Kong: Evidence from a natural experiment. *Pacific Economic Review*, 2020, 1–29.

Zhang, X.C., Jia, Y.D., & Lv, T.T. (2020). The impacts of the US dollar index and the investors' expectations on the AH Premium: A macro perspective. *China Economic Journal*, 13(3), 249–269.

Chapter 6

Volatility Spillover Effects of H-Share and A-Share on ADR

This chapter investigates the cross-market volatility spillover effects using stock index data and data from 29 Chinese companies cross-listed in Hong Kong and the US during 2001–2020. We find evidence of bidirectional volatility spillover effects between H-shares (A-shares) and ADRs, and the net effect is more pronounced when domestic stock market volatility and economic policy uncertainty rise. The net spillover effect from H-shares to OTC market ADRs is stronger than that to Main Board ADRs, while the net spillover effects from A-shares to these two are similar. High analyst coverage or the hiring of offshore accounting firms reduces the net spillover effect of H-shares (A-shares) on ADRs. Given the uncertainty in China–US financial relations, eligible Chinese companies should be encouraged to seek a listing in Hong Kong and give full play to the role of H-shares in guiding ADR price movements, making Hong Kong a distribution center for the overseas listing of Chinese stocks.

1. Introduction

On May 20, 2020, the US Senate passed the HFCAA, which prohibits companies from being listed in the US if they fail to comply with PCAOB audit requirements for three consecutive years. President Trump signed the bill in December 2020, and the SEC adopted interim final rules to implement the HFCAA in March 2021. As a result, Chinese stocks now face higher compliance costs and delisting risks than before.[1] Even so, many Chinese companies are still going public in the US. In 2020, JD.com, NetEase, Yum China Holdings, GDS Holdings, New Oriental Education, and ZTO Express went for a secondary listing in Hong Kong, raising a total of HKD 113.891 billion, accounting for 28.6% of total IPO financing in Hong Kong. Meanwhile, 32 Chinese companies went public in the US in 2020, raising more than USD 13.374 billion.

Meanwhile, some US-listed Chinese stocks have sought listing in mainland Chinese stock markets, HKEX, or other overseas exchanges. Related analyses have mainly focused on the pros and cons from theoretical perspectives but have failed to provide quantitative evidence, particularly about the interactions of cross-listed stocks. This chapter fills this gap by investigating the spillover effects of 29 cross-listed Chinese stocks and presents empirical evidence that H-share price volatility affects ADR prices. Morcover, we investigate the influencing factors, including economic policy uncertainty and corporate governance.

The contributions of this chapter are twofold. First, the research topic is timely and of interest in the policy field, as it sheds light on the listing choices of US-listed Chinese stocks. Second, the chapter documents empirical evidence of spillover effects from H-share (A-share) to ADRs at the index and individual stock levels and investigates the heterogeneity of the spillover effects related to company characteristics.

The rest of this chapter is organized as follows. Section 2 provides a literature review. Section 3 briefly describes the sample and research design. Section 4 presents the empirical results and analysis. Section 5 concludes and proposes policy implications.

2. Literature Review

2.1 *Spillover effect across markets*

Information spillover between financial markets has been widely studied. Theoretically, due to incomplete information, investors may infer information from price changes in other markets and use it to manage their portfolios, generating impacts on risk valuation and portfolio diversification (King & Wadhwani, 1990). Pretorius (2002) classifies explanations of

[1]On January 11, 2021, China Mobile, China Telecom and China Unicom suspended stock trading on the NYSE to start the delisting process.

comovement among different stock markets into three categories, namely, contagion effect (such as information), economic integration (such as trade), and stock market characteristics (such as stock market volatility and industrial similarity). Empirical studies focus on spillover effects among developed economies or between developed and emerging economies (Eun & Shim, 1989; Kim *et al.*, 2016; Prasad *et al.*, 2018). Koutmos and Booth (1995) reveal asymmetric spillover effects, where spillover effects of negative shocks are more substantial than those of positive ones. In addition, studies about cross-asset spillovers aim to provide information on the risk transmission paths of the economy after a shock (Diebold & Yilmaz, 2012).

There are two main research methods for studying volatility spillover effects. The first method is to use the generalized autoregressive conditional heteroskedasticity (GARCH) and related models. This method quantifies the volatility spillover effect with the coefficient of the ARCH term, and stock index data are commonly used (Ahmed & Huo, 2019; Qi Liang *et al.*, 2015). The second method is to construct a spillover index from forecast-error variance decompositions associated with a vector autoregression (Diebold & Yilmaz, 2009, 2012). In addition, regime-switching and stochastic volatility models are also applied to study spillover effects (Zheng & Huo, 2013). Given that the second method can generate a time series for further analysis, we use the second method in this chapter.

2.2 *Factors related to the stock market spillover effect*

Some factors affect the stock market spillover effect, including stock market volatility, market sentiment, macroeconomics, and economic policy uncertainty. According to the contagion model of King and Wadhwani (1990), the magnitude of the contagion coefficients increases with volatility. Prasad *et al.* (2018) find that the determinants of net spillovers between markets include the relative volatility of markets, relative stock market turnover, and macroeconomic news indices. Eiling and Gerard (2015) argue that market development and trade openness are essential in emerging stock market linkages. Zheng and Liu (2018) show that the volatility spillover effects among international stock markets are on the rise, which can be explained by economic fundamentals and market contagion and is positively related to economic policy uncertainty. Su (2020) decomposes volatility spillovers into short-, medium-, and long-term components and finds that the low-frequency components are the main contributors to volatility spillovers across G7 stock markets and that the high-frequency components are highly sensitive to market event shocks.

Regarding studies on China, Zhou *et al.* (2012) studied the spillover effects between the Chinese and world equity markets and found that the volatility of the former has had a significantly positive impact on other markets since 2005, particularly those of Hong Kong and Taiwan. Xu (2017) found that the Shanghai-Hong Kong Stock Connect increased the bidirectional volatility spillover between the mainland and Hong Kong stock markets, while the southbound volatility spillover exceeded the northbound volatility spillover. Mainland market factors such as the price–earnings ratio, size and changes in investor sentiment also affect the volatility spillover effects.

In addition, corporate governance affects stock market investors' decisions and stock prices. Chung and Zhang (2011) find that institutional investors are more willing to invest in well-governed firms. Lei *et al.* (2012) use A-share data from 2006 to 2009 to show that good corporate governance promotes the continuity and stability of a company's business and enhances investor confidence, further affecting stock prices. Liang *et al.* (2020) investigated A-share listed companies from 2007 to 2016 and found that corporate governance characteristics may amplify the risk of stock price collapse.

2.3 *Issues related to US-listed Chinese stocks' listing on other exchanges*

Chinese stocks have been listed in the US since the early 1990s. As of June 1, 2020, 362 Chinese stocks were listed in the US, and 248 are currently still listed and traded in the US stock market. Chinese companies mainly issue ADRs to bypass the strict requirements of US law on registration procedures, financial statements, and information disclosure that apply to directly issuing shares (Rao, 1999). The quality of US-listed Chinese stocks varies. Some companies have problems that jeopardize Chinese stocks' credibility, such as irregular operations, financial fraud, poor corporate governance, and the exploitation of cross-border regulatory loopholes (Dai & Liu, 2016). Investor confidence and trust in Chinese stocks were shaken in 2010 and 2020. The former shock was accompanied by a wave of delisting and class action lawsuits, while the latter was triggered by the financial fraud of Luckin Coffee and exacerbated by tightened regulations and sanctions from the US government.

Listing on China's stock market can improve the performance and valuation of US-listed Chinese companies and promote China's stock market in the long run (Li, 2017). However, becoming listed as H-shares is easier than becoming listed as A-shares. On the one hand, the VIE structure makes it difficult for some Chinese companies to be listed as A-shares (Liu & Lin, 2015). Companies must dismantle their VIE structure or spin off part of their business for listing as A-shares (Peng, 2016), or they must issue Chinese depositary receipts. On the other hand, the HKEX implemented new rules in 2018 to allow the listing of eligible pre-revenue biotech companies and companies with a weighted voting right structure. Coupled with Hong Kong's advantage as an international financial center and the institutional design of the stock connects, the Hong Kong market has become one of the preferred destinations for listing new economy companies and the secondary listing or dual listing of Chinese companies. In addition, ADR and H-shares are fungible financial assets. In general, H-share prices are slightly lower than ADRs, reflecting the impact of information asymmetry and investors' preference for dividend yield and liquidity (Zhang *et al.*, 2022).

3. Data and Empirical Method

3.1 *Research method*

This chapter uses the TVP-VAR method[2] to construct a volatility spillover index. Diebold and Yilmaz (2009, 2012) introduced a volatility spillover index (DY index) based on the forecast variance decomposition of a VAR model to measure the dynamics of aggregate and directional spillover effects between markets. Antonakakis and Gabauer (2017) constructed a volatility spillover index based on the TVP-VAR model. Their index portrays the dynamics of the coefficients and the conditional heteroskedasticity characteristics of the data by incorporating time-varying intercepts and stochastic fluctuations to overcome the limitations of the rolling window VAR approach (including sample loss, window width selection,

[2]A description of the methodology is omitted since we use the existing methods to construct the spillover effect indices. We thus refer interested readers to Diebold and Yilmaz (2009, 2012), Antonakakis and Gabauer (2017), and Zheng and Liu (2018).

and outlier effects). According to Zheng and Liu (2018), this approach can prevent the estimation results from being affected by the trend changes in volatility and conditional heteroskedasticity, making the estimation results more comparable across periods.

In addition, this chapter uses panel data analysis to investigate the factors influencing the volatility spillover effects. Following Fernández-Rodríguez *et al.* (2016), Prasad *et al.* (2018), and Su (2020), this chapter considers the following factors that may alter the volatility spillover effects: (1) macroeconomic variables, including CPI and economic policy uncertainty; (2) stock market variables, such as relative volatility (RelStockVol); and (3) a sentiment variable, proxy by the implied volatility index (VIX). The entire sample includes 29 cross-listed companies. Due to data availability, this chapter considers the impact of corporate governance on cross-market volatility spillovers for a subsample of 13 companies. Given the small number of companies and the large number of observations per company, we use fixed-effect panel regression models for the empirical analysis.

3.2 *Data description*

This analysis utilizes data on both indices and individual stocks. For index-level analysis, we use the Hang Seng China Enterprises Index and the BNY Mellon Hong Kong Classic ADR Index (referred to as the HK ADR Index; data begin on January 8, 2015). The data are obtained from the Wind Economic Database and DataStream databases, respectively. For comparison, we also analyze the spillover effects between the A-share and ADR indices using the CSI 300 index and the S&P/BNY Mellon China Select ADR Index (referred to as the CN ADR Index). Data are obtained from the Wind Economic Database and the S&P Dow Jones Indices website, respectively, and the data start on January 3, 2011. Figure 1 shows that the domestic indices and their corresponding ADR indices are highly synchronized. The correlation coefficient between the Hang Seng China Enterprises Index and the HK ADR Index is 0.62, and the correlation coefficient of index volatility (with a standard deviation of 21 working days) is 0.66. The correlation coefficient between the CSI 300 Index and the CN ADR Index is 0.81, and the correlation coefficient of index volatility is 0.47.

At the individual stock level, we use daily data for 29 Chinese companies cross-listed in Hong Kong and the US from January 2001 to December 2020. A list of companies is presented in Tables A1 and A2.

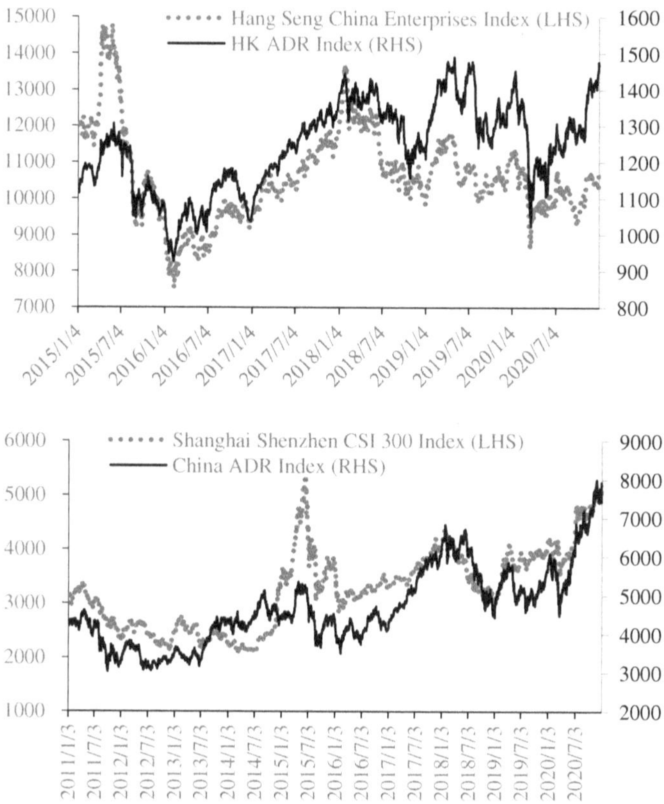

Figure 1. Stock indices: ADR, Hong Kong and Mainland China.

Source: Wind Economic Database, DataStream.

The data on individual stock prices, Hong Kong and US stock indices, CPI, and other macro variables are obtained from the Wind Economic Database. EPU data are monthly frequencies and are obtained from Baker *et al.* (2016).[3] VIX data are obtained from the Chicago Board of Trade. The corporate governance data of the 13 triple-listed companies are obtained from the CSMAR database. Variable definitions and data sources are shown in Table 1.

The descriptive statistics of the variables are shown in Table 2. For the entire sample, the spillover effects of ADR on H-shares or A-shares are

[3]Baker *et al.* (2016) use textual analysis methods to measure economic policy uncertainty and update and republish the index at http://www.policyuncertainty.com/.

Table 1. List of variables.

Variable Category	Variables	Definition	Source	Data Description
r^H, r^{ADR}, r^A		Stock price changes	Wind Economic Database	Panel Data (Daily)
σ^H, σ^{ADR}, σ^A		Annualized volatility of stock price changes	Calculated by the authors	
		Explained Variables		
DY^{vol} [H-ADR]		Net volatility spillover effect of H-shares on ADRs	Calculated by the authors	Panel Data (Daily)
DY^{vol} [A-ADR]		Net volatility spillover effect of A-shares on ADRs		
		Explanatory Variables		
Macro variables	dCPI	CPI Difference between Hong Kong and the US	Wind Economic Database	Monthly
	EPU	Economic Policy Uncertainty Index	Baker *et al.* (2016)	Monthly
Stock Market Variables	RelStockVol	Relative stock market volatility (window of 21 trading days). H-ADR equals the Hang Seng China Index volatility divided by HK ADR Index volatility. A-ADR equals the CSI 300 Index volatility divided by the CN ADR Index volatility.	Wind Economic Database	Daily, (HK)2015/1/8-2020/12/31, (CN)2011/1/3-2020/12/31
Sentiment	VIX	Implied Volatility of S&P 500 Index Options	Chicago Board of Trade	Daily, 2001/1/2-2020/12/31

Corporate Governance	$D_{Location}$	Dummy variable. 1 = independent director and listed company share a location. 0 = different locations. For companies with multiple independent directors, the work location of independent directors with accounting expertise prevails.	CSMAR	Annual panel data
	D_{Big4}	Dummy variable. 1 = The auditor is a Big 4 accounting firm in China.		
	$D_{OffshoreAudit}$	Dummy variable. 1 = The auditor is an offshore accounting firm.		
	$N_{Analyst}$	The number of analysts that publish reports about the company.		
	$N_{Reports}$	The number of research reports about the company.		

Note: The annualized volatility of stock price change such as σ^H is $\hat{\sigma}_{it} = 100\sqrt{365 \cdot \tilde{\sigma}_{it}^2}$ according to Diebold and Yilmaz (2012), where $\tilde{\sigma}_{it}^2 = 0.361[\ln(P_{it}^{max}) - \ln(P_{it}^{max})]^2$.

Table 2. Descriptive statistics of variables (2001–2020).

Variables	Number of Observations	Mean	Standard Deviation	Minimum	Maximum	Unit Root Test
Panel Data						
DY^{vol} [H-ADR]	97,135	−2.187	4.051	−49.064	12.545	26.479***
DY^{vol} [A-ADR]	47,214	−0.891	3.296	−33.251	19.781	32.069***
Time Series						
DY^{vol} [H-ADR] Index	1,488	−0.644	3.224	−9.033	7.930	−2.951**
DY^{vol} [A-ADR] Index	2,525	−0.356	2.474	−12.045	6.174	−4.602***
RelStockVol	1,488	1.349	0.399	0.408	2.971	−4.303***
lnVIX	5,032	2.905	0.382	2.213	4.415	−5.915***
lnEPU (Hong Kong Region)	239	4.781	0.535	3.136	6.053	−7.724***
lnEPU (China)	240	4.614	0.696	3.166	6.495	−4.066***
dCPI (Hong Kong Region)	240	−0.308	2.613	−6.100	4.900	−3.164**
dCPI(China)	240	0.274	1.724	−3.800	4.700	−3.243**
Corporate Governance (Annual Panel Data)						
D_{Big4}	203	0.473	0.500	0	1	—
$D_{OffshoreAudit}$	215	0.930	0.255	0	1	—
$N_{Analyst}$	204	19.284	11.132	1	49	—
$N_{Reports}$	204	43.324	32.308	1	168	—

Note: lnVIX and lnEPU denote the natural logarithm of VIX and EPU, respectively. The Fisher-type unit-root test is used for the panel data, and the statistics listed in the table are modified inv. chi-squared. The Dickey–Fuller test is used for the unit-root test of the time series data.

stronger than the reverse spillover effects, mainly due to the spillover effects in extreme situations. The unit root test shows that the main variables are all stationary. Tables 2 show the descriptive statistics of stock returns and variance. ADR returns were higher than A-shares and H-shares before the launch of the Shanghai–Hong Kong Stock Connect, but the volatility of ADR returns is higher than that of A-shares and H-shares.

4. Empirical Analysis

4.1 *H-share and A-share spillover effects on ADR: Stock index*

The spillover effects of stock price indices are shown in Figure 2. The mean spillover effect is dominated by spillover from ADRs to H-shares and A-shares, while the volatility spillover effect depicts bidirectional spillover features. The spillover effects of A-shares and H-shares on ADR show different dynamic characteristics. After the US Senate passed the HFCAA on May 20, 2020, the spillover effect of ADR on H-shares gradually weakened and was replaced by a net volatility spillover from H-shares to ADR, whereas A-shares do not show such characteristics.

The analysis of stock indices (Table 3) shows that higher stock market volatility in H-shares (A-shares) due to China's economic policy uncertainty is significantly and positively correlated with the net volatility spillover effect from H-shares to ADR. After we control for year effects, the coefficient on CPI becomes insignificant. These stock market and economic factors have higher explanatory power for the net volatility spillover effect of A-shares to ADR than H-shares.

4.2 *H-share and A-share spillover effects on ADR: A panel data analysis*

The results of the panel data analysis are depicted in Table 4. The findings are as follows: (1) Stock market relative volatility (RelStockVol) is significantly and positively related to the spillover effect. It is robust across subsamples, indicating that higher domestic stock market volatility transmits to ADR (a significant increase in the net volatility spillover effect) and is consistent with the findings of Prasad *et al.* (2018). (2) Implied volatility (VIX) is positively correlated with net volatility spillover

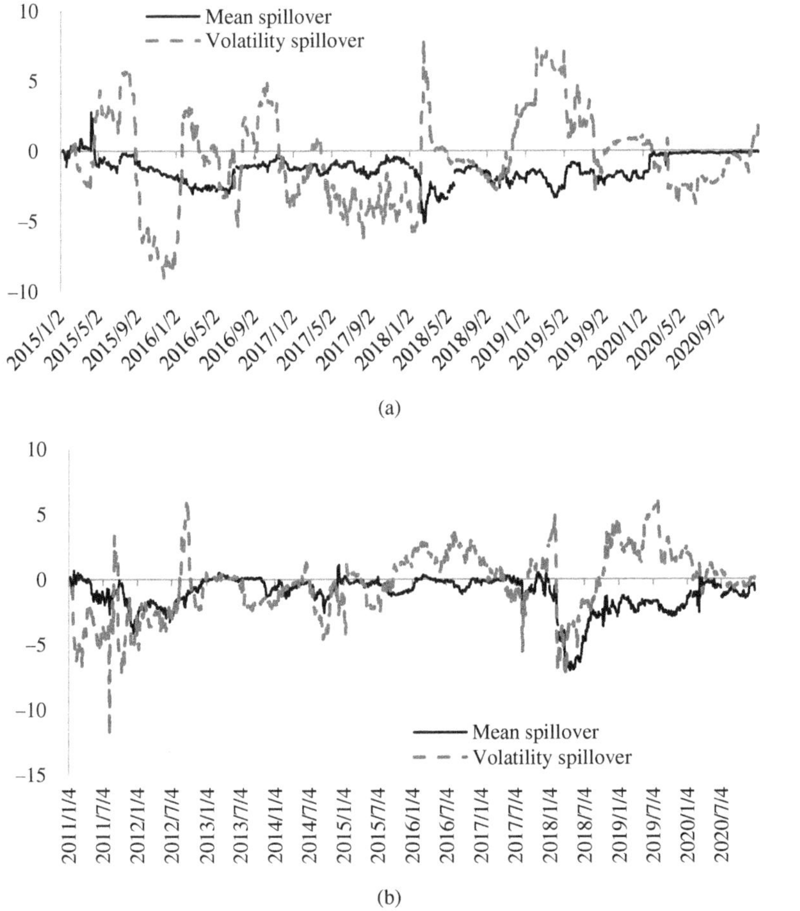

Figure 2. Net spillover effect of Stock Price Index: (a) H-shares on ADR; (b) A-shares on ADR.

effects. A rise in VIX implies increased investor sentiment about the stock market and an enhanced spillover effect. This means that the market sentiment indicator can partly explain the short-term volatility spillover effect in the stock market, which is consistent with Su (2020). However, the influence of the VIX has weakened since May 20, 2020 (the date the US Senate passed the HFCAA), suggesting that investors became more sensitive after the event. (3) Domestic EPU is positively related to the net

Table 3. Factors influencing the volatility spillover effects of stock indices.

	H→ ADR		A→ ADR	
Variables	**(1)**	**(2)**	**(3)**	**(4)**
dCPI	0.320***	0.041	0.101**	−0.051
	(0.053)	(0.071)	(0.048)	(0.048)
lnEPU	1.165***	−0.054	1.785***	0.754***
	(0.183)	(0.171)	(0.089)	(0.141)
RelStockVol	−0.236	1.962***	0.277**	0.371***
	(0.236)	(0.230)	(0.112)	(0.100)
lnVIX	−0.437*	−0.176	−2.039***	−0.280*
	(0.250)	(0.292)	(0.152)	(0.150)
Constants	−5.180***	−4.093***	−4.053***	−6.887***
	(1.195)	(1.188)	(0.577)	(0.840)
Number of observations	1,465	1,465	2,503	2,503
Adjusted-R^2	0.052	0.333	0.176	0.536
Year Effect	×	√	×	√

Note: Standard deviations are in parentheses. *, **, and *** indicate significance at the 10%, 5%, and 1% levels, respectively.

spillover effect. (4) The impact of macroeconomic variables represented by CPI on the spillover effect varies with time.

Compared to Main Board ADRs, ADRs traded on the US OTC market[4] (D_{OTC}) are subject to a stronger volatility spillover from H-shares. The difference in volatility spillover from H-shares and A-shares is insignificant. This finding is consistent before and after the passing of HFCAA. In other words, China can use the significant spillover effect of H-shares on ADRs (especially those traded in the OTC market) and seize the opportunity for the secondary listing or dual listing of US-listed Chinese stocks to make Hong Kong a distributional center for the overseas listing of Chinese stocks. This action could also strengthen H-shares' role in guiding the price fluctuations of US-listed Chinese stocks and facilitate

[4]The OTC market has lower requirements for listed companies and lower liquidity. Eligible listed companies can apply for transfer from the OTC market to the Main Board.

Table 4. Factors related to the volatility spillover effects.

Dependent Variable: DY^{vol} [H-ADR] or DY^{vol} [A-ADR]								
	HK				CN			
Variables	**Full Interval**		**Since the HFCAA**		**Full Interval**		**Since the HFCAA**	
dCPI	0.158***	0.158***	−0.174***	−0.174***	−0.025	−0.025	−0.456***	−0.456***
	(0.012)	(0.012)	(0.017)	(0.017)	(0.021)	(0.021)	(0.043)	(0.043)
lnEPU	0.213***	0.213***	0.365***	0.365***	0.147***	0.147***	−0.451	−0.451
	(0.042)	(0.042)	(0.081)	(0.081)	(0.039)	(0.039)	(0.323)	(0.323)
RelStockVol	0.601***	0.601***	0.231***	0.231***	0.504***	0.504***	1.042***	1.042***
	(0.055)	(0.055)	(0.088)	(0.088)	(0.050)	(0.050)	(0.209)	(0.209)
lnVIX	0.539***	0.540***	0.003	0.003	0.277***	0.277***	−0.469	−0.469
	(0.058)	(0.058)	(0.167)	(0.167)	(0.067)	(0.067)	(0.327)	(0.327)
D_{OTC}	—	1.780**	—	1.875*	—	−0.259	—	−1.203
	—	(0.835)	—	(1.125)	—	(0.443)	—	(1.218)
Constants	−5.729***	−6.471***	−4.488***	−5.264***	−2.808***	−2.728***	3.735	4.105*
	(0.546)	(0.606)	(0.907)	(1.003)	(0.332)	(0.352)	(2.464)	(2.492)
Number of observations	35,626	35,626	3,733	3,733	29,922	29,922	1,947	1,947
Number of stocks	29	29	29	29	13	13	13	13
Adj-R^2	0.011	0.011	0.040	0.040	0.004	0.004	0.099	0.099

Note: Within the group, R^2 is reported.

mainland investors leveraging Stock Connect to increase equity holdings of high-quality Chinese stocks.

4.3 *The impact of corporate governance on volatility spillover effects*

As shown in Tables 5 and 6, corporate governance variables significantly correlate with volatility spillover effects. (1) Consistency in the workplace between independent directors and listed companies is not significantly

Table 5. Influences of corporate governance on H-share volatility spillover.

	Dependent Variable: DY^{vol} [H-ADR]			
Variables	**(1)**	**(2)**	**(3)**	**(4)**
dCPI	0.277***	0.292***	0.113***	0.146***
	(0.023)	(0.023)	(0.024)	(0.023)
lnEPU	0.478***	0.444***	0.358***	0.370***
	(0.066)	(0.066)	(0.065)	(0.065)
RelStockVol	–0.401***	–0.361***	–0.909***	–0.885***
	(0.085)	(0.085)	(0.086)	(0.085)
lnVIX	2.034***	2.145***	2.149***	2.208***
	(0.136)	(0.137)	(0.134)	(0.134)
D_{Big4}	0.116	—	—	—
	(0.091)	—	—	—
$D_{OffshoreAudit}$	—	–1.003***	—	—
	—	(0.131)	—	—
$\ln N_{Analyst}$	—	—	–2.304***	—
	—	—	(0.095)	—
$\ln N_{Reports}$	—	—	—	–1.953***
	—	—	—	(0.080)
Constants	–9.721***	–9.025***	–1.903***	–1.705**
	(0.629)	(0.629)	(0.684)	(0.691)
Number of observations	15,301	15,301	15,301	15,301
Number of stocks	13	13	13	13
Adj-R^2	0.052	0.055	0.087	0.088

Table 6. Impacts of corporate governance on A-share volatility spillover.

Dependent Variable: DY^{vol} [A-ADR]				
Variables	**(1)**	**(2)**	**(3)**	**(4)**
dCPI	0.457***	0.415***	0.366***	0.397***
	(0.035)	(0.035)	(0.034)	(0.034)
lnEPU	–0.100*	–0.183***	0.801***	0.830***
	(0.060)	(0.059)	(0.066)	(0.064)
RelStockVol	–0.101	0.025	–0.112	–0.045
	(0.077)	(0.077)	(0.075)	(0.075)
lnVIX	0.369***	0.593***	0.434***	0.521***
	(0.124)	(0.123)	(0.121)	(0.120)
D_{Big4}	–0.176**	—	—	—
	(0.087)	—	—	—
$D_{\text{OffshoreAudit}}$	—	–2.382***	—	—
	—	(0.124)	—	—
$\ln N_{\text{Analyst}}$	—	—	–2.733***	—
	—	—	(0.099)	—
$\ln N_{\text{Reports}}$	—	—	—	–2.545***
	—	—	—	(0.082)
Constants	–1.354**	0.319	1.585***	2.515***
	(0.579)	(0.576)	(0.548)	(0.528)
Number of observations	15,264	15,264	15,264	15,264
Number of stocks	13	13	13	13
Adj-R^2	0.016	0.039	0.064	0.077

correlated with H-share volatility spillover but is negatively correlated with A-share volatility spillover. Since the stocks of listed companies in the three regions are based on a common operating entity, this difference may indicate that A-share and H-share investors hold different views on the role of independent directors in corporate governance. (2) Companies audited by offshore accounting firms have weaker net volatility spillover effects of H-shares or A-shares on ADRs. This may be related to the requirement that domestic accounting firms receive approval from the CSRC to submit audit work papers to the SEC. (3) Firms with more market attention ($N_{Analyst}$, $N_{Reports}$) and higher information transparency have weaker volatility spillover effects. This further confirms the stronger spillover effects of H-shares on OTC ADRs.

Comparing the data in these two tables with those in Table 4, we see that corporate governance variables have significantly stronger explanatory power for the volatility spillover effect of H-shares than A-shares. In other words, even if it is challenging to enhance the market attention of stocks or adjust the corporate governance structure in the short term, companies can play an essential role in guiding ADR prices by going public in Hong Kong rather than in mainland China.

4.4 *Discussion*

4.4.1 *Spillover effects of A-shares to H-shares*

The volatility spillover from H-shares to ADR may partly originate from A-shares since such shares can spill over to ADR both directly and indirectly (through H-shares). The remaining origins of such spillover stem from the Hong Kong economy or stock market and include, for example, the influencing factors analyzed above. Therefore, the volatility spillover from H-shares to ADR may be greater or less than that of A-shares.

We measure the dynamic AH volatility spillover effect based on the CSI 300 index and the Hang Seng SME index, as shown in Figure 3.

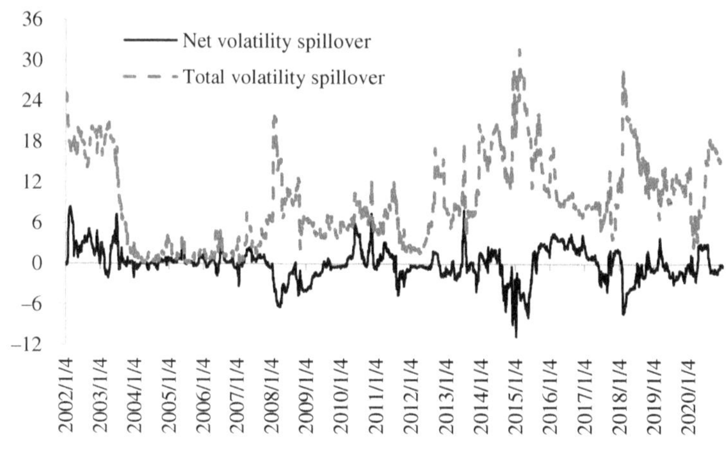

Figure 3. Volatility spillover effects of A-shares on H-shares.

The results indicate a bidirectional spillover between A-shares and H-shares. Moreover, three main periods are characterized by a longer duration of volatility spillover from H-shares to A-shares, corresponding to the global financial crisis in 2008, the period between the launch of the Shanghai–Hong Kong Stock Connect pilot in 2014 and the end of 2015, and the inclusion of A-shares in the MSCI in 2018. Since 2014, the bidirectional volatility spillover between A-shares and H-shares has strengthened, reflecting the enhanced capital and information flows between the two stock markets brought by the stock connects.

4.4.2 *Robustness test*

The results are robust for individual stocks with weekly data and adjusted volatility. Specifically, we refer to Diebold and Yilmaz (2009) to construct a real stock return series, i.e., $r_{i,t} = (1+i_{i,t})/(1+\pi_t)-1$, where weekly nominal returns $i_{i,t} = \ln(P_{i,t}) - \ln(P_{i,t-1})$, $\pi_t = \sqrt[4]{CPI_t}$, and CPI_t are month-on-month CPI. The weekly stock return volatility is defined as

$$\tilde{\sigma}^2 = 0.511(H_t - L_t)^2 - 0.019[(C_t - O_t)(H_t + L_t - 2O_t) - 2(H_t - O_t)(L_t - O_t)] \\ - 0.383(C_t - O_t)^2$$

where H_t and L_t are the natural logarithms of the week's high and low prices, respectively, O_t is the natural logarithm of the Monday open price, and C_t is the natural logarithm of the Friday close price.

5. Conclusions and Policy Implications

This chapter uses stock indices and panel data of cross-listed companies to document bidirectional volatility spillover effects between domestic stock prices and ADR prices. The volatility spillover effect of H-shares (A-shares) on ADR increases with the rising volatility of China's stock market and a rise in the domestic EPU. In other words, domestic stock prices have a guiding effect on ADR prices. Moreover, the higher analyst attention of listed companies, or the hiring of overseas accounting firms, is conducive to reducing the information asymmetry of ADR investors and moderating their sensitivity to H-share (A-share) volatility. The net spillover effect of H-shares to OTC market ADR is stronger than that of Main Board market ADR, while the difference between the net spillovers of A-shares to the two is insignificant.

The results indicate the benefits of also listing US-listed Chinese stocks in Hong Kong. First, doing so gives full play to the volatility spillover effects of H-shares to ADRs, strengthens the influences of domestic stock prices on ADR prices, reduces ADR investors' information asymmetry, and decreases the reputational risk of US-listed Chinese companies. Second, it leverages Hong Kong's status as an international financial center and can facilitate regulatory cooperation, strengthen listed companies' corporate governance, enhance domestic regulators' discourse, and improve investors' trust in Chinese stocks and the Chinese stock market. The findings are also of referential value to Chinese companies that remain listed in the US on enhancing market attention and hiring overseas accounting firms.

Appendix

Table A1. List of dual-listed Chinese companies.

		H-share		ADR		A-share	
Number	**Abbreviated Company Name**	**Code**	**Listing Date**	**Code**	**Listing Date**	**Code**	**Listing Date**
1	Sinopec Shanghai Petrochemical	0338	1993/7/26	SHI	1993/7/26	600688	1993/11/8
2	Guangshen Railway	0525	1996/5/14	GSH	1996/5/14	601333	2006/12/22
3	Eastern Airlines	0670	1997/2/5	CEA	1997/2/4	600115	1997/11/5
4	Southern Airlines	1055	1997/7/31	ZNH	1997/7/30	600029	2003/7/25

(Continued)

Table A1. (*Continued*)

Number	Abbreviated Company Name	H-share		ADR		A-share	
		Code	Listing Date	Code	Listing Date	Code	Listing Date
5	Huaneng Power International	0902	1998/1/21	HNP	1994/10/5	600011	2001/12/6
6	PetroChina	0857	2000/4/7	PTR	2000/4/6	601857	2007/11/5
7	China Petroleum & Chemical	0386	2000/10/19	SNP	2000/10/18	600028	2001/8/8
8	Aluminum Corporation of China	2600	2001/12/12	ACH	2001/12/11	601600	2007/4/30
9	China Life Insurance	2628	2003/12/18	LFC	2003/12/17	601628	2007/1/9
10	China Mobile	0941	1997/10/23	CHL	1997/10/22	—	—
11	China Unicom	0762	2000/6/22	CHU	2000/6/21	—	—
12	CNOOC	0883	2001/2/28	CEO	2001/2/27	—	—
13	China Telecom	0728	2002/11/15	CHA	2002/11/14	—	—
14	BeiGene	6160	2018/8/8	BGNE	2016/2/3	—	—
15	Alibaba	9988	2019/11/26	BABA	2014/9/19	—	—
16	NetEase	9999	2020/6/11	NTES	2000/6/30	—	—
17	JD.COM	9618	2020/6/18	JD	2014/5/22	—	—
18	Tsingtao Brewery	0168	1993/7/15	TSGTY	1996/2/1	600600	1993/8/27
19	Jiangxi Copper	0358	1997/6/12	JIXAY	2003/10/7	600362	2002/1/11
20	Yankuang Energy	1171	1998/4/1	YZCAY	1998/3/27	600188	1998/7/1

21	Ping An Insurance	2318	2004/6/24	PNGAY	2005/3/28	601318	2007/3/1
22	CLP Holdings	0002	1980/1/2	CLPHY	1997/11/3	—	—
23	Techtronic Industries	0669	1990/12/17	TTNDY	1994/1/1	—	—
24	China Overseas Land & Investment	0688	1992/8/20	CAOVY	2008/11/3	—	—
25	Lenovo Group	0992	1994/2/14	LNVGY	1995/3/28	—	—
26	Hong Kong TV	1137	1997/8/4	HKTVY	1999/11/2	—	—
27	Beijing Capital International Airport	0694	2000/2/1	BJCHY	2008/11/3	—	—
28	Semiconductor Manufacturing International Corporation	0981	2004/3/18	SMICY	2004/3/17	—	—
29	Tencent Holdings	0700	2004/6/16	TCEHY	2008/10/20	—	—

Notes: We excluded the following companies from the sample: nine companies that have been delisted from the US stock market (such as Angang Steel), nine foreign companies cross-listed in Hong Kong and the US (such as HSBC Holdings), and US-listed Chinese companies with a short cross-listing history. This table includes US Main Board ADRs (numbers 1–14) and OTC market ADRs (numbers 18–29). The Guangshen Railway was delisted from the NYSE and listed on the OTC market on November 16, 2020, with the stock code adjusted to GSHHY.

Table A2. Descriptive statistics of stock price returns and variance.

	Mean			Variance		
	H	**ADR**	**A**	**H**	**ADR**	**A**
			Index			
Full sample	0.051	0.028	0.044	1.886	1.132	1.652
(a) 2007-2014.11.16	0.027	—	0.030	2.216	—	1.887
(b) 2014.11.17-2020.5.19	0.002	0.011	0.044	1.392	1.104	1.571
(c) 2020.5.20-2020-12.31	0.099	0.170	0.209	1.197	1.338	1.291
Tests for equal means or variances						
(a) & (b)	0.024	—	–0.014	–0.824***	—	–0.315***
(b) & (c)	–0.096	–0.159	–0.165	–0.195**	0.234***	–0.280***
			Individual Stock Panel Data			
Full sample	0.073	0.105	0.066	2.900	7.252	3.108
(1) Before 2006	0.116	0.170	0.118	3.291	7.875	3.650
(2) 2007-2014.11.16	0.073	0.130	0.050	3.010	9.563	3.194
(3) 2014.11.17-2020.5.19	0.019	0.015	0.035	2.291	2.370	2.504
(4) 2020.5.20-2020-12.31	0.162	0.133	0.127	2.772	2.816	2.157
Tests for equal means or variances						
(1) & (2)	–0.043	–0.040	0.068	–0.281***	1.687***	–0.456***
(2) & (3)	–0.054**	–0.115*	0.015	–0.719***	–7.193***	–0.690***
(3) & (4)	0.143***	0.118**	–0.092	0.481***	0.447***	–0.347***

References

Ahmed, A.D. & Huo, R. (2019). Impacts of China's crash on Asia-Pacific financial integration: Volatility interdependence, information transmission and market co-movement, *Economic Modelling*, 79, 28–46.

Antonakakis, N. & Gabauer, D. (2017). Refined measures of dynamic connectedness based on TVP-VAR. MPRA Working Paper No. 78282.

Baker, R.S., Bloom, N., & Davis, S.J. (2016). Measuring economic policy uncertainty, *The Quarterly Journal of Economics*, 131(4), 1593–1636.

Chung, K. & Zhang, H. (2011). Corporate governance and institutional ownership. *Journal of Financial Quantitative Analysis*, 46, 247–273.

Dai, Danmiao & Liu, Xiliang (2017). Literature review of financial fraud in Chinese concept stock companies. *Financial Development Research*, 2017(1), 11–19 (in Chinese).

Diebold, F.X. & Yilmaz, K. (2009). Measuring financial asset return and volatility spillovers, with application to global equity markets. *Economic Journal*, 119, 158–171.

Diebold, F.X. & Yilmaz, K. (2012). Better to give than to receive: Predictive measurement of volatility spillovers. *International Journal of Forecasting*, 28, 57–66.

Eiling, E. & Gerard, B. (2015). Emerging equity market comovements: Trends and macroeconomic fundamentals. *Review of Finance*, 19, 1543–1585.

Eun, C. & Shim, S. (1989). International transmission of stock market movements. *Journal of Financial and Quantitative Analysis*, 24(2), 241–256.

Fernández-Rodríguez, F., Gómez-Puig, M., & Sosvilla-Rivero, S. (2016). Using connectedness analysis to assess financial stress transmission in EMU sovereign bond market volatility. *Journal of International Financial Markets, Institutions and Money*, 43, 126–145.

Grossmann, A. & Ngo, T. (2020) Economic policy uncertainty and ADR mispricing. *Journal of Multinational Financial Management*, 55, 1–19.

Hu Qiuling, Mary (2011). Volatility spillover effect analysis of China's stock market and bond market. *Financial Research*, 2011(10), 198–206 (in Chinese).

Kim, S.W. & Rogers, J.H. (1995). International stock price spillovers and market liberalization: Evidence from Korea, Japan, and the United States. *Journal of Empirical Finance*, 2(2), 117–133.

King, M. & Wadhwani, S. (1990). Transmission of volatility between stock markets. *Review of Financial Studies*, 3(1), 5–33.

Koutmos, G. & Booth, G.G. (1995). Asymmetric volatility transmission in international stock markets. *Journal of International Money and Finance*, 14(6), 747–762.

Lei Guangyong, Wang Wen, & Jin Xin (2012). Corporate governance quality, investor confidence and stock returns. *Accounting Research*, 2012(2), 79–86 (in Chinese).

Li Gao (2017). Analysis of the characteristics and impact of the privatization and spin-off of Chinese concept stocks returning to A-shares. *Securities Market Bulletin*, 2017(11), 42–48 (in Chinese).

Liang Qi, Li Zheng & Hao Xiangchao (2015). Internationalization of China's stock market: From the perspective of information spillover. *Economic Research*, 50(4), 150–164 (in Chinese).

Liang Shangkun, Xu, Canyu, & Wang, Ruihua (2020). Board faultlines and stock price crash risk. *China's Industrial Economy*, 2020(3), 155–173 (in Chinese).

Liu, Jipeng & Lin, Weiran (2015). VIE model double moral hazard and regulatory recommendations. *Introduction to the Securities Market*, 2015(10), 4–12 (in Chinese).

Pastor, L. & Veronesi, P. (2012). Uncertainty about government policy and stock prices. *The Journal of Finance*, 67, 1219–1264.

Peng, Tao (2016). Research on the return of Chinese concept stocks to domestic capital markets. *International Economic Cooperation*, 2016(10), 92–95 (in Chinese).

Prasad, N., Grant, A., & Kim, S.J. (2018). Time varying volatility indices and their determinants: Evidence from developed and emerging stock markets. *International Review of Financial Analysis*, 60, 115–126.

Pretorius, E. (2002). Economic determinants of emerging stock market interdependence. *Emerging Markets Review*, 3(1), 84–105.

Rao Huimin (1999). The development of Chinese enterprises listed overseas ADR way. *China's Industrial Economy*, 1999(2), 39–41 (in Chinese).

Su, X. (2020). Dynamic behaviors and contributing factors of volatility spillovers across G7 stock markets. *The North American Journal of Economics and Finance*, 53, 101218.

Xu, Xiaoguang, Liao, Wenxin, & Zheng, Zunxin (2017). Inter-industry volatility spillover effect and formation mechanism under the background of Shanghai-Hong Kong Stock Connect. *Quantitative Economic and Technical Economic Research*, 34(3), 112–127 (in Chinese).

Zheng, T. & Huo, H. (2013). Reexamining the time-varying volatility spillover effects: A Markov switching causality approach. *North American Journal of Economics and Finance*, 26, 643–662.

Zheng Tingguo & Liu Tangyong (2018). Analysis of stock market volatility spillover effect and its influencing factors. *Economics*, (Quarterly), 17(2), 669–692 (in Chinese).

Zhou, X., Zhang, W. & Zhang, J. (2012). Volatility spillovers between the Chinese and world equity markets. *Pacific-Basin Finance Journal*, 20(2), 247–270.

Chapter 7

Future Directions

A-shares have a persistent price premium relative to H-shares and ADRs, which surged after the launch of Shanghai–Hong Kong Stock Connect in 2014. To accelerate the establishment of the new dual-circulation development pattern, China should enhance the capital account convertibility of the RMB, further promote the flexibility of the RMB exchange rate, strengthen the integration between China and the international financial market, and improve the price discovery efficiency of the domestic stock market. Moreover, China could take the issuance of RMB-denominated Chinese stocks in Hong Kong as a breakthrough to establish a layered, effective, and stable financial system and promote international circulation, creating a better environment for domestic circulation.

1. Deepen the Financial Opening-up and Exchange Rate Reform

1.1 *Price premium of A-shares relative to H-shares and ADRs*

After three decades of development, China's stock market has become the second-largest stock market in the world, but it is not yet fully aligned with the international financial market. More than 1,500 companies have been listed abroad, with approximately 140 are cross-listed. Financial institutions and policymakers are concerned about the stock prices of China's cross-listed companies. The first concern is that domestic stock prices are persistently higher than offshore prices (that is, they have a price premium). The second concern is that the premium of cross-listed A-shares and H-shares surged even after the connectivity between the mainland and Hong Kong stock markets tightened, particularly after the launch of the Shanghai–Hong Kong Stock Connect at the end of 2014.

The data of 116 Chinese companies show that since 2002, the A-ADR premium has averaged approximately 30%, the AH premium has averaged 35%, and the ADR-H premium of 15 cross-listed companies has averaged only approximately 0.1. The low spreads between H-shares and ADRs indicate a high degree of integration between the Hong Kong and US markets, while the significant premiums for A-shares relative to H-shares and ADRs indicate market segmentation between the mainland and offshore markets. Market segmentation affects investors' valuation through multiple channels at the macro, meso, and micro levels, thus affecting the AH and A-ADR premiums.

1.2 *Financial liberalization and exchange rate reform have reduced A-ADR and AH price premiums*

Differences in the stock prices of cross-listed companies mainly stem from the capital flow and exchange rate regime (macro level), trading mechanism and market liquidity (meso level), stock liquidity, and information asymmetry (micro level) in different markets. Arrangements of the US and Hong Kong stock markets are more conducive to price discovery, stock trading, and risk management, including higher financial openness and more flexible exchange rates.

The influencing factors of the stock price premium manifest the immaturity of the Chinese stock market. Unlike the price premium between mature stock markets, the A-ADR price premium is mainly related to capital market liberalization, the speculative motives of A-share investors, and a lack of stock liquidity. Market sentiment is more important in explaining the AH premium than the A-ADR premium, indicating limited investor rationality in the mainland stock market. The shares of overseas investors (approximately 5%) and institutional investors (20%) in A-shares are much lower than those in H-shares and in the US stock market. Given this, mainland China stock markets feature more speculative trading, a higher turnover rate, and a shorter investment horizon, which restrain the stock market's price discovery efficiency.

China's financial market opening-up and exchange rate regime reform have reduced the cross-market price premium. We construct a two-country, two-stage theoretical model and show that increased financial openness, expectations of RMB appreciation, and decreased information asymmetry reduce A-ADR and AH price premiums. The results are supported by an empirical analysis.

First, financial openness enhances price discovery efficiency, thus narrowing cross-market price premiums. We introduce three financial openness indicators, namely, the ratio of foreign assets and liabilities to GDP; the ratio of foreign assets and liabilities, excluding foreign exchange reserves, to GDP; and a dummy variable for the launch of the Shanghai–Hong Kong Stock Connect in November 2014. Panel data analysis in static and rolling windows shows that the effect of financial liberalization in narrowing the A-ADR and AH premium is more significant before 2017 and weakens marginally after 2017. The surge in the AH premium after the launch of the stock connects is caused by factors such as exchange rates, while the stock connects enhance the price discovery efficiency of A-shares.

Second, exchange rate reform has improved the role of the RMB as a pricing currency. Since the "811" exchange rate reform in 2015, the impact of the expected changes in the onshore exchange rate on the A-ADR premium has increased significantly, while the impacts of the USD index on the A-ADR and AH premiums have weakened accordingly, confirming the effectiveness of China's market-oriented exchange rate reform. Meanwhile, the lower priority of expected RMB exchange rate movements among the influencing factors reflects foreign investors' increased acceptance of China's exchange rate fluctuations.

1.3 *Policy recommendations*

In the face of geopolitical risks, an increasing number of Chinese stocks may be delisted from the US and seek listing in Hong Kong or mainland China. It is necessary to further promote the development of the A-share market and the convergence of the A-share market with international financial markets, thus attracting overseas investors and promoting the dual circulation of the economy. The following initiatives can help enhance the price discovery efficiency of A-shares, narrow the A-ADR and AH price premiums, and increase the international influence of China's capital market.

First, the connectivity between the A-share market and international markets should be enhanced, and the opening-up of China's financial markets should be advanced. China should accelerate the launch of an international board, improve its registration system, enhance the capital account convertibility of the RMB, and introduce new measures to facilitate overseas investors' purchase of A-shares. China should also further expand the scale of the institutional opening-up of the financial sector and strengthen the sector's macroprudential management and regulatory capacity.

Second, the flexibility of the RMB exchange rate should be enhanced, and exchange rate expectations should be stabilized. The RMB exchange rate regime should be reformed, and the financial market should be opened up in a coordinated manner. The reform of the international monetary and financial system should be actively promoted, cooperation with other central banks on bilateral currency swaps and the international use of RMB should be encouraged, and the two-way fluctuation of the RMB's exchange rate should be strengthened.

Third, listed Chinese companies should set reasonable dividend payout ratios, thus encouraging domestic long-term institutional investors. The CSRC needs to improve the governance and delisting mechanism of listed companies, reform stock market rules to enhance liquidity, weaken the influence of speculative trading and market sentiment on stock prices, and promote the price discovery efficiency of the domestic stock market.

2. Issue RMB-Denominated Chinese Stocks in Hong Kong

In the context of strategic competition between China and the US, it is necessary to steadily promote RMB internationalization and capital account liberalization. It is critical to leverage Hong Kong's status as an international financial center and the stock connect mechanism. We suggest allowing US-listed Chinese companies to issue RMB-denominated stocks simultaneously in Hong Kong and mainland China. In this way, domestic investors can buy RMB-denominated Chinese stocks through the stock connects, promoting the bidirectional opening-up of the capital market and forming a "reservoir" of offshore RMB. At the same time, the dedicated account management of the stock connects will facilitate the monitoring of RMB fund flows and ensure that the outbound flow is used solely to purchase RMB-denominated Chinese stocks. Our proposal has the following benefits over the current approaches to RMB internationalization and capital account liberalization.

First, the current approach pursues capital account liberalization in an asymmetric manner, encouraging capital inflow but controlling capital outflow. The lift of the QDII quota has limited influence because residents are reluctant to invest if there is no suitable investment subject. The current stock connect mechanism requires RMB investments and remittances to be converted into Hong Kong dollars, which affects the exchange rate and foreign exchange reserves. In contrast, our proposal guides residents to invest abroad in a controllable manner and invest in stocks of familiar companies. Doing so can reduce the risk of a domestic asset bubble and will not cause shock to foreign exchange reserves and exchange rates. If our proposal is followed, domestic funds can conveniently enter the Hong Kong market to purchase RMB assets, and a balanced two-way opening-up will help mitigate domestic asset bubble risks. Meanwhile, the southbound capital flow for purchasing RMB assets in the Hong Kong market will not cause a reduction in China's foreign exchange reserves or fluctuations in the RMB exchange rate. Capital flows can be closely monitored in dedicated accounts based on the stock connects, and the risks can be prudently managed.

Second, to maintain currency stability, the central bank issues RMB central bank bills to extract RMB in the offshore market, which reduces the willingness of foreign institutions to hold RMB and does not help with RMB internationalization. The PBC's current practice of using central bank notes to maintain the stability of the RMB exchange rate results in the actual inaccessibility of RMB funds abroad. In contrast, our proposal is conducive to forming an offshore RMB "reservoir" but does not disturb the RMB exchange rate. Three "reservoirs" of the RMB are needed to promote RMB internationalization: the domestic interbank bond market, the exchange of foreign exchange reserves under a flexible exchange rate regime, and the offshore asset market. Creating a "reservoir" of investable offshore RMB without affecting the exchange rate is essential. If our proposal is implemented, the stock of RMB in the offshore market will increase if domestic RMB outbound investment in RMB-denominated Chinese stocks is promoted. At the same time, the development of the RMB asset market will attract foreign investors, thus forming a "reservoir" of offshore RMB and promoting RMB internationalization.

Third, our proposal can reduce the excessive dependence of Hong Kong's financial system on the US dollar and ease the pressure on the linked exchange rate system. For decades, Hong Kong has served as a re-export hub, and over 70% of the re-export trade has been denominated in the US dollar. Currently, in addition to trade, finance has become increasingly crucial for Hong Kong. The Hong Kong stock market is dominated by mainland companies, which account for approximately 50% of all listed companies and more than 70% of the market capitalization. These mainland assets are currently denominated in Hong Kong dollars and essentially valued in US dollars. The US has revoked Hong Kong's unique economic status and may yet introduce financial sanctions to undermine Hong Kong's status as an international financial center. Our proposal, if implemented, would gradually foster a larger RMB-denominated financial market in Hong Kong and weaken the influence of the US dollar on Hong Kong's financial system.

Fourth, our proposal can facilitate the fundraising of domestic internet technology and financial technology companies and address data security concerns for Chinese technology companies listed in the US. US-listed Chinese companies have a total market capitalization of USD 0.9 trillion by the end of 2023, equivalent to 14% of the total market capitalization of HKEX and 8% of the total market capitalization of A-shares. Technology lies at the core of Sino-US competition. Most US-listed Chinese technology companies are high-quality and belong to fields where China may make breakthroughs. The external environment faced by US-listed Chinese stocks is no longer friendly, and there is an urgent need to make proper arrangements for their listing in Hong Kong or mainland China. The dual listing of Chinese stocks in both Hong Kong and mainland China in RMB can provide enough financing for companies, level the prices of domestic and foreign financial assets, and improve the efficiency of the domestic financial market.

Part III

Bond Market

Chapter 8

History of the Opening-up of the Bond Market

Since the 1980s, China has been continuously advancing the reform and opening up of its bond market. The Chinese bond market has been the second largest bond market in the world since 2016. Currently, China's bond market comprises three main submarkets: the interbank market, the exchange market, and the over-the-counter market. As the primary component, the interbank market operates as a wholesale market for block trading, with participation from various institutional investors. It accounts for approximately 86% of the outstanding volume of the Chinese bond market. The exchange market, on the other hand, functions as a retail market for centralized bidding trading and facilitates block trading. The over-the-counter market, an extension of the interbank market, operates as a retail market.

The Chinese bond market continues to open up and improve with the growing diversity of its market participants. Foreign issuers and investors are becoming more involved in the domestic bond market, a process referred to as "bringing in". Simultaneously, the access of domestic issuers and investors to overseas market participation, known as "going global", has expanded. As of the end of 2023, the outstanding balance of bonds in custody amounted to RMB 157.9 trillion, and overseas institutions held RMB 3.72 trillion, or 2.4%, of the outstanding bonds in custody in China's bond market.

1. Bringing in Foreign Investors and Issuers

1.1 *Foreign investors*

Foreign investors are increasingly engaged in the Chinese bond market as it continues to open up. The PBC introduced the *Measures for Administration of Bond Transactions in the National Interbank Bond Market* on April 30, 2000, enabling foreign bank branches engaged in RMB business to participate in the China Interbank Bond Market (CIBM). In 2005, the Pan-Asian Bond Index Fund became the first foreign institutional investor to enter the interbank bond market. Subsequently, several corporate banks and branches of foreign banks in China, such as HSBC, Standard Chartered, Citigroup, and JPMorgan Chase, became members of the NAFMII. In May 2008, JPMorgan Chase Bank (China) Co. Ltd. became the first foreign bank to qualify as an interbank bond market maker. In January 2009, the CBRC approved wholly foreign-owned banks and Sino-foreign joint venture banks to trade and underwrite (non-financial) corporate bond financing instruments in the interbank bond market, thereby granting foreign banks access to the domestic corporate bond market. As of March 28, 2023, 11 foreign-funded corporate banks or branches were listed as cash bond market makers in the interbank bond market. Among them, Deutsche Bank, BNP Paribas, HSBC, JPMorgan Chase, DBS, and Standard Chartered Bank are comprehensive market makers. The remaining four foreign-funded corporate banks — Bank of East Asia, Citibank, Mizuho Bank, MUFG Bank, and Bank of America Corporation Shanghai Branch — are specialized market makers for credit bonds.

Entry standards for foreign institutional investors into both the interbank bond market and the exchange market have increasingly converged. This unification of standards has resulted in enhanced convenience for these investors. In May 2022, the People's Bank of China, the Securities Regulatory Commission, and the Foreign Exchange Administration issued *Announcement No. 4*, which aimed to further facilitate foreign institutional investors' participation in China's bond market. The announcement introduced measures to streamline the investment process. It allowed foreign institutional investors who had already gained access to the interbank bond market to invest in the exchange market without repetitive applications. Moreover, efforts are now being made to explore and establish inclusive institutional arrangements that are compatible with multilevel trusteeship.

Additionally, the announcement sought to enable two-way fund transfers within the same foreign institutional investor's account in China, thereby facilitating smoother investment operations.

Tax exemption policies associated with foreign investors' involvement in the Chinese bond market have played a crucial role in attracting and encouraging foreign investment. In November 2018, the MoF and the General Administration of Taxation issued the *Notice of the Enterprise Income Tax and Value-Added Tax Policies for Foreign Institutions Investing in the Domestic Bond Market*, outlining the enterprise income tax and value-added tax policies for foreign institutions investing in the domestic bond market. The notice specified that from November 7, 2018, to November 6, 2021, foreign institutions would receive temporary exemptions from corporate income tax and value-added tax on bond interest income derived from investments in the domestic bond market.[1] In December 2021, the MoF and the General Administration of Taxation issued an *Announcement on Extending the Enterprise Income Tax and Value-Added Tax Policies for Foreign Institutions Investing in the Domestic Bond Market*, which extended the enterprise income tax and value-added tax exemption policies for foreign institutional investors participating in the domestic bond market. The policy extension applies until the end of 2025, with the aim of providing ongoing support and encouragement for foreign investors to engage in the interbank bond market (Lei, 2021).[2]

Currently, foreign investors can access the Chinese bond market through direct or indirect means. Direct market entry modes include accessing the interbank market and the exchange market directly through programs such as the QFII and RQFII schemes. Additionally, foreign investors can directly access the interbank bond market through the CIBM. The second option is indirect market entry through the multilevel trusteeship arrangement provided by Hong Kong Bond Connect. Furthermore, an offshore market channel is available for accessing the interbank bond market, although its scale is relatively small. Currently, the GSM mode is the primary mode utilized by foreign investors to invest in the Chinese bond market.

[1]For more details, refer to https://english.www.gov.cn/statecouncil/ministries/202112/02/content_WS61a8ccd9c6d0df57f98e5f24.html.

[2]Lei (2021).

1.1.1 *The QFII and RQFII investment in interbank bond market and exchange bond market*

The QFII and RQFII programs have relatively high entry thresholds geared toward large institutional investors with medium- and long-term investment objectives. The QFII initiative was launched on November 8, 2002, when the CSRC and the PBC jointly issued *Interim Measures on the Administration of Domestic Securities Investment by Qualified Foreign Institutional Investors*. Subsequently, in August 2006, the CSRC, the PBC, and the SAFE issued *Administrative Measures for Domestic Securities Investments by Qualified Foreign Institutional Investors*, which permitted qualified investors to invest in RMB financial instruments approved by the CSRC within the approved investment quota. In December 2011, the CSRC, the PBC, and the SAFE introduced *Measures for Pilot Domestic Securities Investment Made by RMB Qualified Foreign Institutional Investors of Fund Management Companies and Securities Companies*, which expanded the range of participation of overseas institutions and standardized the account management, capital remittance, asset allocation, interbank bond market investment, and information submission of pilot institutions. In March 2013, the PBC, the CSRC, and the SAFE issued the *Pilot RMB Domestic Securities Investment by Qualified Foreign Institutional Investors*. Additionally, the PBC issued the *Notice on Matters Related to Qualified Foreign Institutional Investors to Invest in the Interbank Bond Market*, which allowed qualified QFIIs to invest in the domestic interbank bond market. The SAFE introduced *Regulations on Foreign Exchange Administration for Domestic Securities Investments by Qualified Foreign Institutional Investors* in June 2018. The new regulations eliminated the QFII capital repatriation ratio restrictions and relaxed the lock-up period requirements for QFIIs and RQFIIs. Additionally, the regulations allowed QFIIs and RQFIIs to engage in foreign exchange hedging activities. In September 2019, the restrictions on QFII and RQFII investment quotas and RQFII pilot countries and regions were lifted, significantly enhancing the convenience for foreign investors wishing to participate in the domestic financial market. In September 2020, the CSRC, PBC, and SAFE released *Measures for the Administration of Domestic Securities and Futures Investment by Qualified Foreign Institutional Investors and RMB Qualified Foreign Institutional Investors*, along with accompanying regulations on implementing the provisions. These measures, which became effective on November 1, 2020, integrate the qualifications and system rules for QFIIs and RQFIIs, reduce the access threshold, and significantly expand the scope of investment. By the end of May 2020, before the foreign exchange bureau ceased updating, the number of approved QFIIs was 295, with an investment quota of 116.259 million US dollars. In addition, there were 230 approved RQFIIs, with an investment quota of RMB 722.992 billion.

1.1.2 *Direct investment in the interbank bond market (CIBM direct)*

The CIBM direct model was initially implemented for overseas central bank institutions, RMB clearing banks, and other institutions. However, in recent years, this model has expanded to include all qualified investors to enable them to invest directly in the interbank bond market. The PBC issued the *Notice of the PBC on Issues Concerning the Pilot Program on Investment in the Interbank Bond Market with RMB Funds by Three Types of Institutions Including Overseas RMB Clearing Banks* in August 2010 to support the pilot program for cross-border trade RMB settlement. This notice allowed three types of institutions[3] to use the RMB funds obtained from their central bank monetary cooperation, cross-border trade, and investment in RMB business within the approved limit to invest in the interbank bond market. In July 2015, the PBC issued the *Notice Concerning Bond Purchase Transactions in the Interbank Bond Market by the Overseas RMB Clearing Banks and Overseas Participation Banks* and established a framework for these institutions to conduct bond repurchase transactions in the interbank bond market. Overseas central bank institutions, international financial organizations, and sovereign wealth funds are now subject to a simplified filing system for market entry with no established limit. Moreover, the investment scope for these institutions has been broadened to include repurchasing, lending, forwarding, interest rate swapping, forging forward interest rate agreements, and conducting other transactions, in addition to dealing in cash bonds (Xu *et al*., 2017).[4] In February 2016, the PBC issued an *Announcement on Matters Concerning Further Improving the Work Related to Qualified Institutional Investors' Entrance into the Interbank Bond Market*. This announcement allowed overseas financial institutions and their issued investment products and

---

[3] Overseas central banks or monetary authorities, RMB clearing banks in Hong Kong and Macao, and overseas participating banks in cross-border RMB trade settlement.

[4] Xu *et al*. (2017).

medium- and long-term institutional investors, such as pension funds, charitable funds, and endowment funds, to invest in the interbank bond market through filing and independently determine their investment scale. This meant that foreign institutional investors could directly enter the interbank bond market. By the end of 2022, a total of 1,071 foreign institutional participants entered the interbank bond market.[5]

1.1.3 *Investing in the interbank bond market through the northbound bond connect*

The Bond Connect program is a mode of infrastructure interconnection and multilevel trusteeship that facilitates "one point access" and is designed to attract small- and medium-sized foreign institutional investors. This scheme allows international investors to allocate RMB-denominated bond assets efficiently without changing their business habits and having to ensure compliance with the laws and regulations of the mainland market (Xu *et al.*, 2017). In June 2017, the PBC issued the *Interim Measures for the Administration of Mutual Bond Market Access between Mainland China and Hong Kong SAR*, which regulates the interconnection and cooperation between the mainland and Hong Kong bond markets, also known as the Bond Connect. This includes the Northbound Bond Connect (launched on July 3, 2017) and Southbound Bond Connect (launched on September 24, 2008). As of June 2023, the total amount of mainland bonds held by overseas institutions through Bond Connect exceeded RMB 3.1 trillion. The trading volume of Bond Connect rose from RMB 31 billion in the first month of its opening in 2017 to more than RMB 970 billion in May 2023. The trading volume of Northbound Bond Connect accounts for 70% of the overall trading volume of foreign investors in the mainland interbank bond market. The number of overseas institutions participating in Bond Connect rose from 178 in 2017 to 822 by the end of May 2023.

1.1.4 *Foreign investors' participation in the offshore bond market*

Foreign investors have several options for participating in the offshore bond market, including the Free Trade Zone and Macao MOX.[6] The Free

---

[5] *Source*: CCDC Research, *China Bond Market Overview (2022)*.

[6] China (Macao) Financial Assets Exchange Co. Ltd.

Trade Zone allows investors to access corporate bonds issued by domestic and overseas institutional investors through free trade accounts opened in the China (Shanghai) Pilot Free Trade Zone. The scope of investors includes international institutional investors within and outside the free trade zone. Investors can obtain "one-point access" to accounts opened in international securities depositories and can invest through the free trade zone electronic platform or the counter market establishment in the zone. The bond market in the free trade zone sits between the domestic market and the traditional offshore market. The Macao MOX model, established in July 2019 as a partnership between the Central Clearing Corporation and Macao MOX, offers investors with a streamlined method to access the offshore bond market. This model allows investors to open accounts in Macao and trade directly through subsidiary accounts opened by the Macao MOX in the CCDC.

1.2 *Overseas issuers*

The issuance of RMB-denominated bonds, also known as Panda bonds, by overseas institutions in China began in 2005. In February of that year, the PBC, MoF, NDRC, and CSRC issued *Provisional Administrative Rules on the Issuance of RMB-denominated Bonds by International Development Institutions*, which enabled eligible international development institutions to issue RMB-denominated bonds in China. The first batch of issuers of Panda bonds were the International Finance Corporation and the Asian Development Bank, which issued RMB 1.13 billion and RMB 1 billion of RMB-denominated bonds, respectively, on October 9, 2005, through the interbank bond market. However, during this period, China's financial openness was limited, and the convenience of overseas institutions in financing in China's bond market was insufficient. As a result, the issuers were limited to development financial institutions, and Panda bonds were issued on a small scale, with a cumulative issuance of only RMB 5 billion from 2005 to 2010.[7] On September 16, 2010, the PBC, MoF, NDRC, and CSRC issued the revised *Provisional Administrative*

[7] In October 2005, the International Finance Corporation and the Asian Development Bank issued bonds totaling RMB 1.13 billion and RMB 1 billion, respectively, in the interbank bond market. In 2006, the International Finance Corporation issued RMB 0.87 billion in Panda bonds. In 2009, the Asian Development Bank issued RMB 1 billion in Panda bonds. In 2010, Mitsubishi UFJ Financial Group issued RMB 1 billion in Panda bonds.

Rules on the Issuance of RMB-denominated Bonds by International Development Institutions, which allowed issuers to directly remit the RMB funds raised from bond issuance overseas for use and to transfer RMB funds from overseas for the repayment of RMB-denominated bond principal and interest. This expansion of the use of funds overseas helped increase Panda bond issuance. In November 2014, Daimler AG became the first foreign entity to issue Panda bonds. Since then, the issuers of Panda bonds have expanded to include foreign governments, commercial banks, nonfinancial enterprises, and industrial enterprises, making the bond market more open to the outside world than before.

Since 2015, the convenience of issuing Panda bonds has improved, and the scale of issuance has grown rapidly. In 2015, the scale reached RMB 13 billion, and in 2016, it reached RMB 126.2 billion. In March 2016, Panda bonds were admitted to the bond market of the stock exchange. In September 2018, the PBC and the MoF issued new regulations known as the *Interim Measures for the Administration of Bonds Issued by Overseas Issuers on Interbank Market*, which replaced the previous regulations for international development institutions. The new regulations clarified the conditions and application procedures for overseas institutions, such as foreign government institutions, international development institutions, legal persons of financial institutions and legally registered nonfinancial enterprises overseas, to issue bonds in the interbank bond market. They also standardized regulatory authorities, issuing entities, intermediary institutions, information disclosure, accounting standards, and other matters, further improving the coordination and uniformity of Panda bond supervision and the transparency of the issuance system. On December 2, 2021, the PBC and SAFE issued a *Notice on Matters Concerning the Proceeds Management for RMB-Denominated Bonds Issued by Overseas Issuers in China* (Revised Draft for Comments), which encouraged overseas institutions to collect, pay, and use the funds raised from the domestic issuance of bonds cross-border in the form of RMB, providing new development opportunities for Panda bonds.

According to the PBC, by the end of August 2023, a total of 434 Panda bonds had been issued by overseas institutions in China's bond markets with a cumulative volume of RMB 740.22 billion. According to the Wind Economic Database, the issuance of Panda bonds in 2023 was RMB 154.47 billion, a year-on-year increase of 81.6%, which accounted for 0.22% of the total issuance in China's bond market (RMB 157.9 trillion) during the same period.

To support China's Belt and Road Initiative, in March 2018, the Shanghai and Shenzhen Stock Exchanges formulated a *Notice on Launching the Pilot Program of "Belt and Road" Bonds*, which stipulated that relevant government institutions, enterprises, and financial institutions could issue Belt and Road bonds for financing on the Shanghai and Shenzhen Stock Exchanges. The Belt and Road bond pilot program takes advantage of China's strong financing capabilities in the bond market and plays a positive role in supporting the construction of Belt and Road projects.

In August 2016, the World Bank issued bonds in the China interbank market, denominated in SDR and settled in RMB, with a total issuance of 500 million SDR.

2. Domestic Issuers and Investors Go Global

2.1 *Overseas issuance of bonds by domestic entities*

In March 2000, the State Development Planning Commission and the PBC issued a notice titled *Opinion of the State Development Planning Commission and the People's Bank of China on Further Strengthening Administration of External Bond Issuances*, which established a management system for overseas debt issuance by domestic entities. In 2003, the *Interim Measures for the Management of Foreign Debts* were introduced further to standardize the borrowing of foreign debt by domestic entities. These measures included regulations on borrowing foreign debt and external guarantees, the use of foreign debt funds, foreign debt repayment and risk management, and foreign debt supervision. These measures aimed to improve the efficiency of the use of foreign debt funds by domestic entities. Since 2015, China's foreign debt management policy has undergone reform, and the management system for domestic entities to issue foreign debt has changed from an approval system to a record system. This change has significantly enhanced the convenience of foreign debt issuance. In September 2015, the NDRC issued the *Notice of the NDRC on Promoting the Reform of Managing the External Debt Issuance by Enterprises with a Record-filing and Registration System 2015*, which canceled the approval of the quota of foreign debt issued by enterprises and implemented the record and registration system. Building on the pilot project, the PBC issued the *Notice of the PBC on Implementing Full-coverage Macro-prudent Management of Cross-border Financing Nationwide 2016*, extending the macroprudential management policy of full-caliber cross-border financing across the country. Matters in relation to macro-prudential management for cross-border financing are subject to *Notice of the People's Bank of China on Matters Concerning the Macro-Prudential Management for Full-covered Cross-border Financing* that was implemented in 2017. A key parameter in macro-prudential management is a macro-prudential adjustment parameter, a multiplier that decides the upper limit of outstanding cross-border financing available to an institution. The parameter has been adjusted constantly according to economic situations. For example, it was raised from 1 to 1.25 in October 2022 and further raised to 1.5 in July 2023, which further expanded enterprises and financial institutions' funding sources. Besides, in 2017, the SAFE issued the *Circular of the State Administration of Foreign Exchange on Further Advancing Foreign Exchange Administration Reform to Enhance Authenticity and Compliance Reviews*, allowing debtors to repatriate funds under domestic and foreign guarantees for domestic use. Relevant policies further facilitate the cross-border financing of domestic institutions and promote the rapid growth of the overseas bond issuance scale of domestic entities.

Currently, domestic entities primarily issue three types of bonds in the offshore market: Chinese foreign currency bonds, offshore RMB-denominated bonds (mainly dim sum bonds), and free trade zone bonds.

2.1.1 *Chinese-issued foreign currency bonds*

Chinese-issued foreign currency bonds are bonds denominated in foreign currencies and issued by Chinese-funded enterprises overseas. These bonds are typically issued in US dollars, euros, Hong Kong dollars, Singapore dollars, and other currencies, with Chinese-issued US dollar bonds being the most common. The rapid expansion of the scale of Chinese-funded foreign currency bonds in recent years is closely related to the overseas macro environment, the difference in the cost of issuing bonds at home and abroad (exchange rate and interest margin), and regulatory policies on domestic bond issuance. Chinese-issued US dollar bonds are also known as "Kungfu Bonds", and the scale of their issuance has experienced rapid growth since 2015, when enterprises' issuance of foreign debt became subject to record registration, and after 2017, when funds were allowed to be transferred back to China for use.[8] According to Wind Economic Database, by the end of 2023, the cumulative issuance of Chinese-issued foreign currency bonds was USD 1,976.7 billion, with corporate bonds and financial bonds accounting for the largest proportion, at approximately USD 1,279.8 billion and USD 561.1 billion, respectively. There are 4,326 outstanding Chinese-issued foreign currency bonds with a balance of USD 1105.8 billion, among which 2,598 Chinese-issued US dollar bonds total approximately USD 827.4 billion, and 97 Chinese-issued euro bonds total approximately USD 24.6 billion.

2.1.2 *Offshore RMB-denominated bonds*

In June 2007, the PBC and the NDRC issued *Interim Measures for the Administration of the Issuance of RMB-denominated Bonds in Hong Kong Special Administrative Region by Domestic Financial Institutions*. These measures allowed eligible domestic financial institutions to issue RMB-denominated bonds in Hong Kong, commonly known as "dim sum bonds". The aim was to use the RMB funds deposited in Hong Kong to stimulate the Hong Kong bond market. In May 2012, the NDRC issued the *Notice on Relevant Matters Concerning the Issuance of Renminbi Bonds in the Hong Kong Special Administrative Region by Domestic Non-financial Institutions*. The notice also regulated issuance conditions, approval processes, fund use, and other related matters, which vigorously promoted the development of the RMB-denominated bond market in Hong Kong. In May 2015, the State Council issued *Guiding Opinions on Promoting International Production Capacity and Equipment Manufacturing Cooperation*. This policy supported the China Development Bank, the Export-Import Bank of China, and domestic commercial banks in issuing and using RMB-denominated bonds overseas and lifted the

---

[8]Due to a significant increase in leverage caused by large-scale borrowing by a number of real estate companies, local government financing platforms, and others, the NDRC and the MoF issued a notice in May 2018 titled *Notice of Improving the Market Restraint Mechanism and Strictly Preventing Foreign Debt Risks and Local Debt Risks*. The notice emphasized increased regulatory oversight before and after borrowing to prevent risks.

geographical restrictions on issuing RMB-denominated bonds overseas. This policy further promoted the internationalization of the RMB and facilitated the development of the offshore RMB-denominated bond market.

In recent years, offshore RMB-denominated bonds' issuing subjects and geographical scope have been expanding. The changes have included the issuance of "Lion City Bonds" in Singapore, "Goethe Bonds" in Germany, "Triumph Bonds" in France, and "Fuji Mountain Bonds" in Japan. The development of the offshore RMB-denominated bond market is beneficial for the interaction between the onshore and offshore bond markets and for promoting the internationalization of the RMB.

2.1.3 *Shanghai free trade zone bonds* (*Mingzhu bond*)

The Shanghai Free Trade Zone has a diverse range of bond issuers, such as domestic and foreign financial institutions, sovereign institutions, and nonfinancial enterprises. The funds raised from these bonds are typically used for projects that align with national industrial policies and relevant business fields, as well as supplementary working capital and other purposes. The use of funds is flexible, allowing for a variety of uses. The CCDC serves as the registration agency for bonds issued in the Shanghai Free Trade Zone. These bonds can be listed on multiple platforms, including the Hong Kong Stock Exchange and the MOX. On December 8, 2016, the Shanghai Municipal Government issued RMB 3 billion of local government bonds to institutional investors inside and outside of the Shanghai Free Trade Zone. This was the first bond issued in the pilot trade zone after its establishment. On November 8, 2019, Nanjing Southeast State-Owned Asset Investment Group Co., Ltd., issued RMB 1 billion of free trade zone bonds. In 2021, Shanghai Real Estate Properties (Group) Co. Ltd. successfully launched two offshore bonds on May 14 and October 18 in the Shanghai Pilot Free Trade Zone. By the end of 2022, 72 Mingzhu bonds have been issued in the Shanghai Free Trade Zone, with a scale of approximately RMB 50 billion.[9]

In 2009, the MoF started issuing sovereign bonds denominated in RMB and US dollars to the international market in Hong Kong, following the central government's plan to promote the opening up of the financial

[9] *Source*: CCDC Research, *China Bond Market Overview (2022)*.

industry and support Hong Kong's economic and social development. The issuance scale of these bonds has steadily expanded, and the term structure has been optimized over time. The MoF selects executing agencies in Hong Kong interbank and exchange markets to promote market efficiency, provides bilateral quotations to the secondary market, and guides and promotes market transactions. The maturity varieties of overseas sovereign bonds are constantly enriched, providing a pricing benchmark for the overseas financing of domestic institutions and attracting global investors. The successful and continuous issuance of overseas sovereign bonds and relevant institutional arrangements are helping improve China's sovereign debt and foreign debt maturity structures, reduce overseas financing costs for domestic institutions, and deepen the opening up of the bond market. Since November 2018, the PBC has regularly issued offshore central bank bills in Hong Kong, which enriches RMB investment products and liquidity management tools in the Hong Kong market, promotes the formation of a Hong Kong offshore yield curve, and accelerates the process of RMB internationalization. In July 2019, the MoF issued RMB 2 billion of treasury bonds in Macao for the first time, which was welcomed by the offshore market and accelerated the development of the Macao bond market. Overall, in recent years, the issuance of RMB government bonds, financial bonds, and corporate bonds in the offshore market has been increasing, with diversified issuance methods and locations, which promotes the development of the offshore RMB market.

2.2 *Investors Go Global*

Currently, institutional investors invest in overseas bonds through various channels, including the QDII and RQDII and the Southbound Bond Connect of the Bond Connect program. QDIIs and RQDIIs can also carry out overseas bond investment through the Southbound Bond Connect.

2.2.1 *QDIIs and RQDIIs*

QDII refers to a domestic institution which has been approved by relevant authorities to invest in overseas securities and other financial products. Such institutions include commercial banks, securities companies, fund management companies, insurance institutions, trust companies, and other similar entities. QDII programs allow qualified domestic institutions to invest their funds or raise funds from domestic institutions and individuals in overseas markets and products as permitted by laws and regulations and relevant departments, except for the overseas use of banks' own funds.

QDIIs: In June 2004, the CIRC issued the *Notice on Issues Relating to the Investment of Foreign Exchange Insurance Funds in Overseas Stocks*. In August 2004, the CIRC and PBC issued *Interim Measures for the Control of Overseas Use of Insurance-Related Foreign Exchange Funds*. In April 2006, the PBC issued *Announcement No. 5*, allowing eligible banks to pool RMB funds from domestic institutions and individuals to purchase foreign exchanges within a specific limit for investment in overseas fixed-income products. That same month, the PBC, CBRC, and SAFE issued *Interim Administrative Measures for Commercial Banks to Provide Overseas Wealth Management Services*, which broadened investment channels for domestic residents and promoted the balance of international payments. In July 2007, the CSRC issued *Trial Measures for the Administration of Overseas Securities Investment by Qualified Domestic Institutional Investors*. These measures stipulated that the QDII qualification of domestic institutional investors must be approved by the CSRC, the investment quota must be filed with the SAFE, the funds must be deposited by domestic banks, and overseas investment consultants and securities service institutions can be entrusted to buy and sell securities as agents. In 2007 and 2008, four and five QDII funds were issued, respectively. However, the QDII program was impacted by the 2008 financial crisis and developed slowly in subsequent years.

RQDIIs: In November 2014, the PBC issued the *Notice on Matters Concerning the Overseas Securities Investment of RMB Qualified Domestic Institutional Investors*. This notice stipulated that qualified RMB investors can use their own RMB funds or raise RMB funds from domestic institutions and individuals to invest in RMB-denominated products in overseas financial markets, except for the overseas use of banks' own funds. The notice expanded the scope of two-way circulation channels for RMB funds (Xu *et al.*, 2017). However, at the end of 2015, due to the large fluctuation of the RMB exchange rate, business related to RQDII was suspended. In May 2018, the General Office of the PBC issued the *Notice on Further Clarifying Matters Concerning the Administration of the Overseas Securities Investment of RMB Qualified Domestic Institutional Investors*, including macro-prudential management and information submission requirements.

As of the end of 2023, 186 QDII had been approved, with an investment amount of 165.52 billion USD. It should be noted that the approval system for the QDII quota is different from that of the RQDII quota, which is subject to the actual raised scale. Apart from the QDII and RQDII programs, domestic investors can also invest in overseas markets through other channels, such as Qualified Domestic Limited Partners (QDLPs) and Qualified Domestic Investment Enterprises (QDIEs).

2.2.2 *Southbound bond connect*

On September 15, 2021, the PBC and the Hong Kong Monetary Authority jointly announced that the Southbound Bond Connect would launch on September 24, 2021. The mainland investors initially included 41 banking financial institutions (excluding non-bank financial institutions and rural financial institutions) among primary dealers of the PBC's open market business in 2020. QDIIs and RQDIIs can now also carry out overseas bond investment through the Southbound Bond Connect program. The counterparty is temporarily the "southbound" market maker designated by the Hong Kong Monetary Authority. The investment scope of the Southbound Bond Connect model is currently limited to securities issued overseas and traded in the Hong Kong bond market. The total annual and daily limits for net outflows of cross-border funds through Southbound Bond Connect are currently set at RMB 500 billion and RMB 20 billion, respectively. The opening of the Southbound Bond Connect is expected to improve institutional arrangements for the two-way opening of the Chinese bond market and create more opportunities for domestic investors to allocate assets in the international financial market. It will also help reinforce Hong Kong's role as a bridgehead and hub linking the mainland and global markets, integrate Hong Kong into the overall national development situation, and maintain the long-term prosperity and stability of Hong Kong.

3. Bond Market Index

3.1 *The inclusion of Chinese bonds in the world's top three bond indices*

Major international bond indices have successively included Chinese bonds in their indices. On March 1, 2017, Bloomberg released two fixed-income indices that combined RMB-denominated Chinese bonds with their global indices, called the "Global Aggregate + China Index" and "EM Local Currency Government + China Index". This marked the first time that onshore RMB-denominated bonds were included in global index series. On March 6, 2017, Citibank announced that China's onshore bonds met the conditions for inclusion in its related emerging market and regional government bond indices, such as the Emerging Markets Government Bond Index (EMGBI), Asian Government Bond Index (AGBI), and Asia Pacific Government Bond Index (APGBI). Due to the large size of the Chinese market, Citigroup launched the EMGBI-Capped index and AGBI-Capped index, in which the weight of Chinese bonds was at its highest, at 10% and 20%, respectively (Xu *et al.*, 2017). In April 2019, Bloomberg gradually began including Chinese government bonds and policy bank bonds denominated in RMB in the Bloomberg Barclays Global Aggregate Index (BBGA) over the next 20 months. In February 2020, JPMorgan Chase added nine Chinese government bonds to its flagship global emerging market government bond index series. In November 2018, FTSE Russell included Chinese government bonds on the market watch list of the FTSE World Government Bond Index (WGBI). In October 2021, RMB government bonds were officially included in the FTSE World Government Bond Index (WGBI), and their weight has been gradually increasing. Their weight is expected to reach approximately 5.25% within 36 months, that is, once they are fully included in September 2024. As Chinese bonds have become included in the three major global bond indices, a large number of overseas funds have increased their holdings of Chinese bonds.

3.2 *RMB-denominated bond index system has become a reference benchmark for international bond market investment*

In October 2016, the yield curve of three-month medium-term treasury bonds was added to the SDR interest rate basket. On May 2, 2018,

ChinaBond Pricing Center Co. Ltd., working with the World Bank, released two interest rate indices to measure the income level of monetary assets. The first index is called the ChinaBond SDR CNY 3-Month Constant Maturity Index, which measures the trend of return on investment based on the three-month fixed-term treasury bond yield. The second index is called the China Bond Financial Institutions CNY Excess Reserves Interest Rate Index, which measures the cumulative return on investment based on the interest rate of RMB excess reserves of financial institutions.

In October 2018, ChinaBond Pricing Center Co. Ltd., and the overseas information provider IHS Markit jointly launched the China Bond iBoxx index in Shanghai. This index is subject to the supervision of the IOSCO and EU Benchmarks Regulation (BMR) standards and focuses on government bonds and policy bank bonds that are in high demand among foreign investors (Li, 2021).[10] ChinaBond Pricing Center Co. Ltd. has also developed a series of ChinaBond Green-Bond Indices, and RMB-denominated bond index funds that use ChinaBond benchmarks have been listed overseas. The ChinaBond price index system is designed to promote the formation of fair bond prices and improve market transparency.

4. Assessment of the Opening-up of the Bond Market

The opening-up process of China's bond market was slow prior to 2016. However, the pace of opening up accelerated after the removal of quota restrictions on foreign investors that year and the launch of the Bond Connect program in 2017. In recent years, various policies have been introduced and implemented, resulting in significant progress in the bond market's opening up.

Investors now have broader access to the Chinese bond market, with simplified procedures and improved market connectivity. Foreign investors can invest in the interbank bond market via three channels: CIBM Direct, the QFII and RQFII programs, and Bond Connect. They can invest not only in cash bonds but also through bond repurchasing, lending, forwarding, interest rate swapping, establishing FRAs, and

[10] Li (2021).

engaging in other transactions. Technical issues such as DVP-based settlement, block trades, and settlement dates have now been resolved. The rules linking the interbank bond market and the exchange bond market, which were issued in 2022, have facilitated the rapid increase of foreign investor holdings in Chinese bonds. Moreover, the investor structure has become more diversified. All three major international index providers have added Chinese government bonds to their indices, which reflects the widespread recognition of the opening-up of the Chinese bond market. However, it should be noted that the proportion of Chinese bonds held by foreign investors is still relatively small, and most of the bonds held by international investors are government and policy bank debts.

The issuers in the Chinese bond market include sovereign countries, multilateral development banks, financial institutions, and nonfinancial companies. Overseas issuers can also issue Panda bonds denominated in RMB and Mulan Bonds denominated in SDR in China. The Panda bond market is positioned as an international market, and its issuance mechanism has been continuously improved. It has a broad international investor base, including overseas central bank institutions. In recent years, the depth and breadth of the Panda bond market have further expanded. To meet the needs of green and low-carbon economic transformation, the dealers' association has launched green bonds, sustainable development Panda bonds, and carbon-neutral Panda bonds. By the end of 2021, foreign investors held approximately 25% of Panda bonds, making them the onshore bond product with the highest proportion of foreign investors.

As intermediaries, foreign financial institutions are allowed to underwrite government bonds, financial bonds, and nonfinancial corporate bonds in China in compliance with regulatory requirements. China opened up its credit rating industry in 2017. Currently, Standard & Poor's and Fitch Ratings have established wholly owned subsidiaries in China to conduct bond rating business. By attracting foreign professional financial service institutions and fostering a "catfish effect", domestic institutions are paying more attention to improving their service quality and compliance management, which is beneficial for building an efficient and transparent bond market.

The liquidity of the Chinese bond market has increased rapidly in recent years but still faces many constraints. In 2023, the total turnover of cash bond trading in the interbank bond market reached RMB 307.3 trillion, with the daily average standing at RMB 1234.16 billion, with a year-on-year increase of 13%. The liquidity gap between Chinese government bonds and US government bonds is also narrowing, and the turnover rate of the Chinese bond market has exceeded that of Japan, South Korea, and Singapore. However, Chinese bond investors often hold bonds until maturity, leaving room to enhance the liquidity of the bond market. To further improve liquidity, China's government can optimize the yield curve of its national debt and strengthen its benchmark role. It can also optimize the secondary-market-making support mechanism to improve the bond price discovery function. Moreover, improving the management of bond lending can meet the diverse trading needs of market participants and effectively enhance the liquidity of the bond market.

While Chinese bonds' inclusion in major international indices has enhanced global recognition, the influence of the Chinese bond index remains relatively limited. The inclusion of Chinese bonds in major international bond indices has increased the global recognition of the Chinese bond market and attracted the participation of more foreign investors. On the other hand, it is also crucial for the index compiled by China to become an essential investment benchmark for global investors. This is the fundamental purpose of opening up the bond market.

In general, the Chinese bond market adheres to the pattern of developing in a market-oriented, law-based, and internationalized way and continuing its high-level two-way opening up. As China is the world's second-largest economy with stable economic growth and robust bond market development, global investors can benefit from China's economic growth and diversify their risks by investing in the country's financial market. In 2021, the Chinese government reiterated its commitment to further promoting a higher level of openness in the financial industry, thus enhancing policy transparency and stability for investors. The reform and innovation of the bond market have continued progressing, and risk hedging instruments have become increasingly diverse. The degree of marketization, legalization, and internationalization has also increased, and the channels for overseas institutions to enter China's financial market have become more accessible. The overall market environment has become more favorable for investors.

References

CCDC. (2019). Brief History of Bond Market Development in New China. Beijing: Beijing Times Chinese Book Company (in Chinese).

Lei, C. (2021). Bond market opening up: From history to the future. *China Forex*, 22, 8–12 (in Chinese).

Li, B. (2021). Driving the opening up of the bond market through the main channel. *Bond Market*, 2021(8), 72–78 (in Chinese).

Xu Zhong, Zhang Xuechun, Cao Yuanyuan, Tang Yingwei, & Wan Tailei. (2017). To promote the reform and development of financial markets with opening up. 2017. Jingshan Report (Report 6). Hangzhou: China Finance 40 Forum (in Chinese).

Xu, Z., Zhang, X., Cao, Y., Tang, Y., & Wan, T. (2017). Promoting financial market reform and development through opening up. *New Financial Review*, 2017(5), 135–160 (in Chinese).

Chapter 9

The Opening of China's Bond Market: Chinese Firms' Onshore and Offshore Bonds

This chapter evaluates the opening of China's bond market by analyzing the yields of offshore and onshore bonds of Chinese enterprises from January 2016 to March 2020. The main findings are twofold: First, Bond Connect has strengthened connectivity of the offshore and onshore bond markets, and the influence of the onshore bond market. Before the launch of Bond Connect, the yield of onshore and offshore bonds of Chinese enterprises fluctuated significantly; since its launch, however, the domestic market has started to lead the changes in offshore market yield, and the changes in yields of both markets have become more synchronized, flexible, and market-oriented. Second, the increased flexibility of RMB exchange rate has significantly stabilized bond yields and enhanced the co-movements of offshore and onshore bond markets. Since the US dollar to RMB exchange rate surpassed 7, the coefficient and significance of the long-term cointegration relationship between offshore and onshore bond markets have increased significantly. In particular, with the introduction of the dollar and carry factors, the equilibrium error term significantly impacts the offshore and onshore bond markets, the degree of market integration is significantly enhanced, and the co-movements are much closer.

1. Introduction

China's bond market, the second largest in the world, has opened up in recent years, and its linkages with international capital markets have been enhanced. Domestic investors can invest in offshore markets through QDII, RQDII, QDLP, QDIE, and the offshore branches of domestic financial institutions. At the same time, foreign entities can now issue and invest in China's bond markets. Two watershed events marking the opening up of the Chinese bond market were the launch of Bond Connect in July 2017, and the US dollar to RMB exchange rate surpassing 7 in August 2019. Bond Connect allows international investors to invest in the Chinese bond market using the financial infrastructure and legal framework of Hong Kong. Seven was the psychological ceiling of the US dollar to RMB exchange rate, and the breakthrough event marked a shift of RMB foreign exchange rate policy to a more flexible and market-oriented regime. By the time of writing (end of June 2020), the Chinese offshore bonds outstanding have reached USD 1.1 trillion, and more than 900 foreign institutions own RMB 2.6 trillion in domestic bonds outstanding, accounting for 2.4% of the total. Furthermore, China's bond market is being integrated into the international capital market by participating in all three major international bond indexes, namely, BBGA, GBI-EMGD, and WGBI.

Nevertheless, some of the rules and practices of China's bond market do not align with international best practices. First, less developed derivative markets have reduced the depth of the bond market in China and in turn limited its price discovery capacity, liquidity, and effectiveness. The bond derivatives are restricted to transaction-based and interest swaps, while the derivatives for price discovery and risk management are yet to be developed (Xu, 2018). By 2019, the derivatives of our bond markets amounted to less than RMB 20 trillion, around 1/5 of the base bond assets, far below those in the US, Japan, and other developed markets. Second, limited financial innovations have reduced the bond market liquidity. Given limited bond buyout repo, standard bond futures, and credit default swaps, the bond market transactions are not active. In 2019, the turnover ratio of China's onshore bonds was a mere 1.9 and that of corporate credit bonds only 0.7, far below those of the US Treasury Bond (10) and corporate bond (2). Third, banks with low-risk preference are the main bondholders in China, and for long-term asset allocation purposes, they normally hold bonds for life. In comparison, overseas bond markets are dominated by institutional investors with high-risk preference, which invest in bonds for transaction and speculative purposes (Yi, 2020). Furthermore, some bond ratings in China are too high to reflect risks. The situation is aggravated by the expectation of non-default; as a result, the yields of corporate bonds are mainly term premiums, not credit premiums (Ji & Cao, 2017).

According to the theory of Interest Rate Parity (IRP), the yield of corporate bond equals the sum of risk-free interest rate and credit premium. Given risk-free interest rate, the same issuer should face similar credit premium in different markets. However, the aforementioned factors have resulted in a yield gap between onshore and offshore bonds issued by the same Chinese firms, and this gap may become wider because China's capital account is not fully convertible and the RMB foreign exchange rate mechanism is not sufficiently flexible. Simple statistics show that the average yield gap between offshore investment-grade US dollar bonds and domestic high-grade bonds issued by the same Chinese firms from January 2016 to July 2020 is 0.64%. The gap varies with the introduction of Bond Connect and the enhancement of RMB foreign exchange flexibility. Specifically, prior to the launch of Bond Connect, the yield gap averaged 0.72%, while subsequently, it averaged 0.61%; while in the period before the US dollar to RMB exchange rate surpassed 7, the average yield gap was 0.57%, but this reduced to 0.54% after the breakthrough event. It may lead to some arguments that policy changes have effectively reduced the onshore and offshore yield gap, yet to date, no quantitative studies have been conducted in this area.

This chapter evaluates the policy impacts on the process of Chinese bond market opening. After determining the structural breakpoints of bond yield volatility, we segregate the sample into three periods (pre-Bond Connect, post-Bond Connect, and after RMB exchange rate dropped below 7). Further, we study the long-term correlation, the mean, and the volatility spillover effect between onshore and offshore bond markets based on IRP theory. To control the common share of global systematic variation, we introduce US dollar index and carry trade index as controlling variables.

There are two main findings: First, Bond Connect has enhanced the effective connectivity and impacts of onshore markets. Prior to Bond Connect, the onshore and offshore bond yields of Chinese firms were both relatively volatile; after its launch, the onshore yields became more flexible and market-oriented, and the yield gap of onshore and offshore bonds reduced by 11 base points. Second, enhanced RMB foreign exchange rate flexibility has stabilized bond yield and enhanced the effective connectivity of onshore and offshore markets. Specifically, after August 6, 2019, when the USD to RMB surpassed 7, the RMB exchange rate flexibility improved, as did the long-term correlation of onshore and offshore bond markets. In particular, after introducing the US dollar index and carry trade index, the equilibrium error demonstrates significant impacts on both onshore and offshore markets, and both are able to actively adjust the pricing level to reach the new equilibrium. In other words, the market integration and co-movement have been significantly enhanced.

This chapter contributes to the existing literature in the following three areas: First, this is the first academic chapter to quantify the policy impacts of Bond Connect and foreign exchange rate reform. Second, this chapter focuses mainly on the volatility and correlation of the corporate onshore and offshore bond markets and examines their co-movement. Third, this is the first academic chapter to use data from Bank of America Merrill Lynch as the return rate index of Chinese corporate investment-grade US dollar bonds, and above-AAA and AAA five-year average medium-term bond yield as the yield index of domestic Chinese corporate high-grade US dollar bonds from China Bond Pricing Center (CBPC).

This chapter has four sections. Following this introductory section, Section 2 reviews the related literature. Section 3 details empirical analysis such as model specifications, selection of indicators and their statistical description, and empirical results after considering foreign exchange rate expectations, US dollar factor, carry trade, and other controlling variables. Section 4 concludes with policy suggestions.

2. Literature Review

2.1 *Bond yield: Factors for onshore and offshore markets*

Interest rate parity is the basis for analyzing the co-movement between onshore and offshore bond markets. According to the IRP theory, all expected returns of all monetary assets in different countries should be the same; otherwise, the arbitrage opportunities will lead to similar expected returns of the same assets. Nevertheless, the conditions for IRP may not hold, even in developed countries with fully convertible capital accounts and integrated financial markets (Engle, 2014). It is because IRP only is applicable in a perfect market with no information asymmetry, transaction costs, or market friction. In reality, such assumptions never hold (Bekaert *et al*., 2007; Engle, 2014). Moreover, investors normally prefer home country assets and have difficulties in diversifying their portfolios in different markets, even with free capital movement (Lewis, 1995; Obsfeld & Rogoff, 2001). The existence of transaction costs and market friction and the noted heterogeneity of assets from different countries are important factors that hold back IRP (Stenfors, 2019).

According to IRP theory, exchange rate is neutral for bond issuance and investment, and expectations or costs of foreign exchange rate are critical for the yield of corporate bonds. Miyajima *et al*. (2015) viewed foreign exchange rate risk, default risk, and liquidity risk linked to exchange rate as the main risks for international bond investors. Among these, the volatility of foreign exchange rate is the determinant for overseas investors.

The yield gap between onshore and offshore markets is mainly due to foreign exchange expectations or costs. In this regard, the US dollar index is used as a proxy, given the US dollar's dominant role in the financial markets. The consensus of the existing literature on the relationship of offshore corporate bonds and US dollar index is that the two are positively related for high-rated bonds in normal times. However, the relationship is uncertain for high-yield bonds. This is because high-rated bonds can provide investors with near-risk-free and high-yield US dollar assets (Gambacorta *et al*., 2020). In normal times, when the Fed starts to tighten its monetary policy, the global US dollar liquidity also tightens, and the US dollar appreciates. Given that global investors (mainly risk-averse entities such as reserve managers and asset-allocating institutional investors) prefer low-risk and highly liquid assets, they normally prefer investment-graded US dollar debt similar to the US treasuries and are therefore willing to pay a premium (CGFS, 2020). Meanwhile, the rising US dollar index comes with rising costs for non-US debt issuers and hence less US dollar debt issuance (Bruno & Shin, 2020). According to the demand and supply relationship, because US dollar appreciation increases the prices of investment-rated corporate US dollar debt, the US dollar index is negatively related to the US dollar bond yield. The lower-rated firms, however, face higher default risks and other uncertainties. These firms are forced to pay higher debt costs, and their dollar bond yield may even be positively related to the US dollar index.

In crisis periods, the US dollar's function as a safe currency may cause uncertain or even positive relationship between the investment-graded dollar bond and the US dollar index. During the 2007/2008 international financial crisis period, and in March 2020 when the US received the shock of COVID-19, the panic in global financial markets led to a high US dollar index and US dollar shortage (Rose & Spiegel, 2012; McCauley & Schenk, 2020; Aldasoro *et al*., 2020) and the dumping of all types of credit debt (including investment graded and high-yield bonds) (Hordahl & Shim, 2020). This is also confirmed by various CIRP studies after the global financial crisis (Du *et al*., 2018; Jiang *et al*., 2018).

Another determinant of corporate offshore bond yield is carry trade, which is closely related to the interest rate gap (Hardy & Saffie, 2019; Banerjee *et al*., 2020). IRP is based on the assumption that financial institutions can arbitrage in the foreign exchange market and money market when capital can flow freely. Engle (2014) further points out that the carry trade of non-financial entities and individuals in different markets and among different assets significantly impacts the long-term equilibrium relationship between interest rate and foreign exchange rate in different countries. Xiao and Wang (2014) find that although the co-movement of offshore and onshore RMB-denominated bond markets was low and volatile from 2010 to 2013, the development of the offshore bond market stabilized the co-movement to some degree in the later period. Empirical studies by Huang *et al*. (2018) and Ding *et al*. (2019) on the scale and yield of the offshore bonds of Chinese firms also find that carry trade is an essential reason for offshore issuance, given that high-risk firms with industrial policy constraints are more willing to conduct speculative carry trade and expand their overseas bond issuance. Huang *et al*. (2018) further note that firms with higher risks or policy constraints have more incentive to engage in speculative carry trade, thereby expanding offshore bond issuance.

2.2 *Empirical methods of markets' co-movement*

Co-movement of financial markets means a positive correlation exists between financial asset prices in different markets (Barberis *et al*., 2005). As such, the co-movement between offshore and onshore markets means that the volatility of bond yields is inter-connected; that is, a change of yield in one market may cause a change of yield in the other market. Therefore, increased co-movement of onshore and offshore bond markets means a higher degree of domestic market openness. According to IRP theory, a higher degree of market openness carries with it increased impacts of carry trade and foreign exchange rates on onshore bond yield. Therefore, the co-movement of onshore and offshore markets can be used to evaluate the openness of the bond market in China.

Most studies find a positive relationship among financial markets among advanced countries. Sutton (2000) conducted Monte Carlo simulation of quarterly data of 10-year bond yields of the US, UK, Germany, Japan, and Canada, and found positive co-movement. Christiansen (2014) used panel regression of daily data of J.P. Morgan's 1-year to 10-year government bonds of 17 European countries and found higher degrees of co-movement for countries in the EU than for those not yet in the EU, for countries that had joined the EU earlier than for those that had joined later, and for countries not in crisis than for those in crisis.

Emerging economies (EM) are more vulnerable to external shocks, so the co-movement between EM and advanced markets (AM) is relatively low. Bunda *et al.* (2009) computed rolling correlation coefficients of daily bond yield data of 18 EMs between 1997 and 2008 and found that shocks of EM or AM are contagious among countries and markets. Égert & Kočenda (2007) adopted DCC-GARCH to examine co-movement among three advanced countries (UK, France, and Germany) and three EMs (Czech Republic, Poland, and Hungary) and found that co-movement was higher among advanced countries and lower among EMs.

The related studies on co-movement between the onshore and offshore markets in China mainly focus on RMB foreign exchange rate, government bonds, and equity prices. Ding *et al.* (2014) examined the relationship between offshore and onshore spot foreign exchange rates and RMB Non-Deliverable Forward (NDF) rate, while Ding *et al.* (2020) use VECM-BEKK-GARCH to examine the impacts of the US dollar and carry trade on the spillover effects of onshore and offshore RMB foreign exchange rate volatility. In addition, Huo & Ahmed (2017) and Ma *et al.* (2019) used GARCH and GO-GARCH, respectively, and identified a significantly higher correlation between the Shanghai Composite Index and Hang Seng Index after the introduction of Shanghai–Hong Kong Stock Connect. Studies of the bond markets focus on government bond yield. Zhou *et al.* (2015) employed bi-variate BEKK-GARCH and found that onshore government bond and financial bond have one-way spillover effect on offshore bonds. In a study using the DCC-GARCH-BEKK(1,1) model, Feng & Wang (2016) analyzed the term structure of onshore and offshore government bonds of different maturity and found that among all types of bonds, volatility spillover impacts are most substantial among 10-year government bonds.

There are two shortcomings in the existing studies concerning the empirical methods: First, most studies use multi-period regressions to examine the impacts of important events, but the periods are selected with strong objectivity. Chow test (Chow, 1960) is the traditional way to identify the structural breakpoint, while expanded versions of this method by Andrews (1993) and Andrews & Ploberger (1994) are used to find the breakpoint when no specific timing is needed in advance. The expanded method is now known as the Quandt–Andrews test. In addition, the Makov institution switch model, first used by Engel & Hamilton (1990), applies standard deviation to identify the breakpoint of exchange rate volatility. This chapter combines the Makov institution switch model with the Quandt–Andrews test to identify the structural breakpoints of the bond yield volatilities.

The second shortcoming of the existing studies is that most focus on government bonds, while few papers directly examine the onshore and offshore corporate bond markets. To explore the daily data of onshore and offshore bond market co-movement, we refer to the existing research and employ VECM-BEKK-GARCH. Specifically, VECM can describe the long-term equilibrium relationship of the onshore and offshore bond yields, the diagonal matrix of GARCH-BEKK can describe the error term of the model, and GARCH can specify the error term of high-frequency daily data. These help in analyzing the co-movement of the onshore and offshore bond markets. Compared with the traditional GARCH model and other multi-variate GARCH models (e.g., VECH and DCC-GARCH), BEKK-GARCH can better identify the spillover effect of other markets' volatilities (Engle & Kroner, 1995).

3. Empirical Analysis of the Co-movement of Offshore and Onshore Bond Yields

3.1 *Model setting and data*

3.1.1 *Onshore and offshore corporate bond yields*

At present, China's bond market is not fully integrated with the international bond market in terms of credit rating and market depth. In order to avoid the impact of structural differences between the offshore and onshore bond markets, this chapter mainly selects the yields of offshore Chinese corporate investment-grade US dollar bonds with high credit rating and the yield of domestic high-grade bonds for empirical study. Specifically, this chapter selects the return rate of the Chinese corporate investment-grade US dollar bond index of Bank of America Merrill Lynch as the return rate index of Chinese corporate investment-grade US dollar bonds (IVUSD). The average duration of Chinese corporate investment-grade US dollar bonds of Bank of America Merrill Lynch is about 5 years. Regarding domestic medium-term bonds, this chapter selects above-AAA and AAA five-year average medium-term bond yield as the yield index of domestic Chinese corporate high-grade US dollar bonds (IVCN).

3.1.2 *Exchange rate spread and other control variables*

In this chapter, the main influencing factors of global shocks, such as the dollar factor and carry factor, are introduced as control variables. For the dollar factor (USDIndex), this chapter takes the dollar index published by the Federal Reserve, which should be significantly negatively correlated with Chinese corporate investment-grade dollar yield in normal economic times. For carry factor (CarryIndex), this chapter uses the studies of Bruno & Shin (2017) and Ding *et al.* (2019) as reference to select the onshore and foreign money market spread after adjustment for the implied volatility of foreign exchange options (i.e., the difference between the overnight repo and the federal funds rate divided by the implied volatility of overnight foreign exchange options).

Following the theory of Covered Interest Rate Parity (CIRP), the simple dynamic regression can be described as follows:

$$y_t^* = \alpha + \beta_1 y_t + \beta_2 \Delta s_{t+1} + \beta_x X_t + \varepsilon_t, \tag{1}$$

where y_t^* is IVUSD; y_t is IVCN; Δs_{t+1} is the spread between forward exchange rate (NDF)[1] and spot exchange rate (CNY).[2] X_t represents the control variables, including dollar factor (USDIndex) and carry factor (CarryIndex). The descriptive statistics are reported in Table 1.

---

[1] We select 1 year RMB Non-Deliverable Forward (NDF).

[2] We select the USD/CNY spot exchange rate (CNY).

Table 1. Descriptive statistics of bond yields.

	Mean	Standard Deviation	Skewness	Kurtosis	Normality Test	Observations
			2016/01/06–2020/03/13			
IVUSD	3.4569	0.5570	0.6025	−0.7368	231.41**	947
IVCN	4.1133	0.6421	0.2283	−0.9150	73.608**	947

Notes: The significance levels are displayed as *** for 1%, ** for 5%, and * for 10%.
Sources: Bank of America Merrill Lynch; China Central Depository & Clearing Co. Ltd. (CCDC); China Bond Pricing Center Co. Ltd. (CBPC).

3.2 *Structural breakpoint of bond yield*

This part adopts two methods to analyze the volatility of China's onshore and offshore bond yields; specifically, Engel & Hamilton's (1990) Markov switching model and the Quandt–Andrews Chow breakpoint test are used to detect the potential structural changes to determine the structural breakpoint of bond yield fluctuations.

3.2.1 *Markov switching model*

To analyze the volatility of onshore and offshore bond yields in China, this chapter adopts Engel & Hamilton's (1990) Markov switching model and refers to the method proposed by Ventosa-Santaulària *et al.* (2015) to find the structural break of the volatility of onshore and offshore bond yields in China according to the variance of bond yields. The regression model can be described as

$$y_t^* = \begin{cases} \mu_0 + \beta_1 y_t + \beta_2 \Delta s_{t+1} + \varepsilon_t, & \text{if } s_t = 0 \\ \mu_1 + \beta_1 y_t + \beta_2 \Delta s_{t+1} + \varepsilon_t, & \text{if } s_t = 1 \end{cases}, \tag{2}$$

where $\varepsilon_t \sim N[0, \sigma^2]$ is the residual, which follows normal distribution, y_t denotes the change data of the bond yield time series, and s_t is an unobserved random variable. The mean can be written as a function in the form: $\mu(s_t) = \begin{cases} \mu_0 & \text{if } s_t = 0 \\ \mu_1 & \text{if } s_t = 1 \end{cases}$, β_i is a vector of parameters, and ε_t follows the Gaussian white noise. In this Markov switching model, the unobserved random variable s_t is assumed to follow the first-order Markov chain, defined by the ergodic transition probabilities between the states i and j, and

$$p_{ij} = P[s_{t+1} = i | s_t = j], \tag{3}$$

where the ergodic transition probabilities p_{ij} can be characterized by the following matrix if there are two regimes:

$$P = (p_{ij}); \text{ or } P = \left(\begin{array}{c|cc} & s_t = 0 & s_t = 1 \\ s_{t+1} = 0 & p_{11} & 1 - p_{22} \\ s_{t+1} = 1 & 1 - p_{11} & p_{22} \\ \Sigma & 1 & 1 \end{array} \right). \tag{4}$$

This chapter uses the nonlinear Markov model to study the relationship between onshore and foreign bond yields (Chinese corporate offshore investment-grade dollar bond yields and domestic high-grade credit bond yields) and risk-free spreads under different structural states. Table 2 and Figure 1 show the empirical results of the two-regime MS model from January 6, 2016 to March 13, 2020.

In Table 2, the standard deviations of the two regimes are asymmetric. Regime 0 has a larger standard deviation, while regime 1 has a smaller standard deviation. At the same time, the constant term under the two regimes is significantly positive, and there is a significant spread of bond yields at home and abroad. The sustainability of each regime is very strong. When the market is under a certain regime, the probability that the next period is still under the same regime is very high, close to 98%. The period from March 21, 2017, to August 17, 2017, is identified by the model as Regime 1. The estimated results show that the onshore and foreign bond yield spreads during this period were small and the volatility was relatively low. The main reason for the strong bond market demand in China during this period was the expectation of RMB appreciation. Enhanced expectations of offshore yuan appreciation boosted demand for dim sum bonds in Hong Kong and for onshore bonds.

Table 2 shows that regime 1 includes the period from August 6, 2019, to January 14, 2020, in the sample estimate, indicating that the standard deviation change of bond yields after August 6, 2019, was also relatively stable. At 9:33 a.m. on August 5, 2019, China's onshore RMB

Table 2. Estimation results with Markov Switching Model for bond yields 2016/01/06–2020/03/13.

Markov Model Parameters

	β_1	β_2	μ_0	μ_1	σ_0	σ_1	p_{11}	p_{22}
IVUSD $_t$	0.0335***	−0.0078	4.0907***	2.9788***	0.3282***	0.0576***	0.9848***	0.9798***
	(0.0000)	(0.6320)	(0.0000)	(0.0000)	(0.0103)	(0.0025)	(0.0053)	(0.0071)

Regime Classification

Regime 0	Days	Avg. Prob.	Regime 1	Days	Avg. Prob.
2016-01-06–2016-03-24	52	0.999	2016-03-30–2016-06-07	44	0.982
2016-06-08–2017-02-07	133	0.989	2017-02-08–2017-03-01	16	0.935
2017-03-02–2017-03-20	13	0.957	**2017-03-21–2017-08-17**	**95**	**0.987**
2017-08-18–2017-09-18	20	0.903	2017-09-19–2017-11-29	47	0.984
2017-11-30–2018-05-07	98	0.979	2018-05-08–2018-05-23	11	0.930
2018-05-24–2018-06-01	7	0.848	2018-06-04–2018-09-10	68	0.987
2018-09-11–2019-01-25	86	0.985	2019-01-28–2019-03-05	21	0.943
2019-03-06–2019-08-05	98	0.992	**2019-08-06–2020-01-14**	**103**	**0.989**
2020-01-15–2020-03-13	35	0.981			

Notes: The dependent variable $IVUSD_t$ is Chinese corporate offshore investment-grade dollar bond yields. $IVCN_t$ is domestic high-grade credit bond yield. Δs_{t+1} is the offshore and onshore risk-free spread corresponding to the bilateral exchange rate. The exchange rate is the change in the 100-log difference of the CNY price. p_{11} and p_{22} are variance transition probabilities. The standard errors are shown below the estimates. The significance levels are displayed as *** for 1%, ** for 5%, and * for 10%.

Sources: CFETS; Bank of America Merrill Lynch; CCDC; CBPC.

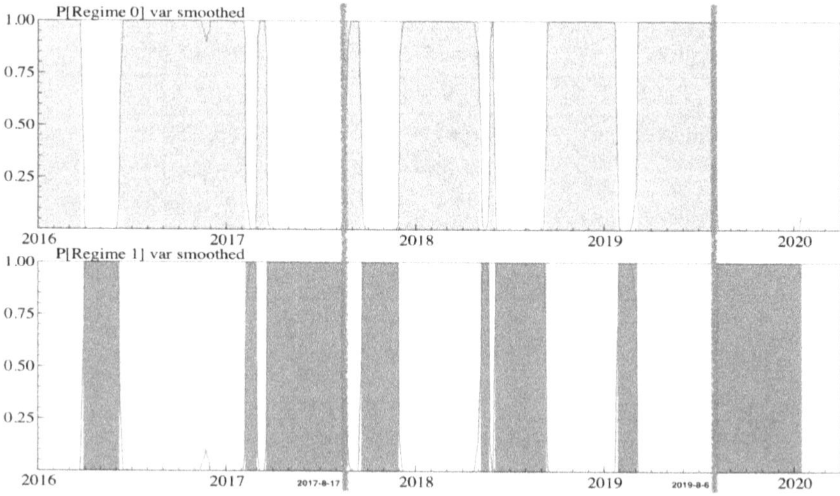

Figure 1. Smoothed probabilities of two regimes for bond yields, January 6, 2016 to March 13, 2020.

against the US dollar "broke 7", reaching 7.0056, with the daily reference rate falling below 6.90.

3.2.2 *Structural breakpoints*

According to the Markov Switching Model, there are two dates of stationary fluctuation period: August 17, 2017, and August 6, 2019. Before and after these two dates, the onshore and foreign bond yields fluctuate less, and the duration is longer. The corresponding events were the official launch of Bond Connect in Hong Kong on July 3, 2017, and the RMB onshore spot exchange rate against the US dollar breakthrough past 7 on August 5, 2019. To further investigate the accuracy of the breakpoints, in this part, the Quandt–Andrews breakpoint test is used to detect the significance of the above two dates: First, OLS with HAC error term is used in regression equation (1). Second, the Quandt–Andrews Breakpoint Test is conducted on the above two breakpoints for the three sample periods (whole sample equation, samples A, and B). The results are shown in Table 3.

As reported in Table 3, the Chow breakpoint test results show that the two breakpoints on August 17, 2017, and August 6, 2019, and the breakpoint test results of the two sub-samples (samples A and B) are all very significant.

Table 3. Chow breakpoint test results.

Breakpoints	**2017-08-17**	**2019-08-06**
	Whole Sample Equation: 2016-1-06–2020-03-13	
F-statistics	75.4684	25.1158
Prob.	0.0000***	0.0000***
Loglikelihood	204.1690	72.9448
	Sample A 2016-1-06–2019-08-05	Sample B 2017-8-18–2020-03-13
F-statistics	298.4512	190.9603
Prob.	0.0000***	0.0000***
Loglikelihood	605.9894	404.0432

Notes: The significance levels are displayed as *** for 1%.

Based on the above two methods and various data analysis results, the following conclusions can be drawn: First, both approaches show that August 17, 2017, and August 6, 2019, are significant structural breakpoints. Second, the period from March 21, 2017, to August 17, 2017, coincides with the period before and just after the launch of Bond Connect in China, indicating that the bond yield fluctuates less after the launch. Before Bond Connect, the yield of onshore and offshore bonds of Chinese enterprises fluctuated greatly. Since the introduction of the Bond Connect mechanism, the domestic market has become the dominant market, and the volatility of offshore and onshore bond yields of Chinese enterprises has become more flexible and market-oriented. Third, August 6, 2019, coincided with the RMB onshore spot exchange rate against the US dollar dropped below 7. Usually, the anticipation of exchange rate depreciation will lead to capital outflows. However, from August 6, 2019, to January 15, 2020, offshore and onshore bond yields showed a relatively stable volatility. Since the RMB against the US dollar broke 7, the movement of the RMB market exchange rate has indeed become more flexible, and the fluctuation of exchange rate with market supply and demand can promote the stability of bond yield.

3.3 *VECM-BEKK-GARCH model*

The VECM model is as follows:

$$Y_t = BZ_t + E_t \tag{5}$$

and

$$\mathrm{Y}_t = \begin{pmatrix} \mathrm{DIVUSD}_t \\ \mathrm{DIVCN}_t \end{pmatrix}; \quad \mathrm{Z}_t = \begin{pmatrix} 1 \\ \mathrm{ect}_{t-1} \\ \Delta \mathrm{s}_{t+1} \\ \Delta \mathrm{y}_{t-1} \\ \cdots \\ \Delta \mathrm{y}_{t-p} \\ \mathrm{Control}_t \end{pmatrix}, \tag{6}$$

where Y_t is the dependent variable; $\Delta\mathrm{ect}_{t-1} = \mathrm{DIVUSD}_t - \beta\mathrm{DIVCN}_t$ is the error correction term; Δs_{t+1} is the spread between forward exchange rate (NDF) and spot exchange rate (CNY); p is the lag length; $\mathrm{Control}_t$ is the control variable, including dollar factor (dlUSDIndex) and carry factor (dCarryIndex); E_t is the random error term matrix.

The Engle & Kroner (1995) BEKK-GARCH model is as follows:

$$\mathrm{H}_t = CC' + A\mu_{t-1}\mu'_{t-1}A' + B'H_{t-1}B, \tag{7}$$

where $H_t = \begin{bmatrix} h_{11,t} & h_{12,t} \\ h_{21,t} & h_{22,t} \end{bmatrix}$ is conditional variance–covariance matrix and represents the conditional variance of onshore and offshore bond yield residual term; $\mathrm{A} = \begin{bmatrix} \alpha_{11} & \alpha_{12} \\ \alpha_{21} & \alpha_{22} \end{bmatrix}$ is the ARCH term coefficient matrix, used to measure the influence of lag order residual term on the conditional variance of the current period; $\mathrm{B} = \begin{bmatrix} \beta_{11} & \beta_{12} \\ \beta_{21} & \beta_{22} \end{bmatrix}$ is the GARCH item coefficient matrix, used to measure the influence of the lag order conditional variance on the conditional variance of the current period; CC′ is the intercept matrix; $\mathrm{C} = \begin{bmatrix} c_{11} & 0 \\ c_{21} & c_{22} \end{bmatrix}$ is the lower triangular matrix that represents the constant term of the equation.

In the variance equation, matrices A and B reflect the volatility spillover effect between onshore and offshore bond yields. The diagonal elements of matrix A reflect the ARCH effect of onshore and offshore markets, which is used to measure the influence of the residual term on the conditional variance of the period. The diagonal elements of matrix B reflect the GARCH effect of onshore and offshore markets, which is used to measure the influence of the lagged conditional variance on the current conditional variance. By expanding the conditional variance, we can get the following:

$$h_{11,t} = c_{11}^2 + \sum_{j=1}^{n}\sum_{i=1}^{n}\alpha_{i1}\alpha_{j1}\mu_{i,t-1}\mu_{j,t-1} + \sum_{j=1}^{n}\sum_{i=1}^{n}\beta_{i1}\beta_{j1}h_{ij,t-1}, \tag{8}$$

$$h_{12,t} = c_{11}c_{12} + \sum_{j=1}^{n}\sum_{i=1}^{n}\alpha_{i1}\alpha_{j2}\mu_{i,t-1}\mu_{j,t-1} + \sum_{j=1}^{n}\sum_{i=1}^{n}\beta_{i1}\beta_{j2}h_{ij,t-1}, \tag{9}$$

$$h_{22,t} = c_{22}^2 + \sum_{j=1}^{n}\sum_{i=1}^{n}\alpha_{i2}\alpha_{j2}\mu_{i,t-1}\mu_{j,t-1} + \sum_{j=1}^{n}\sum_{i=1}^{n}\beta_{i2}\beta_{j2}h_{ij,t-1}, \tag{10}$$

where $h_{11,t}$ is the variance of offshore bond yields, $h_{12,t}$ is the covariance of onshore and offshore bond yields, and $h_{22,t}$ is the variance of onshore bond yields.

The diagonal elements in matrix A reflect ARCH volatility spillover effect (volatility aggregation); the secondary diagonal element α_{12} reflects the impact transmission of offshore bond yields to onshore bond yields; α_{21} reflects the impact transmission of onshore bond yields to offshore bond yields. The main diagonal elements of matrix B reflect the continuous effect of fluctuations in onshore and offshore markets. β_{12} reflects the volatility transmission of offshore bond yield to onshore bond yield, while β_{21} reflects the volatility transmission of onshore bond yields to offshore bond yields. The off-diagonal elements of matrix A and matrix B determine the volatility spillover effect between offshore bond yields and onshore bond yields.

This chapter divides the data samples based on these two structural breakpoint dates of August 17, 2017, and August 6, 2019. The first period is pre-Bond Connect, from January 6, 2016, to August 17, 2017. The second period, post-Bond Connect, is from August 18, 2017, to August 5, 2019. The third period is from August 6, 2019, to March 13, 2020, and is labeled "RMB Breaks 7".

First of all, to ensure the validity of the model results, Augmented Dickey–Fuller (ADF) tests were conducted. The results show that the level data cannot reject the null hypothesis of having a unit root while the first difference data can, confirming that the variables are stationary as I (1) process. Therefore, the data of this chapter were processed as follows: Chinese corporate offshore investment-grade dollar bond yields and domestic high-grade credit bond yields, and the carry factor (CarryIndex), were subjected to the difference treatment; the onshore and offshore risk-free spreads, and the dollar factor (USDIndex), were treated with log difference. The processed data all passed the ADF test at the 1% significance level.

Second, according to the AIC criterion, this chapter finds that the optimal lag length of the VAR model is 4. Since the co-integration model makes the first difference to the level data, this chapter finds that the optimal lag length is 3.

Then, this chapter conducted the Johansen Co-integration Test for each of the three sample periods. The findings show at least one long-run co-integration relationship between onshore and offshore bond markets, implying a long-term equilibrium relationship between them. Therefore, this chapter adopts the VECM model to obtain the sequence of error correction terms for BEKK-GARCH estimation, and the results are shown as follows.

3.3.1 *Long-term co-integrating relationship*

This chapter estimates the VECM co-integration equation between onshore and offshore bond yields of Chinese enterprises in three different periods with the addition of the control variables dollar factor and carry factor. The estimated results are as follows:

As seen from Table 4, the estimated result shows no significant difference between the original equation and the control variable equation,

Table 4. Estimation results of VECM.

	Original Equation		**Control Variables Equation**	
	dIVUSD	dIVCN	dIVUSD	dIVCN
	Pre-Bond Connect (2016-1-6–2017-8-17)			
Cointegration Equation	IVUSD−0.6320*IVCN (0.0874)		IVUSD−0.6402*IVCN (0.0859)	
Adj. R^2	0.0226	0.2848	0.0889	0.2918
	Post-Bond Connect (2017-8-18 to 2019-8-5)			
Cointegration Equation	IVUSD−0.8671*IVCN (0.0531)		IVUSD−0.8673*IVCN (0.0528)	
Adj. R^2	0.0261	0.1678	0.0228	0.1704
	The RMB Breaks 7 (2019-8-6 to 2020-3-13)			
Cointegration Equation	IVUSD−0.8282***IVCN (0.0069)		IVUSD−0.8271***IVCN (0.0075)	
Adj. R^2	0.1407	0.1458	0.1316	0.1495

Notes: The significance levels are displayed as *** for 1%. The control variable equation is the result of adding dollar factor (USDIndex) and carry factor (CarryIndex) to the original equation.

indicating that the long-term co-integration relationship between onshore and offshore bond yields is relatively stable whether the control variable is added or not.

With regard to the results for three different periods, in the original equation estimation results for Pre-Bond Connect, the long-term equilibrium relationship between onshore and offshore bond yields of Chinese enterprises can be expressed as IVUSD=0.6320*IVCN. Before the launch of Bond Connect, the long-term equilibrium linkage between offshore bond yields and onshore bond yields was low, with a correlation coefficient of only 0.632, indicating the low degree of integration of onshore and offshore bond markets.

However, with the introduction of Bond Connect, according to the original equation estimation results, the long-term equilibrium relationship between onshore and offshore bond yields of Chinese enterprises can be expressed as IVUSD=0.8671*IVCN. The coefficient of onshore and offshore bond yields is significantly higher than during the Pre-Bond Connect period, reaching more than 0.8. After the RMB Breaks 7 event, the long-term equilibrium relationship of onshore and offshore bond yields is IVUSD=0.8282*IVCN. Although the coefficient drops slightly, the degree of significance increases. This means that the launch of Bond Connect has increased capital flows, and since the RMB Breaks 7, the exchange rate depends more on the market supply and demand. In the process of China's gradual opening up of the financial market, the onshore and offshore bond yields gradually begin to tend to change synchronously, which also indicates that the degree of integration between China's bond market and the international financial market has made a qualitative leap since the launch of Bond Connect.

3.3.2 *Pre-bond connect*

Table 5 shows the GARCH-BEKK model estimation results for the Pre-Bond Connect period. According to the results of the mean equation, the yield of offshore bonds is significantly affected by the yield of onshore bonds, and the yield of onshore bonds is also affected by the yield of offshore bonds. When the first lag of onshore bond yield rises by 1%, the offshore bond yield rises by 0.126%. When the second lag of the offshore bond yield rises by 1%, the onshore bond yield rises by 0.133%.

This chapter adopts the Wald test to conduct the joint test (see Table 8). The results show a two-way mean spillover effect between

Table 5. Estimation results of GARCH-BEKK model in pre-bond connect period.

	Original Equation		Control Variables Equation	
	Mean Equation of Pre-Bond Connect			
	dIVUSD	**dIVCN**	**dIVUSD**	**dIVCN**
Constant	0.0014	−0.0012	0.0013	−0.0003
	(0.0026)	(0.0019)	(0.0021)	(0.0019)
$dIVUSD_1$	−0.0840*	−0.0200	−0.0594	−0.0450
	(0.0507)	(0.0481)	(0.0506)	(0.0326)
$dIVUSD_2$	0.0799*	0.1332**	0.0549	0.0806
	(0.0462)	(0.0528)	(0.0505)	(0.0529)
$dIVUSD_3$	0.0952**	−0.0609	0.1078**	−0.0010
	(0.0431)	(0.0436)	(0.0458)	(0.0471)
$dIVCN_1$	0.1264***	0.3615***	0.1030**	0.3279***
	(0.0309)	(0.0488)	(0.0482)	(0.0633)
$dIVCN_2$	−0.0485	0.0045	−0.0562	0.0527
	(0.0331)	(0.0452)	(0.0471)	(0.0534)
$dIVCN_3$	−0.0997***	−0.0186	−0.0380	−0.0365
	(0.0388)	(0.0435)	(0.0307)	(0.0439)
S_t	0.0097	−0.0177**	−0.0008	−0.0144*
	(0.0088)	(0.0081)	(0.0083)	(0.0079)
Ect	−0.0083***	0.0020	−0.0054	0.0027
	(0.0030)	(0.0029)	(0.0034)	(0.0025)
dlUSDIndex			1.4020***	0.4183
			(0.3322)	(0.4264)
dCarryIndex			−0.0370	0.0787*
			(0.0343)	(0.0406)
	Conditional Variance Equation of Pre-Bond Connect			
α_{11}	0.1969**		−0.2762***	
	(0.0856)		(0.0981)	
α_{12}	0.3266***		0.0842	
	(0.0983)		(0.1045)	
α_{21}	−0.1137**		0.0254	
	(0.0524)		(0.0712)	
α_{22}	0.4753***		0.6516***	
	(0.1033)		(0.1060)	

(*Continued*)

Table 5. *(Continued)*

	Original Equation	Control Variables Equation
	Conditional Variance Equation of Pre-Bond Connect	
β_{11}	0.9307***	0.9551***
	(0.0245)	(0.0278)
β_{12}	0.0932*	0.1947***
	(0.0528)	(0.0311)
β_{21}	0.0697	−0.0053
	(0.0432)	(0.0457)
β_{22}	0.7214***	0.6056***
	(0.0000)	(0.0867)

Notes: The control variable equation is the result of adding dollar factor (USDIndex) and carry factor (CarryIndex) to the original equation. The significance levels are displayed as *** for 1%, ** for 5%, and * for 10%. α_{12} reflects the ARCH volatility effect of offshore bond yield to onshore bond yield; α_{21} reflects the ARCH volatility effect of onshore bond yield to offshore bond yield. β_{12} reflects the GARCH volatility effect of offshore bond yield to onshore bond yield, while β_{21} is the GARCH volatility effect of onshore bond yield to offshore bond yield.

onshore and offshore bond yields, indicating that the trend of domestic and foreign bond yields will impact each other. When introducing the control variable, it is found that the offshore bond yield is significantly affected by the dollar factor, while the onshore bond yield is affected by the carry factor, and the mean spillover effect is significantly weakened.

The conditional variance equation in Table 5 shows a significant spillover effect between the two markets. Similarly, the joint test results of the conditional variance equation in Table 8 also show a significant spillover effect. This indicates that abnormal shocks will have an impact on the conditional volatility of both offshore and onshore markets. When the dollar factor and carry factor are under control, the volatility spillover effect from the onshore bond market to the offshore market disappears, which indicates that the dollar factor and the carry factor absorb the volatility transmission from the onshore to the offshore market.

According to the coefficient of ARCH spillover effect in Table 5, the offshore market volatility effect will be transmitted to the onshore bond market, which means the offshore market shock will increase the volatility of the onshore market bond yields. However, when introducing the control variables (dollar factor and carry factor), the ARCH spillover effect (aggregation) between the onshore and offshore markets disappears, which indicates that dollar factor and carry factor absorb the shock transmission between onshore and offshore markets.

According to the coefficient of GARCH spillover effect in Table 5, there is GARCH spillover effect from the offshore market to the onshore market, but the spillover effect from the onshore market to the offshore market is not significant. However, when introducing the control variables, the GARCH spillover effect from the offshore market to the onshore market is enhanced, which indicates that the volatility (persistent) transmission from the offshore market to the onshore market is not absorbed immediately, and it takes more time for the market to react to the impact of the dollar factor and the carry factor.

3.3.3 *Post-bond connect*

From the mean equation in Table 6, it can be seen that the onshore market has a significant influence on the offshore market, while the onshore

Table 6. Estimation results of GARCH-BEKK model in post-bond Connect period.

	Original Equation		**Control Variables Equation**	
	Mean Equation of Post-Bond Connect			
	dIVUSD	**dIVCN**	**dIVUSD**	**dIVCN**
Constant	0.0012	−0.0008	0.0015	−0.0006
	(0.0014)	(0.0011)	(0.0016)	(0.0012)
$dIVUSD_1$	0.0296	0.0433	0.0296	0.0388
	(0.0973)	(0.0387)	(0.0939)	(0.0385)
$dIVUSD_2$	−0.05712	−0.0244	−0.0586	−0.0076
	(0.0906)	(0.0387)	(0.0970)	(0.0358)
$dIVUSD_3$	−0.1040	0.0071	−0.1040	0.0010
	(0.0861)	(0.0275)	(0.0842)	(0.0305)
$dIVCN_1$	−0.1191**	0.3863***	−0.1191**	0.3550***
	(0.0492)	(0.0496)	(0.0468)	(0.0516)
$dIVCN_2$	0.0594	0.0251	0.0579	0.0517
	(0.0633)	(0.0472)	(0.0675)	(0.0537)
$dIVCN_3$	−0.0170	0.1056**	−0.0170	0.0906*
	(0.0630)	(0.0483)	(0.0690)	(0.0519)

(Continued)

Table 6. (*Continued*)

	Original Equation		Control Variables Equation	
	Mean Equation of Post-Bond Connect			
S_t	−0.0015	0.0064	−0.0017	0.0043*
	(0.0073)	(0.0067)	(0.0066)	(0.0061)
Ect	−0.0040**	−0.0010	−0.0038*	−0.0009
	(0.0018)	(0.0014)	(0.0022)	(0.0015)
dlUSDIndex			−0.2167	0.4596*
			(0.2929)	(0.2585)
dCarryIndex			0.0117	0.0434*
			(0.0326)	(0.0228)
	Conditional Variance Equation of Post-Bond Connect			
α_{11}	0.4339**		0.4422***	
	(0.1095)		(0.1435)	
α_{12}	−0.0673		−0.0724	
	(0.0675)		(0.0672)	
α_{21}	0.0572		0.0441	
	(0.0819)		(0.0902)	
α_{22}	0.4184***		0.4566***	
	(0.0806)		(0.0786)	
β_{11}	0.8574***		0.8527***	
	(0.0320)		(0.0442)	
β_{12}	0.0199		0.0214	
	(0.0300)		(0.0349)	
β_{21}	−0.0530		−0.0588	
	(0.0731)		(0.0782)	
β_{22}	0.7981***		0.7919***	
	(0.0472)		(0.0457)	

Notes: The control variable equation is the result of adding dollar factor (USDINDEX) and carry factor (CarryIndex) to the original equation. The significance levels are displayed as *** for 1%, ** for 5%, and * for 10%. α_{12} reflects the ARCH volatility effect of offshore bond yield to onshore bond yield; α_{21} reflects the ARCH volatility effect of onshore bond yield to offshore bond yield. β_{12} reflects the GARCH volatility effect of offshore bond yield to onshore bond yield, while β_{21} is the GARCH volatility effect of onshore bond yield to offshore bond yield.

market is not affected by the offshore market. When introducing the control variables, the onshore market still impacts the offshore market, and both the dollar factor and carry factor impact the onshore bond market. The onshore bond market is also affected by bilateral exchange rate differential. Meanwhile, the equilibrium error term significantly impacts the offshore bond yields. If the yield gap between domestic and foreign bonds expands, the offshore bond market adjusts spontaneously to rebuild the equilibrium relationship between the two markets. From the joint test results in Table 8, we find that the mean spillover effect exists from the onshore market to the offshore market whether or not control variables are introduced into the mean value equation, but there is no such effect from the offshore market to the onshore market. The results of the conditional variance equation show no volatility spillover effect between onshore bond yields and offshore bond yields.

In the Post-Bond Connect period, the onshore market is more likely to determine the trend of bond yields, and the onshore bond yields are affected by dollar factor, carry factor, and exchange rate differential. It contrasts the Pre-Bond Connect period when the dollar factor could only influence the offshore bond yields, while the carry factor could only influence the onshore market. In the Post-Bond Connect period, the onshore market becomes dominant, and the global shock represented by the dollar factor and the carry factor begins to affect the onshore bond yields.

3.3.4 *The RMB breaks 7*

The RMB breaking 7 in August 2019 is a symbolic event that indicates the increasing flexibility of the exchange rate.

From the mean equation in Table 7, we find that the offshore market has a significant impact on the onshore bond market regardless of whether the control variables are introduced. With the introduction of the control variables, the equilibrium error term has a significant influence on both the onshore and the offshore market. Specifically, in response to increasing spread, the two markets adjust spontaneously to rebuild the equilibrium relationship. It indicates that the exchange rate is more fitted with the market supply and demand, and the degree of marketization of the bond market has been significantly enhanced.

Table 7. Estimation results of GARCH-BEKK model in the RMB breaks 7 period.

	Original Equation		Control Variables Equation	
	Mean Equation of RMB Breaks 7			
	dIVUSD	**dIVCN**	**dIVUSD**	**dIVCN**
Constant	−0.0081**	−0.0015	−0.0052	−0.0012
	(0.0038)	(0.0019)	(0.0037)	(0.0017)
$dIVUSD_1$	−0.0141	0.0055	0.0266	−0.0002
	(0.1148)	(0.0245)	(0.1026)	(0.0260)
$dIVUSD_2$	0.0556	0.0162	0.0708	0.0032
	(0.0772)	(0.0316)	(0.0759)	(0.0253)
$dIVUSD_3$	0.0211	0.0807***	0.0294	0.0865***
	(0.0951)	(0.0236)	(0.0764)	(0.0245)
$dIVCN_1$	−0.2157	0.1633*	−0.1699	0.2058**
	(0.1493)	(0.0865)	(0.1168)	(0.0962)
$dIVCN_2$	0.0097	0.0902	−0.0701	0.0420
	(0.1140)	(0.0740)	(0.1053)	(0.0649)
$dIVCN_3$	0.2207	0.2357***	0.0761	0.2165***
	(0.1567)	(0.0488)	(0.1205)	(0.0655)
S_t	0.0199	0.0085	0.0164	0.0061
	(0.0180)	(0.0062)	(0.0185)	(0.0056)
Ect	−0.0684	0.0431	−0.0947**	0.0456**
	(0.0474)	(0.0189)	(0.0418)	(0.0225)
dlUSDIndex			−2.6918**	−0.4893
			(1.3236)	(0.3324)
dCarryIndex			−0.0641	−0.0018
			(0.0545)	(0.0090)
	Conditional Variance Equation of RMB Breaks 7			
α_{11}	0.6165**		0.7410***	
	(0.2122)		(0.1390)	
α_{12}	−0.0193		−0.0331	
	(0.0554)		(0.0341)	
α_{21}	0.7168**		0.4258	
	(0.2956)		(0.4720)	
α_{22}	1.1550***		1.1830***	
	(0.2292)		(0.3249)	

(Continued)

Table 7. (*Continued*)

	Original Equation	Control Variables Equation
	Conditional Variance Equation of RMB Breaks 7	
β_{11}	0.7325***	0.6399***
	(0.2124)	(0.0915)
β_{12}	0.0830**	0.0965***
	(0.0382)	(0.0336)
β_{21}	−0.1983	−0.1131
	(0.2695)	(0.1835)
β_{22}	0.4082**	0.4624**
	(0.1659)	(0.1960)

Notes: The control variable equation is the result of adding dollar factor (USDINDEX) and carry factor (CarryIndex) to the original equation. The significance levels are displayed as *** for 1%, ** for 5%, and * for 10%. α_{12} reflects the ARCH volatility effect of offshore bond yield to onshore bond yield; α_{21} reflects the ARCH volatility effect of onshore bond yield to offshore bond yield. β_{12} reflects the GARCH volatility effect of offshore bond yield to onshore bond yield, while β_{21} is the GARCH volatility effect of onshore bond yield to offshore bond yield.

The conditional variance equation in Table 7 shows a significant ARCH spillover effect from the onshore bond yield to the offshore bond yield, where the onshore bond market shock will improve the offshore bond market volatility (but not vice-versa). However, when introducing the control variables, the ARCH spillover effect disappears. This indicates that the dollar factor and carry factor can absorb the shock transmission of both the onshore market and offshore market. From the coefficient of the GARCH spillover effect, it can be seen that there are significant GARCH volatility spillover effects from the offshore market to the onshore market whether or not the control variables are introduced.

From the joint test of conditional variance equation in Table 8, it can be seen that there are spillover effects between onshore and offshore bond yields. When the control variables are introduced, the volatility spillover effect from the onshore bond market to the offshore bond market disappears, indicating that the dollar factor and carry factor affect the volatility transmission between the two markets. All the above results show that since the RMB Breaks 7 event, the co-movement between the onshore bond market and the offshore bond market has been greatly improved, and the degree of integration between the two markets has been significantly enhanced.

Table 8. The joint test results of spillover effect in three periods.

	Pre-Bond Connect		Post-Bond Connect		The RMB Breaks 7	
H0	**Original Equation**	**Control Variables Equation**	**Original Equation**	**Control Variables Equation**	**Original Equation**	**Control Variables Equation**
	Joint test results of mean equation					
No mean spillover effect from onshore to offshore bond yields	24.5994***	7.7824*	6.6780*	7.6570*	3.4317	3.4021
No mean spillover effect from offshore to onshore bond yields	8.4043**	3.9373	1.8165	1.1476	13.3224***	18.3023***
	Joint test results of conditional variance equation					
No volatility spillover effect from onshore to offshore bond yields	5.3995*	0.4287	0.6237	0.5700	6.6470**	1.0004
No volatility spillover effect from offshore to onshore bond yields	12.5119***	39.1679***	1.2350	1.5523	7.1845**	9.0711**

Notes: The significance levels are displayed as *** for 1%, ** for 5%, and * for 10%. All the results in the table are chi-square statistics of Wald test.

4. Conclusions

This chapter conducts an empirical study of onshore and offshore bond yields and evaluates the opening and policy impacts of China's bond market based on interest rate parity theory. The results show that Bond Connect has enhanced the effective connection of onshore and offshore bond markets, as well as the importance of the onshore market. First, the long-term correlation coefficient of the onshore and offshore bond markets increased from 0.63 to 0.87 after the introduction of Bond Connect. Prior to Bond Connect, the offshore bond market was affected only by the dollar factor, while the onshore market was affected by the carry trade factor, and the inter-connection of the two markets was loose and unstable. After the launch of Bond Connect, both the US dollar and carry trade factors started to affect the bond yield of the onshore market, and the integration level of the two markets improved. Second, the onshore market has started to lead the offshore market in pricing. Prior to Bond Connect, there existed volatility spillover effects in both the offshore and onshore markets, indicating that the bond yield of each market might lead to that of the other. However, after controlling for the US dollar and carry trade factors, both the volatility spillover effect from onshore to offshore market and the mean spillover effect from offshore to onshore market disappear. Nevertheless, after the introduction of Bond Connect, there is still a mean spillover effect from the onshore market to the offshore market.

Moreover, the improved RMB foreign exchange rate flexibility has also played a notable role in stabilizing bond yields and improving the effective connection of onshore and offshore bond markets. First, after August 2019, the long-term correlation coefficient increased to 0.83. Second, since August 2019, the dollar factor affected only the offshore market, and the impacts of US dollar, carry trade, and foreign exchange costs on the onshore market have been moderated. Specifically, the offshore market carries the mean spillover effects on the onshore markets, while the two markets have mutual volatility spillover effects. In particular, after controlling for the US dollar factor and carry trade, the long-term equilibrium error term reduces, and the bond yield gap can have notable impacts on both onshore and offshore bond markets. The above findings illustrate that, with the increased RMB exchange rate flexibility to enlarge onshore and offshore bond yields, the two markets will adjust accordingly to reach a new equilibrium. Moreover, the integration of the two markets is notably enhanced, their mutual impact is strengthened, and their co-movement is closer.

Academicians should continue to pay attention to the progress of RMB exchange rate reform, capital account convertibility, and the related impacts on China's onshore and offshore bond markets. Moreover, with the increase in holdings of RMB-denominated bond assets by foreign investors, some researchers may be interested in exploring the potential impacts of derivative market development in China and the impact of rising foreign ownership on the connectivity of the onshore and offshore bond markets.

References

Aldasoro, I., Ehlers, T., McGuire, P., & von Peter, G. (2020). Global banks' dollar funding needs and central bank swap lines. *BIS Bulletin*, 27.

Andrews, D.W.K. (1993). Tests for parameter instability and structural change with unknown change point. *Econometrica*, 61(4), 821–856.

Andrews, D.W. & Ploberger, W. (1994). Optimal tests when a nuisance parameter is present only under the alternative. *Econometrica*, 62(6), 1383–1414.

Banerjee, R., Hofmann, B., & Mehrotra, A. (2020). Corporate investment and the exchange rate. BIS Working Paper, No. 839.

Barberis, N., Shleifer, A., & Wurgler, J. (2005). Comovement. *Journal of Financial Economics,* 75(2), 283–317.

Bekaert, G., Wei, M., & Xing, Y. (2007). Uncovered interest rate parity and the term structure. *Journal of International Money and Finance*, 26(6), 1038–1069.

Bruno, V. & Shin, H. (2017). Global dollar credit and carry trades. *Review of Financial Studies*, 30(3), 703–749.

Bunda, I., Hamann, A.J., & Lall, S. (2009). Correlations in emerging market bonds: The role of local and global factors. *Emerging Markets Review*, 10(2), 67–96.

Chow, G.C. (1960). Tests of equality between sets of coefficients in two linear regressions. *Econometrica: Journal of the Econometric Society*, 28(3), 591–605.

Christiansen, C. (2014). Integration of European bond markets. *Journal of Banking & Finance*, 42, 191–198.

Committee on the Global Financial System (CGFS). (2020). US dollar funding: An international perspective. BIS CGFS Papers No. 65. https://www.bis.org/publ/cgfs65.htm.

Ding, D.K., Tse, Y., & Williams, M.R. (2014). The price discovery puzzle in offshore Yuan trading: Different contributions for different contracts. *Journal of Futures Markets*, 34(2), 103–123.

Ding, D., Huang, Y., & Zhou, Y. (2019). China's offshore corporate dollar bonds. In: *The Future of China's Bond Market*, IMF, Chapter 16, pp. 357–379.

Ding, J., Hu, H., & Ye, W. (2020). Dynamic study of onshore and offshore RMB exchange rates: From the perspective of dollar and carry factor. *Journal of Financial Research,* 6, 78–95 (in Chinese).

Du, W., Tepper, A., & Verdelhan, A. (2018). Deviations from covered interest rate parity. *Journal of Finance*, 73(3), 915–957.

Égert, B. & Kočenda, E. (2007). Interdependence between Eastern and Western European stock markets: Evidence from intraday data. *Economic Systems*, 31(2), 184–203.

Engle, C. (2014). Exchange rates and interest parity. In: Gopinath, G., Helpman, E., & Rogoff, K. (eds.), *Handbook of International Economics*, Vol. 4. Elsevier, pp. 453–522.

Engel, C. & Hamilton, J.D.A. (1990). Long swings in the dollar: Are they in the data and do markets know it? *The American Economic Review*, 80(4), 689–713.

Engle, R.F. & Kroner, K.F. (1995). Multivariate simultaneous generalized ARCH. *Econometric Theory*, 11(1), 122–150.

Feng, Y. & Wang, L. (2016). Research on the volatility spillover of offshore and onshore RMB-denominated bond market based on interest rate term structure. *International Economics and Trade Research*, 32(7), 53–63 (in Chinese).

Gambacorta, L., Mayordomo, S., & Garralda, J. (2020). Dollar borrowing, firm-characteristics, and FX-hedged funding opportunities. BIS Working Paper, No. 843.

Hardy, B. & Saffie, F. (2019). From carry trades to trade credit. BIS Working Paper, No. 773.

Hordahl, P. & Shim, I. (2020). EME bond portfolio flows and long-term interest rates during the Covid-19 pandemic. *BIS Bulletin*, 18.

Huang, Y., Panizza, U., & Portes, R. (2018). Corporate foreign bond issuance and interfirm loans in China. NBER Working Paper, No. 25413.

Huo, R. & Ahmed, A.D. (2017). Return and volatility spillovers effects: Evaluating the impact of Shanghai-Hong Kong stock connect. *Economic Modelling*, 61, 260–272.

Ji, Z. & Cao, Y. (2017). Credit risk premium or market liquidity premium? An empirical study on the pricing of credit bonds in China. *Journal of Financial Research*, 2, 1–10 (in Chinese).

Jiang, Z., Krishnamurthy, A., & Lustig, H. (2018). Foreign safe asset demand for US treasuries and the dollar. *AEA Papers and Proceedings*, 108(5), 537–541.

Lewis, K. (1995). Puzzles in international financial markets. In: Grossman, G. & Rogoff, K. (eds.), *Handbook of International Economics*, Vol. 3. North-Holland, pp. 1931–1971.

Ma, R., Deng, C., Cai, H., & Zhai, P. (2019). Does Shanghai-Hong Kong stock connect drive market comovement between Shanghai and Hong Kong? A new evidence. *North American Journal of Economics and Finance*, 50, 100980.

McCauley, R. & Schenk, C. (2020). Central bank swaps then and now. BIS Working Paper, No. 851.

Miyajima, K., Mohanty, M.S., & Chan, T. (2015). Emerging market local currency bonds: Diversification and stability. *Emerging Markets Review*, 22, 126–139.

Obsfeld, M. & Rogoff, K. (2001). The six major puzzles in international macroeconomics. In: Bernanke, B. & Rogoff, K. (eds.), *NBER Macroeconomics Annual 2000*. Chicago: University of Chicago Press, pp. 339–412.

Rose, A. & Spiegel, M. (2012). Dollar illiquidity and central bank swap arrangements during the global financial crisis. *Journal of International Economics*, 88(2), 326–340.

Stenfors, A. (2019). The covered interest parity puzzle and the evolution of the Japan premium. *Journal of Economic Issues*, 53(2), 417–424.

Sutton, G.D. (2000). Is there excess comovement of bond yields between countries? *Journal of International Money and Finance*, 19(3), 363–376.

Ventosa-Santaulària, D., Gómez-Zaldívar, M., & Wallace, F.H. (2015). The real exchange rate, regime changes and volatility shifts. *Applied Economics*, 47, 2445–2454.

Xiao, M. & Wang, X. (2014). The correlation analysis between onshore and offshore RMB-denominated bond markets: A research based on DCC-GARCH model. *Journal of Central University of Finance & Economics*, (S1), 23–30 (in Chinese).

Xu, Z. (2018). Transformation of monetary policy in the high-quality development stage. *Journal of Financial Research*, 4, 1–19 (in Chinese).

Yi, G. (2020). Revisiting China's financial asset structure and policy implications. *Economic Research Journal*, 55(3), 4–17 (in Chinese).

Zhou, X., Li, M., & Liu, T. (2015). Study on co-movement between onshore and offshore RMB-denominated bond markets and its influencing factors. *Studies of International Finance*, 3, 44–53 (in Chinese).

Chapter 10

Applicability of Interest Rate Parity Theory in China: Evidence from Offshore and Onshore Corporate Bond Yields

This chapter examines the applicability of the covered interest rate parity (CIRP) theory in China, using the daily yields of China's investment-grade US dollar bonds and onshore high-grade credit bonds from January 2010 to July 2020 as a sample. The empirical results demonstrate that the CIRP can be applied to China from mid-2017, which can primarily be attributed to the gradual expansion of openness in China's bond market following the introduction of the Bond Connect program. Additionally, the flexibility of the exchange rate has further enhanced the practicality of interest rate parity theory in China, facilitating effective linkages between China's bond market and international markets. Even the impact of the COVID-19 pandemic in 2020 did not alter the aforementioned relationship.

Due to policies such as the incomplete convertibility of the capital account, neither uncovered interest rate parity (UIRP) nor covered interest rate parity has held in China for a long period. CRIP still does not hold in China even after controlling for the influence of the US dollar index, which has been a critical factor in the "iron law" of CIRP effectiveness since the global financial crisis. Since the launch of Bond Connect in the second half of 2017, China's bond market has gradually achieved effective linkage with international markets, creating conditions for the applicability of interest rate parity theory in China. The convergence of onshore and offshore bond yields, considering the impact of the US dollar index and exchange rate costs, indicates a qualitative leap in the integration of China's bond market with international markets. The reform of the exchange rate formation mechanism has positively affected the convergence of onshore and offshore bond yields, further enhancing the applicability of interest rate parity theory in China.

Further empirical tests show that neither certain industries' bonds nor the impact of the COVID-19 pandemic has affected the applicability of interest rate parity in China. Tests of yields on high-grade municipal bonds and real estate enterprise bonds further support the validity of interest rate parity, but the policy premium has had a more pronounced impact on the yields of such corporations, as they are subject to more policy restrictions on onshore and offshore bond issuance. The data since February 2020 suggest that the applicability of interest rate parity in China has not been affected by the COVID-19 pandemic. However, the relationship between onshore and offshore bond yields has been significantly affected, with a large sell-off of China's US dollar bonds, including investment-grade bonds, amid risk aversion and resulting in a sharp rise in yields. The relationships among China's investment-grade US dollar bond yield, the US dollar index, and onshore bond yields have changed significantly, which is the latest example of the impact of changing international financial situations on bond yields.

1. Introduction

As one of the most fundamental theories governing the determination of exchange rates, interest rate parity has long been the focus of theoretical and empirical research, and the free flow of capital is a necessary condition for interest rate parity to hold, as it enables international capital to exploit arbitrage opportunities in different markets and influence the level of exchange rates through changes in the foreign exchange market's supply and demand conditions. In recent years, China's financial liberalization has notably accelerated, with the degree of capital account opening gradually expanding. According to the IMF's statutory measurement standards, China has achieved varying degrees of openness in 37 items out of the 40 capital account subitems across seven major categories. Based on the IMF's actual measurement criteria, China's openness level reached 70% in 2019, with foreign direct investment (FDI) open at 91.7%, capital and money markets at 64%, and derivatives and other instruments at 50%.[1] Consequently, the interconnectivity between onshore and international financial markets has further strengthened, and the foundational conditions for establishing interest rate parity theory in China are becoming more sophisticated.

According to interest rate parity theory, the role of exchange rates should be neutral for bond issuance and investment, and exchange rate expectations or controlling exchange rate costs should be taken into account when examining onshore and foreign rates of return. However, due to the incomplete convertibility of China's capital account, previous literature has mostly argued that China does not possess the basic conditions for interest rate parity to hold. In recent years, the degree of openness in China's bond market has been increasing.[2] The launch of the Bond Connect program in 2017 greatly enhanced the efficiency and integration of the interconnection between onshore and foreign bond markets, providing a new background and conditions for exploring the applicability of interest rate parity. Bond Connect, which officially came into operation in July 2017, bypasses infrastructure arrangements such as clearing, custody, and information disclosure, as well as policy differences in regulation and taxation through the connection with Hong Kong's financial market infrastructure. This allows offshore investors to access and invest in the onshore bond market through a one-point approach, providing a more convenient channel for global investors to participate in China's financial market than before. By the end of June 2020, nearly 900 offshore legal entities from over 60 countries and regions had entered China's bond

[1] The speech delivered by LU Lei on September 26, 2020, entitled *Building a New Pattern of Financial Market Opening for the Next Five Years* at the Global Asset Management Forum Shanghai Summit.

[2] Opened in the early 1990s, China's bond market has become the second largest bond market in the world. Since as early as the beginning of the 21st century, China has been promoting the two-way opening of the bond market through multiple approaches. One is the "going out" approach, which means investing in the offshore bond market through QDII, RQDII, QDLP, QDIE, etc., or through the trading platform of offshore branches of onshore financial institutions; the other is the "bringing in" approach, which allows international institutions to issue RMB-denominated bonds in the interbank market, and enables offshore investors to directly participate in China's bond market through channels such as the QFII, RQFII, and Bond Connect programs. As of the end of June 2020, the proportion of bonds held by offshore institutions accounted for 2.4% of all bonds in China, which is much higher than the proportion of foreign investment in the stock market, foreign exchange market, and derivatives market.

market, with offshore institutions issuing more than 400 billion yuan of RMB-denominated bonds and holding RMB-denominated bond balances of approximately RMB 2.6 trillion yuan, growing at an annual rate of nearly 40% since 2017.

Based on a literature review on interest rate parity, this chapter explores the applicability of interest rate parity theory in China, starting with an analysis of the factors of the offshore and onshore bond yields of China's enterprises. Through a comparison of the yield rates of China's investment-grade corporate US dollar bonds with those of onshore high-grade credit bonds since 2010, as well as an econometric analysis on the relationships among the index of ChinaBond Pricing Center Co. Ltd., for China's investment-grade offshore US dollar bonds, the corresponding onshore bond index, and the onshore and foreign bond yields of different ratings and specific industries, an attempt is made to verify the applicability of interest rate parity theory in China while investigating the relationship and influencing factors of onshore and foreign bond yields.

The empirical results of this chapter indicate that China has effectively linked with international markets, and market openness has created conditions for the applicability of interest rate parity theory in China. On the one hand, the reform of exchange rate marketization has promoted the convergence of corporate onshore and offshore bond yields. On the other hand, after the Bond Connect program commenced, the convergence of corporate onshore and offshore bond yields, considering the impact of the US dollar index and exchange rate costs, indicates a qualitative leap in the integration of China's bond market with international markets. However, due to the incomplete opening of China's capital account, the space for corporate arbitrage is relatively limited. In addition, empirical analysis verifies the impact of industrial policies on the difference in onshore and offshore bond yields for urban investment and real estate enterprises, and the COVID-19 pandemic that began in 2020 has also significantly affected onshore and offshore yields.

This chapter is the first academic work to describe an empirical study conducted on the relationship between onshore and offshore bonds of China's funded enterprises from the perspective of bond yields, and it verifies the applicability of interest rate parity in China both theoretically and empirically. This chapter also has the following points of significance for the current research on China's onshore and offshore bond markets. First, unlike previous empirical studies that mainly focused on the issuance scale of China's corporate offshore bonds (Huang *et al.*, 2018; Ding *et al.*, 2019), this chapter primarily focuses on the relationship between corporate onshore and offshore bond yields and their influencing factors. Second, the empirical research data are unique, as the yield rates of China's investment-grade funded enterprise US dollar bonds from Bank of America Merrill Lynch and those of onshore high-grade credit bonds have rarely been used in former studies. The ChinaBond investment-grade US dollar bond index and the corresponding onshore bond index from the ChinaBond Pricing Center are also used here for the first time in academic research. Third, this chapter examines the policy effects of the Bond Connect program and exchange rate system reform and analyzes the shortcomings in China's capital account liberalization and the impact on investors.

2. Literature Review

Interest rate parity theory holds that the expected returns on all monetary assets in different countries should be equal; otherwise, there will be arbitrage space, and market arbitrage mechanisms will eventually combine the expected returns of similar assets across countries. Depending on whether the forward foreign exchange market is considered, interest rate parity theory can be classified into two different sub-theories: uncovered interest rate parity (UIRP) and covered interest rate parity (CIRP). UIRP states that, under the influence of market arbitrage mechanisms, the interest rate differential between two countries is equal to the expected change in the exchange rate of the currencies of the two countries; that is, the difference between the onshore interest rate and the foreign interest rate is equal to the expected appreciation (depreciation) of the onshore currency. CIRP, on the other hand, argues that if there is a forward foreign exchange market, the interest rate differential between two countries is equal to the forward premium (discount) of the onshore currency. The sub-theories of UIRP and CIRP are consistent in principle: If the forward exchange rate premium (discount) is regarded as the expected exchange rate change, then the forward exchange rate can serve as an important indicator for the spot exchange rate (Macdonald & Taylor, 1992). The most significant difference is that CIRP introduces the forward foreign exchange market, which implies that no restrictive conditions are made for investors' risk preferences, while UIRP takes investor risk neutrality as an assumption. However, both UIRP and CIRP face great challenges in empirical research, and the discussion surrounding their establishment conditions remains an ongoing topic in international economics research.

2.1 *UIRP*

Empirical research on the validity of UIRP has long been a focus in theoretical discussions. On the one hand, compared to CIRP, UIRP imposes stricter assumptions on investor risk preferences, assuming investors' risk appetite to be neutral. On the other hand, whether UIRP holds is crucial in evaluating the effectiveness of government interventions in the foreign exchange market. This is because, according to UIRP, government interventions in the foreign exchange market cannot effectively alter the spot exchange rate level related to future spot exchange rate expectations, which means that government intervention in the foreign exchange market is often ineffective unless interest rate adjustments are allowed (Henderson & Sampson, 1983). Therefore, many scholars have conducted extensive tests on the validity of UIRP.

Many early empirical studies on the effectiveness of UIRP showed that it does not hold up to scrutiny. Cumby & Obstfeld (1981, 1984) found that future spot exchange rates derived from UIRP relationships often deviated significantly from forward exchange rates, and the currencies of countries with high interest rates often do not depreciate as predicted in theory but rather appreciated further, indicating the existence of "excess returns" and long-term arbitrage opportunities in the market. This phenomenon is known as the "UIRP puzzle" or the "forward premium puzzle", which remains one of the most famous theoretical enigmas in international economics (Obstfeld & Rogoff, 2001; Engle & Zhu, 2019).

As research on the UIRP puzzle has deepened and with the continuous enrichment of market data and improvements in econometric methods, recent studies conducted in both developed economies and emerging markets indicate a decreasing significance of the UIRP puzzle. Overall, UIRP still holds, with its validity being more evident in economies with fixed exchange rate arrangements (Engle & Zhu, 2019).

2.1.1 *UIRP puzzle: Foreign exchange risk premium, rational expectation deviation, and market incompleteness*

The discussion on the factors of UIRP effectiveness is mainly divided into three aspects: foreign exchange risk premium, rational expectation deviation, and market incompleteness. The “risk premium hypothesis” in the foreign exchange market was originally proposed by Fama (1984). By testing the hypothesis of forward exchange rate premiums between nine major currencies in countries, such as France, Germany, and Japan, and the US dollar, Fama argued that the risk premium is the main reason for deviations between exchange rate expectations and forward exchange rates. This hypothesis has been widely examined and confirmed. Many researchers have used partial equilibrium analysis based on the consumption capital asset pricing model (C-CAPM) or general equilibrium models based on rational expectations (optimal consumption decisions) to theoretically characterize the risk premium factor in UIRP (Lewis, 1995) and have tested the impact of risk premium on UIRP through measures such as exchange rate fluctuations (variance), risk-adjusted forward exchange rate returns (Sharpe ratio), and exchange rate expectation surveys (Hochradl & Wagner, 2010; Jorda & Taylor, 2012; Ince & Molodtsova, 2017).

Although the risk premium can explain the UIRP puzzle well, it fails to explain the variations of “excess returns”, particularly when the magnitude is considerable. This gives rise to rational expectation deviation theory (Froot & Frankel, 1989; Frankel & Froot, 1991), which mainly comprises the heterogeneous market model and learning process theory. The heterogeneous market model suggests that there is likely to be a group of investors in the foreign exchange market who are not necessarily rational. These investors have a higher risk appetite and can obtain higher investment returns than other investors. From the perspective of expectation formation, rational expectation deviation is equivalent to a learning process related to changes in the exchange rate regime. Most of the early empirical research samples on UIRP violations were concentrated in the 1970s and 1980s, which was a critical period for countries transitioning from fixed exchange rate regimes to floating exchange rate regimes. Since the changes in investors’ exchange rate expectations are continuously revised with the evolution of the exchange rate regime, issues such as the exchange rate regime evolution and sample selection may be more important than other factors for testing UIRP (Engle, 2014).

Market incompleteness significantly impacts the foreign exchange trading behavior of market participants, which is closely related to the “home bias puzzle” (Lewis, 1995) and is an important factor in determining whether the theory of UIRP holds true. From the investor perspective, onshore investors are often more familiar with and prefer onshore assets. Coupled with real costs, such as currency conversion costs, market segmentation and government restrictions on investment, it is difficult for investors to diversify their investment portfolios uniformly on a global scale, even if capital can flow freely. Obstfeld & Rogoff (2001) further pointed out that market incompleteness can lead to significant transaction costs due to factors such as market segmentation, price stickiness, imperfect competition, and transaction fees. After all, a completely frictionless situation does not exist in real financial markets, and market transaction costs will exist in the long term, which is an important cause of UIRP violations (Bekaert *et al.*, 2007). Moreover, transaction costs and market friction also result in distinct heterogeneity among assets in different countries, and the differences in risk premiums between different countries also make it difficult for interest rate parity to hold (Wong *et al.*, 2016; Stenfors, 2019).

2.1.2 *UIRP in developed and emerging markets*

Early empirical studies on UIRP primarily took developed countries' currencies as samples, finding that the testing results were better for high-inflation countries (e.g., Italy) than low-inflation countries (e.g., Germany), and most UIRP tests based on long-term data affirmed the validity of the theory. argued that the inflation risk of high-inflation countries could often be predicted by the market, and their currencies tended to depreciate as expected by the market. In addition, the effectiveness of UIRP testing based on long-term exchange rate data was notably superior to the exchange rate forecast of short-term interest rates (usually less than one year, mostly three months). Since exchange rate expectation is equal to the sum of the future spot exchange rate and the risk premium and the risk premium is influenced by uncertainties such as inflation and growth, it is difficult for short-term data to reflect changes in long-term expectations (Colacito & Croce, 2013; Bansal & Shaliastovich, 2013), which could be a significant reason for the deviation of forward premiums. Therefore, many scholars have conducted empirical analyses using long-term exchange rate changes and long-term yield data (5 or 10 years) (Alexius, 2001; Chinn & Meredith, 2004; Chinn & Quayyum, 2012; Boudoukh *et al.*, 2016), and they have found that when using such data, UIRP is valid.

After considering factors such as risk premiums and expectations biases, some scholars have utilized new empirical research methods to conduct empirical analyses on the conditions for UIRP holding up in developed economies, which would confirm the long-term validity of UIRP. Lothian & Wu (2011) tested the time-varying characteristics of UIRP regression coefficients in the United Kingdom, France, and the United States over 200 years using methods such as subsample regression and rolling regression. They found that failure to quickly adjust expectations after institutional changes leads to the ineffectiveness of UIRP (learning process), but UIRP still holds in the long run. Lothian (2016) conducted empirical research on historical data from 17 developed countries over an average of nearly 160 years, further supporting the long-term validity of UIRP. Sarantis (2006) and Baillie & Chang (2011) utilized exponential and logarithmic smoothing transition models (ESTR/LSTR), respectively, to test the nonlinear effects of time-varying risk premiums and different market trading strategies on UIRP. Cho (2018) examined the impact of structural changes on interest rate parity using a multiple regime smoothing transition autoregressive model (Multi Regime STAR) with samples from six developed countries, including the United States, the United Kingdom, and Japan.

With the deepening globalization of finance and foreign exchange markets, many studies have devoted attention to emerging economies, revealing that such economies are more in line with UIRP during normal economic periods (Bansal & Dahlquist, 2000; Alper *et al*., 2009; Frankel & Poonawala, 2010; Miah & Altiti, 2020). The empirical research by Loring & Lucey (2013) of samples including the period of the global financial crisis (2004–2011) demonstrates that both advanced and emerging economies qualify for interest rate parity conditions. Frankel & Poonawala's (2010) empirical research indicates that the deviation of forward exchange rates is insignificant for emerging economies during normal periods (1996–2004). Based on empirical research on the exchange rate of 12 emerging economies and 15 developed countries against the US dollar from 2007 to 2016, Miah & Altiti (2020) found that the degree of deviation of forward exchange rates decreased significantly. In general, the emerging market economy is more in line with UIRP conditions during normal periods, while during crisis periods, risk premiums and rational expectation biases have a significant impact on the deviation of forward exchange rates of all countries. However, the level of uncertainty in emerging developing countries is relatively high, which contradicts the risk premium hypothesis. The reasons for this contradiction are similar to those of UIRP testing, which usually holds true in developed countries with high inflation. In many emerging market economies with unsound economic fundamentals, the market is often more accurate in predicting their long-term exchange rate trends than it is in other contexts, leading to more favorable UIRP testing effects.

2.2 *Violations of CIRP after the financial crisis*

CIRP has long been regarded as one of the very few international parity conditions that have been well verified by empirical research (other international parity conditions include the law of one price, purchasing power parity, and the international Fisher effect), and foreign exchange market participants mainly price exchange rates and interest rates under CIRP conditions (Dooley & Isard, 1980; Taylor, 1989). This is because the forward exchange ratc represents a locked-in exchange rate expectation or cost, and if the interest rate does not correspond with the forward exchange rate, there will be a certain risk-free arbitrage opportunity. Since the global financial crisis, CIRP, the "iron law" in international finance, has frequently been broken, mainly evidenced by the abnormal fluctuations of foreign exchange swap points (Borio *et al.*, 2016). Similar to the forward exchange rate, market participants can determine future exchange costs through foreign exchange swaps and obtain US dollar financing by exchanging foreign currency for dollars instead of borrowing dollars directly in the spot market. The difference between the cost of foreign exchange swap US dollar financing and spot US dollar financing is the foreign exchange swap point. According to CIRP, under frictionless and complete market conditions, the foreign exchange swap point should be close to zero. However, during the global financial crisis and the 2011 European debt crisis, the US dollar cost of foreign exchange swap financing for major currencies such as the euro and the yen has consistently been significantly higher than the cost of spot dollar financing. This indicates a large deviation from CIRP, especially since 2014, as both types of costs have exhibited continuous and systemic deviations (Avdjiev *et al.*, 2019).

The continuous deviation of foreign exchange swap points since the global financial crisis results from the combined effect of changes in global US dollar supply and demand. From the supply side, due to stricter financial regulations imposed after the crisis, banks, as traditional US dollar suppliers in the foreign exchange market, are subject to more stringent restrictions on leverage and liquidity ratios, resulting in a significant decline in their ability and willingness to participate in foreign exchange market arbitrage (Borio *et al.*, 2016; Sushko *et al.*, 2018; Du *et al.*, 2018). In addition, different types of banks have varying financing costs and balance sheet expansion capabilities, leading to market segmentation and ineffective arbitrage mechanisms, which impede the functioning of the law of one price (Rime *et al.*, 2017). From a demand perspective, the demand of various market entities to hedge the risk of the US dollar exchange rate, the shortage of US dollar liquidity, and the strengthening of the US dollar index are important reasons for the deviation from CIRP. Since the global financial crisis, the demand for US dollar financing for non-US banks, insurance, pensions, and other financial institutions and non-financial enterprises has increased significantly (Borio *et al.*, 2016; Sushko *et al.*, 2018). During the crisis, an increased demand for US dollar liquidity (US dollar safe asset) strengthened the US dollar index. This further elevated the "shadow price" of the US dollar leverage of banks, restrained the supply of US dollars by banks, and exacerbated the shortage in meeting the US dollar demand. As a result, there was a significant positive correlation between the US dollar index and the deviation from CIRP (Ivashina *et al.*, 2015; Avdjiev *et al.*, 2019). Since 2014, the monetary policies of major central banks, such as those in the US, Europe, and Japan, have diverged significantly, which is also an important reason for the deviation from CIRP (Iida *et al.*, 2016; Cerutti *et al.*, 2019).

Skinner & Mason (2011) found that similar to the UIRP puzzle, risk premium and market incompleteness are important reasons for the violation of CIRP in emerging market countries. Since the global financial crisis, the violation of CIRP is mainly due to the strong demand for exchange rate risk hedging in US dollar financing and the decline in market capacity, which distorts the market arbitrage mechanism to some extent, reduces the breadth and depth of the foreign exchange market, and weakens the effectiveness of hedging exchange rate risk. Lee (2003) discovered quite early on that insufficient liquidity in the foreign exchange market is an important reason why the KRW/US dollar CIRP condition does not hold. The analysis of HKD/US dollars by Fong *et al.* (2010) also indicates that market liquidity risk and credit risk are significant contributors to the breakdown of CIRP. Suh & Kim (2016) pointed out that CIRP should consider the actual market segmentation situation in emerging developing countries, which they supported with empirical analysis of the South Korean foreign exchange market.

2.3 *Relevant literature on the applicability of interest parity theory in China*

Due to the limited openness of China's capital account and the limited exchange rate flexibility and financial market depth, Chinese scholars have long argued that China's interest rate parity should consider the friction coefficient of transaction cost factors or institutional factors. Studies in this area mainly use short-term interest rate data from the money market. Many empirical studies have shown that the exchange rate between RMB and USD does not satisfy the interest rate parity condition (Cheung *et al.*, 2006; Wang, 2010, 2015).[3] Noted that exchange rate fluctuations cannot explain whether China's interest rate parity holds. Empirical analysis of RMB appreciation pressure and foreign exchange reserves derived from CIRP conditions shows that foreign exchange market intervention is an important factor. Additionally, the relatively limited depth of China's bond market also restricts price discovery ability, liquidity, and efficiency, which affects the establishment of the interest rate parity condition. First, the main participants in China's bond market are banks with a low-risk appetite and long-term asset allocation. Due to strict market access restrictions, the development of China's financial derivatives market is lagging behind that of other countries, and the asset-backed securities market still needs improvement. Second, the development of innovative instruments such as the buyout repo market, standard bond forwards, and credit default swaps is limited, resulting in low market activity and bond market liquidity.[4] Third, the

---

[3]Although there are some studies showing that CIRP still holds in China, most research does not support the establishment of China's UIRP and CIRP due to factors such as capital controls.

[4]In 2019, the turnover rate of spot bond trading in China's debt financing instruments was 1.9 times, and the turnover rate of spot bond trading in corporate bonds was less than 0.7 times. Compared with the treasury market and credit bonds of the US, which have a turnover rate of approximately 10 times and 2 times, respectively, the gap is obvious.

credit ratings of China's bond market are inflated and cannot reflect the real risk of bonds. In particular, under the rigid payment expectations of the past, the credit spread of credit bonds mainly reflected the term premium rather than the credit risk premium. However, there has been no research using China's bond market data to test the validity of interest rate parity.

The empirical analysis of the establishment conditions for interest rate parity in China provides support for the influence of factors such as the risk premium hypothesis, rational expectation deviation, and market incompleteness. Regarding the risk premium, Kim & Cho (2011) found that even after the market risks related to capital flows are considered, UIRP in China still holds. Using a nonlinear threshold unit root model, Chang & Su (2015) showed that risk factors such as capital flows, foreign exchange market efficiency, and the degree of currency integration have a significant impact on the validity of UIRP between RMB and the currencies of eight Asian countries. Although the test of demonstrated that the impact of the time-varying risk premium is insignificant, the low risk-adjusted foreign exchange arbitrage return is an important factor affecting the establishment of UIRP in China. Regarding rational expectation deviation, examined the influence of trader heterogeneity expectations and found significant heterogeneity characteristics in the exchange rate expectations of RMB. In terms of market incompleteness and transaction costs, introduced the transaction cost variable of capital flow based on the cost-plus method and used staged cointegration analysis to show that the uncovered interest arbitrage parity of RMB is still valid in the long run. Wang (2015) found that credit risk and lack of liquidity in the foreign exchange market caused by foreign exchange controls and market frictions are important reasons for the continuous deviation of RMB and US dollar CIRP. Compared the effects of risk premium and capital controls and found that the impact of transaction costs resulting from capital controls is significantly greater than that of risk premium, which is an important reason for the violation of CIRP theory in China. Xiao & Liu (2016) also argued that transaction costs significantly impact the validity of RMB UIRP. UIRP tends to hold in areas with lower transaction costs, and the central bank's intervention in the foreign exchange market and changes in cross-border arbitrage returns cause an even more severe deviation of UIRP.

3. Model and Data

3.1 *Econometric model setting*

Currently, tests of the UIRP puzzle are mainly divided into two categories: the indirect method and the direct method. The indirect method formula was proposed by Fama (1984):

$$s_{t+1} - s_t = \alpha + \beta(f_t - s_t) + \epsilon_t, \tag{1}$$

where s_t and f_t are the spot exchange rate and forward exchange rate in period t, respectively (direct quote). The advantage of this method is the availability of forward exchange rate data, but this formula implies the premise of establishing CIRP and is actually a joint test of UIRP and CIRP. Therefore, many studies use the direct method formula:

$$s_{t+1} - s_t = \alpha + \beta(i_t - \mathrm{i}_t^*) + \epsilon_t, \tag{2}$$

where i_t and i_t^* are the onshore interest rate and foreign interest rate in period t, respectively.

Using UIRP and CIRP, it is easy to derive Formula (1) and Formula (2). Whether the indirect or direct method formula is used, if the interest rate parity condition holds, then theoretically, $\alpha = 0$, $\beta = 1$. However, most empirical studies show that $\beta < 1$ and usually even $\beta < 0$, which is the so-called "forward premium puzzle".

According to UIRP, $(1 + i_t) = (1 + i_t^*)\frac{E_{[s]t+1}}{s_t}$, therefore, $i^* \approx i_t - (E_{[s]t+1} - s_t)$. Similarly, according to the CIRP, we can obtain $i^* \approx i_t - (f_t - s_t)$. Both the direct method and the indirect method for the empirical test of UIRP are derived from this condition. However, neither Formula (1) nor Formula (2) takes into account other factors that may affect interest rate parity or offshore bond yields. To this end, we adopt the following econometric model:

$$i^* = \alpha + \beta_1 i_t + \beta_2 \Delta s_{t+1} + \beta_x X_t + \epsilon_t, \tag{3}$$

where X_t are other control variables. Formula (3) is also the basic econometric model used in this chapter.

It can be seen that interest rate parity theory is the analytical benchmark for analyzing corporate onshore and offshore bond yields. Formula (3) is an empirical analysis based on UIRP, taking the corporate offshore bond yield as the dependent variable and the corporate onshore bond yield relationship and its influencing factors as independent variables. After the exchange rate cost (Δs_{t+1}) is controlled or the expected change in the exchange rate ($E\Delta s_{t+1}$) is considered, this formula is equivalent to testing the conditions of CIRP and UIRP. Theoretically, the corporate bond yield equals the sum of the risk-free interest rate and the credit premium. For issuers of the same type, the credit risk is the same, and the difference between the corporate onshore and offshore bond yields mainly reflects the difference between the onshore and foreign risk-free interest rates. After the exchange rate cost is considered, the onshore and offshore bond financing costs or the onshore and offshore bond investment income of the enterprise should be the same. According to Formula (1) or Formula (2), when the degree of the free flow of capital is higher, the degree of integration of financial markets among countries will be higher (i.e., lower differences in risk preferences, expected deviations, transaction costs, and asset heterogeneity), and the interest rate parity condition can then be established; furthermore, there should be $\beta_1 = 1$ at this time.

3.2 *Main indicators and data selection*

3.2.1 *Corporate onshore and offshore bond yields*

We primarily investigate the relationship between the yields of China's offshore-rated investment-grade US dollar bonds with high credit ratings and the yields of onshore bonds with high credit ratings. This is because there are significant differences between China's bond market and the bond markets of major developed economies in terms of market depth, investment policies, and credit ratings. Among them, the factors influencing the yields of corporate onshore and offshore bonds with higher credit risk are highly complex, the relationship between the two is uncertain, and their trends may even deviate, making them difficult to compare directly. Due to the stricter offshore credit ratings for enterprises, the credit spreads of investment-grade US dollar bonds are relatively small, and they are mainly held by risk-averse institutional investors who prioritize asset allocation, which is not much different from the onshore market structure.

Chinese enterprises have been conducting bond financing (mainly US dollar-denominated) in offshore markets since the early 21st century. Bank of America's Merrill Lynch introduced the Asian Dollar Investment-Grade Corporate China Issuers Index (ACCG) quite early, which tracks the performance of China's investment-grade US dollar-denominated bonds in the US and the Eurodollar market as a subindex of the institution's Asian Dollar Investment-Grade Corporate Bond Index. The qualified bonds in the sample have a minimum remaining maturity of one year, an issuance period of at least 18 months, and a minimum circulation size of USD 150 million and are fixed-rate bonds. The rating of sample bonds is determined based on comprehensive considerations of the three major international rating agencies. ACCG data can be traced back to April 30, 2008, with high market recognition.

We select the yield of this index as the indicator for China's investment-grade US dollar bonds. Since the average duration of the index is approximately 5 years, we select 5-year average ChinaBond valuation yields of onshore medium- and short-term notes with AAA+ and AAA ratings as the indicator for yields of onshore high-grade credit bonds against China's investment-grade US dollar bonds.

To ensure robustness, we also utilize the ChinaBond investment-grade US dollar bond index and its corresponding yield data since 2018 to empirically test the relationship between onshore and offshore bond yields and the effectiveness of interest rate parity (see Section 4.5 for details).

3.2.2 *Exchange rates and other control variables*

We use the 1-year US dollar/CNY exchange rate swap (swap1y) to indicate exchange rate costs. China has introduced primary derivative products such as forwards, foreign exchange swaps, and options, which can meet the basic hedging needs of market exchange rate hedging. As the RMB exchange rate adopts a direct quote, a positive and larger foreign exchange swap indicates a higher depreciation of the RMB exchange rate, and there should be a significant negative correlation between foreign exchange swaps and the yield of investment-grade offshore US dollar bonds in such cases.

Regarding discussions on CIRP violations after the global financial crisis and relevant research on the impact on offshore bond yields, we select the US dollar index and arbitrage factors as control variables. The US dollar index we use is the nominal US dollar index published by the Federal Reserve (January 2006 = 100). Existing research generally suggests that under normal circumstances, the yield of high-grade offshore US dollar bonds is positively correlated with the US dollar index, while the relationship between high-yield offshore US dollar bonds and the US dollar index appears uncertain. This is because high-grade offshore US dollar bonds provide investors with an approximately risk-free and high-yield US dollar alternative asset, and the appreciation of the US dollar will drive up the prices of high credit-rated corporate US dollar bonds (Gambacorta *et al.*, 2020). However, in a crisis, the function of the US dollar as a safe-haven currency may lead to an uncertain relationship (or even a significant positive correlation) between the yields of high credit-rated US dollar bonds and the US dollar index (as well as onshore bond yields). This is primarily due to global financial market panic, which results in a surge in the US dollar index and a shortage of the US dollar, leading to massive selloffs of various types of credit bonds (including investment-grade bonds and high-yield bonds issued by non-US entities) (Rose & Spiegel, 2012; Hordahl & Shim, 2020).

Drawing on the research of Bruno & Shin (2017) and Ding *et al.* (2019), we adopt the onshore and offshore money market spreads adjusted considering the implied volatility of foreign exchange options (that is, the difference between the overnight pledge repo rate and the federal funds rate divided by the implied volatility rate of overnight foreign exchange options) as the carry index. The carry trade closely associated with the onshore and offshore spreads is a significant factor affecting offshore bond yields and notably influences the long-term equilibrium relationship between interest rates and exchange rates in different countries. (Engle, 2014; Banerjee *et al.*, 2020). Under free capital flow, the carry index should exhibit a significant negative correlation with the yield of China's investment-grade corporate US dollar bonds. However, due to policy restrictions on the corporate issuance of US dollar bonds, China's capital account has not been completely opened, and the carry index variable may not be significant.

3.3 *Preliminary data analysis*

According to Formula (3), and referring to the research of Huang (2019), we first examine the relationship between corporate onshore and offshore bond yields based on whether we consider the factor of exchange rate cost. This allows us to make a preliminary assessment of the degree of openness of China's bond market. As shown in Figure 1, the yields of onshore high-grade credit bonds are generally higher than those of China's investment-grade corporate US dollar bonds, which is consistent with the fact that the spread between China and the US is typically primarily positive. During the sample period, the average spread between IVCN

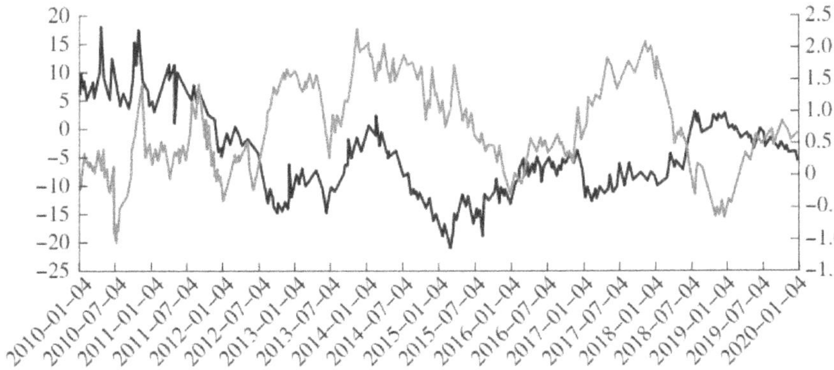

Figure 1. The spread between onshore and offshore corporate bonds (%).

and IVUSD was 0.75%. Before and after the implementation of the Bond Connect program on July 3, 2017, the average spreads were 0.78% and 0.66%, respectively. Although the average spread converged by only 11 basis points after the program's implementation, it is difficult to conclude that onshore and offshore bond yields are converging. However, after the exchange rate costs of USD/CNY are considered, the average spread becomes negative. After the adjustment of one-year foreign exchange swaps, the average yield of onshore bonds is lower than that of offshore bonds, with an average yield spread of −4.3% during the sample period. Of course, most negative spreads are related mainly to the cost of foreign exchange swaps. If we choose shorter-term forward exchange swaps for adjustment (such as one-week, one-month, or three-month exchange rate swaps), the average spread tends to be close to zero or positive. These findings are similar to those presented by Huang (2019). Additionally, the average spreads before and after the implementation of the Bond Connect program were −4.6% and −3.6%, respectively, with a difference of 100 basis points. This significant narrowing of the onshore and offshore bond spreads indicates a substantial increase in the degree of integration between China's bond market and the international market.

The Bond Connect program has also had a significant impact on the yield spreads (Figure 2), particularly right after its implementation,

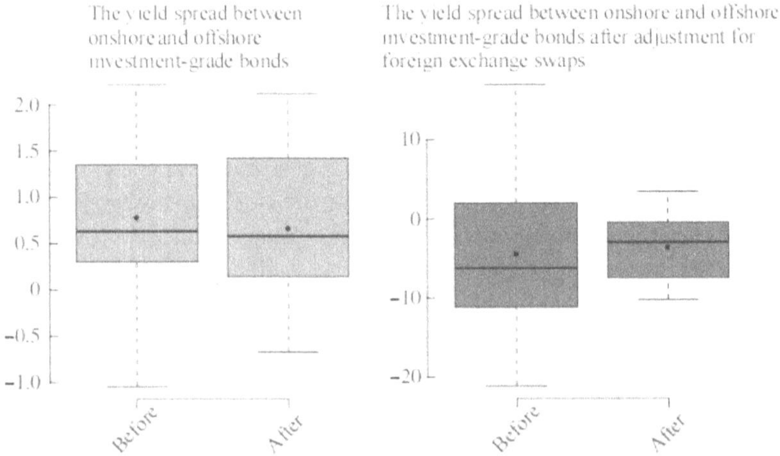

Figure 2. Box plots of the average spread between onshore and offshore bonds before and after the bond connect commenced operations (after adjustment for foreign exchange swaps).

when the convergence of onshore and offshore bond yields adjusted by foreign exchange swaps is more significant. The dispersion of onshore and offshore bond spreads after the implementation of the program is significantly higher than before (with standard deviations of 0.66 and 0.76, respectively, before and after July 1, 2017), suggesting that the onshore and offshore bond yields did not converge. However, after exchange rate costs are taken into account, the corporate onshore and offshore bond yields converge, as reflected in the decreased dispersion of corporate onshore and foreign bond spreads after the implementation of the Bond Connect program (with standard deviations of 8.10 and 3.77, respectively, before and after July 1, 2017). Additionally, although there is a significant difference in the mean of the onshore and offshore bond spreads regardless of whether there have been adjustments using foreign exchange swaps, it is indicated by the mean equivalence t-test that the p-value of the mean equivalence t-test of unadjusted onshore and offshore bond spreads is 0.013, which is significant at the 5% level. Moreover, the p-value of the mean equivalence t-test of onshore and offshore bond spreads adjusted by foreign exchange swaps is even more significant at the 1% level, indicating that considering the cost of foreign exchange fluctuations helps in comparing the corporate onshore and offshore bond yields.

4. Empirical Analysis

4.1 *Results with full sample*

Based on the analysis of influencing factors of corporate offshore bond yield, this section takes China's investment-grade corporate US dollar bond yield as the dependent variable and the onshore high-grade credit bond yield as the independent variable to conduct regressions and test the relationship between corporate onshore and offshore bond yields while considering the exchange rate cost and controlling variables such as the US dollar index and arbitrage opportunity. As the global financial crisis and the impact of COVID-19 may have significantly affected corporate onshore and offshore bond yields, this section analyzes daily data from January 4, 2010, to January 23, 2020. However, data for the carry index are only available from January 4, 2016 onwards. The significance test (t-test) adopts the heteroscedasticity and autocorrelation consistent standard error proposed by Newey–West (1987).

Table 1 presents the results of a simple regression analysis for China's investment-grade corporate US dollar bond yields and onshore high-grade credit bond yields. The most notable point of interest is that the Wald coefficient test shows that all equations reject the null hypothesis of the IVCN coefficient being equal to 1 at the 1% significance level, indicating that although there is a significant positive correlation between corporate onshore and offshore bond yields in the overall sample regression, their changes are not synchronized. The degree of integration between China's bond market and foreign bond markets remains relatively limited, and interest rate parity is not entirely established. This conclusion is consistent with the majority of previous empirical studies on interest rate parity in China.

Table 1 also reveals the following aspects: First, corporate onshore bond yields and foreign bond yields consistently exhibit a positive correlation at the 1% level of significance, indicating that China's bond market and the international bond market have achieved an effective connection, while the IVCN coefficients are all less than 1, suggesting that onshore bond yields are significantly higher than foreign bond yields, which aligns with the fact that the onshore and offshore interest spreads are typically mostly positive. Second, the exchange rate swaps are consistently negatively correlated with IVUSD at the 1% level of significance, which is in line with theoretical analysis. When the exchange rate cost is considered,

Table 1. Yields of China's investment-grade corporate US dollar bonds and onshore high-grade credit bonds (with IVUSD as the dependent variable).

Independent Variable \ Sample Period	2010-01-04–2020-01-23			2016-01-04–2020-01-23	
Constant	2.1138** (0.1728)	2.3969** (0.1399)	3.4074** (0.4278)	2.0682** (0.1992)	1.8659* (1.0673)
IVCN	0.3631*** (0.0386)	0.3545** (0.0293)	0.2903*** (0.0371)	0.4752*** (0.0513)	0.4755** (0.0479)
Swap1y	—	−0.0481*** (0.0034)	−0.0451*** (0.0036)	−0.0849** (0.0126)	−0.0839*** (0.0135)
USDindex	—	—	−0.0075** (0.0030)	—	0.0018 (0.0094)
Carryindex	—	—	—	−0.1894 (0.1588)	−0.2065 (0.1642)
R^2	0.1812	0.5663	0.5758	0.6524	0.6459
S.E.	0.5339	0.3887	0.3845	0.3208	0.3204
F	539.1***	1584.3***	1093.8***	613.2***	460.7***
C (2) = 1 Wald Chi-Square Statistics	272.9***	485.3***	366.5***	104.5***	119.7***

Notes: The numbers in brackets are the Newey–West robust standard deviations, and the significance levels are indicated with *** for 1%, ** for 5%, and * for 10%, the same as the following.

the US dollar index is negatively correlated with IVUSD at the 5% level of significance, while the carry index does not exhibit significant regression coefficients with IVUSD. This indicates that from the perspective of onshore and offshore yields, there is limited arbitrage space for corporate offshore bond financing, which is also related to the incomplete openness of capital accounts and relatively low carry returns in China. Third, if the US dollar index and the carry index are simultaneously controlled, these two variables both become insignificant, and the sign of the US dollar index changes, indicating the presence of collinearity. Fourth, after the exchange rate swap factor is considered, the adjusted R-squared of the regression equation largely increases from less than 0.2–0.57, while further control of the US dollar index and the carry index does not result in a pronounced increase in the adjusted R-squared, suggesting that the exchange rate cost is a more crucial factor than the onshore and offshore bond yield. Since the carry index variable is insignificant, it is not included in the subsequent econometric analysis.

4.2 *Bond connect: OLS and MGARCH-BEKK model*

In this section, we first conduct an OLS regression analysis on the relationship between onshore and offshore bond yields before and after the formal operation of the Bond Connect program, with July 3, 2017, serving as the demarcation point. Table 2 shows that the coefficients of each variable in the regression results are all satisfactory. The Wald coefficient test indicates that although the regression coefficients of onshore bond yields were positive before Bond Connect launched, they are significantly smaller than 1, and all significantly reject the null hypothesis of being equal to 1. After the implementation of the Bond Connect program, if other variables are not taken into account, the regression coefficient of onshore bond yields still rejects the null hypothesis of equality to 1 at the

Table 2. Yields of China's onshore and offshore corporate bonds before and after the implementation of the bond connect program (with IVUSD as the dependent variable).

Independent Variable \ Sample Period	2010-01-04–2017-06-30			2017-07-03–2020-01-23		
Constant	1.8230***	2.3309***	4.5639***	2.4616***	0.1330	3.9999*
	(0.1689)	(0.1503)	(0.4156)	(0.4398)	(0.2392)	(2.2973)
IVCN	0.4274***	0.3660***	0.2349***	0.3424***	0.9720***	0.8503***
	(0.0378)	(0.0308)	(0.0342)	(0.1006)	(0.0610)	(0.0989)
Swap1y	—	−0.0427***	−0.0341***	—	−0.1576***	−0.1617***
		(0.0033)	(0.0037)		(0.0073)	(0.0071)
USDindex	—	—	−0.0170***	—	—	−0.0293*
			(0.0031)			(0.0179)
R^2	0.2688	0.6180	0.6469	0.1029	0.7881	0.7934
S.E.	0.5158	0.3729	0.3586	0.4933	0.2521	0.2492
F	666.4***	1459.9***	1101.6***	57.00***	1151.2***	780.8***
C (2) = 1 Wald Chi-Square Statistics	229.8***	422.8***	501.8***	45.17***	0.2109	2.2925

1% significance level. However, once the exchange rate cost is taken into account, regardless of whether the US dollar index is controlled or not, the IVCN coefficient fails to reject the null hypothesis of being equal to 1, which is the null hypothesis of the establishment of interest rate parity. It can be seen that interest rate parity became applicable in China after the Bond Connect program commenced, and corporate onshore and offshore bond yields showed a synchronous change trend. It also indicates a qualitative leap in the integration between China's bond market and the international financial market.

Theoretically, the higher the degree of openness of a country's bond market is, the stronger its correlation with the international bond market, and the more apparent the phenomenon of volatility spillover effects between onshore and offshore markets; i.e., the volatility of the market itself spreads to the outside. To further test the role of the Bond Connect program on the correlation between onshore and offshore bond markets and the applicability of interest rate parity, we adopt Engle & Kroner's (1995) multivariate asymmetric MGARCH-BEKK model to characterize the volatility and cross-impact between the onshore and offshore bond markets to illustrate the changes in the interaction and guidance relationship between the two markets. Here, we take the yield of China's investment-grade corporate US dollar bonds and the yield of corresponding onshore high-grade credit bonds as the main variables for analysis, with a lag order of 3. The specific results are as follows:

It can be seen from Table 3 that before the implementation of the Bond Connect program, there was mutual influence between onshore and

Table 3. Estimation results of MGARCH-BEKK before and after the implementation of the bond connect program.

Sample Period	**2010-01-04–2017-06-30**		**2017-07-03–2020-01-23**	
Independent Variable	**Mean Equation**			
	IVUSD	***IVCN***	***IVUSD***	***IVCN***
Constant	0.0105	0.02575	−0.1254***	0.0353***
	(0.0291)	(0.0160)	(0.0011)	(0.0027)
$IVUSD_{t-1}$	0.9999***	0.02462	0.9673***	0.0448***
	(0.0149)	(0.0113)	(0.0021)	(0.0014)
$IVUSD_{t-3}$	0.0168***	−0.0210***	−0.0599***	−0.0397***
	(0.0058)	(0.0025)	(0.0007)	(0.0005)

(*Continued*)

Table 3. (*Continued*)

Sample Period	2010-01-04–2017-06-30		2017-07-03–2020-01-23	
Independent Variable	**Mean Equation**			
	IVUSD	***IVCN***	***IVUSD***	***IVCN***
$IVUSD_{t-3}$	−0.0242	−0.0027	0.0914***	−0.0027***
	(0.0194)	(0.0100)	(0.0006)	(0.0001)
$IVCN_{t-1}$	0.0293***	1.4269***	−0.0815***	1.3426***
	(0.0087)	(0.0115)	(0.0009)	(0.0003)
$IVCN_{t-2}$	−0.0487***	−0.3809***	0.1223***	−0.2885***
	(0.0006)	(0.0145)	(0.0009)	(0.0004)
$IVCN_{t-3}$	0.0223*	−0.0484***	−0.0210***	−0.0611***
	(0.0090)		(0.0010)	(0.0004)
Swap1y	−0.000003	0.0000017	−0.000009	0.00001***
	(0.000003)	(0.0000017)	(0.000004)	(0.000002)
USDindex	0.00004	−0.000197	0.0004***	−0.0002***
	(0.0001)	(0.000088)	(0.00001)	(0.000003)
Independent Variable	**Conditional Variance Equation**			
α_{11}	0.1728***		0.4584***	
	(0.0421)		(0.0962)	
α_{12}	0.0373		−0.0123	
	(0.0324)		(0.0375)	
α_{21}	0.0011		0.0241	
	(0.0290)		(0.0816)	
α_{22}	0.3618***		0.4080***	
	(0.0466)		(0.0762)	
Independent Variable	**Conditional Variance Equation**			
β_{11}	0.9861***		0.8494***	
	(0.0050)		(0.0543)	
β_{12}	−0.0041		−0.0002	
	(0.0053)		(0.0165)	
β_{21}	−0.0032		−0.0272	
	(0.0139)		(0.0434)	
β_{22}	0.9117***		0.8393***	
	(0.0266)		(0.02964)	

Note: α_{12} refers to the ARCH fluctuation effect of offshore bond yields on onshore bond yields, α_{21} is its inverse interpretation, β_{12} is the GARCH fluctuation effect of offshore bonds on onshore bond yields, and β_{21} is its inverse interpretation.

offshore bond yields, and neither exchange rate swaps nor the US dollar index has a significant relationship with onshore and offshore bond yield influences, indicating that onshore and offshore bond yields have little connection with exchange rates and US dollar price fluctuations. However, after the program is implemented, both onshore bond yields and exchange rate swaps, as well as the US dollar index, become significant at the 1% level, and offshore bond yields and the US dollar index also become significant at the 1% level. These changes indicate an apparent improvement in the linkage between China's onshore and offshore bond markets.

The joint test results from Table 4 reveal a bidirectional mean effect between onshore and offshore bond yields before the program begins. After the Bond Connect program commences, this bidirectional mean spillover effect continues, indicating a close relationship and mutual influence between onshore and offshore bond yields. However, the joint test results suggest no volatility spillover effect between the offshore and

Table 4. Results of the joint test.

Sample Period	**2010-01-04–2017-6-30**	**2017-07-03–2020-1-23**
H_0	**Results of Joint Test of Mean Equation**	
There is no mean spillover effect of onshore bond yields to offshore bond yields	100395.6***	781937.6***
There is no mean spillover effect of offshore bond yields to onshore bond yields	80.3***	34719.3***
H_0	**Results of Joint Test of Conditional Variance Equation**	
There is no mean spillover effect of onshore bond yields to offshore bond yields	1.7178	0.5676
H_0	**Results of Joint Test of Conditional Variance Equation**	
There is no mean spillover effect of offshore bond yields to onshore bond yields	0.1382	0.4014

Notes: The results in the table are all Wald chi-square statistics.

onshore markets. The volatility of the two markets during different periods remains relatively independent, meaning that the substantial volatility in one market does not lead to significant fluctuations in the other market. The spillover effect of volatility between the two markets is not evident. From the perspective of market risk, this means that the risks in offshore and onshore markets are relatively isolated, and the transmission of market risk is insignificant. To a certain extent, this shows that although the linkage between China's bond market and the international market has significantly improved since the Bond Connect program began, this link remains relatively lower than that of major developed countries and the international market since the capital account has not yet been fully liberalized,[5] which indicates that there will be higher requirements for China's financial opening in the future.

4.3 *Bond Connect and the reform of the exchange rate formation mechanism*

In Tables 1–4, it can be seen that since the operation of the Bond Connect program commenced, the yields of corporate onshore and offshore bonds with high-grade credit ratings have converged, and interest rate parity applies to China. Introducing dummy variables, we conduct a robustness test on the impact of the program on the degree of correlation between onshore and offshore markets and interest rate parity. Due to the preparation time needed for foreign institutions to enter China's bond market through filing and account opening procedures after the launch of the Bond Connect program, the scale of bonds held by foreign institutions through that program in the first three months of its opening is over RMB 70 billion, accounting for less than 10% of the total holdings by offshore institutions at that time,[6] and there is a certain time lag in the effect of the

[5]For example, according to data from Bloomberg, from July 2011 to June 2020, the correlation coefficients between China's 10-year treasury bond yield and the treasury bonds with the same maturity of the United States, the United Kingdom, Japan, and euro area countries were 0.32, 0.24, 0.20, and 0.23, respectively; these figures were significantly lower than those of major developed countries and many emerging market countries.

[6]Before the operation of the Bond Connect program, foreign institutions mainly entered the market directly through means such as offshore central banks, RMB clearing banks in Hong Kong and Macau, and offshore participating banks, as well as participating in China's bond market through channels, such as QFII and RQFII.

policy. Therefore, the dummy variable for Bond Connect implementation (Dum1) is set to 0 before August 31, 2017, and 1 after that.

The exchange rate cost is crucial in comparing the relationship between corporate onshore and offshore bond yields and interest rate parity, which allows us to consider the impact of the reform of the market-oriented exchange rate formation mechanism. Since the implementation of managed free floating in July 2005, China has steadily promoted the reform of market-oriented exchange rate formation mechanisms. On August 11, 2015, the quotation mechanism of the central parity rate of RMB was adjusted, requiring market makers to issue quotations with reference to the closing exchange rate of the interbank foreign exchange market on the previous day to better reflect changes in market supply and demand. However, under the anticipation of RMB depreciation at that time, China's foreign exchange market and capital flows experienced sharp fluctuations. To this end, China started publishing the RMB exchange rate index in December 2015, emphasizing the need to increase the reference to a currency basket, and in early 2016, a preliminary mechanism of "closing rate + exchange rate changes of a currency basket" for the central parity rate was established, somewhat strengthening policy guidance for the formation of the central parity rate. In May 2017, a countercyclical adjustment factor was introduced to increase the weight of policy adjustments. As cross-border capital flows and the supply and demand of the foreign exchange market in China tended to approach equilibrium, from early January to August 23, 2018, the countercyclical adjustment factor briefly returned to a neutral position to reduce policy interventions. Due to the deterioration of the external economic environment, since 2019, China has intensified its efforts to reform the exchange rate formation mechanism. The spot exchange rate and the central parity rate of USD/RMB both "broke 7" on August 5 and August 8, 2019, respectively, further weakening specific exchange rate targets, and exchange rate formation then became more responsive to market supply and demand. For this reason, a dummy variable (Dum2) for exchange rate reforms is set to 1 during periods of higher marketization in the exchange rate formation mechanism (from August 11 to December 31, 2015; from January 2 to August 23, 2018; and after August 5, 2019) and 0 for other dates. For robustness considerations, we set an exchange rate dummy variable (Dum3) to 0 before August 5, 2019, and 1 afterward.

When introducing dummy variables into the regression, we follow Wooldridge's (2012) method and multiply the dummy variables by IVCN

Table 5. Bond connect, the market-oriented reform of the exchange rate, and yields of China's onshore and offshore corporate bonds (with IVUSD as the dependent variable).

Independent Variable \ Sample Period	2010-01-04–2020-01-23				
Constant	4.2340*** (0.4288)	3.7307*** (0.4522)	3.2118*** (0.4267)	3.7621*** (0.4378)	4.3694*** (0.4114)
IVCN	0.2409*** (0.0350)	0.2745*** (0.0364)	0.2811*** (0.0379)	0.2455*** (0.0360)	0.2074*** (0.0339)
Swaply	−0.0417*** (0.0038)	−0.0448*** (0.0037)	−0.0466*** (0.0036)	−0.0468*** (0.0037)	−0.0441*** (0.0039)
USDindex	−0.0136*** (0.0030)	−0.0099*** (0.0033)	−0.0046 (0.0030)	−0.0088 ***(0.0032)	−0.0134 ***(0.0030)
IVCN*Dum1	0.0385*** (0.0146)	—	—	—	0.0336** (0.0172)
IVCN*Dum2	—	0.0364*** (0.0140)	—	0.0719*** (0.0117)	0.0598*** (0.0152)
IVCN*Dum3	—	—	−0.1176*** (0.0128)	−0.1711*** (0.0125)	−0.1750*** (0.0132)
R^2	0.5829	0.5831	0.5971	0.6217	0.6261
S.E.	0.3813	0.3812	0.3746	0.3631	0.361
F	844.4***	845.2***	895.2***	793.6***	673.8***
C (2) = 1 Wald Chi-Square Statistics	470.1***	369.6***	361.9***	437.2***	545.1***

to examine the specific effects of reforms on the coefficient of the variables. As shown in Table 5, the regression results of all equations are relatively satisfactory. Only the US dollar index of the equation with Dum3 controlled is insignificant (with a *p*-value of 0.12), while all other variables are significant at the 5% level. Furthermore, the coefficient for Dum1 is significantly positive, indicating that the operation of the Bond Connect program improved the relationship between onshore and offshore bond yields, thus creating conditions for interest rate parity. The coefficient for Dum2 is also significantly positive, suggesting that market-oriented exchange rate reform facilitates the convergence of onshore and offshore bond yields and the integration of markets, thereby enhancing the applicability of interest rate parity in China. However, the coefficient for

Dum3 is significantly negative, likely related to the expectations of RMB depreciation caused by the market's excessive pessimism about the deteriorating foreign exchange environment. Even after we control for Dum2 and Dum3, the variables remain significant, indicating a clear impact of the market-oriented reform of the exchange rate. Moreover, when we simultaneously control for the dummy variables of Bond Connect implementation and exchange rate reform, the regression results remain highly satisfactory, demonstrating the robustness of the econometric tests.

4.4 *The impact of COVID-19*

After the outbreak of the COVID-19 pandemic in late January 2020, the market risk appetite significantly decreased, leading to noticeable adjustments in China's US dollar bond market. In particular, the COVID-19 pandemic intensified in foreign regions at the end of February and beginning of March 2020, causing market panic spread and a "dollar shortage". Global risk assets were largely sold off, and China's US dollar bonds experienced a sharp decline, especially in the high-yield segment.[7] During the two weeks from March 9 to March 22, 2020, the overall price of China's US dollar bonds dropped by 7.1%, of which investment-grade bonds fell by 5% and high-yield bonds by 11.7%. In the first quarter of 2020, the overall return of China's US dollar bonds was −2.00%, of which the investment-grade bond was flat and slightly positive (0.62%), the high-yield bond was −7.19%, and China's high-yield real estate US dollar bond was −8.26%. Due to the soaring issuance costs of US dollar bonds, most investors stayed on the sidelines, and the issuance volume of China's US dollar bonds decreased to USD 15.26 billion and USD 15.37 billion in February and March 2020, respectively. Especially since mid-March 2020, due to the sharp correction in the secondary market, the primary market issuance of China's US dollar bonds almost reached a standstill. However, buoyed by optimistic factors such as the conclusion of the US–China trade agreement, the issuance volume of China's US dollar bonds in January was relatively high (USD 25.96 billion), and the overall issuance scale of China's US dollar bonds in the first quarter of 2020 remained substantial, reaching USD 56.59 billion, thus representing a quarter-on-quarter and

[7]On the situation of China's USD bond market in this sector since the COVID-19 pandemic began, refer to *Research Report on China's Dollar Bonds (Q1 and Q2 2020), China's Dollar Bonds under the Shortage of USD Liquidity. (2020). China Forex, 8 (in China's).*

year-on-year growth of 23.7% and 11.6%, respectively. With the Federal Reserve System actively rescuing the market and releasing abundant US dollar liquidity by leading other central banks to carry out currency swaps, the international market's risk aversion has gradually eased since the second quarter of 2020. The US dollar index gradually declined in early June 2020 after hovering at a high level. The credit spreads of global investment-grade and high-yield bonds significantly narrowed, and investors' risk appetite slowly recovered, which further drove the recovery of China's US dollar bond market. In the second quarter of 2020, the primary market issuance of China's US dollar bonds amounted to only $39.41 billion, representing a decrease of 30.4% quarter-on-quarter and 42.0% year-on-year; this figure comprised USD 5.06 billion in April, USD 7.26 billion in May, and USD 27.09 billion June. The total return of China's US dollar bonds in the secondary market also turned from negative to positive (4.95%), with investment-grade bonds reporting a return of 2.95% and high-yield bonds sharply rebounding to 9.30%. Therefore, the relationship between corporate offshore bond yields and the US dollar index under the impact of COVID-19 remains uncertain and may exhibit a significant positive correlation.

In addition to the changes in the international market environment, since the end of January 2020, China has implemented large-scale pandemic response policies, leading to reasonable and ample liquidity in the onshore financial market and overall loose funds and a significant decline in bond market yields. Coupled with the effective control of the pandemic in China and other factors, the trend of China's corporate onshore and offshore bond yields deviated to a certain extent during the initial two months of the global outbreak of COVID-19. It was not until mid- to late May 2020 that China's monetary policy began to be flexible and more moderate, the risk aversion of international financial markets was effectively eased, and the relationship between corporate onshore and offshore bond yields gradually returned to normal. To this end, we introduce a dummy variable (Dum4) for regression samples from the period of the COVID-19 pandemic to examine the specific impact of the pandemic, with a value of 1 starting from February 3, 2020, and 0 otherwise, and the sample period is extended to July 10, 2020. For robustness, we controlled for Dum1 and Dum2 separately to observe the effects of Bond Connect implementation and the market-oriented exchange rate reform.

Table 6 presents the regression results for samples from the COVID-19 pandemic period starting in February 2020. If we only consider the exchange rate cost, onshore bond yields are not significant. The

Table 6. The impact of the COVID-19 pandemic on the yields of China's onshore and offshore corporate bonds (with IVUSD as the dependent variable).

Sample Period / Independent Variable	2017-07-03–2020-07-10						2010-01-04–2020-07-10			
Constant	3.2802***	−4.6002***	0.4175*	0.3756	−0.4351	−0.6345	3.4163***	3.3762***	4.1408***	4.1224***
	(0.3805)	(1.1199)	(0.2317)	(0.2434)	(2.1312)	(1.9660)	(0.1473)	(0.4260)	(0.4283)	(−0.1905)
IVCN	0.0062	0.3692***	0.8994***	0.8977***	0.9284***	0.9302***	0.3119***	0.2902***	0.2443***	0.2478***
	(0.1502)	(0.0907)	(0.0587)	(0.0611)	(0.0911)	(0.0841)	(0.0140)	(0.0369)	(0.0350)	(0.0158)
Swap1y	−0.0743***	−0.0761***	−0.1499***	−0.1543***	−0.1495***	−0.1535***	−0.0451***	−0.0454***	−0.0424***	−0.0431***
	(0.0159)	(0.0074)	(0.0068)	(0.0077)	(0.0074)	(0.0082)	(0.0011)	(0.0036)	(0.0037)	(0.0012)
USDindex	—	0.0056***	—	—	0.0064	0.0076	−0.0084***	−0.0069***	−0.0128***	−0.0128***
		(0.0079)			(0.0159)	(0.0149)	(0.0010)	(0.0010)	(0.0013)	(0.0014)
IVCN*Dum4	—	—	0.1377***	0.1258***	0.1328***	0.1187***	—	0.1178***	−0.1278***	−0.1390***
			(0.0303)	(0.0325)	(0.0363)	(0.0392)		(0.0223)	(0.0241)	(0.0128)
IVCN*Dum1	—	—	—	—	—	—	—	—	0.0357***	0.0242***
									(0.0059)	(0.0064)
IVCN*Dum2	—	—	—	0.0353***	—	0.0360***	—	—	—	0.0260***
				(0.0114)		(0.0115)				(0.0060)
R^2	0.6036	0.869	0.8204	0.8338	0.8205	0.8346	0.5996	0.6132	0.6188	0.6214
S.E.	0.1637	0.0954	0.2553	0.2457	0.2554	0.2453	0.3855	0.379	0.3763	0.3749
F	79.95***	223.2***	1105.3***	909.5***	815.9***	719.3***	1259.6***	999.7***	818.6***	689.0***
C (2) = 1 Wald Chi-Square Statistics	43.80***	48.35***	2.9403*	2.8027*	0.6185	0.6894	2413.1***	370.5***	465.1***	2280.5***

exchange rate cost is a more important factor in dominating China's US dollar bond yields during the COVID-19 pandemic. All variables pass the significance test when further controlling for the US dollar index, but the US dollar index shows a significant positive correlation. Additionally, the regression analysis of the COVID-19 pandemic samples indicates that the US dollar index significantly enhances the overall degree of interpretation of the regression equation (with R^2 increasing from 0.6036 to 0.8690). This adequately demonstrates that during the COVID-19 pandemic, China's US dollar bonds have been heavily sold off due to a decrease in investors' risk appetite, and the rapid strengthening of the US dollar significantly has affected the yields of China's US dollar bonds.

By introducing dummy variable regression, we find that since the Bond Connect program began, the relationship between offshore bond yields and variables such as onshore corporate bond yields and exchange rate swaps has been still relatively stable, and both are significant at the 1% level. However, due to the impact of the COVID-19 pandemic and the rapid strengthening of the US dollar index, the US dollar index variable is not significant. Controlling for the dummy variable of the pandemic leads to a noticeable change in the sign, indicating the potential presence of collinearity issues. After the pandemic dummy variable is controlled, the sign changes notably, indicating the possible presence of collinearity problems.

To our delight, the regression results covering samples during the COVID-19 pandemic period indicate that considering only the exchange rate cost will cause the rejection of the null hypothesis of the IVCN coefficient being equal to 1 at the 1% significance level, while the introduction of the pandemic dummy variable will cause the rejection of the null hypothesis that the IVCN coefficient is equal to 1 only at the 10% significance level. If the US dollar index is further controlled for, although there is a collinearity issue, the null hypothesis of the IVCN coefficient being equal to 1 cannot be rejected. The above results indicate that the convergence trend of corporate onshore and offshore bond yields since the Bond Connect program was launched has not been impacted by the pandemic, and the interest rate parity condition is still valid. Additionally, if the sample is expanded to include the period before the Bond Connect program began, the regression results of all variables, including the US dollar index, are relatively satisfactory. Moreover, regardless of whether it is the regression for overall samples or samples since Bond Connect commenced, the dummy variable of market-oriented exchange rate reform

(Dum2) is significant. Thus, the econometric analysis results of the relationships among the variables in this chapter are robust and reliable.

4.5 *Robustness test with China's investment-grade offshore US dollar bonds*

In May 2019, the ChinaBond Pricing Center released China's Investment-Grade Offshore US dollar Bond Index, which covers bonds denominated in US dollars and issued in offshore financial markets by China's onshore institutions (including government agencies, financial institutions, and other onshore enterprises and foreign-invested enterprises) and offshore enterprises or branches controlled by China's onshore natural persons or institutions. The index takes December 31, 2017, as the base date and 100 as the base point value, with the capability of tracking data back to January 2, 2018. The ChinaBond Pricing Center provides an index of China's investment-grade offshore US dollar bonds that includes bonds with all remaining maturities and issuances, as well as price indices for various types of bonds issued by the corresponding entities in the onshore bond market, enabling us to better compare the relationship between onshore and offshore bond indices of similar issuers. Similar to China's Investment-Grade Corporate US Dollar Bond Index from the Bank of America's Merrill Lynch, where the average duration of sample bonds is approximately 5 years, the average maturity of sample bonds in the index from ChinaBond is 4.8 years.

We separately test the onshore and offshore full price index and flat price index from the ChinaBond Pricing Center (the former includes undistributed interest, i.e., full price = flat price accrued interest). Since the independent variable is the bond price index, the theoretical relationship between the US dollar bond index and variables such as foreign exchange swaps and the US dollar index is the opposite of that of the yield. Considering the relatively short sample period, we only control for Dum3 as a control variable for the reform of exchange rate marketization, and Dum4 is introduced to examine the specific impact of the COVID-19 pandemic.

From Table 7, it can be observed that except for the corporate onshore bond yields in the regression of samples from the COVID-19 pandemic period and the US dollar index in the full price index equation, while controlling for the exchange rate reform dummy variable, the regression results of other variables are relatively satisfactory and are all

Table 7. Relationship between China's investment-grade offshore US dollar bond index and the onshore bond index of corresponding entities.

Independent Variable \ Dependent Variable	Full Price Index	Full Price Index	Full Price Index	Full Price Index	Full Price Index	Flat Price Index	Flat Price Index	Flat Price Index	Flat Price Index	Flat Price Index
Sample Period	2018-01-02–2020-01-23	2018-01-02–2020-01-23	2018-01-02–2020-01-23	2018-01-02–2020-06-01	2020-02-03–2020-06-01	2018-01-02–2020-01-23	2018-01-02–2020-01-23	2018-01-02–2020-01-23	2018-01-02–2020-06-01	2020-02-03–2020-06-01
Constant	−16.64***	−16.232***	2.1548	7.0740	60.04**	−41.00***	−32.84***	−10.62	−1.7400	68.92**
	(6.0540)	(5.752)	(−10.306)	(9.4958)	(19.28)	(8.0736)	(8.1782)	(−13.164)	(11.922)	(16.83)
Corresponding Offshore Bond Yield	1.1093***	0.9435***	0.8385***	0.8160***	0.2994	1.3486***	1.0329***	0.9047***	0.8682***	0.1911
	(0.0577)	(0.0953)	(0.1069)	(0.1020)	(0.2098)	(0.0775)	(0.1207)	(0.1321)	(0.1247)	(0.1828)
Swap1y	0.3731***	0.4011***	0.3258***	0.3025***	0.1619*	0.4057***	0.4354***	0.3506***	0.3230***	0.1818**
	(0.0275)	(0.0293)	(0.0447)	(0.0371)	(0.0921)	(0.0293)	(0.0286)	(0.0484)	(0.0390)	(0.0834)
USDindex	—	0.1471**	0.0816	0.30592	0.0931*	—	0.2139***	0.1354**	0.0910**	0.1134***
		(0.0579)	(0.0587)	(0.0406)	(0.0491)		(0.546)	(0.0602)	(0.0412)	(0.0413)
Corresponding Offshore Bond Yield*Dum3	—	—	0.0081**	0.0097***	—	—	—	0.0087**	0.0112***	—
			(0.0034)	(0.0031)				(0.0035)	(0.0030)	
Corresponding Offshore Bond Yield*Dum4	—	—	—	−0.0068**	—	—	—	—	−0.0086***	—
				(0.0030)					(0.0032)	
R^2	0.8203	0.8297	0.8409	0.9046	0.3797	0.7733	0.7984	0.813	0.8868	0.4391
S.E.	0.8222	0.7971	0.7713	0.7616	0.6112	0.8738	0.8209	0.7914	0.7812	0.5494
F	1141.6***	795.8***	646.1***	1070.1***	14.69***	852.8***	646.8***	531.4***	883.3***	18.79***
C (2) = 1 Wald Chi-Square Statistics	3.584*	0.3517	2.2841	3.2503*	11.15***	20.21***	0.0745	0.5207	1.1168	19.58***

significant at least at the 5% level. Moreover, except for the corresponding subject onshore bond index in the regression of samples from the COVID-19 pandemic period and the full price index regression controlling for the exchange rate reform variable and the COVID-19 pandemic variable, of which the coefficients reject the null hypothesis of being equal to 1 at the significance levels of 1% and 10%, respectively, all other regression equations fail to significantly reject the null hypothesis of being equal to 1, indicating the establishment of interest rate parity. The regression of samples from the COVID-19 pandemic period shows that both exchange rate cost and the US dollar index variable are significant at least at the 10% level and have signs consistent with the theory, but the corporate onshore bond price index is insignificant. This may be related to the fact that the sample does not include data from June 2020, when China's US dollar bond market markedly recovered, further supporting the conclusion of the previous theoretical analysis that the relationship between variables may change significantly during the crisis period. Based on the above analysis, the econometric conclusions in this chapter are robust and reliable.

At the same time as the release of ChinaBond's index on China's investment-grade offshore US dollar bonds, the ChinaBond Pricing Center also began releasing information on the yield curve of China's investment-grade US dollar bonds. Referencing international ratings, this information is subdivided into six credit ratings from A + to BBB-, and the data can be traced back to December 28, 2017. The yield curve of China's investment-grade US dollar bonds is updated daily based on reliable market prices. For bonds without market prices, the curve is adjusted using market prices from the same issuer and comparable companies. The critical tenor yield is determined using reliable market prices, and the yield curve with complete maturity is obtained through interpolation using the Hermite model. The ChinaBond Pricing Center provides information on the onshore bond yields of corresponding entities for the sample bonds in the ChinaBond index for China's investment-grade offshore US dollar bond yields, allowing for analysis of the relationship between corporate onshore and offshore bond yields for the same entity. Yields of China's five-year investment-grade US dollar bonds at the A+ to BBBB-level and onshore bonds of corresponding entities are selected to test the relationship between variables before the outbreak of the COVID-19 pandemic.

As shown in Table 8, the regression results of China's US dollar bond yields with different ratings are highly satisfactory. The regression

Table 8. Yields of China's investment-grade offshore US dollar bonds and the onshore bonds of corresponding entities (sample period: 2017-12-28–2020-01-23).

Independent Variable \ Dependent Variable	A+ Level US dollar Bond	A Level US dollar Bond	A– Level US dollar Bond	BBB+ Level US dollar Bond	BBB Level US dollar Bond	BBB– Level US dollar Bond
Constant	3.0715	3.9146	4.2793*	3.5010	4.1284**	5.0829**
	(2.5030)	(2.4907)	(2.3226)	(2.6080)	(2.2529)	(2.4298)
Corresponding Offshore Bond Yield	1.0911***	1.0279***	0.9527***	1.0917***	0.9606***	1.0120***
	(0.0577)	(0.1122)	(0.0975)	(0.1179)	(0.0909)	(0.0979)
Swap1y	−0.1312***	−0.1194***	−0.1312***	−0.1354***	−0.1169***	−0.1233***
	(0.0075)	(0.0074)	(0.0075)	(0.0076)	(0.0072)	(0.0077)
USDindex	−0.0345***	−0.0393***	−0.0396***	−0.0361***	−0.0376***	−0.0446**
	(0.0182)	(0.0182)	(0.0170)	(0.0188)	(0.0164)	(0.0175)
R^2	0.8224	0.8106	0.825	0.8187	0.8352	0.8356
S.E.	0.2292	0.2344	0.2233	0.2309	0.2187	0.2336
F	756.1***	700.7***	769.9***	737.8***	827.5***	830.5***
C (2) = 1 Wald Chi-Square Statistics	0.6434	0.0621	0.2348	0.6074	0.1912	0.0149

coefficients of the corresponding entities' onshore bond yields for all equations do not reject the null hypothesis of being equal to 1, indicating that the interest rate parity condition still holds. Given the exchange rate cost and the US dollar index, the corporate onshore and offshore bond yields exhibit a synchronized pattern of changes, further confirming the robustness and reliability of the econometric findings presented in this chapter.

In December 2019, the ChinaBond Pricing Center released the yield curves of China's investment-grade US dollar bonds in specific industries, including the municipal and real estate industries, which have faced stricter restrictions on offshore bond issuance in recent years than they did before. China's investment-grade US dollar bonds in the municipal industry are classified into five credit ratings ranging from A to BBB–, while those in the real estate industry are categorized into three credit ratings from BBB+ to BBB–. The data can be traced back to December 28, 2018. The ChinaBond Pricing Center provides information on the yield curves of onshore bonds corresponding to China's investment-grade US dollar bonds of municipal and real estate enterprises. We select five-year corporate onshore and offshore bond yields and conduct econometric analysis on samples before the outbreak of the COVID-19 pandemic.

From Table 9, it can be observed that in the regression of municipal US dollar bonds, except for the fact that the US dollar index in the BBB-level equation is not significant and has a contradictory sign to the theory, indicating a possible collinearity issue, all other variables are significant at the 1% level, and the econometric results are relatively satisfactory. However, even after the exchange rate cost is considered and the US dollar index is controlled for, the variable coefficient of the corresponding onshore bond yields of municipal US dollar bonds remain positive but significantly less than 1. This suggests that the issuance of municipal bonds is more influenced by non-market factors, and market incompleteness could be an important reason for the lack of support from the results for interest rate parity. Unlike municipal enterprises, real estate enterprises are subject to many policy restrictions on onshore bond issuance and stricter controls on offshore bond issuance qualifications and funds. Since the second quarter of 2018, real estate enterprises have been allowed to use only offshore bond issuance for repaying maturing debts to avoid default and are restricted from using offshore debt funds to invest in

Table 9. Yields of China's investment-grade municipal US dollar bonds, real estate bonds, and corresponding onshore bonds (sample period: 2018-12-28–2020-01-23).

Bond Industry Type	Municipal Bond					Real Estate Bond		
Dependent Variable / Independent Variable	A Level US dollar Bond	A– Level US dollar Bond	BBB+ Level US dollar Bond	BBB Level US dollar Bond	BBB– Level US dollar Bond	BBB+ Level US dollar Bond	BBB Level US dollar Bond	BBB– Level US dollar Bond
Constant	11.38***	8.9462***	15.11***	15.83***	14.19***	9.3155***	0.2030	4.2682
	(2.2663)	(1.9109)	(2.1202)	(2.5062)	(1.8687)	(1.9672)	(2.8377)	(2.6585)
Corresponding Offshore Bond Yield	0.5386***	0.5419***	0.4904***	0.5195***	0.2888***	0.6267***	0.0820	−0.2170
	(0.0759)	(0.0635)	(0.0821)	(0.0911)	(0.0916)	(0.1080)	(0.1253)	(0.1334)
Swap1y	−0.1037***	−0.0984***	−0.0951***	−0.0947***	−0.0832***	−0.1122***	−0.0967***	−0.0879***
	(0.0080)	(0.0072)	(0.0080)	(0.0096)	(0.0084)	(0.0081)	(0.0126)	(0.0112)
USDindex	−0.0876***	−0.0598	−0.1093***	−0.1160***	0.0920	−0.0707***	0.0334	0.0103
	(0.0189)	(0.0154)	(0.0174)	(0.0202)	(0.0160)	(0.0169)	(0.0237)	(0.0226)
R^2	0.7995	0.8773	0.8399	0.8149	0.7896	0.8196	0.608	0.5197
S.E.	0.1674	0.115	0.148	0.1657	0.1501	0.16	0.1545	0.1646
F	329.7***	591.1***	433.6***	364.0***	310.3***	375.7***	128.2***	89.43***
C (2) = 1 Wald Chi-Square Statistics	36.98***	52.05***	38.57***	27.84***	60.26***	11.95***	53.64***	83.21***

onshore and offshore real estate projects or supplement operating funds.[8] To avoid the negative impact of default on their offshore market ratings and related businesses, many real estate companies have no choice but to issue bonds at a higher cost, with the bond yields including a higher policy risk premium. Therefore, it can be understood that the relationship between the yields of real estate corporate onshore and offshore bonds at the BBB and BBB-levels is not significant, and there is even an abnormal phenomenon in which the onshore and offshore yields of BBB-level bonds deviate from each other.

5. Conclusions and Policy Implications

As the first article to verify the applicability of interest rate parity theory in China using offshore and onshore bond yields, this work shows that interest rate parity in China has held true since the Bond Connect program was implemented. In line with the findings of most China-specific studies, the empirical research on onshore and foreign bond yield in this chapter indicates that interest rate parity (UIRP and CIRP) has not held for long periods of time, with capital controls being an important factor determining this duration. Furthermore, CIRP still does not hold true in China even after controlling for the US dollar index, which has been a key factor in the "iron law" of CIRP effectiveness since the global financial crisis. Since 2017, with the acceleration of China's financial liberalization, especially after the implementation of the Bond Connect program, there has been no significant difference between corporate onshore and offshore bond yields considering the exchange rate cost, and taking the US dollar index into account does not change the conclusion. This chapter provides strong empirical support for the validity of the covered interest rate parity

---

[8]In May 2018, the National Development and Reform Commission and the Ministry of Finance jointly issued the *Notice by the National Development and Reform Commission and the Ministry of Finance of Improving the Market Constraint Mechanism and Strictly Preventing Foreign Debt Risks and Local Debt Risks*. In 2019, the National Development and Reform Commission further tightened the filing management of offshore bond issuance by real estate and municipal enterprises. Although the People's Bank of China and the State Administration of Foreign Exchange adjusted the full-scale macroprudential adjustment parameters for cross-border financing in March 2020, expanding the space for the offshore debt financing of China's-funded enterprises, the policy adjustment does not apply to real estate and municipal enterprises.

condition in China and indicates the effectiveness of China's foreign exchange market.

This chapter examines the degree of openness of China's bond market from the perspective of the relationship between offshore and onshore bond yields. Through an empirical analysis of the yield rates of China's investment-grade US dollar bonds from Bank of America's Merrill Lynch and onshore and offshore yields for similar high credit-rated enterprises since 2010, we confirm that China's bond market has effectively connected with the international bond market. However, the changes in corporate onshore and offshore bond yields are not synchronized, indicating that the integration degree of China's bond market and foreign bond markets is still limited. Specifically, the US dollar index significantly impacts the yield of China's US dollar bonds, suggesting that the exchange rate cost is an important factor in corporate onshore and offshore bond yields. Furthermore, although China–US interest rate differential provides potential space for interest rate arbitrage, the impact of interest rate arbitrage on corporate onshore and offshore bond yields is not significant due to the incomplete opening of China's capital account, which differs from conclusions drawn in the existing literature.

The empirical analysis in this chapter can also validate the effectiveness and existing problems of China's exchange rate regime reform and financial market opening policy. First, China's exchange rate regime reform has played a positive role in the convergence of corporate onshore and offshore foreign bond yields, but the US dollar index has a significant impact on China's offshore bond yields, indicating that there is still room for further improvement in the flexibility of the RMB exchange rate. Second, after the Bond Connect program was launched, the trend of corporate onshore and offshore bond yields considering exchange rate costs has significantly converged, indicating an increased degree of integration between the onshore and offshore bond markets. Third, China's capital account has not been completely opened, which limits the space for corporate arbitrage. Fourth, urban investment and real estate enterprises face more policy restrictions on issuing bonds and experience a more pronounced impact of policy premium on bond yields. Fifth, the relationship between corporate onshore and offshore bond yields has been significantly affected by the COVID-19 pandemic, with a large selloff of China's US dollar bonds, including investment-grade bonds, due to risk aversion and resulting in a sharp rise in yields. The relationship between China's investment-grade US dollar bond yields and the US dollar index and onshore bond yields has changed significantly, which is the latest example of the impact of macroeconomic changes on bond yields.

This chapter provides an empirical basis for systematically promoting the opening of the bond market in China. Systematic financial market opening requires further improved exchange rate flexibility and capital account convertibility. At the technical level, liberalizing market access for interest rates and credit derivatives and promoting the development of the foreign exchange derivatives market can also effectively reduce the interest rate risk, credit risk, and exchange rate risk of bond investment and provide better investment and financing opportunities for enterprises. There are still many issues worthy of additional research. The first is the influencing factors of high-yield US dollar bonds in China and the specific reasons that may lead to the deviation between the onshore and offshore yields of high-yield corporate bonds. The second is the impact of onshore and offshore bond market issuers and investor structure on corporate onshore and offshore bond yields and the relationship between onshore and offshore yields of enterprises with different types of ownership. The third is the impact on corporate onshore and offshore bond yields and the direction of possible policy improvement in the basic implementations of liquidation, custody, and information disclosure, as well as specific differences in taxation and regulatory standards. The fourth is the degree and particular measures of the internationalization of RMB and capital account opening, as well as the essential measures for development, the extent of market deepening, and the specific impacts of the onshore foreign exchange and bond market on corporate onshore and offshore bond yields.

References

Alexius, A. (2001). Uncovered interest parity revisited. *Review of International Economics*, 9(3), 505–517.

Alper, C., Ardic, O., & Fendoglu, S. (2009). The economics of the uncovered interest parity condition for emerging markets. *Journal of Economic Surveys* (Wiley), 23(1), 115–138.

Avdjiev, S., Du, W., Koch, C., & Shin, H. (2019). The dollar, bank leverage, and deviations from covered interest parity. *American Economic Review: Insights*, 1(2), 193–208.

Baillie, R. & Chang, S. (2011). Carry trades momentum trading and the forward premium anomaly. *Journal of Financial Markets*, 14(3), 441–464.

Banerjee, R., Hofmann, B., & Mehrotra, A. (2020). Corporate investment and the exchange rate. BIS Working Paper, No. 839.

Bansal, R. & Dahlquist, M. (2000). The forward premium puzzle: Different tales from developed and emerging economies. *Journal of International Economics*, 51(1), 115–144.

Bansal, R. & Shaliastovich, I. (2013). A long-run risks explanation of predictability puzzles in bond and currency markets. *Review of Financial Studies*, 26(1), 1–33.

Bekaert, G., Wei, M., & Xing, Y. (2007). Uncovered interest rate parity and the term structure. *Journal of International Money and Finance*, 26(6), 1038–1069.

Borio, C., McCauley, R., McGuire, P., & Sushko, V. (2016). Covered interest parity lost. *BIS Quarterly Review*, September, 45–64.

Boudoukh, J., Richardson, M., & Whitelaw, R. (2016). New evidence on the forward premium puzzle. *Journal of Financial and Quantitative Analysis*, 51(3), 875–897.

Bruno, V. & Shin, H. (2017). Global dollar credit and carry trades. *Review of Financial Studies*, 30(3), 703–749.

Cerutti, E., Obstfeld, M., & Zhou, H. (2019). Covered interest parity deviations. NBER Working Papers, No. 26129.

Chang, H. & Su, C. (2015). Uncovered interest parity and monetary integration in East Asian countries based on China. *Journal of International Trade & Economic Development*, 24(4), 451–464.

Cheung, Y., Chinn, M., & Fujii, E. (2006). The Chinese economies in global context. *Journal of the Japanese and International Economies*, 20(1), 128–153.

Chinn, M. & Quayyum, S. (2012). Long horizon uncovered interest parity reassessed. NBER Working Papers, No. 18482.

Chinn, M. & Meredith, G. (2004). Monetary policy and long-horizon uncovered interest parity. *IMF Staff Papers*, 51(3), 409–430.

Cho, D. (2018). On the persistence of the forward premium in the joint presence of nonlinearity, asymmetry, and structural changes. *Economic Modelling*, 70(C), 310–319.

Colacito, R. & Croce, M. (2013). International asset pricing with recursive preferences. *Journal of Finance, American Finance Association*, 68(6), 2651–2686.

Cumby, R. & Obstfeld, M. (1981). A note on exchange-rate expectations and nominal interest differentials. *Journal of Finance*, 36(3), 697–703.

Cumby, R. & Obstfeld, M. (1984). International interest rate and price level linkages under flexible exchange rates. In: Bilson, J. & Marston, R. (eds.), *Exchange Rate Theory and Practice*. Chicago: University of Chicago Press, pp. 121–151.

Ding, D., Huange, Y., & Zhou, Y. (2019). China's offshore corporate dollar bonds. In: *The Future of China's Bond Market*. IMF, Chapter 16, pp. 357–379.

Dooley, M. & Isard, P. (1980). Capital controls, political risk and deviations from interest rate parity. *Journal of Political Economy*, 88(2), 370–384.

Du, W., Tepper, A., & Verdelhan, A. (2018). Deviations from covered interest rate parity. *Journal of Finance*, 73(3), 915–957.

Engle, C. (2014). Exchange rates and interest parity. In: *Handbook of International Economics*, Vol. 4, pp. 453–522.

Engle, R. & Kroner, K. (1995). Multivariate simultaneous generalized ARCH. *Econometric Theory*, 11(1), 122–150.

Engle, C. & Zhu, F. (2019). Exchange rate puzzles. BIS Working Paper, No. 805.

Fama, E. (1984). Forward and spot exchange rates. *Journal of Monetary Economics*, 14(3), 319–338.

Fong, W., Valente, G., & Fung, J. (2010). Covered interest arbitrage profits. *Journal of Banking & Finance*, 34(5), 1098–1107.

Frankel, J. & Froot, K. (1991). Exchange rate forecasting techniques, survey data and implications for the foreign exchange market. NBER Working Paper, No. 3470.

Frankel, J. & Poonawala, J. (2010). The forward market in emerging currencies. *Journal of International Money and Finance*, 29(3), 585–598.

Froot, K. & Frankel, J. (1989). Forward discount bias. *Quarterly Journal of Economics*, 104(1), 139–161.

Gambacorta, L., Mayordomo, S., & Garralda, J. (2020). Dollar borrowing, firm-characteristics, and FX-hedged funding opportunities. BIS Working Paper, No. 843.

Henderson, D. & Sampson, S. (1983). Intervention in foreign exchange markets. *Federal Reserve Bulletin*, November, 830–836.

Hochradl, M. & Wagner, C. (2010). Trading the forward bias. *Journal of International Money and Finance*, 29(3), 423–441.

Hordahl, P. & Shim, I. (2020). EME bond portfolio flows and long-term interest rates during the Covid-19 pandemic. *BIS Bulletin*, 18.

Huang, H. (2019). China onshore insights: A new way to look at China's corporate bonds. *HSBC Euromoney Fixed Income Research Survey*, May.

Huang, Y., Panizza, U., & Portes, R. (2018). Corporate foreign bond issuance and interfirm loans in China. NBER Working Paper, No. 25413.

Iida, T., Kimura, T., & Sudo, N. (2016). Regulatory reforms and the dollar funding of global banks. Bank of Japan Working Paper, No. 16-E-14.

Ince, O. & Molodtsova, T. (2017). Rationality and forecasting accuracy of exchange rate expectations. *Journal of International Financial Markets*, 47(C), 131–151.

Jorda, O. & Taylor, A. (2012). The carry trade and fundamentals. *Journal of International Economics*, 88(1), 74–90.

Ivashina, V., Scharfstein, D., & Stein, J. (2015). Dollar funding and the lending behavior of global banks. *Quarterly Journal of Economics*, 130(3), 1241–1281.

Kim, H. & Cho, J. (2011). A test of the revised interest parity in China and Asian emerging markets. *Emerging Markets Finance and Trade*, 47(Sup. 4), 23–41.

Lee, S. (2003). Deviation from covered interest rate parity in Korea. *East Asian Economic Review*, 7(1), 125–141.

Lewis, K. (1995). Puzzles in international financial markets. In: Grossman, G. & Rogoff, K. (eds.), *Handbook of International Economics*, Vol. 3. North-Holland, pp. 1931–1971.

Loring, G. & Lucey, B. (2013). An analysis of forward exchange rate biasedness across developed and developing country currencies. *Emerging Markets Review*, 17(C), 14–28.

Lothian, J. (2016). Uncovered interest parity: The long and the short of it. *Journal of Empirical Finance*, 36(C), 1–7.

Lothian, J. & Wu, L. (2011). Uncovered interest rate parity over the past two centuries. *Journal of International Money and Finance*, 30(3), 448–473.

Macdonald, R. & Taylor, M. (1992). Exchange rate economics: A survey. *IMF Staff Papers*, 39(1), 1–57.

Miah, F. & Altiti, O. (2020). Risk premium or irrational expectations? *North American Journal of Economics and Finance*, 51(C), 1–22.

Newey, W. & West, K. (1987). A simple, positive definite, heteroskedasticity and autocorrelation consistent covariance matrix. *Econometrica*, 55(3), 703–708.

Obstfeld, M. & Rogoff, K. (2001). The six major puzzles in international macroeconomics. In: Bernanke, B. & Rogoff, K. (eds.), *NBER Macroeconomics Annual 2000*. Chicago: University of Chicago Press, pp. 339–412.

Rime, D., Schrimpfand, A., & Syrstad, O. (2017). Segmented money markets and covered interest parity arbitrage. BIS Working Papers, No. 651.

Rose, A. & Spiegel, M. (2012). Dollar illiquidity and central bank swap arrangements during the global financial crisis. *Journal of International Economics*, 88(2), 326–340.

Sarantis, N. (2006). Testing the uncovered interest parity using traded volatility, a time-varying risk premium and heterogeneous expectations. *Journal of International Money and Finance*, 25(7), 1168–1186.

Skinner, F. & Mason, A. (2011). Covered interest rate parity in emerging markets. *International Review of Financial Analysis*, 20(5), 355–363.

Stenfors, A. (2019). The covered interest parity puzzle and the evolution of the Japan premium. *Journal of Economic Issues*, 53(2), 417–424.

Suh, S. & Kim, Y. (2016). Covered interest parity and arbitrage paradox in emerging markets. *Pacific-Basin Finance Journal*, 38(C), 161–176.

Sushko, V., Borio, C., McCauley, R., & McGuire, P. (2018). The failure of covered interest parity FX hedging demand and costly balance sheets. BIS Working Paper, No. 590.

Taylor, M. (1989). Covered interest arbitrage and market turbulence. *Economic Journal*, 99(396), 376–391.

Wang, Y. (2010). Anomaly in China's dollar–RMB forward market. *China & World Economy*, 18(2), 96–120.

Wang, Y. (2015). Convertibility restriction in China's foreign exchange market and its impact on forward pricing. *Journal of Banking & Finance*, 50(C), 616–631.

Wong, A., Leung, D., & Calvin, N. (2016). Risk-adjusted covered interest parity: Theory and evidence. Hong Kong Institute for Monetary Research Working Papers, No. 16/2016.

Wooldridge, J. (2012). *Introductory Econometrics: A Modern Approach.* Cengage Learning.

Afterword: Financial Opening and Security

In recent years, deglobalization, regional conflicts, the distressed global financial order, and misused financial sanctions have added to concerns about financial opening and security. Against this background, it is useful to summarize the experiences and lessons from China's financial opening up over the past few decades and clarify the future direction of China's financial opening. More importantly, it is critical that economic and financial development plays a key role in China's financial security and national security.

I. China's Financial Opening-up Has Occurred through Various Channels and in a Gradual Manner

Over the past 40 or more years, China has moved up in the global financial ranks. In 2023, the country's equity value totaled close to RMB 78 trillion (62% of GDP), second only to that of the US. The total bonds in depositories surpassed RMB 156.9 trillion (125% of GDP), ranking second in the world. By the end of 2023, bank assets totaled RMB 409.7 trillion (325% of GDP), making China first in the world by this metric. China accounts for five of the ten largest banks in first-tier capital and assets.

With the country's enhanced financial sector, the government has promoted China's financial opening. At the end of June 2023, foreign investors held 4.0% of A share equities and 2.2% of onshore bonds. Other foreign presence in China includes, among others, foreign banks, insurance companies, fund management companies, and securities companies. Of these, foreign banks accounted for 1.2% of China's banking sector (partly because Chinese banks have expanded too rapidly over the past few decades), and foreign insurance companies held a market share of 11%. However, the openness of most advanced countries is higher than that of China, with international investors accounting for 16.7% of the US equity market, 57.7% of the UK equity market, and approximately 30% of the Japanese and Korean equity markets. Moreover, international investors also hold 30%, 30%, 14%, and 20% of the treasury bonds of the US, UK, Japan, and Korea, respectively, showing that these countries are more open than China. Another important indicator of China's financial opening is the internationalization of RMB, and its share in the Special Drawing Rights increased from 10% to 12.28% in May 2022.

Nevertheless, the opening of the financial sector lags behind that of the economic and trade sectors. Over the past two decades, China has accounted for more than 15% of the world economy and 12% of global trade and contributed to more than 30% of global growth. However, the country's financial opening cannot match the importance of China's economy and trade. Although the RMB ranks third in trade finance, fourth in payment, and fifth in reserves, it accounts for a mere 2–5% of the total, far behind the USD, and lower than the euro, pound sterling, and Japanese yen. In comparison, the economies of the US, the UK, and Japan accounted for 13.4%, 2%, and 3.3% of the 2023 global economy, respectively, while in December 2023, the USD, pound sterling, and Japanese yen accounted for 82.84%, 0.19%, and 1.3% of global trade finance, respectively, and 47.54%, 6.92%, and 3.83% of global payments, respectively. In Q3 2023, these three currencies accounted for 54.6%, 4.5%, and 5.0% of the global foreign reserves, respectively.

The financial opening in China has mostly followed a channeled and phased manner. First, the opening of equity and bond markets has occurred mainly through special channels of the HK, London, New York, and other exchanges, and fund transfers are performed in special accounts of custodian banks according to specific regulations. In 2022, China and the Hong Kong Connect program expanded to wealth management products and ETFs, further widening the growth potential of cross-border funds, yet they operate only in new or expanded channels. In addition, prior to RMB internationalization in 2008, external financial services were mainly related to the country's current account; afterward, trade demands became the main driver in the first seven years, and since 2017, equity investment and related foreign exchange transactions have become the main drivers for cross-border fund flow. International payments in RMB are made mostly in the major channels of trade, and bond and equity, as securities and individual outward investment are still limited.

Policy measures in recent years have indicated that the Sino-US trade war and other US containment measures have not slowed the pace of China's financial opening. In fact, China has accelerated its pace. During 2019–2020, China expanded and then lifted foreign ownership ceilings in banks, insurance companies, fund management, and equity industries, facilitating Hong Kong's entry into onshore equity and bond markets. These measures, together with the inclusion of Chinese equity and bonds in indices of MSCI, Moody's, and the like, have enhanced China's cross-border fund flow.

As the financial opening has promoted fund flow and enhanced market competition, it has also added to the requirements of financial regulations. Fund inflow means that foreign funds can share the growth dividends of China. On the one hand, this inflow increases competition among Chinese and foreign financial institutions and raises market efficiency; on the other hand, it also adds the challenges of market volatility and supervision.

II. Reflections on the Financial Opening in the New Context

We must now reflect on the lessons and experiences of the financial opening over the past few decades. First, the financial opening has been based on demands from trade and economic activities, driven by the markets. That is, the policies have mainly been designed to support market-driven demand and serve economic entities. On the one hand, international investors have the desire to enter Chinese financial markets and allocate RMB-denominated assets, while domestic investors need to diversify risks to invest overseas. On the other hand, China has evolved to become the second largest economy and trade country, the largest buyer and consumer of many commodities. With an improved institutional setup for an open economy, China has the capacity to serve domestic and international investors.

Second, the approach of financial opening has been phased, with pilots first and expansion coming next; most importantly, reforms in key areas are conducted at critical points in time. For example, the Chinese economy and market were mostly stable during the period of 2013–2015; however, China must open certain areas in order to join the SDR. Once China breaks through these bottlenecks, the country can maximize the gains from its opening measures.

Third, it is critical to actively communicate with markets, financial institutions, and firms to design the policy measures needed. Lessons can be learned from the period of policy flipping in 2015–2016. At this time, policy measures were taken to reduce market volatilities, with some effective short-term impacts as well as significant long-term negative consequences. In retrospect, the principle for policy design should be minimizing market distortions and economic entity interventions. Under this principle, automatic market adjustments should be applied first, market expectations should be guided in a timely manner, and the understanding of overseas markets should be enhanced.

Additionally, China's financial opening must be considered in the new geopolitical context. In the short to medium term, the global financial rules and infrastructure remain in the hands of the US and other advanced countries, while exclusion from the international financial system means trade stagnation, economic recession, and financial risks. The most recent example is the sanctions placed on Russia after February 24, 2022, which almost paralyzed Russia's external economic and financial connections.

Specifically, the future directions of global financial asset allocation, payment systems, foreign reserves, and international monetary systems must be reflected upon before designing a new approach to China's future financial opening up. First, the investment philosophy of environmental, social, and governance (ESG) is changing, and ESG evaluations are being amended. ESG evaluations are mainly applied to risks in the environment, social performance, and corporate governance of projects and firms, as well as their long-term development capacity. Recently, some rating firms have considered the inclusion of new geopolitical variables in ESG evaluations (Pratsch, 2022). Second, countries such as India, Iran, Russia, and Vietnam have been exploring payment systems outside of SWIFT, indicating that the balance among international payment systems may be changing. Such a change may open a window for the CNY payment system in the future. Third, dollar-denominated assets are more vulnerable than other assets, given the added financial and capital market sanctions for geopolitical purposes (Bridgewater). At the same time, China's foreign exchange rate is mainly market-driven, and the country's massive foreign exchange reserve is mainly the result of insufficient domestic demand and insufficiently open capital accounts. Thus, China needs to learn from Japan and shift more official foreign exchange to firms and residents. Fourth, although the trust in the USD has been slowly decreasing, the currency remains the symbol of the US' comprehensive strength. That is, the international monetary system is expected to remain relatively stable in the short to medium term.

In the current period of great changes, China should upgrade its financial opening via continued efforts to improve the financial system and follow the path of transparent, controlled, and phased opening. Against the background of deglobalization, it is well known that further opening is the only option, as China's financial supply chain is highly externally dependent. Only with further and upgraded opening can China mingle and compete in international markets and better serve international investors. On the one hand, if China continues to develop, its market will continue to be attractive to international investors, and sharing the country's development dividends with international investors can improve China's international status. On the other hand, upgraded financial openings can help improve China's financial system efficiency and competitiveness and better support the country's economic development. A secluded financial system can only mean lower efficiency and less stability.

III. Financial Security Strategy Must Pay Attention to Both Security and Development

Financial security in the present geopolitical background is characterized by multifaceted financial bundling. This means that China should go beyond the financial framework when analyzing financial security issues. That is, financial security can only be achieved with economic development, given the current global geopolitical background. First, there is no absolute financial security, and such security must be integrated into the development of a country. Second, the key issue in China's financial security is not foreign exchange reserves but the business environment. Only with an improved business environment can China improve its technology innovation and thereby its financial security. Third, the most significant financial insecurity comes from cutting off from the outside world. Financial security can increase only with deeper integration in international trade and international financial markets.

1. **There is no absolute financial security, and security and development are indivisible**
   Security and development are highly interrelated. Without economic development and technological innovation, there will be no security, let alone financial security.
2. **The core issue of China's financial security is not foreign reserves but the business environment**
   Financial security can only come with an improved business environment. Since the global pandemic began in 2020, regulatory policy changes and resonance have deteriorated the business environment in China and partially contributed to fund and investment outflow. In addition, there are many red lights and very little encouragement for private investment and platform companies. More notably, a worsened business environment has negatively affected technology innovation, as fewer private inputs have been provided for research and development. Furthermore, without an enabling business environment, technology cannot be developed, recognized, and marketized.
3. **The worst choice for financial security would be sealing off the country. High-level financial security only comes with deepened participation in international trade and financial markets**
   First, RMB internationalization should be enhanced, especially its role in commodity pricing. The international monetary system is evolving, and insufficient RMB internationalization will put China in the hands of the reserve currency countries. If China can enhance its competitiveness, especially in terms of its governance level, the credibility of RMB can increase accordingly, thus facilitating RMB internationalization. In addition, as the oil–dollar link dries up, the US will no longer seek to export USD through oil imports, and the SWANA region will need to find alternative currencies. If the RMB can play a role in settling oil, its role as an international pricing currency can grow drastically.

Second, the core issue in China's financial security is not excessively large foreign reserves or the fact that USD assets dominate foreign reserve investment. In fact, USD is the most important strategic advantage a country can have, and using USD helps the US maintain its strategic advantage. Over the short to medium term, China can learn from Japan, that is, by letting firms and residents hold more foreign exchange by amending the Foreign Exchange Management Law.

Third, China should develop its bond market and upgrade its overseas financial product supply. Many efforts are needed, including (1) improving bond market rules and regulations, as well as market infrastructure and connections among infrastructure; (2) enriching bond products to enhance the bond market and expand bond market inclusion; and (3) improving the supervision of intermediaries such as underwriters, accounting firms, law firms, and rating agencies. In addition, China can do more to increase the international competitiveness and impacts of its bond market by facilitating the issuance of Panda Bonds, domestic firms' overseas issuances, and two-way bond investment between mainland China and Hong Kong. Moreover, new products based on treasury bonds can also increase the overseas supply of RMB-denominated financial products.

In summary, China's financial opening hinges on the country's domestic strength and financial supervisory capacity, and the keys are economic development and national governance. If China can maintain a certain level of growth speed, strengthen its intellectual property protection, and stabilize the policy expectations of investors, the country steadily advance its financial opening.

Reference

Pratsch, M. (June 16, 2022). How the new geopolitical reality affects ESG. OMFIF.

Index

E

F

www.ingramcontent.com/pod-product-compliance
Lightning Source LLC
Jackson TN
JSHW010916090525
83698JS00002B/185
9789819803217